FROM CONFINEMENT
TO CONTAINMENT

In the series *Asian American History and Culture*, edited by Cathy Schlund-Vials, Shelley Sang-Hee Lee, and Rick Bonus. Founding editor, Sucheng Chan; editors emeriti, David Palumbo-Liu, Michael Omi, K. Scott Wong, and Linda Trinh Võ.

ALSO IN THIS SERIES:

Patricia P. Chu, *Where I Have Never Been: Migration, Melancholia, and Memory in Asian American Narratives of Return*

Cynthia Wu, *Sticky Rice: A Politics of Intraracial Desire*

Marguerite Nguyen, *America's Vietnam: The* Longue Durée *of U.S. Literature and Empire*

Vanita Reddy, *Fashioning Diaspora: Beauty, Femininity, and South Asian American Culture*

Audrey Wu Clark, *The Asian American Avant-Garde: Universalist Aspirations in Modernist Literature and Art*

Eric Tang, *Unsettled: Cambodian Refugees in the New York City Hyperghetto*

Jeffrey Santa Ana, *Racial Feelings: Asian America in a Capitalist Culture of Emotion*

Jiemin Bao, *Creating a Buddhist Community: A Thai Temple in Silicon Valley*

Elda E. Tsou, *Unquiet Tropes: Form, Race, and Asian American Literature*

Tarry Hum, *Making a Global Immigrant Neighborhood: Brooklyn's Sunset Park*

Ruth Mayer, *Serial Fu Manchu: The Chinese Supervillain and the Spread of Yellow Peril Ideology*

Karen Kuo, *East Is West and West Is East: Gender, Culture, and Interwar Encounters between Asia and America*

Kieu-Linh Caroline Valverde, *Transnationalizing Viet Nam: Community, Culture, and Politics in the Diaspora*

Lan P. Duong, *Treacherous Subjects: Gender, Culture, and Trans-Vietnamese Feminism*

Kristi Brian, *Reframing Transracial Adoption: Adopted Koreans, White Parents, and the Politics of Kinship*

Belinda Kong, *Tiananmen Fictions outside the Square: The Chinese Literary Diaspora and the Politics of Global Culture*

Bindi V. Shah, *Laotian Daughters: Working toward Community, Belonging, and Environmental Justice*

Cherstin M. Lyon, *Prisons and Patriots: Japanese American Wartime Citizenship, Civil Disobedience, and Historical Memory*

Shelley Sang-Hee Lee, *Claiming the Oriental Gateway: Prewar Seattle and Japanese America*

Isabelle Thuy Pelaud, *This Is All I Choose to Tell: History and Hybridity in Vietnamese American Literature*

Christian Collet and Pei-te Lien, eds., *The Transnational Politics of Asian Americans*

Min Zhou, *Contemporary Chinese America: Immigration, Ethnicity, and Community Transformation*

A list of additional titles in this series appears at the back of this book.

FROM CONFINEMENT TO CONTAINMENT

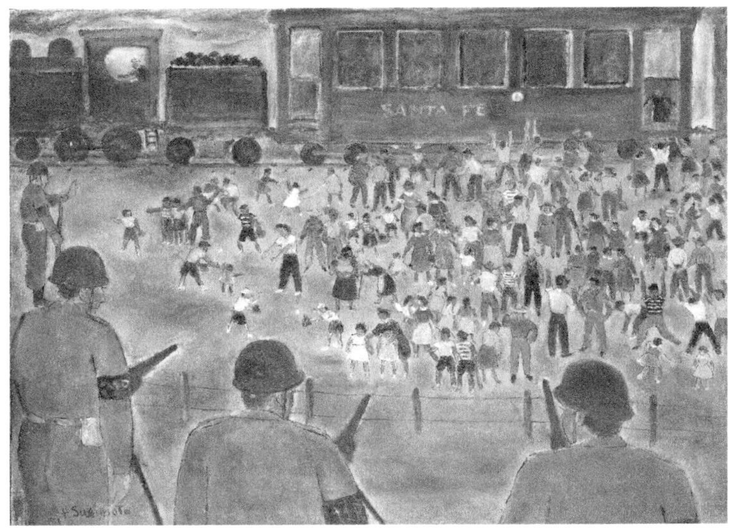

Japanese/American Arts during the Early Cold War

EDWARD TANG

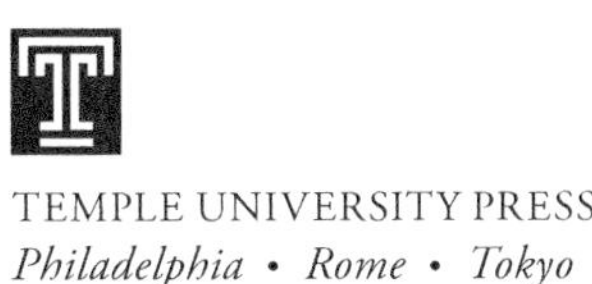

TEMPLE UNIVERSITY PRESS
Philadelphia • Rome • Tokyo

TEMPLE UNIVERSITY PRESS
Philadelphia, Pennsylvania 19122
tupress.temple.edu

Library of Congress Cataloging-in-Publication Data

Names: Tang, Edward, author.
Title: From confinement to containment : Japanese/American arts during the
   early Cold War / Edward Tang.
Description: Philadelphia : Temple University Press, 2019. | Series: Asian American
   history and culture | Includes bibliographical references and index. |
Identifiers: LCCN 2018021198 (print) | LCCN 2018021748 (ebook) |
   ISBN 9781439917503 (E-book) | ISBN 9781439917480 (hardback : alk. paper) |
   ISBN 9781439917497 (paper : alk. paper)
Subjects: LCSH: Japanese American art—20th century—Themes, motives. |
   Arts, Japanese—20th century—Themes, motives. | Arts and society—United
   States—History—20th century. | Arts and society—Japan—History—20th century. |
   BISAC: SOCIAL SCIENCE / Ethnic Studies / Asian American Studies. |
   HISTORY / United States / 20th Century. | HISTORY / Asia / Japan. |
   LITERARY CRITICISM / American / Asian American.
Classification: LCC NX512.3.J32 (ebook) | LCC NX512.3.J32 T36 2019 (print) |
   DDC 704.03/956073—dc23
LC record available at https://lccn.loc.gov/2018021198

♾ The paper used in this publication meets the requirements of the American National
Standard for Information Sciences—Permanence of Paper for Printed Library Materials,
ANSI Z39.48-1992

Printed in the United States of America

9 8 7 6 5 4 3 2 1

For Sam, Bessie, Andy, and Brendan

Author's Note

JAPANESE NAMES APPEAR, according to Japanese usage, with the family name preceding the given name. Japanese American names appear, according to Western usage, with the given name preceding the family name.

Contents

Acknowledgments

I am fortunate to have received a great deal of help in writing this book. Several institutions were instrumental in providing not only research material but also prompt responses to my queries. I thank the staffs at the Charles E. Young Research Library, the University of California, Los Angeles (UCLA); the Bancroft Library, the University of California, Berkeley; the Knight Library, Special Collections, the University of Oregon; the Special Collections and University Archives, Stanford University; the Harvard-Yenching Library, Harvard University; the Wisconsin Historical Society; the Margaret Herrick Library of the Academy of Motion Picture Arts and Sciences; the Modern Museum of Art; the Brooklyn Museum; the Smithsonian American Art Museum; and the Japanese American National Museum (JANM). Peter Hanff at the Bancroft Library and Jamie Henricks at JANM were especially helpful.

I could not have put these archives to use without funding from various sources. I received a National Endowment for the Humanities Summer Stipend that covered an assortment of expenses. My home institution, the University of Alabama, was also generous in providing aid. I won a Research Grants Committee (RGC) award at the university level, as well as two grants from the College of Arts and Sciences' College Academy for Research, Scholarship, and Creative Activity (CARSCA), established by Dean Robert F. Olin. The Department of American Studies provided support from the Carla and Cleo Thomas Fund and from my two-year Clarence C. Mondale Faculty Fellowship.

My gratitude extends to those laboring in Asian American studies and related fields who welcomed and tested my ideas for this project. Much of this process began with my visit to UCLA, where Lane Ryo Hirabayashi, David Yoo, and Stacey Hirose were generous with their advice and encouragement. Since then, through conferences at the American Studies Association, the Association for Asian American Studies, and other forums, I have enjoyed friendships with a host of supportive scholars. While sharing a shuttle van ride to the airport after one gathering years ago, Cathy Schlund-Vials introduced herself and then invited me to present at the University of Connecticut's Asian American Studies Institute. This book developed further from my participation on panels and in other exchanges with Eiichiro Azuma, Leslie Bow, Kim Brandt, Elena Creef, Greg Robinson, and Stephen Sumida. Several of Eiichiro's suggestions changed the direction and the nature of the book for the better. Elena and Leslie were present at the start of the project and inspired me with their own work. Greg was a marvelous fount of information, always ready with particular leads, reassurance, and excellent choices in restaurants. At various venues, Steven Doi, Victor Jew, and Brian Niiya imparted valuable insights as well. Kim Brandt, Mary Ting Yi Lui, and Ellen Wu were kind in sharing their scholarship with me. In the early stages of formulating my thoughts, Min Hyoung Song, who was then the editor of the *Journal of Asian American Studies,* guided a draft article on Hanama Tasaki to publication with precision and professionalism. Also during this process, Eiichiro Azuma, Naoko Shibusawa, John Shy, and John J. Stephan lent crucial perspectives to my understanding of Tasaki. Emily Anderson came to my aid by sending me her English translation of Henry Sugimoto's unpublished memoirs. Madeleine Sugimoto was encouraging in my brief exchanges with her and provided vital information about her father's life and work. Koji Arizumi was more than willing to communicate with librarians in Tokyo and Wakayama, Japan, on my behalf. Finally, Fred Whiting organized the Americanist Faculty Workshop at the University of Alabama, a hospitable site where I presented my ideas on two occasions.

As for the Department of American Studies and my wonderful colleagues, I could not have asked for a better working environment. Lynne Adrian, Jolene Hubbs, Stacy Morgan, and Eric Weisbard read various forms of my writing, from book proposals and fellowship applications to introduction and chapter drafts. Throughout the two decades that I have known her, Lynne has perused almost everything I have written and has kept me centered on the important issues. Jolene, with her loathing of modifiers, vagueness, and passive voice, worked the chapter on Yamaguchi Yoshiko into shape. She, Han, and Geneva also served as amiable hosts, entertaining me during two research visits to the Bay Area. Always the devoted friend, Stacy lent his expertise to the chapter on Henry Sugimoto, adding intellectual heft and exactitude to my outlook on modern art. He was gracious, too, in guiding me through the process of obtaining copyright permissions and image reproductions. Eric helped with his forceful questioning of my arguments, structure, and wording, which vitalized mundane first-attempt fellowship statements and informed my later writing. Mike Innis-Jimenez, Rich Megraw, Jeff Melton, and Mairin Odle are equally ideal co-workers, willing to reach consensus on difficult issues and quick to laugh and sympathize over the shared joys and challenges of academic life. The same is true for the administrative staff, Veronica Pruitt and Neva Newman, who manage the office with good cheer and patience.

Temple University Press has been a terrific institution to work with. My editor, Sara Cohen, saw promise in the project and steered it through to publication with a deft touch. Several readers for the press, including Greg Robinson, Cathy Schlund-Vials, and Naoko Shibusawa were thoughtful and dedicated in their comments and suggestions, improving the final product in many ways. My appreciation extends to the various staff members, Ann-Marie Anderson, Gary Kramer, Nikki Miller, and Joan Vidal among them, who helped make the process as straightforward as possible. I am also grateful for Ginny Perrin's copyediting.

My final thanks go to the Tang family. Although my father, Sam, passed away before I began my doctoral work many years ago, he set the model for what a life in teaching and research could accomplish. My mother, Bessie, still inspires me with her enduring support, humor and toughness, and passion for storytelling. My brother, Andy, like my father, departed too soon. But he helped me see what was important, and I sense how his musings and generosity, fondness for fiction and poetry, and love of good coffee come to life in his remarkable son, Brendan. To all of them I dedicate this work.

FROM CONFINEMENT
TO CONTAINMENT

Introduction

IN SEPTEMBER 1951, the Japanese prime minister, Yoshida Shigeru, and a staff of envoys arrived in San Francisco to attend the peace treaty conference that would signal the end of their nation's postwar occupation by the United States. Newspapers across the country highlighted the historical importance as well as the unusual tenor of the visit. The *New York Times* observed that the official welcome at the airport "was anything but the kind of greeting traditionally extended to treaty signers from a beaten country" because of its cordiality.[1] The presence of Japanese Americans at events honoring the visiting delegation contributed to this sense of reconciliation. When the diplomats landed, a drum and bugle corps with Boy Scouts of Japanese ancestry supplied the ceremonial music. A woman and a child dressed in kimonos then presented bouquets of chrysanthemums and roses to Yoshida and his party. Later that week, the prime minister addressed more than eight hundred attendees at an evening ballroom reception that included federal and state officials and representatives from local Japanese American communities. Yoshida began by confessing his amazement at the new congenial attitude among Americans toward the Japanese. "The pre-war anti-Japanese feeling was strong," the Los Angeles–based *Rafu Shimpo* noted, "and . . . neither he nor Japan expected anything but a treaty of revenge and retaliation."[2] The graciousness of the United States, as displayed by the gathering that night, cheered the dignitaries from Japan. This shared affection among the dinner guests obliged the prime minister to ponder the new turn in transpacific sentiments. For a statesman catering to his audience, the explanation appeared simple enough: Japanese Americans played a vital role in fostering friendlier relations between two former adversaries.

Media attention on exchanges that revealed suddenly improved domestic and international affairs was understandable. Only a few years earlier, Japan was a formidable and hated enemy during World War II. American propagandists painted the Japanese as savage "monkey-men" or rats who devalued human life, caricatures that fueled desires to exterminate them. Wartime public opinion polls even showed that Americans were more willing to kill Japanese soldiers and civilians than to destroy Nazi Germany.[3] Moreover, Japanese Americans were a disparaged populace in the United States, with more than 110,000 of them from the West Coast and some from Hawai'i confined to camps as a supposed military necessity. Following the Imperial Japanese Navy's attack on Pearl Harbor on December 7, 1941, many suspected the loyalties of those with a Japanese background, considering the immigrant Issei generation as "enemy aliens" and their native-born Nisei children as not much better. Their racial and ethnic ties to the ancestral land, as the argument went, trumped whatever feelings of allegiance they pledged to the United States. On February 19, 1942, President Franklin D. Roosevelt signed Executive Order 9066, by which the federal government removed Japanese Americans to seventeen temporary "assembly centers" on the West Coast and then to ten "relocation centers" built in the most harsh and desolate environments in the nation's interior. Other facilities held the more suspect among them. That two-thirds of the civilians imprisoned without trial were U.S. citizens hardly roused concern or protest against this injustice.[4]

Once the Pacific War ended, however, American political and military leaders, journalists, Hollywood filmmakers, and other figures tried to encourage among the public a different understanding of relations at home and abroad. The onset of the Cold War motivated these new circumstances, with geopolitical realignments helping to shift how the nation's mainstream perceived the Japanese and Japanese Americans. Postwar Japan became a valued anticommunist "model ally" in the Pacific theater to contain the machinations of the Soviet Union, China, and North Korea. That the Russians and Chinese had been U.S. allies and the Koreans a colonized people under Japanese sovereignty in World War II only accentuated the transformed global landscape. For their part, Japanese Americans purportedly overcame a traumatizing mass confinement and other acts of racial prejudice, becoming in the process the prototype for a "model minority" that exemplified the best of American values. U.S. Cold War objectives affected how both populations now appeared to possess redeeming characteristics, such as industry, reliability, and honesty, proving capable of appreciating the benefits offered by a liberal democracy.

These transitions in sentiment were astonishing, given what Japan had represented and what Japanese Americans had endured in the United States. The *New York Times* correspondent covering Prime Minister Yoshida's appearance in San Francisco wondered at this turn of events, surmising that the Japanese Americans who greeted him had spent time in the prison camps. Now they were participating in the State Department's ceremonies to receive the leading dignitary of a nation that once dominated East Asia.[5]

As previous scholarship has shown, the changed perceptions of Japan and Japanese Americans were mutually reinforcing, ones intended to soften prior racist beliefs and to encourage cultural understanding among domestic and overseas populations. Ideally then, if Japanese Americans could underscore their U.S. patriotism and integrate into the white mainstream despite a past associated with imperial Japan, the Japanese could reject their militarist desires, embrace democracy, and profess loyalty to the United States as well. These models of postwar conduct could then promote American values and benevolence and help to contain national and international developments.[6]

Labeling Japanese Americans as quiet, persevering, and "almost white" in their presumed beliefs and behaviors lessened the visibility and severity of their wartime confinement and other injustices. As depicted in popular forums, they gained new prominence by apparently recovering without any help to become "success stories" and forgiving any past wrongdoings against them. Media coverage framed Japanese Americans as law-abiding citizens who appreciated the opportunities for assimilation, advancement, and abundance, an alluring vision that coincided with the promises of a postwar American utopia. This later image, however, served to limit any voicing of grievances and to discourage social movements against a governing system that had forsaken them. It also worked to discipline other ethnic minorities, especially Latinos and African Americans, who demanded more state interventions to protect their rights and to rectify structural inequalities. By the mid-1960s, a prevailing logic emerged among sociologists, editorialists, and politicians that if Japanese Americans could flourish in the United States despite whatever setbacks, then others had no excuse for their own failures to enjoy what the nation offered.[7]

Japan and its revived industries became a U.S. base of operations not only to restrict communist influence but also to integrate market and military alliances with developing countries in Asia. Similar to West Germany's role in Europe, Japan played the junior partner to the United States in these efforts, accommodating American and allied troops to fight in Korea and forming trade networks with Southeast Asia and beyond.[8] Presenting the island nation as a reformed state also helped to downplay its imperial past and an evolving U.S. expansionism. Prominent writers familiar with Asia, such as Pearl S. Buck and James A. Michener, endorsed the need for Japan and other nations to help stabilize the region, while denying that the United States was reenacting or furthering its earlier turn-of-the-century imperial ventures. Despite the establishment of overseas military bases and client states, they saw U.S. involvements in the Pacific as opportunities for building friendships with other countries.[9] In this way, American disavowals of postwar empire building coincided with recognizing the pitfalls in showcasing supremacy over peoples of color. As Mary Dudziak explains, a new emphasis on "Cold War civil rights" arose, wherein U.S. statesmen urged a readjustment in racist practices on the home front. These changes were essential to attracting countries with nonwhite populations in the Middle East, Africa, Latin America, and Asia to an American-led global order. Otherwise, the Kremlin had only to suggest that postcolonial nations would experience similar bigoted conduct from the United States. Cold War imperatives to advertise "the American way of life," as opposed to what the communists offered, thus dictated that memories of World War II and perceptions of U.S. racism required reshaping to meet the latest challenges.[10]

Yet such abruptness in reversing earlier animosities in transpacific relations elicited uncertainty among the victors, the vanquished, and the victims. However constructed, the new world order still retained raw traumas and residual prejudices from the past, even as it created other problems.

Exultant after winning a world war, Americans realized that the days of international isolation were over and that the United States had to lead a new global coalition against communism. As John Dower and Naoko Shibusawa have demonstrated, Americans accepted Japan as a junior partner in this fight, in part because of U.S.-made popular images that depicted the defeated nation as infantile and thus submissive.[11] But many continued to distrust Japan, a response with racial overtones intensified by the Pacific War and left to simmer long afterward. Stereotypes of Japanese "inscrutability" and fears of Japan's receptiveness to communism only added further misgivings about a new ally. In truth, mainstream editorialists gathered that the Japanese would not be so compliant under American guidance. *Commonweal* declared in 1951, "The fact remains that Japan cannot be a reliable ally unless the Japanese people are a willing partner of the non-Communist powers." That willingness, the writer intimated, was suspect, as Japan began the process of regaining its sovereignty after the occupation. In the same year, *Newsweek* envisioned a drastic scene: "By joining the Communist East, Japan, as the most advanced country in Asia, can achieve its old aim of dominating China and the rest of the Far East." The magazine conjured the frightening wartime specter of Japan's imperial presence in the region. This time, however, the country would have communist allies to help revitalize its ascendancy. If this opinion sounded melodramatic, others chimed in at similar decibels. Edwin O. Reischauer, the noted Japan specialist at Harvard University and later a U.S. ambassador to that nation, likewise remarked in the *New York Times Magazine* in 1956, "If Japan does not become a major asset for our side, there is always the possibility . . . that she might join the Communist camp." The United States had to keep nurturing democracy in Japan, he cautioned, or else its industrial output and technological savvy, combined with a potential partnership with communist China, would be "the death blow to democratic hopes in Asia." Fears of a reimagined Asiatic horde were palpable: instead of becoming a model ally, the Japanese could join the Chinese as a postwar yellow peril.[12]

This matter gained urgency in the reconstruction of Japan. With a despairing and disillusioned populace, the nation attempted to reformulate past intentions, particularly its militarist ambitions. The demands of the imperial hierarchy had resulted in defeat and exhaustion, leading many Japanese intellectuals to fault previously cherished ideals and institutions, from the emperor on down. Affected by the power and presence of the U.S. occupation, people's everyday language adjusted to acknowledge the benefits of democracy and antimilitarism. Some even satirized Japan's folly in feeding its expansionist appetites. In other cases, however, the occupation itself came under scrutiny and even mockery. To American foreign policy makers, these viewpoints were a constant source of danger that smacked of communist and socialist encouragement. The new Japanese constitution established under American auspices in 1947 renounced war and militarism, guaranteed trade union rights and universal suffrage, provided women with more rights, and protected freedom of speech and assembly, among other issues. But U.S. efforts to contain communism in the Pacific, along with an economic downturn and mass demonstrations in Japan, made American officials anxious about their new ally's susceptibility to Soviet pressure. In response to these concerns, occupation authorities enacted a "reverse-course" policy in which they reinstated to power once-purged Japanese business and government leaders to bolster the country's financial stability. Democratic reforms became less important in this scenario, as U.S.-supported Japanese authorities began suppressing labor groups and other activists that pushed for further social advances. China's establishment of a communist government and the Soviet Union's testing of an atomic bomb in 1949 ensured this more conservative turn by the United States in Japan's rebuilding. The start of the Korean War in 1950 also contributed, rousing Japan's economy through a massive dose of U.S. military spending. But after the occupation ended in 1952, public opinion polls revealed ongoing concerns among Japan's populace. Between 1956 and 1962, for instance, more than 50 percent of respondents regularly opposed having U.S. military bases in Japan, while a range of only 14 to 18 percent favored them. For many Japanese, doubts about, and discontent with, the American presence in their homeland and U.S. influence on their political leadership remained constant.[13]

Alongside these developments, the wartime confinement of Japanese Americans became an "absent presence," as Caroline Chung Simpson phrases it, a painful past unseen and unsaid, yet still extant as a submerged narrative within U.S. triumphal memories of "the Good War." Fearful of communism and enthralled by mass consumerism, most Americans avoided addressing the incarceration of civilians and other egregious actions based on little more than racial prejudice.[14] The formerly imprisoned themselves remained silent about their wartime experiences, with feelings of shame overshadowing, but not dissipating, their hurts, losses, and grievances. When released from the camps, the Issei and Nisei simply wanted to rebuild their lives and sought a return to normalcy. Even so, migrating back to the West Coast or resettling in other regions also meant facing instances of racism, some involving physical violence or the destruction of property. Starting their lives and careers again from almost nothing posed other hardships for Japanese Americans, such as limited work and housing opportunities, not to mention the untold psychological sufferings endured.[15] The confinement and its aftermath thus became something that younger generations did not learn about until decades later. As one elder recalled from that sorrowful time, "When shame is put on you, you try to hide it. We were put into camp, we became victims, it was our fault. We hide it." Another confessed to literally interring his remembrances of confinement: "Before leaving camp, I buried my diary, in which I had written about many bitter memories. . . . I even buried the good memories I had committed to paper."[16] Not until the late 1960s and early 1970s, with persistent civil rights activism, the advent of films and writings on the issue, and the beginnings of the Japanese American redress movement, did many seek public notice and reparations for their earlier misfortunes.[17]

Given these concerns, the dual emergence of Japan as a model ally and Japanese Americans as a model minority within a U.S. Cold War mind-set requires more critical interrogation. This book offers a cultural perspective that includes Japanese and Japanese American voices that spoke within and around such developments.[18] The following chapters provide such an outlook through the lives and works of four figures: the novelist Hanama Tasaki, the actor Yamaguchi Yoshiko, the painter Henry Sugimoto, and the children's author Yoshiko Uchida. In the late 1940s to the early 1960s and beyond, these writers and artists, along with sympathizers in the arts industry (editors, publishers, reviewers, film producers, and others) offered more engaging visions of transpacific relations that played into, but also challenged, the rehabilitated images of Japan and Japanese Americans. The topics these figures brought into public view through their work were wide ranging, yet interrelated. These encompassed the racial legacies of the Pacific War, the migrations between the United States and Japan, the imperial endeavors of both nations, and the wartime confinement of Japanese Americans. Through their varying efforts and interests, the four individuals created public personas and imaginative spaces in cultural forms that allowed audiences to consider domestic and global relations in complex and contradictory ways.

I identify this group of artists and writers as "Japanese/Americans" to denote their heterogeneous backgrounds and concerns that highlighted the influence of transpacific encounters on American Cold War culture. To trace these different yet intertwined and shifting markers of "Japanese" and "American," I adapt David Palumbo-Liu's broader framing of U.S.-Asia relations and their impact on Americans of Asian ancestry. By writing "Asian/American," Palumbo-Liu explains that the solidus "marks *both* the distinction installed between 'Asian' and 'American' *and* a dynamic, unsettled, and inclusive movement."[19] This construct emphasizes the separations formed from the history of legal restraints that disallowed Asians from entering the United States and from the exclusionary practices used against them once they were within the country, where they were still considered "perpetual foreigners." Conversely, each term also merges with, and destabilizes, the meanings of the other, creating new possibilities for understanding or extending what constitutes modern America. The "and/or" positioning thus indicates the concurrent tensions and overlaps that arise from cross-cultural interactions. Important, too, the relationships between signifiers on each side of the divide can change over time, even within a person's identity, outlook, or career. In light of this wide-ranging assessment of Asian/America, more focused work on particular periods and populations becomes necessary as well. The four artists and writers examined here contributed to postwar Japanese/American formations in multiple ways that defied issues of loyalty, citizenship, or national borders, just as these figures were constrained by them.[20] Indeed, the sociopolitical structures and lingering racial prejudices that undergirded the transitions from wartime confinements to Cold War containments—as broadly defined restrictions on bodies, movements, ideas, and images—were very real. This book assesses how the arts in the postwar period offered a range of tools to critique relations at home and abroad that blurred the boundaries and categories that the United States sought to impose on its minority populace and on other nations.

No doubt the doctrine of containment shaped in vital ways how the United States realized its power and possibilities domestically and throughout the world. As Alan Nadel observes, "Because of the United States' unprecedented capacity in the decades following World War II to deploy arms and images, to construct alliances and markets, to dominate global entertainment, capitalize global production, and epitomize global power, containment was perhaps one of the most powerfully deployed national narratives in recorded history."[21] Intended to counter Soviet expansion, American influence on other nations and regions was unsurpassed in its political, cultural, economic, and military scope. Yet containment served domestic as well as global purposes, pervading nearly every aspect of postwar American culture. As several scholars have argued, "containment" proved a useful metaphor for describing and controlling perceived threats within the United States: communist sympathizers in Hollywood, women in the workforce, civil rights activists on the streets, homosexuals in government agencies, among other groups. Containment as an overarching idea thus affected how Americans negotiated and contested their social relations with one another through their understandings of gender and sexuality, race relations, and class antagonisms as well as political, regional, and religious affiliations.[22] The machinery of McCarthyism in government and in public life as well as other repressive measures on the home front, such as racial segregation, certainly constricted the clout and capacity of dissenting voices. But recent critical work demonstrates how these systems of containment were not monolithic but malleable and scattered, unintentionally allowing for opposition to ensue. Alternative viewpoints appeared and persevered, challenging how the nation's political apparatus functioned by coopting its ideals of fairness, domesticity, patriotism, citizenship, and other issues.[23]

This point applies to how Japanese/Americans in the arts became a determined public presence in the early Cold War era, but in more fluid, transnational ways. The backgrounds of the four figures reveal this mixing of nationalities, borrowing of cultures, and combining of domestic and overseas interests as well as the inherent risks involved when proceeding in such directions. The popular but now forgotten novelist Hanama Tasaki was a Hawai'i-born Nisei who fought for Japan in World War II because of the racial discrimination he faced in the United States. Remaining overseas in Japan after the war, he still appealed to his native land to adhere to its democratic ideals when getting involved in Asian affairs. Yamaguchi Yoshiko was a famous Manchuria-born Japanese actor and singer who posed as a Chinese national starring in propaganda films for imperial Japan. In her postwar Hollywood phase, however, she played fictional characters in the process of "becoming American." Henry Sugimoto was a Japan-born Issei artist long troubled by his wartime incarceration, revisiting the topic in his paintings for the rest of his life. But he also embraced the opportunity to become a U.S. citizen, even as he expressed a love for European aesthetics and pictured himself as an artist unbounded by styles, themes, or borders. The children's author Yoshiko Uchida was a California-born Nisei who wrote about the imprisonment of Japanese Americans in popular young-adult books. Yet she also wanted to strengthen U.S.-Asia relations and began her career crafting Japanese folktales to ease the postwar tensions and misunderstandings between her ancestral and native lands.

All of these individuals journeyed between the United States and Japan and to other parts of the globe as well. These travels and wider social contacts informed identities, works, and worldviews that disclosed cosmopolitan sensibilities. Although few of the figures used the term "cosmopolitan" to describe themselves or their projects, they did favor more inclusive interactions between cultures and beyond borders that contested the Cold War's binary distinctions between "us" and "them."[24] At the same time, the artists and writers aligned their understandings of the world with the principles of Cold War liberalism in problematic ways. Contrasted against communism, this set of Western beliefs assumed universal desires among societies for the benefits of democracy, free markets, individual rights, national self-determination, reason, and scientific progress. Yet, since the eighteenth century, the aim of liberal nation-states to implement these concepts and systems has coexisted in tension with what they have enacted against their own populaces and the rest of the world such as labor exploitation, imperial interventions, immigration and trade restrictions, and other policies that have ensured regional, racial, gender, and class hierarchies.[25] As transpacific actors, the four artists and writers acknowledged, even welcomed, liberalism's global influence and inclusive values while critiquing its exclusive practices. But they avoided offering developed political commentary and demonstrated worldliness in the most general sense when appreciating and encouraging the diversity of exchanges among peoples, cultures, and nations. This stance was not about transcending differences so much as accepting and working within them in order to fashion more cooperative communities in the wake of war. The two Nisei authors—Hanama Tasaki and Yoshiko Uchida—cautioned against American aims to unilaterally spread liberal democratic values and practices, and thus U.S. power and influence, throughout the world. They instead advocated for postwar Japan and other nations to cultivate their own versions of peaceful, democratic societies. The two persons born in East Asia—Yamaguchi Yoshiko and Henry Sugimoto—initially identified their cultural affinities and desired public images with China and France, respectively, and not with their ancestral land. By the postwar era, they came to recognize, through creative ventures in film and art, the history of geopolitical friction between the United States and Japan that they hoped to assuage. Each of these positions developed over the course of years, during which these artists and writers adjusted to shifting conditions within nations and continents.[26]

More specifically, the aftershocks of communal wartime suffering informed the four figures' thoughts on, and encounters across, the Pacific. The series of conflicts in Asia and their repercussions in the United States stirred among them a desire to nurture affective links among different populations that, in turn, inspired how they approached their work. For those living in Japan, but originally from elsewhere (Hanama Tasaki and Yamaguchi Yoshiko), enlarging their career prospects meant attracting American audiences wary of rising U.S. commitments in East Asia. To accomplish this goal, the writer faced and the actor masked their feelings of war guilt about imperial Japan's destruction of China. For the Issei and Nisei figures based in the United States (Henry Sugimoto and Yoshiko Uchida), incorporating the Japanese diaspora as subject matter gave broader and deeper meaning to their imaginative labors. These efforts arose from an urge to confront the haunting anguish of their wartime confinement. In this manner, we can see how they all occupied interstitial positions. Although enjoying the privileges gained as world-traveling cultural producers, they were also vulnerable to state power as displaced or exploited subjects. The group thus disclosed perspectives that were historically situated and in dialogue with social and political developments in the United States and abroad. Having incurred suspicion, discrimination, imprisonment, and other hindrances, they were attentive to how U.S. interventions and anxieties regarding global affairs intersected to shape definitions of race and national belonging.

This book converges with, and builds on, prior work that links Asian American studies and Cold War studies, but with a focus on the arts as a mode for cultural critique. Scholarship on Japanese Americans has emphasized their wartime incarceration, since it was, and still is, the defining event of their history in the United States. A host of volumes have examined the government policies behind removal and confinement, the inmates' varied experiences and responses, and how Japanese Americans first became seen as model citizens during World War II, with the Nisei's military service and professions of loyalty to the United States.[27] Other works have focused on the postwar period, when changing relations with China, Japan, and Korea affected how the United States saw Asian Americans as threatening aliens and as assimilating subjects.[28] Scholars have also explored how mainstream Americans embraced distant lands and peoples as potential Cold War allies through popular culture. For Christina Klein, interpreting Asia through film, musicals, novels, and other venues provided white Americans a way to comprehend the continent as underdeveloped and immature, and thus requiring U.S. guidance and protection from communists. These forums, as she suggests, helped to create sentimental bonds between U.S. audiences and Asian subjects to integrate and strengthen global alliances. For Naoko Shibusawa, Americans reimagined Japan as a childlike nation in the stages of developing into a junior partner willing to accede to U.S. wishes. This strategy reinforced American hierarchies of power over the Japanese with regard to race, gender, and maturity.[29] Considering the artists and writers in this study discloses the nuanced relationships that Japanese/Americans had with reviewers and audiences when critiquing the wartime confinement and other prejudicial accounts through a transpacific framework. These cultural enactments attract our attention because they spoke to, and moved beyond, the state subjugation of a minority populace and its ensuing rise as a model citizenry that served to shroud this subjugation from public memories of the Pacific War. While doing so, the four figures also exposed the strains of having to navigate their personae and performances between two warring, then allied, nation-states, while entangled in the desires and aggressions of each.

In this rendering, the late 1940s to early 1960s gave rise to fascinating moments when Japanese/Americans developed what Viet Thanh Nguyen calls "flexible strategies" to convey stories.[30] The literary and visual narratives examined here played on the promises of American principles in complex ways when responding to U.S. demands for fidelity and forgetfulness. Rather than choosing between resisting and accommodating these expectations, the four artists and writers negotiated among different ideologies, institutions, and cultural authorities to get their efforts noticed. Adopting such flexible strategies to create cultural forms was a matter of professional survival and adaptability, given that many of the publishers, art critics, filmmakers, and audiences they hoped to attract belonged to the American mainstream. To gain public approval, these individuals evaded or revised particular stances when asserting themselves through the arts. Other moments reveal how they took on the liberal state's ideals to critique its failings, even as they lent credence to its power and potential. But throughout this process, the group still articulated its hopes for, and frustrations with, U.S. encounters with peoples of Asian ancestry at home and abroad.

Chapter 1 examines the brief popularity of the Hawai'i-born novelist Hanama Tasaki (1913–1996). I discuss his once best-selling, but now neglected, antiwar novel, *Long the Imperial Way* (1950), which portrays the sufferings and war guilt of a Japanese soldier in occupied China during the 1930s. Tasaki based the work on his own experiences in China, and he later fought for Japan during World War II, decisions that marked him as "not quite American." Yet his birth in Hawai'i made him "not quite Japanese." The chapter compares this background with postwar fiction and histories about Japanese Americans in Hawai'i that portrayed the Nisei as patriotic and self-sacrificing model citizens, despite whatever past discrimination they faced. Tasaki positioned himself alongside these 1950s narratives as an anti-imperialist reformer, explaining the destructive methods of Japanese expansionism for an American nation reasserting its own presence in East Asia. Reviewers took to his novel's lessons about the limits of imperial desires when debating U.S. involvement in Korea and in the occupation of Japan. Tasaki later revealed broader cosmopolitan yearnings in a second novel, *The Mountains Remain* (1952), when an Imperial Army veteran returns home after the war, willing to consider all points of view—capitalist and communist, traditionalist and reformist—to create a new Japan. This text, however, received less notice from American readers, revealing their rejection of alternatives to U.S. unilateral influence on a postwar ally.

Chapter 2 analyzes the Hollywood arrival of Yamaguchi Yoshiko (1920–2014), a famous Japanese singer and actor, through her films *Japanese War Bride* (1952) and *House of Bamboo* (1955). Known in wartime Asia as an entertainer who played the Chinese love interest of Japanese men for imperial Japan's propaganda films, Yamaguchi shed her Chinese public persona and transformed herself in the postwar era (as "Shirley Yamaguchi") by portraying a Japanese war bride involved with American GIs. I contextualize her new visibility through popular media coverage on the marriages between American servicemen and Japanese women during and after the occupation of Japan. Considering these relationships as part of the intimacies of empire, I examine film reviews and other publicity to show how Yamaguchi and her Hollywood productions intensified American interest in Japan. Her status as a transpacific cosmopolitan, bolstered by her marriage to the celebrated Nisei sculptor and designer Isamu Noguchi (1904–1988), also bestowed attention on Japanese Americans and their mass imprisonment. Yet Yamaguchi's postwar identities and Hollywood movie roles, in which she performed the parallel feats of "becoming Japanese" and "becoming American," served to quell the specters of Japanese and U.S. empire building, while her films reinforced the stereotypes of Japan as a model ally and Japanese Americans as a model minority.

Chapter 3 considers the wartime and postwar art of Henry Sugimoto (1900–1990), an Issei painter incarcerated in the camps at Jerome and Rohwer, Arkansas. Like other imprisoned Japanese American artists, Sugimoto wanted to document his trying experiences and the landscapes in which they occurred. Unlike others who stopped painting after the war or who moved into abstract art, he continued to explore and expand on the themes of incarceration from the 1950s to the 1980s. His postwar art especially divulges a wider transpacific vision of Japanese American history, from the turn-of-the-twentieth-century Japanese immigration and the restrictions placed on it to the wartime confinement and the dropping of atomic bombs on Japan. The postwar era thus reveals how he was still tormented by the wartime incarceration that challenged his sense of American and Japanese identities, destabilizing the "Japanese immigrant becomes an American citizen" success narrative. The chapter traces his developing artistic sensibilities about the confinement period and about U.S.-Japan relations through his adaptations of Mexican muralist and French Postimpressionist influences. Although Sugimoto defined himself as a worldly and apolitical artist, he revealed through his styles and themes a trenchant social critique of war, migration, and imprisonment as interrelated processes.

Chapter 4 focuses on Yoshiko Uchida (1921–1992), a popular, award-winning Nisei author of children's literature, with a career spanning the late 1940s to the early 1990s. This chapter focuses on her earlier works from the late 1940s to the early 1960s that divulged her interest in Japanese culture, when Japan and the United States attempted to restore peaceful relations. Uchida desired to enhance cultural understanding among the younger generations, publishing works about Japanese folktales, while also portraying the interactions of white American, Japanese, and Japanese American protagonists in other books. She admitted that this period of creativity was crucial to understanding herself as both American and Japanese after her release from the camp in Topaz, Utah. As a child, she wanted to be "American, not Japanese," even though her country saw her as "Japanese, not American." The confinement unsettled her ideas about what it meant to be a native-born U.S. citizen, but also helped her appreciate her ancestral culture. In turn, Uchida's valuing of her family's heritage helped her, from the 1970s to the 1990s, to produce books and memoirs about the wartime imprisonment. These later and more well-known works on the confinement had cosmopolitan roots in the early Cold War era, when she wrote about Japanese society and culture, more so than in the later civil rights period of the 1960s and 1970s.

Immigration, war, empire building, occupation, and confinement provided the historical bases from which these four individuals became products and shapers of larger transactions, both beneficial and perilous, between two nations.[31] Surveying the overlaps between these case studies permits us to see not only the relationships between larger global forces but also how the artists and writers responded to them in both critical and compromised ways. In turn, their film, art, and literature made visible to the American public the linked processes of U.S. actions at home and abroad. Their efforts thus reveal how American Cold War culture itself proved susceptible to dissent, critique, and complication from transpacific exchanges, just as the United States could still work to contain these disparate voices and visions because of its Cold War concerns. Within these possibilities and pressures, Japanese/Americans in the arts crafted, claimed, and altered their public presence to interrogate a problematic past while offering more hopeful prospects for the future.

1

Reorienting Empires

Hanama Tasaki's War Guilt and
U.S.-Japan Relations

THROUGHOUT THE 1950s, popular writings in the United States presented Hawai'i and Japan as part of the American strategic defense system
against the growing threat of communism in Asia. Hawai'i was a "ram-
part of the Pacific," as one writer put it, while others described postwar Japan
as a "bulwark" or a "far eastern citadel."[1] In each rendering, the people inhabiting these sites of U.S. occupation not only protected American interests
against communist encroachment but also were on the vanguard of propagat-
ing freedom and democracy to the Asian mainland. Hawai'i was especially
important in this regard when publicized as a multiracial democracy that
showcased American acceptance of ethnic minorities to nonwhite peoples
overseas. Immigrant and native-born Japanese Americans proved crucial to
both locations' positioning within the geographic and ideological struggles
between the United States and the Soviet Union. As U.S. citizens, the Nisei in
particular withstood distrust from the white mainstream during World War
II and became a model of loyalty and patriotism to the American cause. Postwar fiction and historical studies about Hawai'i depicted them as ready and
willing to contribute to the nation's security in troubling times.[2] Meanwhile,
Nisei soldiers serving in the U.S. occupation forces as well as businessmen,
journalists, and others traveling or working in Japan were touted as cultural
ambassadors who could demonstrate to their ancestral homeland the benefits
of living under liberal democratic principles.[3]

One figure who attracted popular attention at this time, but in a very different way, was Hanama Tasaki, a Hawai'i-born Nisei who lived in postwar

Japan. Although forgotten today, he enjoyed a short-lived renown for his anti-war novel, *Long the Imperial Way,* which appeared on the American market in August 1950. The story focuses on the intense emotional and physical struggles of a young Japanese soldier, Takeo Yamamoto, who serves in China during the late 1930s. Takeo's life in the Imperial Army consists of great suffering and brutality. He not only endures harsh military discipline from his superiors but also must participate in the large-scale violence inflicted on the Chinese in both northern and southern provinces. The text traces in bildungsroman fashion Takeo's developing moral conscience as he sporadically embraces, but then rejects, the empire's expansionist aims and the perpetual warfare promised for its soldiers and civilians.[4]

Tasaki based *Long the Imperial Way* on some of his own experiences. The son of Issei laborers, he spent most of his youth in Maui and attended McKinley High School in Honolulu, where he participated in its citizenship club. He enrolled briefly at Oberlin College and then at the University of Hawai'i, and worked in California for a year alongside Japanese American farmers. But something else came to occupy his attention. Roused by Japan's rising power and influence in East Asia, and angered by *haole* (white ruling elite) prejudice in Hawai'i, he traveled to his ancestral land in 1936 to enlist in the Imperial Army, which stationed him in China.[5] He later became a reporter for the *Osaka Mainichi Shimbun* and the Domei News Agency, followed by combat tours in the South Pacific during World War II. Tasaki gained notice for his English-language skills and in 1942 translated for publication the Imperial Rescript declaring war on the United States and Great Britain. After the war, the veteran earned his keep as a livestock farmer, a toy maker, and a refuse hauler in Japan. While recuperating from tuberculosis, he began working on *Long the Imperial Way* to relieve his "guilt complex" wrought from the carnage that the Japanese military unleashed on the rest of Asia.[6]

The author privately published his English-language work in 1949, offering it to Tokyo bookshops that catered to the U.S. occupation forces. He labored in obscurity until an American officer, who appreciated the novel's merits, sent it to the Boston-based publisher Houghton Mifflin. The company then released the book a year later to widespread critical acclaim in the United States.[7] Reviewers hailed *Long the Imperial Way* as one of the first major works of fiction emerging from postwar Japan. The *New York Times* listed it as one of the top 275 books of the 10,000 titles published that year. A *Chicago Daily Tribune* critic went further, including it on his "Ten Books of the Year" list. Another columnist likewise praised the work's qualities in the *Saturday Review of Literature.* As one sign of the novel's mass appeal, *Reader's Digest* distributed Tasaki's text as part of its Condensed Books series. Several enthusiasts even compared *Long the Imperial Way* to such classics as

Erich Maria Remarque's *All Quiet on the Western Front* (1929) and Norman Mailer's *The Naked and the Dead* (1948).[8]

A Japanese novel set in China, written by a Japanese American for a mainstream American audience: given this unusual mix of the book's topic, its author's background, and its reception history, *Long the Imperial Way* presents both challenges and opportunities for contemporary evaluation. Perhaps due to the author's Nisei origins, Asian American studies scholars claim *Long the Imperial Way* as an important, underappreciated work. Indeed, the title occasionally appears on lists in overview essays that call for broader or different ways to analyze Asian American literature.[9] Yet the novel has attracted little to no critical attention, even with the recent emphasis on transnational approaches to interpreting texts.[10] Part of the difficulty in assessing *Long the Imperial Way* lies in its lack of discernible themes that relate to the experiences of Asian Americans. Unlike seminal Japanese American works published during the postwar period—Miné Okubo's *Citizen 13660* (1946), Toshio Mori's *Yokohama, California* (1949), Monica Sone's *Nisei Daughter* (1953), and John Okada's *No-No Boy* (1957)—Tasaki's narrative makes no mention of the Issei and Nisei. In fact, *Long the Imperial Way* provides no commentary on American life and culture. Nowhere does the main protagonist Takeo Yamamoto even long for a chance at the good life in the United States. The text addresses only Takeo and his squad's three-year ordeal in China, charting their disaffection through the mundane and terrifying aspects of military life: marching, scavenging for food, serving on guard duty, skirmishing against guerillas, engaging in all-out battles, and enduring discipline from superiors. No character among them is a Nisei fighting in the Imperial Army. Complicating matters of classification, both Tasaki and *Long the Imperial Way* migrated across the Pacific, but in opposite directions—he to Japan, his work to the United States—testing more conventional definitions of a "minority writer" creating "ethnic literature."[11]

Yet, if *Long the Imperial Way* is not quite Asian American literature, it does reveal important issues concerning the field. For instance, we can see how transpacific movements, shaped by the overlapping imperial histories of the United States and Japan, affected the novel's production, distribution, and reception.[12] Author and text in this way align with Susan Koshy's concept of "minority cosmopolitanism." As she observes, "The topography of literary production and consumption has been transformed as writers and texts travel . . . and writers' locations, audiences, and subject matter resist ready alignment."[13] Here, Koshy argues for the significance of works that address, reconfigure, and result from contacts beyond national borders. She contends as well that such relations are "grounded in the experience of minority subjects," from which writers are conscious of "the constraints of primary attachments, such as family, religion, race, and nation." But they can still convey "the disruptions and asymmetries of intercultural encounter while sustaining an openness to its transformative possibilities."[14] This position seeks to avoid romanticizing transnationalism as a way to exceed or ignore social, political, and racial boundaries by recognizing the levels of institutional pressures enacted on artists from minority backgrounds. At the same time, minority cosmopolitanism valorizes opportunities in cultural expressions that can extend the range of writing beyond those limitations.

Such is the case and more with Hanama Tasaki and *Long the Imperial Way*. As an ethnic minority coming of age in the United States, the author was familiar with the racial constraints enacted on him, even in the multicultural environment of Hawai'i. Yet his service in the Imperial Army as a Nisei (another kind of minority in different circumstances) placed him in a position to oppress other civilian populations, much to his later regret. Interviewed by the *New York Times* in 1950, Tasaki expressed hope that his work would contribute to "a freer exchange of artists, writers and intellectuals" between Asia and the United States. He suggested, too, that these cultural interactions could prompt more peaceful international relations as well as an Asian renaissance of the arts.[15] Like most of the populace in postwar Japan, Tasaki suffered from remorse for, and disillusionment about, what the militarist state imposed at home and abroad. He sought absolution by writing *Long the Imperial Way*, which provided "an outlet for the strong yearning for beauty which replaced the great void after the war."[16] But the novel went beyond a search for personal redemption through artistic endeavors. *Long the Imperial Way* also disclosed to American readers the broader entangling legacies of war and empire building in Asia, detailing the levels of power an imperial state could exert over its citizens, soldiers, and colonial subjects. Just as important, the work exposed the extent to which these populations could oppose, alter, or adapt to this authority, suggesting that it was neither constant nor totalizing.[17] By fictionalizing the disastrous effects of ruling other lands, the novel further posed implicit warnings that some reviewers applied to the U.S. military intervention in Korea and to the continuing occupation of Japan. We can then perceive the author as an important interlocutor in U.S.-Asia relations, outlining through his work the destructive practices of Japanese militarism for a nation reasserting its own influence in the Pacific theater.

The book publicity on Tasaki's Hawaiian upbringing and postwar career in Japan played a vital role in helping readers comprehend these overseas issues. His positioning as a minority cosmopolitan writer relied on his malleable "Japanese" and "American" identities that incorporated, destabilized, and shifted between both categories. His status as a "Japanese/American" author was thus complicated by its varying degrees of indeterminacy. He was "not quite American" due to his alienated racial identity and his tours of duty with the Imperial Army. But he was also "not quite Japanese," having been born and raised in Hawai'i. Tasaki negotiated these cultural worlds by engaging the "absent presence" of his Nisei subjectivity that book reviewers were complicit in reproducing.[18] That is, Tasaki and the promotional material about *Long the Imperial Way* selectively masked and acknowledged aspects of his life story, especially regarding his ethnicity and U.S. citizenship. This hybrid status in turn raised larger, troubling questions about race, empire, and Tasaki's national loyalties, in light of his military service. Even then, he aspired to transcend these issues through his postwar plea for expanding universal rights based on liberal democratic ideals. He thought that this desire could work only if the United States abandoned its aim to impose its values unilaterally and allowed other nations to develop in their own ways. But he still advanced this position from within a liberal framework that downplayed U.S. empire-building efforts, part of which began in Hawai'i. In this way, Tasaki and his novel performed valuable, yet problematic, cultural work for an American public wrestling with its new place and power in the world.

Hawai'i provided an important context for the absent presence of Tasaki's Nisei identity, marking both the visibility of U.S. race relations and the invisibility of American imperial ambitions. Alongside works about Hawai'i published in the early Cold War period, Tasaki's biography for the book's marketing reinforced an emerging narrative about how the islands' Japanese Americans contributed to building and strengthening a democratic society, despite the previous wartime suspicions against them. Yet the concurrent debates over admitting Hawai'i as a state revealed public concerns about assimilating racial Others into the white mainstream. In response, supporters of statehood hoped that Hawai'i's inclusion in the United States would show the world how readily the nation accepted ethnic minorities and countries with nonwhite citizens. This stance was crucial to contest Soviet propaganda about American racism. Tasaki's Hawaiian rearing, as detailed in the promotional material, aligned with these latter priorities. Although the author apparently had rejected the bounty and values offered in Hawai'i to fight for imperial Japan, he now posed as an unwilling conscript caught up in the torrents of war, a theme that pervades *Long the Imperial Way.* Tasaki and his American background, however, presented challenges to book reviewers who described him as a Japanese writer, even though they acknowledged his birth as a U.S. citizen. This matter coincided with how critics deflected charges of American empire building in the Pacific. They did so by highlighting the author's democratic upbringing in Hawai'i and how it contributed to his anti-imperialist portrayal of Japan's wartime aggressions.

Another component of transpacific relations that Tasaki addressed was the U.S. occupation of Japan. Readers praised *Long the Imperial Way* as a rare ethnographic account that humanized the Japanese as victims of militarism and empire building who needed American guidance to point them in the right direction. This depiction corresponded with the broader efforts among U.S. policy makers to gain public support for the Cold War alliance between the United States and Japan. But Tasaki later problematized how this relationship would work. His sequel, *The Mountains Remain* (1952), portrays the veteran Takeo Yamamoto returning to a defeated Japan after surviving the South Pacific campaigns. Although the book later came out in several different languages, American critics mainly ignored it. *The Mountains Remain* sold poorly in the United States, perhaps because it presented the central character pondering multiple options to reconstruct his devastated nation, rather than relying simply on U.S. leadership. The second novel also disclosed Tasaki's further cosmopolitan leanings, from which he dramatized the debates in Japan among reformers and traditionalists, capitalists and communists, Christians and secularists, among others. But the timing of the novel's appearance in 1952 may have worried American readers, given the uncertainty over the directions Japan might take after resuming its sovereignty when the occupation officially ended.

In many ways, then, Tasaki's novels provoked responses that both legitimized and critiqued attempts to contain communism through a U.S. presence in the Pacific. American readers recognized the significance of the author's work, conferring *Long the Imperial Way* in particular with cultural resonance because the text addressed a variety of their fears and aspirations about influencing a geographic expanse that Japan once controlled.

A Nisei amid Two Empires

Hanama Tasaki and other Nisei who journeyed abroad traversed the boundaries between Japanese and American imperial exploits in the Pacific. Diverse reasons impelled this population to venture outside the United States and its territories during the early twentieth century. Many sought educational or employment opportunities in Japan, or in regions under its colonial dominion such as Korea and Manchuria. National and ethnic pride conveyed by Issei parents likewise contributed to the sense that their futures and fortunes coincided with those of fellow Japanese on the other side of the Pacific.[19] Racial prejudice in Hawai'i and on the U.S. mainland motivated these migrations too. Alien land laws, immigration restrictions, denial of naturalization opportunities, housing and employment discrimination, and other exclusionary practices only exacerbated the feeling that the Issei and their progeny would find life difficult within a hostile white nation. More than a few Nisei were sojourners who went to Japan for their education or for prospects in business, journalism, and other occupations, but they eventually returned to the United States. Presenting aspects of "migrant nationalism," to use Mae Ngai's phrase, they admired Japan's show of strength in Asia while retaining the legal and cultural attachments of their American lives. This sense of belonging to two worlds was not inherently stable and coherent, but flexible in how it informed ethnic minority communities' sense of themselves. People's national loyalties overlapped and shifted over time when defining their experiences. Even before the Pacific War erupted, however, maintaining this complicated in-between state was no longer viable. Nations compelled them to choose sides.[20]

Whether an individual served in the armed forces for the United States or for Japan in World War II became the linchpin for determining a Japanese American's allegiance that reverberated well into the postwar era. Hawai'i-born Nisei who fought for the United States in the 100th Battalion and those from the mainland who comprised the 442nd Regimental Combat Team (which later absorbed most of the 100th) have received both popular and scholarly attention, partly because their decorated wartime heroism adhered to the romance of ethnic minority devotion to the American nation, despite the discriminatory practices they faced. As volunteers and draftees, the Nisei serving in these segregated detachments under white officers gained considerable notice for their courage and accomplishments on the battlefields of North Africa and Europe. That the U.S. government imprisoned Japanese Americans because of suspected wartime loyalties to imperial Japan, and that many of the mainland Nisei were fighting totalitarianism overseas for a nation that held their friends and families behind barbed wire, only added to the allure of their patriotism and sacrifices.[21]

After the war, many Nisei veterans and their supporters believed that service in the U.S. military helped to recuperate the image of Japanese Americans as a whole. As Monica Sone wrote in her 1953 memoir, *Nisei Daughter*: "The birth of the Nisei combat team was the climax to our evacuee life, and the turning point. It was the road back to our rightful places."[22] The Japanese American Citizens League (JACL) also publicized these soldiers' heroic deeds. Yet, at the war's onset and afterward, the JACL was a controversial organization within Japanese American communities. The association's leaders, attempting to make the best of the bad situation of removal and confinement, offered assistance to the federal government, in spite of their doubts. The league's moderate-to-conservative bent also alienated more progressive voices that critiqued its stances as unrepresentative of all Japanese Americans. That the organization notified U.S. intelligence agencies about certain persons it suspected as disloyal did not help its image.[23] But the JACL argued that the

Nisei veterans' wartime loyalty and sacrifices legitimated the fight for Cold War civil rights. Mike Masaoka, the executive secretary of the JACL and a 442nd veteran himself, promoted their model minority image to press for rights long denied to them in housing, employment, and education. Nisei veterans became politically active in other areas, especially in Hawai'i, where they challenged the white establishment's hold on the islands by running for local, state, and federal offices. Working with U.S. congressmen and other government officials, Masaoka boasted in 1953 that "the record of the 442nd has been more responsible than any other argument for the corrective and remedial legislation which persons of Japanese ancestry have gained" since the end of World War II.[24] This struggle included obtaining U.S. citizenship and property rights for the Issei, securing small amounts of financial reparations for the losses incurred by the confinement, and calling for Hawaiian statehood. To Masaoka and others in the JACL, the Nisei's military service bolstered their political and moral authority to correct the prewar restrictions on Japanese Americans and the adverse effects of their wartime experiences.[25]

Articles, editorials, and other news features that catered to mainstream audiences highlighted how the Nisei GIs, like the Japanese American populace in general, displayed such admirable traits as adapting to demanding circumstances, showing fidelity in the face of suspicion, and expressing forgiveness of those who wronged them. By focusing on the good behavior of those imprisoned in the camps and especially on the military service of the Nisei, however, many publications excused themselves from examining the broader political and structural reasons for the mass incarceration and other longstanding prejudices against Japanese Americans. *Reader's Digest,* for instance, privileged the 442nd's exploits over the sufferings and grievances of the larger Japanese American population to emphasize the themes of heroism and sacrifice. One writer for the magazine observed in 1956: "The conduct of the evacuated Japanese and, above all, the superb military record of the *Nisei* [italics original] had brought about a reversal in the feelings of most other Americans toward them."[26] Underlining the martial success of one ethnic minority while downplaying prejudicial state power reinforced the standard by which others succeeded or failed as individuals to overcome obstacles. In this way, *Reader's Digest* revealed the wartime racist frenzy against Japanese Americans as incidental to, rather than embedded within, the nation's principles, history, and social structures.

Downplaying racial prejudice in the United States through the Nisei soldiers also helped the postwar nation's overseas objectives. The servicemen provided reassurance in trying times by closing the credibility gap between American ideals and the nation's discriminatory practices toward minorities. "In a day when democracy seems to be diplomatically on the defensive," the

Saturday Review of Literature noted in 1947, "it is heartening to find proof of its vitality" in Hawai'i, where Japanese Americans participated fully in daily life, and with the example of the 442nd Regiment. Arguing that the growth of communism endangered democratic societies, the magazine presented the Nisei's loyalty and service as proof of the nation's fairness and acceptance of a diversified populace. But their war record became the primary allure of democracy's strength. As the article noted, "The thing above all others that lifted the Japanese-Americans from the undeserved abyss of hatred and mistrust was their military record."[27] Others connected the new perception of Japanese Americans with the new direction in U.S.-Japan relations. Viewed through a Cold War lens, valorizing the Nisei soldiers and transforming Japan into an anticommunist ally served to allay American anxieties about world affairs. In 1957, Christopher Rand reported in the *New Yorker* on the rising popularity of Japanese Americans in light of Japan's new role in the Pacific. "In general," he wrote, "the [N]isei, the first crop of real Japanese-Americans, appear to stand well with the public at large, partly because of their fine war record, and partly . . . because of the recent switch in American sentiments toward Japan."[28] Like others, Rand invoked the 442nd as representative of the entire Nisei population, correlating military service with U.S. citizenship. For the author, the Nisei GIs offered a more compelling face for public consumption than the discriminatory past from which they arose.

Hollywood also contributed to these perceptions of the Nisei's martial sacrifices for the United States through the MGM production *Go for Broke!* (1951). Released during the Korean War as a way to link past and present patriotic efforts, *Go for Broke!* was one of the few films that even mentioned the wartime confinement, although it never showed the prison camps themselves. Instead, the war picture valorized the bravery and professionalism of ethnic minority soldiers who remained committed to the nation, from their training on the home front to their overseas campaigns in Europe.[29] The main reason for this focus was that initial attempts at portraying Japanese Americans in the camps ran up against U.S. propaganda efforts during the Cold War. As the film's producer, Dore Schary, admitted years later, what he and his production team learned about the mass incarceration "was so shocking and depressing we felt that in the early years of the Cold War . . . [the topic] would be a disservice."[30] Larry Tajiri, writing for the *Pacific Citizen* in 1955, noted more frankly that federal officials "reportedly feared such scenes would be exploited by the Communists in the cold war, particularly in Asia where the Kremlin and the Chinese Reds had used the story of the mass evacuation of Japanese Americans as Anti-American [*sic*] propaganda."[31] Showcasing the Nisei soldiers became more strategically viable, particularly when advancing American political and military objectives in Asia. In a 1951 letter to Defense Department personnel involved in cooperating with MGM, Schary emphasized the potential overseas appeal of *Go for Broke!* "Since it is quite likely that we may have Japanese regiments fighting on our side in some future upheaval, I think this picture has definite morale and defense values." A film about Japanese Americans fighting for the cause of democracy, he assumed, would benefit how the Japanese saw their own contributions to containing communism in the Pacific. Other Hollywood producers also recognized the film's political importance. William Gordon, an executive at Universal Studios, congratulated Schary: "The film should be of tremendous value in the Far East as an object lesson in our democratic process."[32]

Japanese Americans themselves helped to broadcast how crucial the Nisei's postwar service in the U.S. military was for international relations in the Pacific and, more specifically, for relations with Japan. Part of this strategy was to validate their contributions to, and their model citizenry within, the United States to promote a sense of national belonging. They also saw themselves as potential transpacific mediators between the two nations. Much of the ethnic press reported on Japanese leaders' statements about the Nisei soldiers in this manner. Visiting the United States in 1951, Prime Minister Yoshida Shigeru thanked "the ceaseless effort of the Japanese Americans to have the American public better understand the Japanese." He recognized the Issei and Nisei for the financial and material aid they sent to their ancestral land as it recovered from the wartime devastation. But more than anything else, he declared, the patriotism and sacrifice of the Nisei soldiers during World War II was "the prime factor" in transforming American attitudes toward Japan.[33] Other Japanese officials shared Yoshida's expressions of gratitude for American generosity and forgiveness in light of these contributions toward advancing reconciliation and friendship. In 1950, the *Pacific Citizen* reported that the governor of Tokyo, Yasui Seiichiro, entertained eighty veterans from the 442nd who made up part of the U.S. occupation forces. At the gathering attended by four hundred Japanese statesmen, Governor Yasui "praised the achievements of the Nisei GIs in World War II and declared them an important factor in American-Japanese relations." In 1951, the Japanese vice-minister of foreign affairs, Kusaba Ryuen, noted while visiting Hawai'i the GIs' influence on overseas relations: "The Nisei soldiers . . . gave the people of America and her Allies a new concept of persons of Japanese ancestry." Kusaba even credited the Nisei's military service with contributing to "the favorable peace treaty given Japan."[34]

· Nisei living abroad also accentuated these international ties. George Kiyoshi Togasaki, the president of the English-language *Nippon Times,* a Tokyo-based daily, wrote in 1952 about the effect that Nisei soldiers and linguists in the U.S. forces had on the occupied Japanese. For Togasaki, the Nisei in

Japan did more than act "as a liaison force between the conqueror and conquered." He cited "the psychological effect on the Japanese population of the sight of soldiers of Japanese ancestry in American uniform." This exhibition of American ethnic inclusion undermined the "race war propaganda" of the Japanese militarists.[35] Implied in this argument was that a multiracial democracy was superior, both in social and martial terms, to those that assumed the legitimacy of racial hierarchies. Togasaki avoided mentioning how racial segregation and other forms of discrimination remained alive and well in the United States. Nor did the topic of the mass confinement arise in his work. But he may have understood how these issues would undermine his argument and his sense of ethnic pride in what Japanese Americans were accomplishing overseas. That the United States accepted soldiers of color willing to serve their nation was to him a valuable model for Japan in the workings of American democracy.[36]

Hanama Tasaki and others like him, however, presented another side of the story. The veteran was among approximately five thousand Nisei who left home to enlist in the Japanese military before and during World War II. But much is unknown regarding his specific feelings about, or experiences in, the China campaigns, the Pacific War, and afterward.[37] In interviews later in his life, Tasaki did recall incidences that informed his youth. Although involved with citizenship activities in high school, he distinctly remembered the racial slights his parents encountered in Hawai'i that only served to remind him that his family did not belong. Tasaki was also impressed by the "spiritual strength" of the Issei he met in California and by Japan's ideals in the 1930s for the "Yamato race" to lead a pan-Asian coalition.[38] All of these issues contributed to his joining the ranks of the Imperial Army. This action later resulted in Tasaki's loss of American citizenship, according to the 1940 Nationality Act, when he served in the military of another nation-state. This act, however, did not necessarily foreclose the possibilities for regaining one's citizenship. Several hundred Nisei who fought for Japan's armed forces succeeded in reclaiming their former legal status as American citizens after World War II. Many had been visiting family or tending to other affairs in Japan at the war's outbreak and were then conscripted for duty. To regain their prior standing, they argued that, under Article 503 of the Nationality Act, their U.S. citizenship was still valid if a foreign state forced them to fight against their will. The federal government acquiesced in most cases because it could not disprove the claims of those individuals who said they served under duress. No evidence suggests that Tasaki ever filed papers concerning this matter, and the reasons why he did not are lost to history. Like the majority of Nisei veterans of the Imperial Army and Navy, he remained in Japan for the rest of his life.[39]

This personal history lent a unique perspective to Tasaki's work. The author's literary intervention in postwar American culture emerged from an interstitial state, one that changed over time. Tasaki initially was "not quite American" because of his alienated Nisei identity in the United States and his involvement in the Imperial Army during the 1930s. The ensuing loss of his American citizenship settled the issue legally, if not culturally. Overlapping this period, Tasaki was "not quite Japanese" because he was never fully accepted in Japan due to his Hawaiian background. What also separated him, at least from other postwar Japanese authors, was that the bilingual Tasaki wrote his novel in English.[40] Tasaki thus contributed to a "Japanese/American" sensibility in several ways. In terms of nationality, his being "not quite American" and "not quite Japanese" only reinforced his indeterminate standing among U.S. readers, even though they viewed him mainly as "Japanese" because of his ethnic background. But his occupying of two worlds and yet neither also applies to how he approached his work. In one sense, *Long the Imperial Way* aligns with the literary strategies seen in postwar Japanese writings that sought to confront a militarist past. At the same time, Tasaki interrogated the underpinnings of the Japanese imperium through his embrace of American liberal democratic ideals. This cross-cultural scheme, in turn, affected how U.S. reviewers interpreted the author and his text in expansive, but also limiting, ways regarding issues of race and national belonging.

Book critics offered a variety of opinions when considering the boundaries and the transgressive nature of Tasaki's accomplishments. Edmund Fuller, a *Chicago Daily Tribune* reviewer, credited the writer's birth in Hawai'i and his American education for producing a noteworthy novel in English. "But," the critic proclaimed, Tasaki "is a Japanese."[41] Fuller arrived at this conclusion by citing the author's understanding of the Japanese people as evidenced in the novel. Other columnists followed this lead. The assertion that Tasaki was Japanese only, however, also suggested a desire to resolve for readers a potentially confusing problem about race and loyalty. Asian Americans in the United States, as Cindy I-Fen Cheng observes, were "perpetual foreigners-within" during the Cold War, a view accentuated by international events that created "two Chinas" and "two Koreas." This geopolitical condition heightened suspicion against Americans of Chinese and Korean ancestry, whether they were communist sympathizers or not.[42] The nation's anxieties about communist expansion and infiltration, visualized here through race, also affected Japanese Americans after their mass imprisonment. Addressing doubts about their loyalty, Nisei community spokespersons and others assured those in the white mainstream of Nisei "Americanism" and their ability to assimilate. Given the trauma of mass incarceration, many Nisei during and after the war continued to emphasize their cultural fitness within a nation still ingrained with racial animosities.[43]

Tasaki was ill suited for this narrative because he recalled a past that complicated beliefs about Nisei loyalties. Thus his presence in the public sphere presented difficulties for those who wanted to make sense of *Long the Imperial Way*. Most reviewers chronicled the novelist's American upbringing, which made up more than half of his lifetime by 1950, when he became a public figure. But they curiously avoided characterizing Tasaki as a Nisei. Convenience, ignorance, or discomfort may have led some book critics to locate the author as a national subject in Japan. Intentionally or not, this interpretation simplified Tasaki's transpacific story as well as elided the racial prejudice against Japanese Americans in the United States.

Some did wrestle with the meanings of Tasaki's unusual status. Whereas Fuller and others saw Tasaki's identity as fixed within national borders, one Nisei critic saw it as more fluid. In 1952, Tajiri publicized *Long the Imperial Way* in the *Pacific Citizen*. Assessing the literature produced by Nisei up to that time, he reported on Tasaki's personal history, but appeared confounded on how to classify the work. He clarified that "Tasaki's point of view . . . is that of a Japanese, rather than that of an American who goes to Japan." Like the *Chicago Tribune* reviewer, Tajiri conceded the author's Japanese identity, one rooted in the novel's production and perspective. Yet he differentiated Tasaki from other Japanese writers, noting that "his education in the United States . . . has given him the facility to express that point of view in English, something which none of Japan's recognized novelists is able to do." Tajiri struggled to define Tasaki as a "Nisei writer," but at least sensed the cosmopolitan qualities the author disclosed in being "not quite American" and "not quite Japanese." This uncertainty may have contributed to Tajiri's regret that Nisei readers ignored *Long the Imperial Way*.[44] He offered no possible reasons for this avoidance, but the novel may have raised troubling thoughts among potential Japanese American audiences because Tasaki had fought for Japan. Those with lingering allegiances to their ancestral land still attracted suspicion because they undermined the wartime story of Nisei patriotism to the United States.[45]

The need to establish Japanese American loyalty becomes apparent in the example of Bill Hosokawa, who also critiqued *Long the Imperial Way* for the *Pacific Citizen*. Unlike Tajiri, he avoided calling Tasaki a Nisei, despite acknowledging the subject's American background. Hosokawa did consider *Long the Imperial Way* an "excellent novel." But instead of recommending it for the Nisei, he advocated a version of the text for Japanese readers. "It would be revealing to the bulk of the Japanese masses," he wrote in 1950, "who are convinced their soldiers were noble knights in white armor."[46] A translation eventually appeared, but the text gained little notice in Japan, perhaps because it reminded audiences too much about the Imperial Army's shameful past in China. Yet, as members of the JACL during the 1930s, both Hosokawa and Tajiri embraced the idea of Nisei as transpacific cultural interpreters between the United States and Japan. For them, being pro-Japanese was also being pro-American. They saw no inconsistency in this position, viewing it as simply contributing to better relations between the two nations. By the 1950s, however, Hosokawa was particularly influential in rewriting the Nisei in several works as being completely American, a position also advanced by the JACL.[47] Tasaki and his novel most likely presented an inconvenient reminder about a more dynamic and intricate past regarding Japanese American experiences. Hosokawa, like Fuller beforehand, wanted to stabilize Tasaki's identity and label his work as simply "Japanese." In this case, Hosokawa perceived the work as better suited for markets in Japan in order to reform mistaken beliefs there and as a chance to distance himself from his prior ideals.

Mainstream writers in the United States were more often concerned with transforming Japan into a model ally in the Pacific theater than about Nisei abilities to assimilate at home, especially when public venues began depicting them as model minorities who had supposedly recovered from their wartime imprisonment and made successes of their lives. Standard periodicals such as the *Saturday Evening Post, Reader's Digest, Collier's, Life,* and others enlightened millions of their subscribers throughout the late 1940s and early 1950s as to the extent to which a former enemy could shun its militarist past and take to democratic values and practices.[48] These evaluations of Japan were noteworthy because of its value as a bastion against communism. At the same time, writers understood the ongoing suspicions among the public and called for relinquishing prior wartime anger against Japan to make this new partnership work. In May 1949, as communist forces gained control of China, a *Collier's* editorialist observed that this development "will compel us to change our policies, our opinions and feelings about Japan." As a result, the author declared, "Hates must be forgotten" between the two nations. The State Department encouraged this view. As deputy under secretary for political affairs in the Eisenhower administration and as a former ambassador to Japan, Robert Daniel Murphy acknowledged the past hurts and furies generated from World War II. He noted in 1954 that when thinking of Japan, "we are reminded of Pearl Harbor, of Bataan, of Japanese abuse of war prisoners." Retaining such memories into the Cold War era, however, undermined American interests abroad. "Wherever there is a bitter memory—and there are many—the Communists work to keep old wounds smarting, old hatreds alive." Murphy urged

Americans to stop resuscitating the wartime past and to accept the reality of working with Japan because of its importance as a Pacific ally. That the secretary felt compelled to address these hard feelings against Japan suggests that the State Department took them seriously, dreading how they might subvert diplomatic relations.[49]

Whatever the costs of these new global realignments, *Collier's* magazine in 1956 summarized the stakes at hand: "A Japan harnessed to Russia and Red China could lure what is left of independent Asia into the Red camp and tip the scales fatally against the West. A prosperous Japan on the side of the free world remains a valuable ally."[50] But at this point, the extent of its adaptations to U.S. power was still unclear to American audiences. They did recognize that Japan was in the midst of difficult transitions. The magazine continued: "The new Japan is fermenting a mash of new ideas and old customs . . . mixing political democracy with feudal loyalties." Even so, the political climate there was difficult to discern. "The nation that once meekly did what a handful of leaders told it to," the writer surmised, "is now outspokenly divided on every major issue." With the contentiousness of a more democratic process now supplanting a hierarchical system, Japan revealed something troubling to Americans. Its newly acquired independence meant that no one in the United States could predict the direction the Japanese would take, or the consequences of their actions. The *Collier's* writer expressed hope that American ideals and policies would benefit a new ally, only to fret, "Japan is on her feet—but headed where?"[51]

Other cultural commentators also continued to reveal their misgivings and anxieties about how this new junior partner would proceed in its international relations, especially should a rebuilding Japan fall victim to Soviet and Chinese influences. Two factors contributing to this uncertainty were concerns expressed over Japan's veterans and about U.S. postwar empire building. At times, these worries overlapped with one another. Depicted in American popular culture as subhuman beasts during the Pacific War, soldiers from the demobilized Imperial Army were often bedraggled men who returned to a devastated nation and met with derision for their defeat. Americans began sympathizing with the ordinary troops, separating them as the "good Japanese," who were deemed capable of reform, as opposed to the "bad" militarist leaders, such as Tojo Hideki, who had steered them into such degraded circumstances. By acknowledging the common soldiers' humanity, Americans could then maintain hope for converting Japan into a worthy ally. The forlorn condition of these veterans, however, failed to assuage some U.S. reporters' ambivalence about Japan and its now-wrecked military.[52]

This view became evident in descriptions of veterans resuming their rural and urban lives in postwar Japan. *Life* magazine in 1945 portrayed a nameless veteran-farmer, representing a majority of his kind, as a product of a timeless agrarian culture. Once the war ended, this man "humbly settl[ed] again into his immemorial place in the village" and became "grooved in the involuntary Shintoism of his past."[53] These signifiers of feudal tradition, the writer suggested, emphasized a social stability that would counter any radical change, such as the introduction of communism. But the implied fear was that these ancient proclivities might also check the spread of democracy and modernity in Japan. The journalist Darrell Berrigan likewise noted in 1947 for the *Saturday Evening Post* his mixed feelings about unemployed veterans in the cities. On the one hand, more than a few Japanese began challenging the older generations' restrictive ways and called for democratic reforms. On the other hand, numerous desperate men in Tokyo "are filled with hate," Berrigan observed. "They hate Americans for defeating and humiliating them. They hate Japanese society for the lies the civilian population so blindly swallowed." Searching for steady work, many joined gambling rings or became black market thugs to make ends meet. They indulged in the "spirit of rebellion" amidst a "peaceful [U.S.] occupation."[54] Berrigan presented this situation as destabilizing to a benevolent, nonimperial U.S. presence in the Pacific. Taming the remnants of Japan's armed forces while aiding its citizenry to rebuild was supposed to demonstrate U.S. magnanimity. That discharged soldiers wandered the streets in organized gangs complicated attempts at transitioning Japan into a firmer democratic ally.

The unease about former Japanese soldiers gained further traction once the Korean War began, a sentiment noted in James A. Michener's *The Voice of Asia* (1951). In this collection of essays, the popular author recorded his travels throughout the region as he interviewed people from all walks of life about their views on U.S.-Asian relations. His purpose was to inform American audiences about the importance of understanding and retaining overseas allies. Michener condensed his uncertainty about the Japanese military into one chilling portrait of the veteran Masao Watanabe. Of all the interviews conducted with diverse peoples throughout the Pacific, the author announced, "I remember his most unforgettably." The old soldier appeared to Michener as "rugged, lean, tight-lipped and steel-eyed" with a "peaked cloth cap drawn tight about his bullet head." Such vivid prose painted the veteran as war incarnate. Michener initially wanted to know the extent to which the Japanese accepted their defeat by the United States. Watanabe detailed how he found his calling in the military and admitted that the sole reason why he accepted Japan's surrender was because of the emperor's declaration. Otherwise, he "was quite prepared to die" in his nation's defense if American troops had invaded. If nothing else, Watanabe reinforced Michener's notion of a dedicated, experienced soldier who lived for war.[55]

But Watanabe turned the tables on the author, chiding Michener about U.S. intentions in Asia. As the veteran explained, the Japanese "would never have been kicked around in Korea the way you [Americans] have been." Still dedicated to combat, he further declared, "We could be doing your fighting for you." Watanabe even guaranteed better results since the Japanese could draw on their own prior experiences when occupying Korea.[56] He played on American postwar anxieties about losing Japan and the rest of the Pacific to Soviet dominion by implicitly linking his nation's past designs in Asia to the present aims of the United States. Sooner or later, the old soldier opined, Americans would have to allow Japan an army again to help battle the communists. In this broader view, Watanabe intimated that from earlier confrontations over territorial expansion the Japanese knew something about fighting the Russians, and the Chinese too. A stunned Michener wondered to his subject if the United States could entrust the Japanese with a military force, given their history of imperial desires and destructiveness in the region. The veteran responded, "Probably not . . . [but] to prevent a flood you must build dikes. . . . You'll have to trust us."[57] In Michener's account, Watanabe was an unreconstructed militarist who saw how the political winds had shifted. Containment strategy, or "building dikes" against the flood of communism, exacted a cost for Americans. In this bargain, the former soldier viewed the United States as a temporary means by which Japan could regain control of its own destiny. As U.S. political and military leaders considered rearming Japan to help secure the Pacific theater against communism, these deliberations proved unsettling to Michener and likeminded others because of their continued doubts about a new ally. The author concluded *The Voice of Asia* by disavowing American intentions to create an empire in the Far East, claiming instead that a U.S. presence there would guarantee better, more cosmopolitan relations with Asian peoples. Yet the idea of turning Japan into a militarized stronghold discomforted him, given its past actions and the growing U.S. commitments overseas.[58]

Although most Americans denied that the United States engaged in empire building, several mainstream columnists visiting Japan expressed apprehension over developments that invoked visions of imperialism, especially in light of the U.S. occupation. At the same time that the United States preached the benefits of democracy to the Japanese, the American military government extended its power and influence throughout Japan, controlling political, social, and economic developments there. The disparities between the occupiers and the occupied were readily apparent in the early stages. Food and medical shortages, bombed-out neighborhoods, and other hardships stemming from the war were still daily constants for numerous Japanese. Many had to engage in the black market for necessities. Others peeked into windows of American PX (Post Exchange) shops and commissaries, longing for such "luxury" items as soap, shoes, and cigarettes. That the U.S. military staff members, the occupation troops, and American civilians lived in segregated quarters, dubbed "Little America" in downtown Tokyo, only heightened the lifestyle differences. They hired domestic servants for their families, renamed streets and buildings, and repeated in public notices and private settings the most famous official phrase of U.S. domination in Japan, "By order of the Occupation Forces." The literal and figurative signs of the American military presence were everywhere seen and felt.[59]

In 1949, Stewart Alsop noted in the *Washington Post* that the material well-being of the occupiers "created an almost unbridgeable chasm" between Americans and Japanese. Much of this demonstrated power and influence on the everyday lives of Japanese civilians undermined U.S. prospects in the Pacific, while reinforcing communist propaganda about American imperialism. The prevalence of Coca-Cola, steak dinners, cocktail parties, and golfing trips for American use in Japan only accentuated the exclusionary, rather than the democratizing, character of the United States. "Twentieth Century American Japan," Alsop opined, "has a little in common with Nineteenth Century British India." Compared to earlier empire building, the U.S. occupation provoked anxiety, given that Americans supposedly desired to extend democratic ideals abroad. Alsop admitted that a military occupation was a relationship of disproportionate power and understood the need for such displays over a conquered nation and its people. Yet the journalist was troubled by the military's discriminatory practices, declaring that "the way in which Japan is now being governed by the United States is profoundly politically unhealthy." Helen Mears, writing for the *Saturday Evening Post* in 1950, agreed with this assessment. The "conspicuous privilege" of Americans living in Japan was not sending the appropriate message about U.S. intentions to the rest of the world. Instead, the United States gave "the communists occasion to charge that we live like conquering imperialists," she remarked.[60]

Other American observers offered disquieting portraits of U.S. expansionism, as seen by the Japanese. Demaree Bess, an editor for the *Saturday Evening Post,* noted the gap in perception between Americans and Japanese with regard to the occupation. Traveling to Japan in 1952, he observed that Americans "don't feel that our present relations with the Japanese are imperialistic." Yet, when talking to the Japanese, he noticed that most thought that "America's relationship to Japan is even more imperialistic" than the Soviet attempts to dictate to its communist satellites. This reasoning was based on how the United States "abandoned . . . efforts to reform Japan almost overnight when communist aggression in Korea alarmed us." In other words, Americans appeared less concerned with enacting democratic policies in Japan than with militarizing the Pacific to protect U.S. interests. In 1954, another *Post* reporter interviewed a Japanese veteran who, like Hanama Tasaki, began his career with the Imperial Army in China during the 1930s. The ex-soldier recalled his days on the Asian mainland with nostalgia: "That was a good life, as good as you Americans had it here during the occupation." Shocked by this comment, the *Post* correspondent elaborated that the veteran gave "no indication that he sees any difference between the Japanese occupation of China and the American occupation of Japan." For these writers, American disavowals of empire building were insincere at best when the U.S. occupation conjured images of British, Russian, and Japanese colonizing efforts.[61]

Aloha, Empire

As an Imperial Army veteran born and raised in Hawai'i, Hanama Tasaki offered a narrative salve for American anxieties about Asia in general and about Japan in particular. Portrayals of his early life in the publicity materials for *Long the Imperial Way* meanwhile served to downplay U.S. racism and efforts at empire building. The novel's first-edition dust jacket included the author's biography, which revealed a childhood spent in a multicultural paradise, wherein Tasaki reminisced about his youthful days on the islands, "shrouded in a mist of romanticism," when he played on beaches "with children of every race imaginable in an atmosphere of total understanding and friendship." This illustration of a liberal, multiethnic society cast Tasaki as a product of a tolerant and generous nation. Even as a colonizing presence, the United States supposedly nourished the blossoming of a diverse humanity in its annexed territories, offering a simpler, more fulfilling life amid a tropical New Eden. The framing text of Tasaki's childhood memories of Hawai'i thus personified what readers of *Long the Imperial Way* could fancy as a captivating moment in the history of U.S. expansion that coincided with the nation's Cold War aims. It was a vision that emphasized the value of a racially harmonious democracy while ignoring the realities of a racially dystopian empire.[62]

However imagined and marketed, Tasaki's version of Hawai'i was a rose-colored rendering that disregarded the islands' more complex history and his own family's encounters with racism. In the book publicity, the author submerged any memories or grievances about racial prejudice in Hawai'i, which had contributed to his volunteering for duty in the Imperial Army in the first place. The Cold War most likely played a vital role in this self-depiction. Airing the complex motives that affected how Japanese Americans defined their loyalty or disloyalty might have disrupted mainstream audience expectations and threatened sales of *Long the Imperial Way,* given the patriotic fervor of the times.[63] Yet Hawai'i was not immune from racial discrimination, though it took different forms compared to the U.S. mainland, particularly in light of how the Japanese were treated and contained on the West Coast. Missing in Tasaki's recollections was any mention of a white-ruled plantation system backed by the United States and built on a racial hierarchy that exploited a multiethnic labor force. Since the mid-nineteenth century, the islands' white business and political elites sought to control the Japanese population. Targeted for surveillance were Japanese-language schools, Buddhist temples, and Japanese-language newspapers. White leaders also depicted striking Japanese laborers in the 1920s as a racial menace and a national security threat when the workers demanded higher wages. Planters initially desired to "Americanize" Japanese laborers to reinforce their loyalties but then became flummoxed when these hands asserted their rights on the basis of American principles. In 1931, when Japan invaded Manchuria, the U.S. government began considering the detention of any Japanese immigrant or American citizen who had contacts with Japanese abroad. In this manner, the white ruling elite questioned the loyalty of the Japanese long before any bombs exploded at Pearl Harbor.[64]

Yet the idealized, Cold War version of Hawai'i aligned with what American statesmen wanted to convey globally, as they attempted to fashion anticommunist alliances, especially with developing nations inhabited by nonwhite populations.[65] For U.S. policy makers, Hawai'i was not only a strategic military location in the Pacific but also a site from which to project liberal democratic values to peoples in Asia. In this broader scheme, however, white Americans would have to either confront or dampen their own prejudices. Racists focused on the idea that granting Hawai'i statehood would open Congress to multihued representation and thus signal the end of American civilization. Others countered that including Hawai'i would advertise U.S. goodwill toward the rest of the world. In 1950, when *Long the Imperial Way* appeared amid the start of the Korean War, a variety of popular periodicals accentuated this point. Regarding the Hawaiian population, "what more logical intermediaries to carry an understanding of U.S. democracy to the Orient?" asked a *Business Week* editorialist. Hawai'i, as *Collier's* noted, "is a model of a harmonious living-together by diverse races and cultures." Supporting statehood for this territory was important as well because it "stands on the threshold of the Orient and on the political front line of American democracy." Otherwise, added the *Christian Century,* if the United States rejected Hawai'i from entering the Union on the basis of racial prejudice, "Communist propaganda can be counted on to make the most of . . . white self-interest in its appeal to the peoples of Asia and Africa."[66] The islands' importance to a reconstructing Japan was especially significant in this regard. General Douglas MacArthur, the Supreme Commander of the Allied Powers in occupied Japan, also favored Hawaiian statehood because he felt it would set an example for the Japanese about the benefits of democracy.[67]

Fiction writers, historians, and others in the early postwar years published a number of books on the Japanese in Hawai'i to showcase them as a model minority ready to assimilate into the mainstream of American society. Novels and nonfiction about Hawai'i often portrayed the islands as a vibrant democracy in which people of different backgrounds interacted in a peaceful manner. Many of the postwar histories about Hawai'i begin with December 7, 1941, and how the attack on Pearl Harbor became a flashpoint for assessing the racial progress made from a plantation economy to a multiethnic democracy that disclosed Japanese American patriotism. In John Rademaker's *These Are Americans: Japanese Americans in Hawaii* (1951), the islands "show clearly that the American way of life is so vital, satisfying, and attractive to the people who live [there] . . . that they gave their wholehearted support to its defense and its preservation when it was threatened."[68] Many of the accompanying photographs in Rademaker's work present the islands' Nisei population in regimented group poses that evoke their contributions to the war effort. Pictures of uniformed soldiers predominate, but other portraits include agricultural workers in the fields, children at their school desks, or workers in offices. A politics of respectability, in which propriety and productivity are cherished, is apparent in the photographs. The subjects' clean and pressed clothing, attentive body postures, and smiling or determined facial expressions reveal their aspirations to fit into mainstream American life. Thus, even as the book highlights a society that values diversity in racial backgrounds and in cultural practices, its key visual narrative suggests that Japanese Americans were, and would continue to be, followers and models of established order.[69]

Two fictional works on Hawai'i by Japanese American authors, Shelley Ota's *Upon Their Shoulders* (1951) and Kazuo Miyamoto's *Hawaii: End of the Rainbow* (1964), offer other accounts of Japanese immigrant and native-born experiences that culminate in World War II and afterward. Both works confront the harsh racial realities that Japanese laborers initially encountered. As in the postwar histories of the islands, the novelists also chart the sense of racial progress made through the protagonists' assertion of rights and their improved access to education, employment, goods, and services. Regarding the almost two thousand civilians transported to the U.S. mainland for confinement, each text focuses on their endurance and forgiveness. *Upon Their Shoulders* presents the character Dr. Noda, a curmudgeonly Issei immigrant with sympathies for Japan, who gets arrested and shipped to a prison camp in Arizona. After the war, he returns to Hawai'i with a new appreciation for the United States because of his incarceration on the mainland. "He rather enjoyed the whole interlude," Ota writes. "Once they had been settled in Arizona, it had not been bad at all. Not bad at all." Part of this transformation was due to sympathetic War Relocation Authority (WRA) administrators that Dr. Noda realized were doing their best for the inmates' benefit. In *Hawaii: End of the Rainbow,* Miyamoto's take on the confinement of Hawaiians is similar. A Nisei soldier visits his grandfather in an Arkansas camp, wherein the GI is uneasy about his imprisoned family members while he serves his country. But Seikichi Arata assures his grandson, "We are not bitter about our lot." He does "not . . . blame the United States government" because the confinement of the Issei and Nisei is "for the security of the nation." The grandfather's reasoning, in which he justifies state power and dismisses camp hardships as an understandable necessity, then helps the young soldier realize his own sense of duty. The responses of these forgiving model minority characters thus reassure white readers that U.S. wartime practices against Japanese Americans were not so much racist as actually favorable to their postwar assimilation.[70]

Like the fictional characters in Ota and Miyamoto's novels, Tasaki portrayed himself as a person whose principles stemmed from the liberal, multiethnic environment of Hawai'i in which racial equality had evolved. To do so, he refashioned his past when *Long the Imperial Way* first appeared. One storyline from the book's publicity focused on the author's decision in 1936 to travel to Japan. Rather than recounting his desire to enlist in the Imperial Army because of the racial prejudice his family faced in Hawai'i, he now reported that he had intended "to throw himself bodily into the progressive movement" in Japan to challenge the militarists. The army, however, allegedly conscripted him against his will to fight in China.[71] As in his remembrances of a childhood spent on Hawaiian beaches, Tasaki's account of his journey to Japan suggested a romanticized past that exhibited an early dedication to combating tyranny, one nurtured by his Hawaiian upbringing with American ideals and citizenship. Aside from helping to publicize *Long the Imperial Way,* this strategy also had a broader transpacific context that may have influenced Tasaki's version of events when living in postwar Japan. Revisions of intent were commonplace among the defeated Japanese, in which a traumatized populace rechanneled its everyday language to invent pasts that now accentuated democracy and antimilitarism. This practice in effect warded off feelings of disorientation and aided in adapting to the new circumstances of the U.S. occupation.[72]

Unaware of the author's original aims in Japan, several reviews of *Long the Imperial Way* emphasized this revised aspect of Tasaki's background because it presented a simple but powerful theme: an earnest individual fighting against the machinery of totalitarianism.[73] The narrative's allure in this manner corresponded with the broader precepts of a Cold War universalism advanced by U.S. policy makers, social scientists, and cultural producers. This set of ideals assumed that nations shared similar desires in maintaining the dignity of individuals through liberal democratic systems to counter repressive institutions supported by the Soviet Union. But this vision entailed unilateral action from Americans. That is, presumably higher-based Western civilizations, of which the United States was now the preeminent power, would uplift more primitive, authoritarian, or otherwise ideologically misguided societies through several progressive stages of political and economic development. Later known as "modernization theory" in the early 1960s, this scheme depended on supplying overseas aid and management to integrate developing nations into the American fold and to contain communist advances within said nations. But it also conjured older imperial desires to access and dominate these realms.[74] To Americans, Japan was already modernized in its urban-industrial growth, but was still stuck in feudal ways, having lacked the liberal democratic values to halt its march toward militarism and a catastrophic war. From this standpoint, readers of *Long the Imperial Way* valued the novel because it offered a window into the unwanted world of the Japanese imperial past and of a Soviet-dominated future, when modernizing forces could run amok without proper guidance. It was then up to Americans to spread their ideals and practices abroad to both developed and developing states that, as potential anticommunist allies, knew no better.

Press coverage of Tasaki's education in Hawai'i and on the U.S. mainland supported this metanarrative. As an American-educated author, Tasaki appeared well situated to explain Asia to U.S. readers and to act as a possible agent for American interests in Asia. Asked in a *New York Times* interview about the sources of inspiration for his writing, Tasaki responded that he saw his novel as "a hopelessly complicated maze of a million influences, both Eastern and Western." His was a transpacific work that sought to bridge the cultural divide between the United States and Japan. As I discuss below, *Long the Imperial Way* corresponded with the themes and narrative strategies familiar to postwar Japanese writers when critiquing their nation's prior militarist ambitions. Developing his answer further, however, Tasaki emphasized that "the greater happiness of individuals, the scientific curiosity, the cleanliness, [and] the respect for fair play" were the main Western tenets that guided him.[75] If Americans hoped to transfer their ideals to postwar Japan and to the rest of Asia to thwart communist objectives, then Tasaki presented an example for how his rearing in Western principles informed his resistance against a repressive regime.

Yet Tasaki drew on the cultural capital gained as a Nisei in Hawai'i and on the U.S. mainland to suggest that adopting American values and practices encompassed more than simply exporting democracy to Asia. He continued in the interview by chastising Western powers that had set the pattern for Japan's colonizing efforts in East Asia. "I did not like Western colonialism," he asserted, "more so, because I was raised in the tradition of the American fighters for independence." Invoking the revolutionary founders, he highlighted how his education affirmed the cherished values of American society and culture. But Tasaki proceeded beyond a naïve celebration of these ideals, imploring the United States to adhere to its founding principles and censuring any postwar colonial presence in developing nations. "I am for the early independence of all Asiatic countries," he concluded. Tasaki in this way cautioned the United States and its European allies not to repeat the mistakes of imperial Japan. As a former soldier who participated in occupying other peoples and nations, he knew something about "the inhumanities to which mankind can stoop" in denying freedom to those who desired it. This language corresponded to a lesser extent with his experiences in the United States and its territories as a Japanese American who strived for opportunities, yet encountered discriminatory obstacles. He remained silent about this part of his past for reasons previously mentioned, intimating instead that the changing geopolitical circumstances were neither simple nor straightforward. Asia still required a U.S. presence to contain communism in Korea, he noted, especially because of its proximity to Japan. Tasaki confessed to watching "with alarm the inroads which the very system of absolute government, which I have come to detest with a burning hatred, is making into our beloved Asia."[76] The author thus presented himself as both idealist and pragmatist. He advocated freedom for developing nations, but also supported U.S. involvement overseas, including its provisional occupation of Japan, to hold communism at bay. His underlying message, however, was full of foreboding: the United States was the only anticommunist safeguard in the region, but it had to mind the path taken by imperial Japan.

Reading the Imperial Past and Present

The struggles of Takeo Yamamoto, the young protagonist in *Long the Imperial Way*, showcase the author's intentions to reorient, if not contest, the objectives of empire. Drafted by the Imperial Army, Takeo presents a sympathetic figure caught in a system that transforms ordinary men into trained killers. His title is First-Year Soldier, signifying his lowly position as a new conscript in the army. He must attend to the orders of the Privates First Class, the Reserves (previously discharged privates who have been called up again for service), the noncommissioned officers, the company and battalion leaders, and up the chain of command. Since the Imperial Army requires unquestioning loyalty to the emperor, its hierarchy of personnel emphasizes a set of rituals and regulations that appear at odds with Western military traditions. Takeo and his fellow conscripts must bow to the east, toward the Imperial Palace, memorize and recite the Imperial Rescript, and suffer constant physical punishment from superiors. A farm boy with an elementary school education, Takeo endures the military environment, hoping to earn enough money to buy an ox to ease his parents' workload in the fields back home. But his loyalties toward family, together with the terrors of warfare he encounters, progressively subvert his sense of duty to nation and empire. Takeo's altered consciousness thus prompts him to resist the idea of sacrificing his life for the emperor's glory. Moreover, the young soldier questions the nature of his service and favors his parents over the emperor as the ultimate source of his moral sensibilities.

American reviewers interpreted Takeo's experiences through two intersecting approaches: as an ethnographic study of the Japanese military and as an exercise on Cold War universalism that underscored his resistance to this authoritarian institution. Tasaki's rhetoric of liberal humanism throughout the text supported this view, in which the Imperial Army stood against individual freedom and potential. "Shells of the warm, constructive individuals they were born to become," Tasaki notes, "the men lived unhappily within a perversion which tried not to recognize the ethics, constructiveness, and fair play their souls constantly hungered for in their relations with their fellow men" (39). This wording replays the author's statement to the *New York Times* that emphasized his commitment to Western ideals and to his anti-imperialist advocacy for Asia. Readers focused more on the former point than on the latter because their cultural embrace of universalism made the notion of an American empire invisible to them. Applying liberal values abroad meant denying efforts to place Asians within reach of another military force that benefitted another imperial power.[77] Tasaki, however, was well aware of the disparities between American ideals and practices, just as his experiences in the Imperial Army shattered his former beliefs about Japan's purposes and capabilities in Asia. Writing *Long the Imperial Way* was Tasaki's method of filling these moral fissures within his mind. Thus his Nisei subjectivity, hiding in plain sight in its espousal of democratic principles, achieved creative expression in part through Takeo Yamamoto's pacifist yearnings.

In light of Tasaki's lessons about imperial desires, reviewers of his book employed ethnographic and universalist themes to justify the U.S. military presence in the Pacific, though a few expressed doubts about this strategy. This uneasy mix of interpretations arose from anxieties sparked by the Korean War and by the unknown extent of postwar Japan's willingness to integrate into an American-led alliance. The *New York Times* columnist and playwright Harvey Breit recognized these thematic links, remarking in his August 1950 review of *Long the Imperial Way:* "Because of what is happening in Korea today, because of what happened in Japan yesterday, because of the inscrutably tragic problem that the entire Far East has presented and still presents, this reporter considers the first novel to come to us out of Japan since World War II an arresting and serious event."[78] The text's significance for this reviewer lay in its ability to speak to pressing political issues. Breit emphasized how past and present merged, relating Japanese imperial aggression in Asia to the North Korean invasion of South Korea in June 1950. Implied in this comparison was that the United States had to intervene in another Pacific war to fight against a totalitarian system, this time communism. The reviewer's use of the phrase "inscrutably tragic problem," however, served to reinforce the prevalent Western stereotypes of the "inscrutable Orient" that contrasted against a supposedly rational, benevolent, democratic West. Asia presented a burden to U.S. interests, Breit suggested, requiring the nation's continual involvement and guidance. This orientalist view justified U.S. objectives in the Pacific. As the book critic intimated, military intervention was required to bring potential Asiatic chaos to an American-led liberal democratic order.

Other reviewers took a different tack. The fiction writer Monroe Engel agreed with Breit's assessment but blamed uninformed Americans, not "inscrutable" Asians, for the perilous situation evolving overseas. He noted in *Commentary* that *Long the Imperial Way* "does something at least to pierce our ignorance of the Orient, an area in which it becomes increasingly evident that our ignorance is catastrophic."[79] The novelist Merle Miller, who evaluated Tasaki's book for the *Saturday Review of Literature,* sounded ambivalent too. Few U.S. leaders, he claimed, "ever succeeded in understanding the Japanese—or, as is now more than ever apparent, the Chinese."[80] Miller thought that *Long the Imperial Way* might contribute to rectifying this problem of unfamiliarity with Asia and its peoples. Whichever way literary critics felt about the U.S. handling of developments in the Far East, they valued the novel for its important insights that they felt Americans should heed.

Tasaki's reflections purportedly helped Americans better comprehend how the Japanese thought and behaved in their imperial endeavors, as well as how they might act in their postwar relations with the United States. That Takeo Yamamoto resolves over time to fight for his family, and not for the emperor, "makes the famous *banzai* charges more intelligible," admitted one columnist for *The Nation.* Ray Falk added in the *New York Times* that Tasaki "makes us understand (almost accept) without excusing the primitive behavior of the Nipponese soldier." In the *Chicago Daily Tribune,* Edith Weigle remarked that *Long the Imperial Way* "made the Japanese soldier understandable to the occidental," contributing such valuable insights that it circulated in paperback throughout U.S. Army post exchanges in Japan. Many in the occupation forces, she reported, "read [the novel] with tremendous interest." The assumption here was that erstwhile enemies could surmount their cultural and historical differences through Tasaki's literary work. The United States could then proceed with its universalist, "nonimperial" objective of transforming Japan from its formerly "unintelligible" or "primitive" state into a liberal democratic nation.[81]

Long the Imperial Way in this sense corresponds with what Yoshikuni Igarashi calls "a drama of rescue and conversion" that U.S. policy makers created as an official narrative in their relations with postwar Japan. The underlying intent was to project how the United States "rescued" Japan from its militarist government and "converted" it into a democratic polity under American leadership.[82] Several reviewers of *Long the Imperial Way* invested in this story line, reading Takeo Yamamoto as a figure caught in the grind of Japanese imperialism and as a representative of postwar Japan. The influential *New York Times* critic Orville Prescott observed that Takeo was not so much a developed individual character as he was "a representative of his kind," a common soldier who symbolized the simple desire to survive and to free himself from the oppressive environment of Japanese militarism. A writer for the *Christian Science Monitor* further applied American concerns for rescuing postwar Japan to the novel's protagonist: "We can only hope that with sympathetic, understanding guidance the wilderness experience of Takeo and those like him will not be unduly prolonged." Another likewise claimed in the *Washington Post:* "In Takeo's yearning . . . lies the hope for a new Japan." Critics thus imagined this character as a broader illustration of Japanese aspirations, foiled in the imperial past but supported by the United States in the postwar future.[83]

Takeo Yamamoto thus represented the "good Japanese" in the postwar American mind-set. In this broader context, *Long the Imperial Way* contributed to an expanding body of literature, films, and other cultural forms that marked changing sensibilities in the United States toward the Japanese as being more human and capable allies. Takeo's exploits and suffering for moral knowledge led reviewers to accept the notion that all war is hell, even for the Japanese. Prescott noted that the conscripts, "in their long-suffering patience, in their homesickness, in their dislike of war and their corruption by the brutalities of war, seem like any soldiers."[84] A critic for the *Washington Post* noticed that "Takeo and his comrades have no resemblance to bucktoothed monsters" that dominated U.S. wartime publicity about Japanese soldiers as brute killers.[85] These new sentiments toward Japan coincided with the political necessities of forming new multinational relations in the Pacific. *Long the Imperial Way,* then, presents possibilities for transforming a militarist Japan when Takeo questions his loyalty to the emperor. Once he begins interrogating the ideals behind emperor worship and the causes of war, Takeo discloses to readers his readiness to follow other (read "American") forms of governance.

Hanama Tasaki later provided a less certain perspective on Takeo's imagined willingness to adhere to U.S. objectives, challenging the degree to which Americans could read this character as a good Japanese. Tasaki's only other novel, *The Mountains Remain* (1952), also written in English and published by Houghton Mifflin, is a sequel to *Long the Imperial Way* that portrays Takeo's return to Japan after the Pacific War. Along with family, friends, and acquaintances, the veteran navigates through the tumultuous years of U.S. occupation, debating the influences of democracy, Christianity, the black market, women's rights, land reform, and communism, as the Japanese attempt to restart their lives. Americans in this story are barely mentioned background figures; their authority is invisible but apparent. Here, Takeo's loyalties are determined not by international or ideological alliances but by personal relations among fellow Japanese. He befriends an aristocratic family whose patriarch, Count Imayama, disdains labor unions and land redistribution, even as his daughter Michiyo marries Takeo the struggling farmer, representing the possibilities for a new Japan.

The novel presents the American occupation and its dictates as confusing to the Japanese, to the extent that they create their own meanings from their own interests. "Everything that stressed equality and was radically new seemed like communism" to Michiyo's mother, the countess, "unless an American said it or gave his blessing to it. Then it was 'Occupation policy.'" Michiyo herself converts to Christianity and bases her notions of fairness on her newfound faith, which Takeo later adopts. At another point, Takeo describes to friends his capture by U.S. forces while fighting in the Philippines, where he met Nisei soldiers who tried to help, but failed, when teaching him and other prisoners about American ways. "There were some Nisei who came to talk to us about democracy," Takeo recollected, "but I did not understand much." This brief moment serves to undercut the postwar narrative of Japanese Americans as a model minority who could guide Japan to becoming a model ally with a better awareness and acceptance of U.S. objectives. In these instances, the Japanese instead respond with varying degrees of comprehension or curiosity. They then decide among themselves what the best approach to an issue might be, while negotiating around the American presence in their country. Yet the author's multilayered view of postwar Japanese opinion was not so much about the occupation's effectiveness as it was about the release of new social and political forces in Japan with which the characters had to contend.[86]

Indeed, amid these myriad sentiments expressed in *The Mountains Remain* was the contentious topic of communism, which a few protagonists espouse. Takeo sympathizes with two other Imperial Army veterans, one a former prisoner of the Soviets who became a communist while in their custody, and another who is a communist labor leader whom Takeo hides from occupation authorities. Although Takeo listens sympathetically to these figures' arguments, his camaraderie with them is based more on their shared military service and sufferings. The novel concludes with Takeo accepting, but still weighing, the strengths and weaknesses of each character's position. Like postwar Japan itself, he is trying to find his own way. At the same time, the author attempts to portray his main protagonist in a manner that would attract American readers: Takeo becomes a small landowner and a Christian, two features that ensured against communist seduction. But the text attracted little attention in the United States, perhaps because it presented no memorable American characters, or because the unsettled ending played into the distrust of Japan's intentions, particularly regarding communism. Either way, U.S. critics and audiences ignored *The Mountains Remain.*

Long the Imperial Way offered clearer answers for readers: the obstacles imposed by the Japanese military prevented Takeo from realizing the full extent of liberal democratic ideals. The institutionalized violence exacted on the mind and the body, and how this power translates into empire building, is apparent throughout the text.

How the army permeates every soldier's consciousness is on display throughout *Long the Imperial Way.* The novel opens with Takeo Yamamoto standing guard on the plains of northern China, pondering the ideal of sacrificing one's life for the emperor. Thoughts of death have preoccupied him since his initial experiences at the front. From prior engagements, he recalls seeing mangled corpses and escaping death himself in several instances. Yet he cannot come to grips with his own possible end. Comforting himself by humming patriotic songs and recalling slogans from a magazine he once read, Takeo suddenly determines, "He would die for the Emperor!" (8). Alone in his musings, the young soldier congratulates himself on reaching this point of assurance after giving "free rein to his power of thinking." "Like so many people . . . whose thoughts are usually dominated by the necessity to obey or to be servile to others," the author writes, "Takeo felt a sharp exhilaration when he found himself thinking out a problem under his own free will." His fears thus calmed, Takeo finds meaning in the destruction that surrounds him because of "the conclusion he had reached under his own free volition" (9). This repetitious phrasing of "free" thinking, will, or volition, however, cues readers that Takeo's reasoning is faulty. Although the youth thinks that he voluntarily offers his life to the emperor, the Imperial Army has already preordained the outcome when it drafted Takeo for service.

The author further notes that, once a person becomes a soldier, "his life as an individual ended when he took off his civilian clothes and put on his uniform." "From that moment on," he continues, a soldier's "body and soul belonged to the Emperor" (11). Yet, as discussed below, body and mind also work together, however ineffectually, to resist or reconfigure the empire's bidding. That the Imperial Army transforms an individual's body through martial clothing is only the first phase of domination. Soldiers receive training in obedience through a Foucauldian nightmare of discipline and punishment that reinforces the military hierarchy. For any blunder committed in dress code, weapons maintenance, saluting, or other oversight, Takeo's superiors administer quick, painful slaps to the offender's face. The author explains that punches with fists would be more physically agonizing, but this administration of pain is not the slap's intent. Instead, "slaps with the open hands" and "the great noise they made [were] a powerful demoralizer." This punishment broke any individual will; it "ate into one's heart and squeezed it each time" (33). No slapped soldier could resist such demeaning strikes because insubordination would mean a death sentence. The intent of this grueling punishment is to harden the Imperial Army's men to destroy the emperor's adversaries without questioning orders.

The novel's critique of the Imperial Army coincided with the conditions of writing in postwar Japan, from which many realized and rejected the prior excesses of a militarist state. What the author Tamura Taijiro described in the late 1940s as a "literature of the flesh" became a favored method among several Japanese intellectuals to interrogate the imperial past through the body. "'Thought' has, for a long time, been draped with the authoritarian robes of a despotic government," Tamura contended, "but now the body is rising up in opposition."[87] Because the state controlled information through propaganda and censorship to overwhelm people's consciences, the body became a site of resistance and liberation after the war. In its hunger, fatigue, and sexual desires, the body was the only vessel of reality understood by a perplexed, angry, and desperate populace. Set against a collapsed totalitarian mind-set, the body's assertion of individuality became for the "flesh writers" the basis for democratic struggles to attain more utopian possibilities.[88]

Another way postwar Japanese authors confronted the consequences of imperialism was through what David C. Stahl characterizes as a "literature of survival." The works of Ooka Shohei, especially his novel *Fires on the Plain* (1951), highlight the psychological trauma of outliving the war with only one's guilt intact.[89] Ooka, like Tasaki, was a veteran who sought consolation in writing to allay his feelings of remorse. The protagonist in *Fires on the Plain,* Private Tamura, is a consumptive released from his squad to die alone during the Leyte Island campaign in the Philippines in the last days of the war. The narrative focuses on not only the hardships of surviving the conflict but also the workings of memory—its construction, selectivity, uncertainty, and evasions—that the soldier struggles with from a mental hospital in postwar Japan. The text explores the sufferings of the body, including scenes in which some of the troops on Leyte descend into cannibalism. But Ooka focuses more on the existential meanings of this shocking act and on searching for God's presence. However different in approaches, the "literature of the flesh" and the "literature of survival" overlap in their accounts of the physical and mental torments enacted by the empire on its subjects. In this way, postwar Japanese novels depicting soldiers' sufferings, such as Ooka's *Fires on the Plain* or Takeyama Michio's *The Harp of Burma* (1946–1948), are more artistically accomplished and philosophically engaged than *Long the Imperial Way.* Yet these works never match Tasaki's ethnographic detail about life in the Imperial Army.

Long the Imperial Way's portrayal of the Imperial Army's activities in China, especially its disciplinary cruelties performed on its soldiers, proved instructive for Americans. Examined from a broader perspective, the text was one among many venues that helped them to realize the potential difficulties in steering postwar Japan away from its hierarchical, militarist tendencies and toward the universalist bounty offered by the United States. Cringing at the Japanese army's treatment of its troops, one reviewer noted that the novel revealed "what a tremendous mental chasm lies between Japan's old order and western democratic traditions." Prescott remarked that obedience to the emperor "was born of a culture which had never acknowledged individual rights, which was permeated with ancient feudal ideas and new fascist ideas."[90] Prescott indicted Japan's ancient and modern propensities toward authoritarian rule and indicated that it would behoove the United States to reform these tendencies if the Japanese were to join a more liberal democratic world order. Trumpeting the superiority of Western culture, he valorized the power of free individuals over the oppressive and "alien" culture of Japan. Yet *The Naked and the Dead,* released two years before *Long the Imperial Way,* provided readers with a brutal portrait of American GIs and their crazed leaders in the Pacific War. Critiquing Mailer's novel in 1948, Prescott noted that the fictionalized soldiers presented "a bitter comment on American civilization," from which they emerged as "frighteningly primitive, barren of ideas and ideals, a sad reflection on the social system that left them so intellectually immature."[91] Here, the critic's argument against Japan blinded him from his own previous remarks when making cultural comparisons between Asians and Westerners during wartime. Even then, apprehension about the Japanese arose from this postwar sanctimony: the persistent cultural differences between the two nations would make it harder for Americans to assimilate Japan into their political and economic orbit.

The hope presented in *Long the Imperial Way* lay in the example of Takeo Yamamoto. Although reared in an autocratic culture, he yearns to live his own life and recoils from the harsh demands of the Imperial Army. The constants of mud, fear, and death impel Takeo throughout the campaigns in northern and southern China to experience a "gradual but pronounced" transformation in his moral intuition. "He had started out with a pure, unadulterated desire to perform his patriotism to his Emperor," the author observes, "and, in the performance of it, he had also tried to find a means to accomplish his filial duties to his aged parents" (274). By his second year in the army, Takeo strains to link his obligations to the emperor with those to his parents as intense combat duties persist. He sees officers commit strategic mistakes in battle and his comrades die because of these orders. He observes with horror and disgust how the new recruits endure, like he did, the slapping and screaming from superiors. He begins to recognize that, despite his training to kill them, the Chinese enemy consists of struggling farmers like him. All of these incidents and realizations serve the emperor's will according to the logic of the Imperial Army. But the young soldier "knew that his parents could never condone many of the things which he was forced to perform or witness unrestrainedly at the front in the name of patriotism" (275). Takeo's parents are subordinate to the emperor, as is everyone else in the empire's organic hierarchy. Yet, in the young soldier's mind, they prove a superior source of morality and devotion to a higher being. The emperor exists for Takeo only through the military discipline and destruction he encounters. His parents, then, become for him the wellspring of moral principle and thus of his humanity.

Tasaki traces in other instances how the soldiers' dedication to the emperor, while apparent, is also inconstant. It waxes and wanes in their thoughts, leading them to focus instead on their families back home, especially when facing the dangers of combat. Two related scenes disclose how invoking the emperor appeals to the troops' courage but fails to sustain their understanding of patriotism. Sailing for southern China from the northern provinces, the men celebrate on deck the emperor's birthday with a speech and with full-throated cheers of "*Banzai!*" Absorbed in the moment, Takeo sees the sun, which the emperor symbolizes, rise from the transport's view of the horizon and experiences an "almost supernatural exultation" (242). One of the men even declares, "At a time like that, you don't care if you die!" (238). The soldiers afterward descend into the ship's hold and rid themselves of ceremonial dress, considering the import of their upcoming sacrifices. Some wonder if the emperor has ordinary instincts and desires like them. Perhaps if they could frame their sovereign in a more compelling and personal way, their expected loyalty would make sense to them. The attempts to comprehend the emperor in human terms, however, fall short. "If it were left to our own free will," says Private Hirata, the scholar among them, "no one will come to the front." His assertion, clarified by the dread of impending casualties, situates patriotism with involuntary actions. Defying edicts and rituals that emphasize loyalty to the emperor, he posits that they are actually serving their homes and families. Put in this manner, Takeo more comfortably asserts, "I am really fighting for my folks at home" (244). The others nod in agreement. The troops do not contest, so much as alter, the official intentions of the imperial state by prioritizing their personal ties to family rather than to the emperor. Important as well, they feel no disloyalty or shame in admitting this point to one another.

The soldiers' longing for compassion sometimes includes the Chinese natives they encounter, suggesting the broader sufferings caused by military occupation. Takeo's fictionalized perspective thus differentiates *Long the Imperial Way* from other postwar Japanese writings that avoid confronting the army's maltreatment of civilian populations. In Japan best sellers about the Pacific War focused more often on the noble yet tragic or senseless deaths of Imperial Army soldiers than on the casualties they caused.[92] In the case of *Long the Imperial Way,* Tasaki's authorial empathy may have been another postwar realization, along with his newfound antimilitarism, that helped to alleviate his war guilt. The work nonetheless garnered praise from the overseas press regarding its cosmopolitan inclusion of Chinese viewpoints and memories of the war. One report compared Tasaki to the writer Lin Yutang, both being cultural interpreters between East and West. Another mentioned the London-based author S. I. Hsiung (Xiong Shiyi), who exclaimed about *Long the Imperial Way,* "What [a] hell of a book!" The quote even appeared on the front cover of the 1951 British edition of the novel.[93] This admiration for *Long the Imperial Way* is notable, considering the relative silence in other postwar literature from Japan regarding the Imperial Army's culpability.

Rather than transforming into obedient, merciless killers, Takeo and a few others often sympathize with those whom they are colonizing or fighting. An aged Chinese woman, who reminds Takeo "of his own mother at home," cries in protest when the army appropriates and abuses her donkey (19). Takeo's thoughts and memories of his family, which counter the imperial state's efforts to control him, serve as a moral standard for his behavior when he tries to compensate the elderly woman with his food rations. Later, when his friend Miki disobeys orders to stay away from a restricted Chinese brothel, the *kempei* (military police) catch and beat him for his offense at its headquarters, nearly killing him. Miki floats in semi-consciousness, battered and bleeding in his jail cell, while listening to incarcerated Chinese suspects in other rooms as the *kempei* thrash and interrogate them. Hearing "the wailing of the tortured natives and the screaming of their tormentors," Miki "felt a closer kindredship with these natives than he had ever felt before" (173). The private commiserates with those whom he allegedly must subordinate, asserting his humanity through this shared pain. In this case, the empire's supremacy, embodied in the fists and boots of the *kempei,* is too entrenched to challenge in any physical sense. But in Miki's mind, the regulated boundary between imperial soldier and colonial subject temporarily vanishes.

The soldiers at one point even think the natives may have the better situation in the war, highlighting how empathy forged from brutalizing conditions has its limits. Takeo reflects on being an occupier of a foreign land as opposed to being occupied by an invading force. "It is better to be a noncombatant in a conquered nation than to be a soldier in a winning army," he asserts to his comrades (287). His superior, Third-Year Soldier Oka, agrees, observing that at least the natives are free from military discipline, long marches in foul weather, guard duty on cold nights, and fierce, deadly combat. Takeo continues the argument: unlike soldiers serving abroad, natives have their own homes, no matter how devastated, and their families nearby, no matter how poor. As part of the Imperial Army, however, he fails to consider the natives' possible fear of the Japanese and their relief when the troops avoid damaging their villages or hurting the inhabitants. They strategically offer tea to the passing army, "for they seemed to have decided that it was better to do so than to have the soldiers rummaging roughly through their homes" (286). Yet, in his fatigue and distress, Takeo can articulate only the desires shared between combatants and civilians: a home, a family, and being left in peace.

Lest any soldier think that similar racial features between enemies make for better comprehension of Japan's colonizing efforts, Takeo dismisses the idea. His friend Kan, who is the most exuberant in his patriotism among the group, acknowledges the horrors involved in combat. Like Takeo beforehand, he notes, "The old men and women we saw in the [Chinese] villages are exactly like the ones we see in our own country villages." Kan suggests that the situation might be different if the Japanese fought white soldiers, a comment that predicts the approaching engagement with Americans. He implies that a racial conflict would stir the troops more effectively in their willingness to serve. Takeo rebuffs this nonsense, remarking, "Whomever we fight, it is the same. A war is a war" (352). The young conscript rejects not only war but also the foundations of it. He resists the idea behind Japan's Greater East Asia

Co-Prosperity Sphere, a euphemism that structured its "anti-imperial" efforts to unite the region under its auspices to fight Western colonialism.[94] Takeo's opposition to further war implies that what the Imperial Army procured from Asia is similar to what the Western powers had taken years earlier. Battling European or American armies after enduring the China campaigns would be no different. Only devastation, guilt, and sorrow would ensue. From this perspective, the text's pacifist tone may have assured U.S. readers that Japan as a whole could renounce its militarism. But this point also reinforces Tasaki's cautioning the West in newspaper coverage of his novel to shun the cycles of imperial conquest in the postwar era.

The text's argument for a common humanity among occupiers and the occupied was timely, provoking readers' sensibilities about the Korean War. What the Japanese aggression in China recalled was that the United States might follow suit in Korea, despite whatever differences of circumstance or intent. One episode from *Long the Imperial War* that would become familiar to American GIs focuses on the destruction of a Chinese village that communist guerillas control. Takeo's company takes fire from this site and advances on it, discovering women, children, and the aged cowering in a nearby ditch. Meanwhile, the Chinese guerillas retreat to the countryside. With commanders who are intent on punishing anyone perceived as aiding the enemy, Takeo and his colleagues receive orders to burn the village, even though some realize that the civilians were innocent in this engagement. Fleeing the conflagration alongside newly created Chinese refugees, several soldiers consider the implications of their actions. "They shouldn't let us burn villages," one grumbles. "They shouldn't let us fight wars," another responds (112).

The American public learned from news reports about similar circumstances in Korea. A *Life* magazine feature that appeared in August 1950, the release date of *Long the Imperial Way,* detailed such atrocities. The correspondent observed that the United States had occupied South Korea for several years now. Yet, without further understanding of conditions in Korea, military involvement would not only "court final failure but also . . . force upon our men in the field acts and attitudes of the utmost savagery." These actions already included "the blotting out of villages where the enemy *may* be hiding; the shooting and shelling of refugees who *may* include North Koreans." Incurring civilian casualties adversely affected how the United States could justify its presence in East Asia, given how Soviet publicity already framed American troops there as a destructive imperial menace. In 1951, the *Christian Century* noted "the failure of our propaganda to match that of the Communists in reaching the minds of the Koreans," in part because of the "grandiose promises that we were in no position to fulfill." One significant reason lay with "the habit of our troops . . . of looting as they took over towns and villages."[95]

Long the Imperial Way intensified these concerns for Americans at home. As Miller observed in the *Saturday Review,* Tasaki's "great war novel shows that the soldiers of Nippon fighting in China ten years ago suffered the same sensations and torments that our own soldiers are undergoing today in Korea."[96] In this case, sympathy for Takeo and his fellow soldiers overcame the racial and national divides between the United States and Japan because of the Korean War. Miller empathized with Japanese soldiers as victims rather than as perpetrators of empire, given what American GIs were enduring only five years after the end of World War II. The larger desire among U.S. officials and cultural spokesmen was that the Japanese, because of their revealed humanity, would integrate more willingly into a larger anticommunist alliance. Miller's reference, however, suggested a cautionary tale about asserting imperial power: that American troops, like the Japanese before them, would be caught in a maelstrom of continual misguided conflict. Public opinion polls on the Korean War's early stages validated this position. One showed that 50 percent of Americans believed that the U.S. government was doing a "poor job" in its relations with Asia, particularly with Korea and China. Only 17 percent thought the government was doing a "good job," and 21 percent marked a "fair job." Survey results at the war's conclusion revealed little change in public attitudes. Looking at their polling in 1953, a group of Cornell University sociologists observed, "Instead of consensus, we have partisanship—in place of conviction and faith, we have divided opinion and doubt."[97]

Tasaki's novel reflected these feelings in its critique of waging dubious and dispiriting warfare. Proceeding into his third year of service, Takeo realizes the futility of fighting and even of controlling territory. "The enemy had been routed," the author observes, "but, as usual, only routed, though the papers at home made capital news of the 'victory.' Months had then followed of interminable and wearing combat with guerillas" (347). Tasaki's insertion of "as usual" serves as an Orwellian warning that, despite a short-lived dominance of the field, "victory" is still elusive, like the enemy itself, requiring further military commitment. The final chapter heightens the absurdity of this point when Takeo and his company return to Japan, parading through an unnamed city to their barracks, followed by cheering civilians. They listen to speeches by officials who declare that the nation may invest in future confrontations. Both the governor and the division commander intone the same words to the assembled troops: "The world situation is growing tense," a nod to the impending inferno of World War II (366, 371). Readying the men, the dignitaries address the sanctity of the body, one that sacrifices itself for the larger body politic. "Take good care of your bodies and always keep your personal affairs in good order" for any imminent conflict, the governor advises (371). Takeo, however, becomes enraged as the speeches continue, using his body to express discontent, a character development strategy encouraged by the postwar Japanese flesh writers. Waiting for the discharge service to begin, he relieves himself in the direction of the ceremonial gate that fronts the barracks. This violation in conduct "was a bold act of defiance," notes the author, but the officers themselves are restless and overlook the sacrilege (364). Then, as the governor's words start to blur in Takeo's mind, the young soldier "felt almost like vomiting" (372). This juxtaposition between speeches that glorify empire and Takeo's urinating and desires to throw up emphasizes the body as a site of resistance. Takeo's physique, in actions that punctuate his developing anti-imperialist stance, rejects the notion of serving again as he defiles the grounds on which his training began.

Americans appreciated the impact *Long the Imperial Way* left on their views of the evolving relationship between the United States and East Asia. Alongside its literary significance, the novel offered them an intricate look at Japanese imperialism that corresponded with and challenged American postwar endeavors framed by a universalist righteousness. This perspective derived in part from a selective, intertwined process of public interpretation and Tasaki's self-promotion that relegated his Nisei past to an acknowledged yet absent presence. But the work also made the functions and inclinations of empire more discernible for some U.S. readers troubled by their nation's overseas ventures. As a Japanese/American writer fashioned by two empires, Tasaki sought in turn to reorient both, linking one's prior activities in China with the other's future in Japan and Korea. That receptive audiences in the United States debated his text in light of their nation's involvement in another Asia-Pacific war reveals the cultural scope as well as the artistry of Tasaki's novel. In this context, his was a tremendous, yet now overlooked, achievement from the early Cold War era.

2

Sleeping with the Frenemy

Yamaguchi Yoshiko as Japanese War Bride

YAMAGUCHI YOSHIKO was a movie star who traversed multiple, overlapping worlds. The variations of her stage name from the 1930s to the 1950s suggest as much: she was known in China as Li Xianglan ("Fragrant Orchid"), as Ri Koran (its translation) among the Japanese, and as Shirley Yamaguchi in the postwar United States. Born to Japanese parents in Manchuria, she was fluent in several languages and identified more often with China than with her ancestral homeland. Yamaguchi did not even visit Japan until she was eighteen years old, only to discover how out of place she felt there. Still, she was a citizen and a product of its imperial system. Her father worked for the Southern Manchurian Railway Company (or Mantetsu), which Japan had acquired from its victory in the Russo-Japanese War. The actor began her movie career in 1938 with the Manchurian Film Association (or Man'ei) and performed as well for other studios in propaganda pictures that encouraged the friendly ties between China and Japan. These projects were part of the latter's strategy of asserting its dominance by overseeing "harmonious" relations among Asian peoples through the Greater East Asia Co-Prosperity Sphere. Yamaguchi gained renown in her films playing the Chinese love-interest of Japanese men, interactions that personalized the larger cultural, political, and economic stakes in the region. Man'ei publicists even advertised their star as a Chinese national with Japanese sympathies to maintain audience interest. After the war, however, Kuomintang officials charged Yamaguchi with treason, and she faced possible execution for collaborating with the enemy. Authorities released the actor when she revealed herself as

Japanese, proving that she could not be a traitor to China. Chastised for her ruse, she submitted to repatriation to Japan and appeared in a few productions there. In 1950, Yamaguchi decided to try the American movie market. Hollywood proved a fitting change of venue, when producers at Twentieth Century–Fox cast her in two motion pictures, King Vidor's *Japanese War Bride* (1952) and Samuel Fuller's *House of Bamboo* (1955). In these films, she once again portrayed a woman wooed by members of an occupying force, this time in postwar Japan with U.S. servicemen, to dramatize the new relations between former foes.[1]

The actor's arrival on the Hollywood scene came at a telling moment in not only U.S.-Japan relations but also race relations within the United States. During and after the U.S. occupation, the fraternization between American GIs and Japanese women stirred domestic and international controversy. Most encounters were casual and fleeting, but others developed into committed relationships that resulted in marriage, from which the wives became known as "war brides." During the late 1940s to the early 1960s, roughly thirty thousand of them came to the United States.[2] These unions initially occurred without official sanction from the U.S. military and met with resistance in both Japan and the United States. To the Japanese, native women having sexual relations with foreign occupiers heightened feelings of defeat and despair as well as disgust at the mixed-race progeny created from such pairings. Friends and families of the war brides often reacted with shock and shame.[3] To Americans back in the United States, Japan was a former enemy that still conjured up feelings of distrust or even hatred. Moreover, these interracial couples, if relocated to the United States, would challenge segregation and miscegenation policies that safeguarded white supremacy and immigration restrictions on Asians established since the late nineteenth century. In light of these charged issues, the United States worked to improve its image abroad as a multiethnic democracy to downplay these racist practices and to present a better alternative to communism. It was no coincidence, then, that magazine and newspaper coverage, popular fiction, sociological studies, and Hollywood films throughout the 1950s focused attention on the phenomenon of U.S. soldiers bringing home Japanese wives.[4]

Yamaguchi seemed particularly suited to play a war bride because of her past roles that enacted the intimacies of empire, when Japan metaphorically "wooed" China through fictional characters' romances to justify its expansion and dominance. American-produced narratives of postwar relations gave her another opportunity to embody a conquered, feminized nation, this time Japan, now courted by a benevolent, masculine, white hero personifying the United States. Conveying international alliances through romantic relations, as illustrated by American soldiers wedding Japanese women, was one way for

Hollywood to stage the new turn in global affairs. But these accounts were as much about establishing and naturalizing hierarchies of authority as they were about portraying the acceptance of cultural or racial differences. As Ann Laura Stoler and others have shown, the personal, familial, and sexual relationships developed between occupiers and the occupied reveal the dynamics of how imperial systems exert and extend their sovereignty over subjugated populations beyond military force. Creating laws that forbade miscegenation, restricted migration, instituted hygiene standards, and managed adoptions and child-rearing practices, for instance, demonstrated these methods of rule.[5] Yet unregulated interactions still occurred, despite what a governing bureaucracy documented or attempted to control, as seen in the censured GI–war bride marriages, among other examples. In these cases, intimate affairs remind us not only how nation-states acquire and sustain ascendancy over other territories and peoples but also how resistance or adaptations to this power arise and persist past its reach.[6]

The status of postwar Japan further complicates this framework because it was unlike conventional colonies or newly formed postcolonial states. Having asserted its own modern imperial machinery on the Asian mainland and surrounding islands, the nation enjoyed a favored position within American political, economic, and military structures to help oversee the Pacific theater. Japan's strategic location, rebuilt industries, and past knowledge about the broader swath of Asia proved invaluable to U.S. aims in containing communism and in integrating market economies.[7] As Paul A. Kramer notes about such relationships: "Throughout history, empire-builders have been acutely preoccupied with other empire-builders; networks of modern empire bound rivals together in competitive and cooperative exchange, emulation, and adaptation."[8] These frictions and overlaps were evident in U.S.-Japan relations, especially from the 1930s to the 1950s, providing an important context for understanding Yamaguchi's transnational allure. The two nations not only came to blows in the Pacific War; they also developed as imperial powers almost simultaneously, when procuring colonies and client states at the turn of the twentieth century. In similar fashion, each positioned itself as an exceptionalist, anti-imperial state desiring to enlighten and to liberate other realms and populations. Americans thought of themselves as part of what Thomas Jefferson called an "empire of liberty," while the Japanese advanced the Greater East Asia Co-Prosperity Sphere.[9] As Takashi Fujitani and Yukiko Koshiro have demonstrated, the United States and Japan even shared a disdain for racial mixing, just as they purposefully crafted narratives about it during and after the war to signal the importance of political and cultural partnerships, however contradictory these feelings and intentions appeared.[10] It should be noted that to compare the two nations' designs and development as imperial states is not to ignore their differences in political ideologies, governing systems, levels of applied coercion, availability of resources, scales of occupation, collaborations with native elites, and other factors that were apparent in their approaches to dominating the Pacific. But the significance of Yamaguchi's evolving movie career rests on how she epitomized these countries' intersecting stances on interracial intimacies that validated and disrupted their colonizing presence. In this way, her appearances in Hollywood productions and the publicity about them coincided with broader social and political developments, especially regarding American reactions to Japan as a new ally and to the intimacies occurring between U.S. servicemen and Japanese women.

Yamaguchi's films and star image in Asia and the United States thus exposed the correlations between imperial Japanese and postwar American objectives, when each nation sought to extend its power and influence at home and abroad through cultural forms. Noteworthy too is how different populations read the actor's persona and performances to suit their own ends, oftentimes in defiance of such power and influence. While she posed as a Chinese national, the Japanese actor had to weigh her wartime identities and agendas with the demands of moviegoers in occupied China and imperial Japan. In this balancing act, she realized the freedoms and the dangers involved when seen as belonging to both nations and to neither. Yamaguchi likewise attracted divergent responses to her postwar Hollywood films, with audiences that included mainstream Americans as well as Japanese and Japanese Americans. By this time, however, her nationality became more stabilized as "Japanese." With the end of the war came the end of the "Chinese" performer Li Xianglan/Ri Koran, although fans throughout East Asia still recognized the movie star by these names long afterward. Nevertheless, Yamaguchi went by her Japanese family name in her later film credits. She even played a Chinese protagonist in one postwar Japanese production, *Woman of Shanghai* (1952), but audiences by then saw her as a Japanese actor.[11]

Within the context of U.S.-Japan relations, Yamaguchi's new image, while not as feigned or fluid as before, developed into a different kind of celebrity as she negotiated her postwar identity. This makeover avoided her past complicity in advancing Japan's wartime propaganda and her resulting guilt about it. Promotional material in the 1950s omitted mentioning these matters because of changing geopolitical concerns and alignments. Japan's defeat and new status as a U.S. ally, American desires to build workable partnerships in the Pacific, and China's emergence as a communist state all contributed to this silence over the actor's prior movie career and affection for China.[12] Cultural beliefs about gender roles in the United States also played a significant part in repressing Yamaguchi's war guilt within her public persona. Unlike Imperial

Army veterans, such as Hanama Tasaki, who fictionalized his own feelings of remorse (discussed in Chapter 1), Japanese women as a whole became disassociated from their homeland's prior militarism and empire building. These included the war brides who immigrated to the United States. Americans viewed them, and Yamaguchi in particular, as the image of a revised, yet still docile, "Madame Butterfly," catering to Western male fantasies of Asian women's subordination. This orientalist impression, one grounded in the history of U.S. imperialist desires in Asia at the turn of the twentieth century, also applied to postwar Japan as a whole, reassuring Americans of their ally's love and loyalty. But the purposes and contexts of this U.S. orientalism differed from earlier eras because of the new threat of communism in the region and the lingering doubts about Japan's willingness to embrace democracy and U.S. leadership.[13]

We can see in this configuration of "Japanese/American" how Yamaguchi enacted the parallel processes of "becoming Japanese" and "becoming American." The former describes her transition into a more fixed Japanese persona in her postwar publicity, while the latter addresses her fictional roles as a Japanese war bride assimilating into U.S. society or accepting American influences in her life. Both methods of "becoming" represent narratives about integrating racial Others: not only for Japanese war brides in the American mainstream but also for a suspiciously "mixed" Chinese/Japanese repatriated actor in Japan. From another perspective, Yamaguchi's Japanese/American positioning highlights how the entertainer and popular media coverage simultaneously merged and separated her real-life and onscreen performances to sustain her reconceived celebrity status. Her "becoming Japanese" played an important part in her "becoming American," when Hollywood intimated through her roles as a war bride the broader transitions that a newly reconstituted Japan had to make when conforming to U.S. expectations. In this framing, Japan as a "feminized," subordinate nation would willingly adapt to what the United States wanted it to become. Yet Japan had its own social, political, and economic interests to pursue, which Americans certainly recognized. Japanese moviegoers even interpreted Yamaguchi's postwar Hollywood performances in ways that contested the U.S. film industry's marketing and imagery of their nation. Thus the solidus between signifiers in this Japanese/American construct also illuminates the underlying tensions and divisions between an occupied Japanese populace and an occupying American force, despite their new political partnership.

In contrast, Nisei reviewers saw the commonalities they shared with Yamaguchi as part of a broader transpacific community contributing to the improvement of U.S.-Japan relations and domestic race relations. Indeed, Yamaguchi's Hollywood roles recalled issues at home and abroad that affected how the Nisei imagined her: first, through memories of the mass confinement depicted in *Japanese War Bride* and, second, through the U.S.-Japan discord revealed by the release of *House of Bamboo.* Publicity about Yamaguchi's private life enhanced the visibility of these topics. For example, the actor's marriage from 1951 to 1955 to the renowned Japanese American sculptor and designer Isamu Noguchi epitomized for audiences on both sides of the Pacific this melding of, and the frictions between, two peoples, cultures, and nations. Arriving at the crossroads of interracial and international relations, Yamaguchi offered through her star image and her Hollywood features more intimate ways of realizing these wider challenges.

A Chinese/Japanese/American Movie Star

On February 28, 1946, Yamaguchi Yoshiko waited with two thousand other Japanese nationals at a Shanghai harbor to board a ship headed for Japan. At the conclusion of the Pacific War, the process of repatriating people to their ancestral homelands began, whether or not they were born there, or had ever lived there. Dismantling an empire meant that the Allied victors had to remove Japanese soldiers and civilians from not only China but also Korea, Taiwan, and Southeast Asia, a total of 6.9 million individuals. In turn, almost 2.3 million subjects from occupied regions who had been relocated to Japan for their labor required reinstatement to their native countries. Repatriation also included persons whom the Japanese had transported from one client state to another, such as the 1.5 million Koreans in Manchuria and the tens of thousands in other places formerly under imperial authority. The famed actor's presence at the Shanghai port was one small part of this massive transference of peoples.[14]

Yamaguchi's own repatriation exposed the initial difficulties she faced when attempting to conform to a new established order. That February morning at the harbor was chilly, as she recalled, and the gathered crowd could see their collective breath wafting in the air. The actor was tired and disheveled, having endured a treason trial after being mistaken for a Chinese national and charged with collaborating with the enemy. Kuomintang authorities in Shanghai, like moviegoers throughout China, still saw her as Li Xianglan, the Man'ei-created film persona who besmirched their national pride by starring in propaganda films for imperial Japan. Yamaguchi was arrested and imprisoned, but she eventually confirmed her Japanese citizenship and escaped a likely execution when a friend traveled to Japan to retrieve the family register documents proving the actor's nationality to a Chinese military court. Although the issue appeared resolved, the drama continued at the Shanghai harbor when the officials checking repatriation papers also recognized Yamaguchi as Li Xianglan and prevented her from boarding the ship. Apparently, proper notification of her acquittal had not yet reached them. Yamaguchi tried to explain to the harbor officials that the court had already cleared her of treason charges, but to no avail. She would not be traveling to Japan that day. In the weeks that it took to re-verify her identity, authorities placed the controversial star under house arrest. When all was finally settled with the Chinese government in late March, Yamaguchi proceeded back to the harbor and left on another vessel. She was now a Japanese repatriate (223–256).

These encounters with Chinese officials emphasize how Yamaguchi's multiple identities and the postwar confusion about them created both public interest in her celebrity and dangerous circumstances for her own life. The pressures of presenting such a fluid persona had been building since her interactions with Chinese and Japanese production companies, movie reviewers, and audiences throughout the latter half of the Asia-Pacific War. The revelation of her true nationality and her repatriation to Japan, however, marked her transformation into a less ambiguous film star. In her memoir, Yamaguchi even titled the chapter describing her efforts to leave China as "Farewell, Li Xianglan." In this valediction, she discarded both the glamour and the troubles of her wartime past. Her departure thus concluded a tumultuous period of growing up amid war and occupation, of celebrated renown, of having Chinese friends and admirers, of enduring suspicion and even hatred because of her Chinese and Japanese sympathies, and of shedding a Chinese persona that became too precarious for her. When Yamaguchi's ship from Shanghai arrived in Kyushu, Japan, a crowd of reporters surrounded her, asking for a statement. The actor proclaimed to the press the symbolic demise of Li Xianglan, or the Japanese rendition of this figure. "Ri Koran has died," she remarked. "I now wish to live as Yamaguchi Yoshiko once again" (258). Reclaiming this identity signaled her hopes for transitioning into a more peaceful postwar life.

Yamaguchi Yoshiko's original identity emerged in 1920, when she was born in Fengtian (Shenyang) in Liaoning Province, located in the southern part of northeastern China (or Manchuria). At this time and place, her family background and her coming of age already revealed the difficulties she would have to negotiate when caught between Japanese imperial actions and persistent Chinese nationalism. That her "motherland of China" and her "fatherland of Japan" (as she called them) clashed with each other only made her sympathies for both an empire and its subjects problematic from each side's point of view. Varying levels of distrust about Yamaguchi's intentions lingered among Chinese and Japanese officials, journalists, and audiences throughout the war. The inner turmoil she felt was also considerable. "If I really wanted to become Chinese," she surmised, "I would lose my Japanese character; but if I wished to retain my Japanese self, I would be misinterpreted by the Chinese" (44). Because of these internal conflicts, she often desired to eschew national attachments, even as she ended up serving the interests of the Japanese empire.

This intermingling of peoples and cultures from which Yamaguchi emerged played an important part in Japan's aims to create a cooperative society in Manchuria. In 1931, Japan's Kwantung Army invaded and occupied northeastern China, establishing there a puppet state and renaming the region Manchukuo by the following year. The army became a garrison force, maintaining order through its brutal, imposing presence, while seeking to secure the territory's northern borders against any Russian belligerence. But various factions in Japan had other coinciding plans for the region. To industrialists, fostering an integrated economy with Manchuria was essential to the overall scheme of empire. To agrarian reformers, encouraging the mass migration of Japanese farmers into Manchuria meant relieving population pressures in Japan and extending its influence to the Chinese hinterlands.[15] On another front, Yamaguchi's father was one of the people who had been relocated to China to manage the railway lines and urban planning ventures of Mantetsu that conjoined Japan, Manchuria, and Korea. Japanese leaders thus saw Manchuria as part of a modern, interconnected, multicultural empire. The idea of pan-Asianism outlined this prospect, from which the "harmony of the five races"—Japanese, Chinese, Manchus, Koreans, and Mongolians—announced the rise of a new Asia under Japan's enlightened guidance. This notion, however, also signified the consolidation of Japanese power throughout the region, as those under its rule were quick to discover.[16]

Yamaguchi's upbringing in this environment revealed a cosmopolitan blurring of affiliations, one filled with an appreciation for the arts. She noted that her parents never required her to learn the more conventional aspects of Japanese domesticity, such as cooking, needlework, flower arranging, or the tea ceremony. Instead, they encouraged her interest in music, providing her with lessons in singing as well as in violin and piano (2–3). Under the tutelage of a Russian voice teacher, Yamaguchi included in her repertoire Russian folk songs, classical opera, and other types of Western music. In 1933, at the age of thirteen, she caught the attention of the Fengtian Broadcasting Station. This Japanese-run company wanted to attract Chinese audiences to the cause of "Japanese-Manchurian Friendship" through its playlist of adapted Chinese folk songs and other popular tunes. Since Yamaguchi was conversant in both Mandarin and Japanese, she embodied what the radio station had been seeking. Her vocal skills would later help her film career with Man'ei and other studios that showcased her singing, a talent still enjoyed by listeners throughout Asia to this day (26–28).

Occupying several worlds at once was not unusual for Yamaguchi, given her family roots and interest in China. Her grandfather, Yamaguchi Hiroshi, was a Sinologist. Her father, Fumio, also developed a deep admiration for Chinese culture. Fumio became an instructor of Mandarin for Mantetsu; by way of these lessons, the railway company's Japanese employees could communicate with their Chinese coworkers. As a young girl, Yoshiko attended her father's language classes and soon achieved fluency. So developed were these family interests in China that they extended to personal relationships with the Chinese elite. Fumio agreed to have a friend, General Li Jichun, symbolically adopt Yoshiko as his own daughter, a common cultural practice in China that signified friendship between families. Li was a Japanese collaborator and the president of the Shenyang Bank in Fengtian. As a new member of Li's extended family, Yoshiko took the name "Li Xianglan" to honor her adoptive father's surname (19–21).

Another significant influence on Yamaguchi was Kawakita Nagamasa, a movie producer and the president of the Towa Film Company. Like the actor herself, Kawakita admired Chinese culture and possessed "a cosmopolitan sensibility rarely seen among the prewar Japanese," as she recollected (186). Indeed, her worldly concerns matched his. Yamaguchi observed that the conflict between China and Japan was "so personally painful that it threatened to tear him apart," a sentiment he often expressed to her (187). As a well-connected man, Kawakita diligently promoted Japanese films overseas, bringing Kurosawa Akira's *Rashomon* (1950) to international fame. He also imported Western films to Japan and worked with Chinese production crews and actors. Kawakita maintained contacts with European and American filmmakers too. For instance, one of his friends in the United States was Joseph Bernhard, a producer at Twentieth Century–Fox. In 1950, Bernhard had a project in development, *East Is East,* later renamed *Japanese War Bride,* for which he needed an actor to portray the title character. As a friend of Kawakita's, Yamaguchi came to the Hollywood producer's attention as just the right person for the role (264).[17]

Yamaguchi's life and career up to 1945 thus exposed the entangled histories of Chinese collusion with the Japanese (through the Li family) and Japanese interest in the Chinese (through her family elders and Kawakita) that challenged the conventional contours of national allegiances. These personal connections explain why Yamaguchi could develop both Chinese and Japanese sensibilities, even admitting that she "felt" Chinese when growing up. She once admitted, "I forgot completely that I was Japanese. . . . Living on a vast continent led me naturally to think that we all coexisted as friends, whether any of us was Chinese, Korean, or Russian" (75). Amid this mix of peoples, specific ethnicities or nationalities mattered little to her, as she readily embraced the possibilities and pleasures offered by other cultures.

But since her youthful days in China, Yamaguchi also realized the stark contrasts in Japan's objectives in creating a multiethnic empire. She recalled with horror, when looking out her house window as a child, the Japanese military police interrogating and beating a Chinese man in the early days of occupation (7–8). When first visiting Japan as a teenager, she prompted a policeman's wrath for wearing Chinese clothes and speaking Mandarin to her accompanying Chinese friends. Reading her given Japanese name on her passport, the officer erupted at her hybrid mannerisms, as she described his outburst. "Now look! We Japanese belong to a first-class nation," he lectured her, believing this status threatened when she adopted the habits of an "inferior" culture. "Damn you! Aren't you ashamed of yourself?" he continued (81–82). Yamaguchi saw and experienced enough of Japanese discrimination against inhabitants of Manchuria and elsewhere to know that the espoused harmony among a diverse populace was far from achieved or intended.

Having cosmopolitan interests likewise placed Yamaguchi's friends and family in great peril. Japanese authorities suspected both Yamaguchi's father and Kawakita of having overt Chinese sympathies, putting their lives and their careers at risk. The military police once detained Fumio for questioning about his perceived aiding of "the enemy," since he had many Chinese friends and associates (13). Rumors of potential assassination attempts swirled around Kawakita because he advocated for allowing Chinese film companies to function without imperial oversight (192–193). While also working for Japan's wartime movie industry in Manchuria, Yamaguchi later discovered that she had been under surveillance by Japanese and Soviet agents. Amid the "bewildering profusion of ideologies and ethnicities," she wrote, it was her transnational contacts, and thus her indeterminate loyalties, that attracted suspicion, even though Japanese film companies had encouraged her hybrid identities in the first place to gain wider audiences (183–184).

To facilitate imperial Japan's objective of regional dominance, its movie studios produced storylines about the nation's expansion into other lands as acts of benevolence. Expected viewers included colonial subjects across East Asia as well as Japanese audiences in occupied areas and in the home islands. That Man'ei and other institutions portrayed Yamaguchi as a Chinese actor with Japanese sympathies, who played Chinese protagonists submitting to Japanese supervision, was a vital part of this propaganda strategy.[18] Hers, then, was a double-layered performance incorporating a manufactured public persona that matched her onscreen fictional protagonists' portrayal of the cooperation between subjects and rulers. But within these dynamics, her films and characters conveyed different meanings to different audiences. While viewers could simply enjoy the aesthetic pleasures of Yamaguchi's singing and acting, the political ramifications of her movies were hard to miss. On the one hand, the Chinese saw in Li Xianglan particular characteristics that expressed their defiance and nationalism amid Japan's occupation. On the other hand, the Japanese pondered through Ri Koran the aptness of their imperial presence in China. Two of Yamaguchi's signature films that spawned such reactions were *China Nights* (1940) and *Glory to Eternity* (1943).[19]

China Nights became one of Yamaguchi's most famous and controversial productions, one of many in which she depicted a Chinese woman wooed by a Japanese male hero. Yamaguchi plays the orphan Keiran, a plucky girl who becomes enamored of the Japanese sailor Tetsuo. Initially, Keiran repulses Tetsuo's kindnesses and advances because she hates the Japanese, the war having claimed both her parents and her home. What remains discomfiting to Chinese audiences is the scene wherein Tetsuo becomes impatient and angry with Keiran's resistance to him, and he slaps her. After this abrupt violence, Tetsuo apologizes and Keiran comes to recognize his love for her. She then shares her newly realized feelings for him. As Yamaguchi explained in her memoir, the Japanese producers and viewers understood Tetsuo's blow as stemming from affection. Thus, in a larger sense, a China that required military occupation and its ensuing brutality would come to appreciate what the Japanese were attempting to accomplish for its own benefit. Most Chinese, however, did not see it this way. Although Tetsuo's love for Keiran compelled him to apologize for his violence and to make himself vulnerable to her feelings, Chinese moviegoers were still incensed at her humiliation from this episode, finding her response and the plot development unbelievable (99–100).

Yet, with such a flexible identity, Yamaguchi was able to traverse the lines between imperial dominance, in which she was complicit in Japan's objectives, and native resistance, when sympathizing with the Chinese. *Glory to Eternity,* a joint Chinese-Japanese production, exposes again how various audiences could generate diverse meanings and pleasures from the same film. In this feature, Yamaguchi plays a candy peddler who visits an opium den in 1840s China, a country under British imperial rule. In one famous tune, "The Candy Peddling Song," she wishes that the Chinese would consume the sweets she sold instead of the destructive opium offered by the British. The Japanese producers hoped to present a critique of Great Britain and white imperialism, while portraying themselves as enlightened leaders. But among Chinese movie patrons, the song stirred a resurgent nationalism regarding not only their past under British colonialism but also their present circumstances under Japanese authority (194). However unintended, Yamaguchi's performance and star attraction in the film exposed the vulnerabilities within an empire's acts and intentions.

Indeed, *Glory to Eternity* and the publicity behind it served to boost Yamaguchi's popularity among Chinese audiences. Shortly after the film's release, the actor felt compelled to reveal herself as a Japanese national because her Chinese friends continually expressed anger about her roles that they thought demeaned them. "I was beginning to feel guilty" about these wartime films, she confessed, especially since they "ended up satisfying none other than Japan's egotistical needs" (169). But Yamaguchi's managers pressured her to remain quiet about her identity to maintain the success of the studios and of her own career. When Yamaguchi appeared at a press event, a Chinese reporter, assuming that the actor was also Chinese, asked how she could portray her own people in humiliating fashion in such films as *China Nights.* Yamaguchi cited as an excuse her unknowing youth at the time and apologized for these earlier portrayals. The gathering of journalists then applauded this expression of remorse (200–201). Some evidence suggests that because a few Chinese fans knew, or inferred correctly, about Yamaguchi's Japanese citizenship, her elicited repentance carried added weight when they read in her apology that Japan itself was regretful for its actions against China. On her own behalf, Yamaguchi was able to relay her guilt in a convincing manner because of her personal connections to Manchuria and her interstitial position as a Chinese/Japanese movie star. It was after this incident that the performer's fame in China expanded beyond Manchuria, particularly from record sales of her songs and from the Shanghai movie market. By the postwar era, however, China endured a civil war and emerged a communist nation, while Japan became an American ally. For Yamaguchi, showing remorse over her films was then no longer possible. She now had to disassociate herself from China because of these political shifts and her new acting career in Japan and the United States. Not until the early 1970s, when China and Japan began reestablishing diplomatic relations, did she start another phase of rapprochement with the Chinese by publicly apologizing again for her prior complicity in the wartime propaganda pictures.[20]

Yamaguchi's postwar appearances in Japanese films offer another instance of reworking her identity and "becoming Japanese" as a repatriated actor. Repatriates in Japan were often viewed as not quite Japanese, since they carried the temporary stigma of foreignness themselves, developed from their prior interactions and familiarity with colonized Others in China, Korea, and elsewhere.[21] In this light, Yamaguchi appeared alien and exotic because of her Manchurian background. Some Japanese moviegoers even criticized her for looking "too Chinese" in her postwar films. Others surmised that she was of mixed parentage, a rumor that started during the war (74).[22] Such reactions never dogged Hara Setsuko, another Japanese movie star and Yamaguchi's contemporary. Hara also appeared in imperial propaganda films, also at times as a Chinese woman. But she never adopted a Chinese public persona, instead becoming the archetype of the pure Japanese maiden, as opposed to Yamaguchi's continued ethnic posing and involvement in fictionalized illicit romances. In the postwar years, moviegoers even identified Hara as "the eternal virgin," the chaste, ideal embodiment of modern Japanese womanhood. She personified this type of figure in such Ozu Yasujiro classics as *Early Summer* (1951) and *Tokyo Story* (1953). In these and other productions, Hara played the morally centered protagonist who cared for friends and family while also maintaining her dignity and independence.[23]

Despite Yamaguchi's "mixed" background, the star still fascinated Japanese viewers because her own rehabilitation paralleled postwar Japan's. Yamaguchi's film characters in Japanese productions during the 1950s, as Jennifer Coates observes, produced anxiety and ambivalence among audiences. Because of her past roles as a subjugated woman who also presented an elusive, hybridized exoticism, moviegoers began identifying with this status, seeing in it their own defeat and ignominy. In this affective state, they realized themselves as the feminized and racialized Other, as the Chinese and other Asians had been under Japanese rule. This new condition arose in large part from the racial views of Japan's white American occupiers, who now set the rules and standards for what was or was not acceptable regarding everyday practices, beliefs, and behaviors.[24] We can then see how Yamaguchi's past appearances in propaganda films, in which she portrayed Chinese characters under occupation, ironically provided Japanese audiences with a model of heroic and enduring comportment. The star's power thus stemmed from her ability to offer movie patrons a cultural outlet for their own sense of despair. It also lent credence to the nation's feelings of uncertainty when shifting from an imperial to an occupied state and then to a sovereign state again. Her "becoming Japanese" in this way matched Japan's own efforts at creating a new national identity amid such transformations. This process entailed the Japanese and the actor herself downplaying or reimagining their former roles in cultural exchanges with, and the colonization of, other Asian peoples.[25]

Yamaguchi's transition from a Chinese/Japanese to a Japanese/American actor likewise occurred within the overlapping national and global contexts of U.S.-Japan relations. When "becoming Japanese" as a postwar star in Japan and "becoming American" in Hollywood films, Yamaguchi revealed how her performances, both onscreen and in media coverage, reinforced the desires of each nation. But the actor's career was still lithely transnational, albeit in different ways from her earlier roles. Yamaguchi was already well experienced in portraying characters that crossed cultural, racial, and national boundaries through acts of "transgressive love."[26] In the United States, she elicited diverse reactions among mainstream and Japanese American audiences that corresponded with the nation's postwar anxieties about domestic race relations and international affairs. The Nisei especially saw in her celebrity status their own significance in larger transpacific exchanges between their ancestral and native lands. Yet the actor's participation in Hollywood also discloses how imperial Japan and the United States exerted their power and influence through popular entertainment, not only for home audiences but for the conquered as well. This latter population now included the Japanese.[27] Against this backdrop, it made sense to American filmmakers to present Japan as a model ally and Japanese Americans as a model minority, static cultural framings that aligned with Yamaguchi's more stabilized star image, to promote democratic values and goodwill at home and abroad. But moviegoers in Japan and the United States read the films in ways that challenged these representations. Yamaguchi and the Japanese war bride characters she portrayed became the means by which audiences could then interpret their varying postwar conditions.

Madame Butterfly Redux?

The arrival of Japanese war brides in the United States both confirmed and complicated how the nation could fulfill its interests and responsibilities in the postwar world. Despite the controversy surrounding the women's marriages to American GIs, their visibility on the domestic front helped to advertise racial tolerance and diversity as well as U.S. desires to secure overseas allies to the anticommunist cause. In this manner, the war brides' importance extended beyond public curiosity about their racially anomalous position within the white mainstream. Nor were they and their husbands seen as simply engaged in romances that merged different families, ethnicities, and cultures. To be sure, their marriages held great political and cultural significance during the Cold War because they offered Americans an intimate framework for assessing their nation's race and gender relations at home and dealings with nonwhite populations abroad. The interracial pairings consequently stirred broader national debates about U.S. immigration, citizenship, and miscegenation policies, the roles of women in and outside the household, U.S. relations with Japan and other Asian states, and American abilities to contain communism in the Pacific.[28]

The war brides from Japan presented a unique challenge to U.S. immigration and citizenship policies because of the prior restrictions on Asian populations within and outside the country. When pairings of GIs and Japanese women began with the occupation in 1945, few foreign-born Asians could become naturalized as American citizens. Nor could they gain entry into the United States without extreme difficulty. Congress passed a series of temporary "GI brides bills" between 1945 and 1952 as a partial acknowledgment of these relationships, allowing servicemen to bring their foreign-born wives into the country. But these acts were intended mostly for white women from occupied Germany or from allied European nations. Because of the longstanding limits against Asians, private bills sponsored by individual congressmen and by such organizations as the Japanese American Citizens League (JACL) permitted GIs to circumvent the immigration quotas and to enter the United States with their Japanese wives. The moral logic behind these moves came from emphasizing the men's martial sacrifices, and thus the rights earned from this service, rather than from desires to create a diverse and racially tolerant society by admitting Asian women.[29] The passage of the McCarran-Walter Act in 1952, the same year in which Japan regained its sovereignty, opened the door to legitimizing Asian arrivals by offering them naturalization as part of a Cold War strategy to embrace the "good immigrants." More broadly, it enacted standards for color-blind citizenship in the United States. But the number allocated for admission from Japan was only 185 people per year, and even fewer were to be admitted from other Asian countries. These restrictions revealed a dogged reluctance among U.S. leaders, including the bill's sponsors, Senator Pat McCarran and Congressman Francis Walter, to permit entry to those seen as racial Others. Japanese war brides were exempted from these provisions because of their non-quota status as spouses of American citizens.[30]

What sparked Japanese American interest in the McCarran-Walter Act was its section on naturalization, which gave foreign-born Asians who were already within the United States, particularly the Issei, the opportunity to become citizens. However, as a Cold War document, the legislation included mechanisms to denaturalize and deport subversives, targeting anyone who espoused communism or had ties to any suspicious organizations. The law developed from the Internal Security Act of 1950, also a product of Senator McCarran's efforts, which sought to control immigration through such tactics as detaining or expelling suspects as part of the broader battle against communism.[31] Some Nisei editorialists feared that this state power might be abused, since it invoked memories of Japanese Americans being marked as threats to society, which then resulted in their wartime imprisonment. Yet the JACL, a supporter of the McCarran-Walter Act's passage, argued that what mattered most for Japanese American communities was getting the Issei protected as U.S. citizens. Backing the bill with its anticommunist provisions would also reinforce their model status as loyal Americans. These moves and debates revealed not only how the overlapping issues of citizenship, immigration, and national security affected U.S.-Japan relations but also how Japanese Americans positioned themselves throughout the Cold War.[32]

On the cultural front, American popular media associated the newly arriving Japanese war brides with the figure of Madame Butterfly. One major manifestation of this idea came from John Luther Long's 1898 novella, *Madame Butterfly,* which became a useful narrative for comprehending U.S.-Asian relations. The central character of the book is Cho-Cho-San, a young and innocent Japanese woman who falls in love with the American naval officer Lieutenant Benjamin Franklin Pinkerton. A carefree man, Pinkerton seeks a woman's companionship while stationed in Japan. Winning over the agreeable Cho-Cho-San, he oversees the daily rhythms of her life, convincing her to convert to Christianity, ordering her to speak English in the household, and estranging her from her extended family. Pinkerton then returns to the United States, vowing to come back in the springtime. Meanwhile, Cho-Cho-San gives birth to their son. Pinkerton eventually reappears in Japan, yet unexpectedly with his blond American wife, Adelaide, who determines to take the child back with them to the United States. Mired in grief, Cho-Cho-San tries to commit suicide to maintain her honor. But the cries of her son prompt her to live for his sake. As the story concludes, the two have already disappeared to some unknown future when Adelaide comes for the boy.[33]

This orientalist image of submissive yet wary Asian women had roots in U.S. empire-building efforts at the turn of the twentieth century. Indeed, *Madame Butterfly* appeared in the same year as the Spanish-American War, when the United States defeated Spain and acquired its colonies in Cuba, Puerto Rico, Guam, and the Philippines. Borrowing from western European assertions of racial and cultural superiority over Asian, African, and Middle Eastern peoples, white Americans similarly viewed their nation's imperialism and dominance over native populations through orientalist lenses to legitimate their overseas interventions.[34] These more frequent encounters with racial Others, particularly in Asia, subsequently stoked interest among novelists, playwrights, architects, musicians, artists, designers, and others in "East meets West" styles and themes that influenced domestic consumer tastes. White American women, who had a hand in purchasing choices, adorned their bodies and households in orientalist fashions to reinforce their middle-class or elite status. Acquiring furniture, wallpaper, and artwork, dressing up in kimonos and adopting ornamental hairstyles, or reading romantic novels set in Asia and written by white authors like John Luther Long, were acts of ownership that showcased the broader impact, however indirect, of the nation's imperial endeavors.[35] Long's text gained resonance because it established through fiction how audiences could conceive of international affairs through hierarchical renderings of race and gender relations. The novella held such attraction that the playwright David Belasco wrote a successful New York stage adaptation of it in 1900. The most famous rendition of this story comes from the Italian composer Giacomo Puccini, whose *Madama Butterfly* (1904) and its later variations draw worldwide audiences to this day. Notable in Puccini's reworking is that Cio-Cio-San (as spelled in his version) proceeds in the end to kill herself. This act signified the unsuitability of interracial relations between white men and Asian women.[36]

The appearance of *Madame Butterfly* also coincided with the nation's reception of, and restrictions on, immigrants coming from a variety of different shores. The United States began curbing the influx of migrants from Asia and then from southern and eastern Europe when domestic fears of growing ethnic diversity complicated the nation's needs for industrial and agricultural labor. A few years before the book's release, Congress enacted constraints that targeted Asian populations, including the Page Act of 1875, which controlled the admission of women, and the Chinese Exclusion Act of 1882, directed at laborers. Several years afterward, the informal Gentlemen's Agreement of 1907 limited Japanese entry into the nation. As Susan Koshy notes, U.S. laws that sought to contain relations between Asians and white Americans at the turn of the century disclosed fears of miscegenation within and outside the United States because the act threatened the authority associated with white supremacy. But, as she continues, sexual interactions that occurred overseas were implicitly condoned as part of American empire building, which extended the military and political privileges of white men. Exchanges happening within domestic borders, however, were forbidden, including Asian male–white female pairings, because they would disrupt the nation's established hierarchies. Where these relationships occurred, whether overseas or within the nation, had become as important as why they required controlling. The consequence of geography and the assertion of imperial authority, together with constructed notions of race and gender, thus determined American outlooks and actions on interracial intimacies.[37]

Not surprisingly, the image of Madame Butterfly resounded within American Cold War thinking, when the United States began reasserting its presence in East Asia after the power vacuum left by a conquered Japan and by weakened European allies that could no longer control colonial territories pushing for self-determination. But the ideals of freedom and democracy that informed U.S. participation in World War II and the Cold War altered how Americans understood their own race relations, pushing them to tolerate ethnic diversity as a way of differentiating themselves from fascists and communists. This sentiment, however, did not necessarily translate into equal treatment of nonwhite peoples. As Naoko Shibusawa, Traise Yamamoto, and others have contended, postwar Americans saw their hierarchical relationship with occupied Japan through the themes of race, gender, and maturity in order to accept an erstwhile enemy as a political ally. In this new framing, the Japanese, as a defeated, feminized, and childlike people, would loyally and lovingly serve the interests of the victorious, masculine, and benevolent United States. Interactions between American GIs and Japanese women most clearly personified this association.[38] Notably, more than a few of these war bride marriages occurred with African American or Nisei husbands. But white servicemen became the main face of such interracial unions, and thus of the nation's global relations, because of the power and privileges associated with their race and gender positioning at home and abroad.[39] As depicted in popular culture, the war brides, as embodiments of Japan, presented opportunities for domestic audiences to consider the new extended influence of the United States. Yet persistent anxieties about Japan coincided with concerns about integrating ethnic minority populations at home and anticommunist nations abroad. Japanese war brides offered reassurance that they would willingly adapt to the American mainstream, just as Japan and other countries would willingly join a U.S.-led global alliance against the "red menace."

Popular literature in the United States relied on the romance narrative as a way to comprehend the intricacies and intimacies of international affairs during the Cold War. Unlike prior storylines about a submissive Cho-Cho-San that charmed turn-of-the-century audiences, the idea of wooing postwar Japan came with a lurking suspicion, if not fear, that the Japanese would attract communist rivals. As no ordinary client state, Japan elicited such anxieties because American officials and cultural pundits believed that its strategic military value and its industrial output could tip the geopolitical scales any which way in the Pacific. Worries also arose that the United States, when bestowing democracy and its accompanying bounty to the world, might fail in its suitor role to win over hearts and minds.

Mainstream reporters were apprehensive about losing potential allies to communism, pointing to Japan as a potential victim and recalling their worries about China and its surrender to the Red Army in 1949. This earlier event stirred controversial perceptions of the State Department "allowing" the Chinese to turn in such an unwelcome direction. Now Japan's future was at stake. The prominent journalist Stewart Alsop noted in 1950 that the Soviets would "take advantage of our foolishness in Japan as they did of our foolishness in China." Sooner or later, he lamented, "we shall be asking 'Who Lost Japan?'" To Alsop, the United States remained as clueless as when dealing with China. Other writers agreed with this assessment. *Commonweal*'s 1951 editorial carried a suggestive title, "Second Chance in Asia," but grimly concluded: "We dare not fail in Japan as we have failed in China." *The Nation* magazine also warned in 1955, "If in the future the fearful cry goes up, 'Who lost Japan?' the American obscurantists [in Washington, D.C.] can look to themselves for the answer." These and other articles urged a strengthened American resolve to halt a potential collapse to communism in East Asia. Despite their certainty in U.S. power and superiority, a pervasive feeling among observers suggested that states vulnerable to communist influence might reject American practices and principles.[40]

That the United States viewed postwar Japan in racialized and gendered ways was no accident, considering the extended influence of *Madame Butterfly* and other popular narratives. But when displacing the metaphor of romance onto overseas affairs, U.S. observers revealed not only the gratitude they expected from their Cold War allies but also the concern that Japan might betray American trust and generosity. This positioning only intensified fears about "losing" Japan to communism, or even about Japanese indifference to U.S. aid and incentives. Visiting the country in 1952, the civil rights activists and U.S. diplomats Hugh and Mable Smythe warned in *Phylon*: "An observer in Japan rather suspects that this partner to the shotgun marriage of East and West secretly looks forward to a divorce, albeit an amicable one." "Like all nations," they continued, "Japan is opportunistic, following her self-interest wherever it leads." *The Nation* added in 1955: "Japan and the United States are sworn allies." This partnership, however, "was nevertheless not a union of true love, but rather a marriage of convenience." *Newsweek* also bemoaned Japan's waywardness in light of communism's attractions: "Its flirtations with Red China had sent Japanese-American relations into a tailspin." The editorialist suggested that Japan had wandering eyes for other likely allies and advised U.S. statesmen to be wary of potential unfaithfulness.[41]

Commentators also expressed through the rhetoric of romance their specific unease about Japan's desires to trade with China and the Soviet Union. *U.S. News and World Report*'s subtitle for a 1954 piece, "Communist Wooing Is Winning Friends in Japan," emphasized Japanese dissatisfaction with the amount of American economic aid received. A *Saturday Evening Post* editorial remarked as well: "Although Japanese public officials ordinarily express only the most cloying sentiments of affection for the United States, it is undeniable that important currents of opinion are running against us." Some reporters reproached the Soviets and the Chinese, as well as Japanese socialists and communists, for sowing displeasure with Americans. But others pointed to the United States as also blameworthy. Apprehension about keeping Japan under U.S. dominion revealed itself in a 1955 *Look* magazine piece entitled "Japan: Partner or Problem?" The author noted that Japan's continued economic growth was imperative to containing communism in the region. The situation, however, was becoming dire. Japan enjoyed a brief period of development when the United States spent over two billion dollars there to fight against North Korea and China. Afterward, Japan's economy began to decline, as it had done before the Korean War. The problem was that the Japanese could not achieve self-sufficiency since losing their colonial possessions, which had provided raw materials for their industries. In addition, hardly any country wanted to buy products that postwar Japan offered. As a result, it recorded large trade deficits with Australia, Canada, and the United States for cotton, wheat, rice, and other necessities. In these unstable conditions, the article warned, China would be more than willing to do business with Japan. In a *Saturday Evening Post* article from 1957, "Are We Driving Japan into Red China's Arms?" the writer observed that the United States itself shared responsibility for missteps in its dealings with Japan. Tariffs on Japanese goods, the magazine suggested, made Americans appear too controlling in the relations with their junior partner, obliging Japan to look elsewhere for commercial opportunities. The Nisei press likewise noticed the trade tensions that China introduced into the U.S.-Japan alliance, with the *Pacific Citizen* asking, "How long will the postwar honeymoon between the United States and Japan last?" That such frictions would "hasten the day of reckoning," the editorial surmised, meant that Japanese Americans had to stay informed of overseas events to better enact their roles as transpacific mediators to help ease misunderstandings between the two nations.[42]

Fretting over Japan's objectives in the Pacific extended to depictions of cultural exchanges too. *Newsweek* reported on a 1954 tour of Kabuki dancers and musicians in the United States. But the magazine jealously remarked that "the Communist world has begun to woo Japan" when Soviet dignitaries also requested that a Japanese troupe perform in Moscow. Meanwhile, "Communist China slipped in its blandishments" with its own invitation to engage in a "friendship pact" between Beijing and Tokyo. Other news reports on the difficult courtship of Japan faulted the Japanese themselves. Even if the populace displayed fondness for the United States, some thought this sentiment misplaced. Norman Cousins, the editor of the *Saturday Review of Literature,* opined in 1952 that Japanese affections arose from a foolish delight in American popular culture: "Gum, jive, jazz, tight sweaters, padded bras, yo-yoes [*sic*], comic books, neon lights, dance halls, and chromium trim." These pleasures, he quipped, distracted from the more important matters of developing political democracy in Japan. Cousins complained that the younger generations of Japanese especially "love us for the wrong reasons." A strained U.S.-Japan relationship, suggesting a marriage of convenience, flirtations with the communists, and apparent misunderstandings of U.S. ideals and intentions, disclosed pervasive qualms about not only Japan's loyalties but also American effectiveness in managing global events.[43]

In this light, media attention on Japanese war brides framed them as alleviating anxieties over international relations, emphasizing the wives' apparent love for, and loyalty to, American servicemen. Hollywood productions and popular press coverage on the women contributed to public debates about domestic and overseas affairs by portraying them as incarnations of both the model minority and the model ally.[44]

On the home front, the Japanese wives appeared to successfully adapt to life in the United States, similar to postwar Japanese Americans, whose apparent assimilation offered a forceful retort to reforming structural inequities that adversely affected other ethnic minorities. At first, popular periodicals expressed concerns about how the GI–war bride marriages would work, given the admitted discomfort that white Americans had with racial differences, let alone with mixed-race progeny arising from these relationships. Over time, however, the press scripted the Japanese wives as eager participants in the American way of life, as revealed through their embrace of mass consumerism, their acceptance of gender hierarchies, and their misgivings about communism.[45] In this way, these wives' support of American politics, culture, and consumer goods served to promote the ideological and material wonders that the United States offered to the rest of the world. Their heterosexual relationships with predominantly white men and their establishment of stable nuclear families also assuaged the American mainstream about the continuing power of the nation's Cold War aims. These included not only confronting the threat of communism but also ensuring domestic abundance and solidity by using the example of Japanese brides to prescribe subordinate roles for other minorities and women. This point became clear when commentators favored Japanese women's recognition of gender hierarchies over the behaviors of more "aggressive" or "liberated" white women in the United States. As depicted in various novels, films, and other popular forums, white American women threatened domestic stability because they sought employment outside of the household, were too emotionally unbalanced, or were too demanding of their husbands. Femme fatale characters in film noir and in pulp fiction, or even a meek housewife who accommodates darker personalities within, as seen in the Hollywood production *The Three Faces of Eve* (1957), suggest the range of hazards that white women presented in a postwar world. At the same time, a blockbuster picture like *Sayonara* (1957) displayed Japanese wives catering to their white GI husbands during the U.S. occupation—behavior that stood in distinct contrast to their restive American counterparts.[46]

Regarding international affairs, the Japanese war brides' apparent submissiveness to their spouses paralleled overseas subordination to American leadership, bolstering the idea that Japan would devote itself to the United

States when combating communism and extending global capitalism. The mainstream media in particular invested in the narrative of rescuing, enlightening, or assimilating female racial Others who represented subsidiary regions to demonstrate the benevolence of masculine occupying powers.[47] The idea that Americans were uplifting Japan from feudal ways and thinking, which had prevented the country from progressing to a modern liberal state, became understood through the language and imagery of race and gender relations. Influenced by their male occupiers' values and behaviors, Japanese women came to appreciate the open-minded attentiveness of American suitors. War brides themselves did make conscious decisions to marry GIs to escape from not only restrictive traditions but also the material deprivation and destruction in their homeland. As heads of struggling households when their fathers and brothers became casualties of war, many of the women felt freer to find work with the occupation forces, where they met their future husbands.[48] But even as Americans saw themselves as attempting to enlighten Japan, they also applauded the idea that Japanese women knew their place and the expectations of them. Two accounts from popular periodicals highlight the pervasiveness of these cultural attitudes toward the war brides and how such outlooks related to U.S. Cold War objectives.

One story in the *Los Angeles Times* in 1953 emphasized the steady and assuring presence of Kyoko Ariki, who had married a U.S. corporal while in Japan. The soldier, Claude Batchelor, then left with his unit to fight in Korea, where he became a prisoner of war. During the negotiations for peace, however, Batchelor decided to remain with his communist captors. This act played into American frustrations regarding POWs "turning communist," prompting larger worries about U.S. impotence, malaise, and weak-mindedness at home and abroad. Susceptibility to "brainwashing" was seen as a symptom of physical and mental softening stemming from too much consumerism and domestic affluence, or not enough religious faith and a lack of strong family ties. These issues, many Americans feared, would eventually lead to a break down in individual and national autonomy. Such concerns transferred to overseas conflicts, when communist forces held American soldiers captive in body, mind, and soul.[49] Yet, back in Tokyo, the Japanese war bride, as exemplified by Ariki, became the symbol of resilience in these difficult moments "because of her hatred of Communism" and her appreciation of an American lifestyle.[50] A large photograph of Ariki dressed in Western attire graces the article. In it, she faces the camera in a medium shot with an earnest expression, sitting with pen and paper, ready to encourage her husband to resist communist propaganda and to return to their marriage. No demure Cho-Cho-San, she instead presented a strong-willed persona, but that of a wife who would respect the gendered order of the household, once her husband realized his mistake and reintegrated into domestic stability. This image of the war bride's resolve was thus required for a subordinate partner to withstand a marriage under fire, a situation that paralleled international relations. In this light, even if American GIs in Korea became susceptible to enemy indoctrination, their Japanese wives not only stood firm in their love for their spouses but also represented a faithful, anticommunist Japan that would remain true to the United States in troubling times.

In 1955, *Reader's Digest* presented another war bride, Mieko Miyazaki, whose story embodied American Cold War dreams of an overseas model ally turned domestic model minority. When interviewed for the magazine, she described on the one hand white American women as too competitive when trying to lure potential husbands or when buying clothing. On the other hand, American men were better than their Japanese peers when it came to romance. During her first contacts with them in occupied Japan, U.S. soldiers struck her with their "human-ness, a conviction that human beings are important." As she continued, "It's the quality that makes Americans fight Communism." She also confessed that she experienced no racism when coming to the United States. Miyazaki admitted that she felt lucky when immigrating in 1948, as opposed to the 1920s, when racial prejudice was more extensive. She cited the example of her father, a Japanese diplomat; when he was visiting the United States, someone spat on him. By the postwar era, the nation presented to the war bride not only the apparent racial progress made but also the "beautiful homes, lovely cars and elegant clothes" to which all Americans could aspire. "America is a country where such dreams seem feasible," she remarked. In an interesting twist, *Reader's Digest* first presented Miyazaki as a liberated new woman in Japan when she wrote an article about birth control. The American military government, however, censored her work for unstated reasons. Incensed, she went to an occupation office to lodge her complaint. But she met a GI there, and they soon fell in love. Any reminder of her initial activism then disappeared from the narrative, presumably coopted by her marriage. Although Miyazaki desired to escape a "rigid, tradition-bound life in Japan," her views on reproductive rights became contained when love made her an accomplice to the power of a white American patriarchy.[51]

Yamaguchi Yoshiko negotiated her performances within and against these American understandings of Japanese women. When the actor traveled to the United States in 1950 to test her talents in Hollywood, she teased American reporters that she looked forward to learning how to kiss, a statement designed to attract headlines about the star. Much of her response targeted the Japanese film industry, where caressing was uncommon in movie scenes. Yamaguchi had already appeared in a few productions in Japan showing such acts. In 1948, she told the Japanese press that their country's performers were not skilled enough in on-screen kissing, but Americans certainly were. For their part, U.S. occupation authorities encouraged reforms in Japanese cinema by allowing actors to kiss, hoping to instill among audiences more frankness in public feelings. Much of this impetus came from the desire to spread American cultural values throughout Japan. But other motives were steeped in stereotypes about Asian inscrutability. Such secretiveness, as many Americans saw it, led to the attack on Pearl Harbor in the first place. Hence, U.S. officials wanted to promote openness among the Japanese through popular entertainment that introduced democratic beliefs and practices. Yamaguchi's postwar roles in Japanese movies belonged in part to this American project.[52]

The movie star's public statement about coming to the United States to learn the art of kissing also signified a shift from her previous wartime roles in the intimacies of empire; American men now sought to woo Japanese women. Yamaguchi's gesture implied her willingness not only to be courted and protected but also to be tutored in the affairs of love and sex by white men, thus ensuring their superiority over her. This stance, in turn, suggested the sexual immaturity of Japanese women as a whole, which reflected the political immaturity of Japan, positions that reenacted Lieutenant Pinkerton's dominance over Madame Butterfly. As an entertainer who had already spent years in the limelight, however, Yamaguchi was adept at telling correspondents what they wanted to hear. This skill at negotiating publicity recalls her apology to the Chinese press about her wartime role in *China Nights,* which helped her attract attention for the release of *Glory to Eternity.* In her cultural diplomacy with American reporters, she voiced her anticipated pleasure at embracing Western ideals and behaviors. By doing so, she also allayed U.S. anxieties about Japan, while expanding her professional opportunities to a nation that occupied her country.

Still, promotional material on, and reviews of, Yamaguchi's Hollywood films resorted to simplistic and common archetypes regarding Japanese womanhood and, consequently, postwar Japan in order to demonstrate American supremacy. Movie critics in the United States continually described the actor as "pretty and doll-like," an "exotic film favorite of Japan," or in similar phrases reminiscent of a foreign, submissive Madame Butterfly.[53] This outlook extended to political debates on the reconfigured postwar alliances in the Pacific. For *House of Bamboo,* Twentieth Century–Fox publicists either misunderstood or misrepresented Yamaguchi's life story after World War II, proclaiming that the actor left China to escape from communism rather than because of a postwar repatriation.[54] This storyline highlighted how a reformed Japan, under American tutelage, became an important refuge from the dangers presented by communist China. The strategy also served to diminish Japan's wartime occupation of China, as well as Yamaguchi's own role in that imperial project, within American public memory. Given such publicity, Yamaguchi had to keep silent about her love for, and guilt about, China as her "motherland," as her more complicated relations with that country dissipated in the Cold War spotlight. Meanwhile, postwar Japan, when imagined by the U.S. movie industry as a charming and innocent junior partner, became a safe haven for the actor and for the rest of Asia, a stance that reinforced American aspirations to contain communism in that region.

American uncertainties about Japan and the reassurance provided by war brides, as played by Yamaguchi, were apparent in cultural venues throughout the early Cold War. The actor was well aware of how her Hollywood productions coincided with the growing number of Japanese women marrying their American GI suitors, as briefly noted in her memoir (264). At the same time, she gave little credence to these films because they reached only a modicum of worldwide success. Important as well, her Hollywood pictures aroused tepid, if not angry, reactions in Japan because of their simplistic depictions of its culture. A related problem, as other Japanese complained, stemmed from American dominance of the film industry in their country. Yamaguchi herself noted how U.S. production crews were inattentive to her advice, particularly about portraying Japanese women. *Japanese War Bride* and *House of Bamboo,* however, offered opportunities for cultural commentary beyond the growing disharmony in U.S.-Japan relations. The films and Yamaguchi's presence in the United States also elicited varying Japanese American responses that highlighted this group's interests in domestic and transpacific affairs.

"American Japanese, Like Me"

In 1952, *Japanese War Bride* appeared in theaters across Japan and the United States just as major events symbolically converged with regard to the two nations' concerns. The year marked the official end of the U.S. occupation of Japan, raising questions among both Japanese and Americans about how the new allies would perform on the world stage. On the U.S. home front, Congress passed the McCarran-Walter Act, allowing the Issei and other foreign-born Asians to apply for American citizenship, while also permitting a small annual quota of Asian immigrants to enter the United States in addition to Japanese war brides. The film thus appeared amid debates over national and international belonging, in terms of assimilating racial Others as citizens and as representatives of allied states. The Hollywood production dramatized U.S. Cold War aims by fitting Japanese women and Japan itself within the process of "becoming American" to highlight the power of liberal democratic tenets. At the same time, the presence of Japanese American characters and the references to their wartime imprisonment in the film complicated how this unilateral endeavor would work. Creating their own sense of transpacific collaborations, the Issei and Nisei figures exchange onscreen moments of postwar healing, forgiveness, and self-protection with the Japanese war bride that occur beyond the sight, or the intervention, of white protagonists. These actions, in turn, offered possibilities for Japanese Americans to read the film in ways that differed from the views of mainstream critics.

Although underdeveloped in plot and characters, *Japanese War Bride* is still a rich cultural artifact that reveals the unresolved racial tensions of World War II.[55] As Caroline Chung Simpson suggests, the rising visibility of Japanese war brides in the postwar United States and these women's gradual acceptance by the white populace overshadowed the fact that other Japanese Americans still faced difficulties gaining recognition from mainstream society.[56] *Japanese War Bride,* however, brings these matters to a head. The film begins with an American soldier, Lieutenant Jim Sterling (Don Taylor), who gets wounded while fighting in Korea and recovers in occupied Japan. He falls in love with a Japanese Red Cross nurse, Tae Shimizu (Yamaguchi). After courting and marrying her, Lieutenant Sterling brings her to Salinas, California, to meet his family, whose members react in different ways toward the war bride. As their name suggests, the Sterlings represent the typical all-American, middle-class family that farms its own land and adheres to basic values of decency and hard work. But the sheen wears thin when Tae enters the picture, and some of the Sterlings greet her suspiciously, if not with outright hostility. Complicating these relations further are the neighboring Japanese Americans, the Hasagawas, who had been imprisoned during the war. Composed of an Issei father (William Yokota), his son, Shiro (Lane Nakano), and daughter, Emma (May Takasugi), the Hasagawas welcome Tae, yet still remain cautious when interacting with the Sterlings. Presenting an array of characters in their hurts, doubts, and grievances, *Japanese War Bride* offers a narrative in which neither the white mainstream's approval of Japan as a new ally, nor forgiveness on the part of Japanese Americans, is assured.

When arriving in Salinas, Tae's anticipation and enjoyment of becoming American earns her the glowing affection of her husband, Jim. Dressed in Western clothing, Tae appreciates the bounty of postwar consumerism by going shopping with some of the Sterling women, which serves to reassure audiences of their nation's abundance amid uncertain times. The United States, as Tae sees it, is also filled with the marvels of modern technology and industrial productivity in a pastoral setting. The Sterlings drive her past expansive fields dominated by harvesting machinery, as the camera pans across the scenery in a documentary-like manner. The Hasagawas then show her the vegetable packing plant in which they work, alongside white laborers. Thus the film reveals Japanese Americans as a part of this rural modernity in which U.S. industrialism and consumerism benefit everyone, regardless of race.

Yet Tae's presence in the Sterling household evokes past troubles associated with the Pacific War and with the Japanese American confinement. One of the Sterling's elder white neighbors, Mrs. Shafer, cannot hide her disgust at the mixed marriage. Mourning her son who fought and died at Bataan, Mrs. Shafer tells Jim's mother, "I hate them all!" Tae's racial presence and the war memories she conjures only add to Mrs. Shafer's grief. Occupying the opposite end of the grudge-carrying spectrum is the Issei Mr. Hasagawa, who, along with his children, was incarcerated in the wartime camps. Shiro and Emma have little problem putting the past behind them and visit the Sterlings, bringing a wedding present to Jim and Tae. One medium shot depicts both parties meeting over the white picket fence of the Sterling farm—an image that suggests overcoming barriers. Mr. Hasagawa, however, remains behind in the truck. Like Mrs. Shafer, Mr. Hasagawa cannot move beyond the pains and sorrows of the war. Yet the film minimizes Mr. Hasagawa's feelings when viewers hear a gong on the soundtrack during a close-up shot of his fixed expression. Jim's mother also compares him to a cigar-store Indian, sitting there in stony silence. Mrs. Sterling's comment reduces both Asians and Native Americans to stereotypes but also recalls the groups' shared history of repression and containment, when portions of Indian reservations served as "relocation camps," notably at Gila River and Poston, Arizona, during the war. In several other conversations, Tae asks her husband about the Hasagawas, wondering whether they are friends of the Sterlings. Jim mutters that they are simply neighbors. His uneasy response reveals that he knows about, and wishes to avoid, discussing the removal and confinement of Japanese Americans. Tae's presence and curiosity once more conjure a submerged memory dating back to the war, one that few desire to address, or even to redress. The topic of imprisoning Japanese Americans, however, becomes minimized since Shiro and Emma Hasagawa represent the younger generation that will set priorities for the future.

What proves most interesting about *Japanese War Bride* is the relationship between Tae and the Hasagawas, which dramatizes Tae's becoming American, a process aided by these Nisei neighbors. Once settled in Salinas, Tae looks to the Americanized Hasagawas, and not to the Sterling family, as her model of U.S. citizenship. At one point, Tae refers to the younger Hasagawas as "American Japanese, like me," when the Sterlings show her the fertile farmland that Japanese Americans reclaimed after the war. In another scene, Tae refers to Emma Hasagawa as "a real American, as I hope to be." In these cases, the Nisei Hasagawas provide Tae with a racialized template of how to be an "American." On the surface, the film celebrates a postwar image of American diversity and tolerance as part of the nation's strength, and the Nisei still display their faith in the American creed. As the film suggests, the younger Hasagawas, as paradigms of the model minority, are able to make a living within the white mainstream, despite their Japanese ancestry and the past discrimination against them. Likewise, Tae, as a model ally, will endure the distrust and hatred of some white Americans. But taking a lesson from the Hasagawas, she will surmount these obstacles as well. Thus the Nisei become exemplars of American pluralism, even as the film presents them as stereotyped characters who endure setbacks and forgive past wrongs against them. Yet, on another level, the idea that they will endure racism, despite their citizenship, still lingers. The younger Hasagawas are then the purveyors of democracy as well as the strategists on how to persist in spite of its systematic shortcomings.

One telling exchange about the wartime past occurs between Tae and Shiro, the Hasagawa son. The film gives voice to Japanese American anger when Shiro tells Tae about his family's incarceration during the war. But since Shiro's sister, Emma, had handled it well enough, the elder Mr. Hasagawa's bitterness appears more like an individual's failure to forgive than a nation's structural failure to protect its ethnic minorities. Caught in a different situation, Shiro had been in Japan looking for employment when the war erupted, and authorities there imprisoned him because of his loyalty to the United States. Shiro's enduring ire at Japan thus serves to offset his father's rage at being mistreated back home. In turn, Tae recounts her family's sadness at hearing about the Japanese attack on Pearl Harbor and how they did not support the militarists in Japan. This positioning presents Tae as an innocent bystander rather than a hated enemy. Tae's persona then reinforces how postwar Americans could view the Japanese as infantile and malleable when asserting U.S. authority during the occupation and downplaying their prior racial hostility toward a new Cold War ally. Tae fits the profile here, with her eagerness to please the Sterling family.[57]

Yet the war bride serves another purpose when interacting with the Japanese American characters. Tae and Shiro eventually agree that the old adage of "forgive and forget" is the best one to follow, allowing for the Cold War integration of both the Japanese and Japanese Americans into the nation's interests. The film aligns with other popular venues in presenting this message, as both groups express their desires for freedom, democracy, and material comforts. This scene, however, offers other interpretive possibilities. Tae and Shiro voice their idea of forgiving and forgetting to only each other and not to any white character overseeing their conversations. But they also support one another when acknowledging that this attitude toward the past will help them to survive in, and adapt to, a postwar nation and its expectations of racial minorities.

These insights were apparent to Nisei reviewers, Larry Tajiri the foremost among them. He commended the film in the *Pacific Citizen* for addressing the wartime confinement and for giving Japanese American actors this rare opportunity to appear in a Hollywood production. He also emphasized the importance of showing Japanese and Japanese Americans interacting with each other. In one of his several columns on *Japanese War Bride,* he observed, "It is from Shiro that Tae learns of the problems faced by the Nisei during the war, of the mass evacuation and the relocation camps and of the bitterness that is the residue of that wartime experience." But Tajiri avoided the "forgive and forget" message from the characters' dialogue. Instead, he noted the lingering "bitterness" created from the incarceration, a sentiment he thought would affect his Japanese American readers more forcefully than the film's depiction of model protagonists forgiving white society for its trespasses against them. In another column, Tajiri began not with the interracial romance depicted in the film but with the ongoing racial discrimination faced by Japanese Americans. "The subject of a California community's prejudice against persons of Japanese ancestry," he wrote, was a topic that was "once considered too hot for Hollywood to handle." Now, with the need to address Cold War civil rights, the memories of the wartime confinement still motivated his concerns. The film clarified the postwar condition of Japanese Americans, as depicted by the Hasagawas, who were "still fearful of prejudice and mindful of the . . . mass evacuation and mass detention" and were "living somewhat uneasily" once returned to Salinas. Despite these challenges, Tajiri observed that the Hasagawas were significant characters, "whose friendship helps Tae in her difficult months of adjustment in a strange land."[58]

In other instances, the Japanese American press highlighted the possibilities for cultural exchanges that allowed for postwar reconciliation between the United States and Japan through Yamaguchi's visit and onscreen appearances. Alongside one of Tajiri's reviews of *Japanese War Bride,* the *Pacific Citizen* included news about the impending peace treaty with Japan, proposing the Nisei as "the key link" for "mutual understanding" between the two nations. "Who is in a better position to carry between the two countries the most vigorous concepts of democracy?" the paper asked. The Chicago-based *Scene* magazine also broached this point in its 1950 interview with Yamaguchi. That she recognized the differences among the Nisei in Japan, in Hawai'i, and on the U.S. mainland was impressive enough. More important, though, was her desire to learn American values from them. "I would like to meet Niseis and talk to them, ask questions about democracy and so on," she noted. If Yamaguchi portrayed the process of "becoming American" with the help of the Nisei characters in *Japanese War Bride,* she anticipated this stance through her star image in publicity for the ethnic press. In this context, the

Nisei saw themselves as appropriate models of democracy to help reconstruct postwar Japan, displaying through their apparent recovery and successes the merits of an American lifestyle.[59]

Japanese Americans were likewise pleased by Yamaguchi's appearances and by her public recognition of them. This was particularly evident when Yamaguchi, before her work in Hollywood began, toured several cities in the United States for concerts that showcased her singing. Japanese American audiences from Honolulu to Los Angeles to Chicago appeared in great numbers to see and hear her. As Yamaguchi recollected about these experiences, "I sang with hope that I could offer consolation to the Japanese Americans, as I heard that they had gone through hardships during the war." As part of her playlist, she offered at the Hawai'i venue a hybrid version of Jack Pitman's popular tune "Beyond the Reef" (1948), singing the first stanzas in Japanese and the rest in English. By merging these cultural traits in her celebrity persona and performances, Yamaguchi extended to her listeners not only solace for their wartime sufferings but also a curative pleasure and value in reconnecting with their once disparaged Japanese ancestry.[60] The affective power of these interactions was therefore mutual. The Nisei educated Yamaguchi, and thus Japan, about democracy to help rebuild that nation as a viable ally, while she widened her transnational appeal to the United States and aided their postwar recuperation.

But these transpacific interactions also necessitated that Japanese Americans overlook portions of this intertwined past. When ethnic newspapers announced Yamaguchi's concert appearances, they reminded their readers about Ri Koran's fame and her prior films such as *China Nights*. Yet many avoided mentioning how this stage name and motion picture related to imperial Japan's occupation of China, a troubling point in her history of stardom. The *Nichi Bei Times* disclosed in 1950 that Yamaguchi got her start with the Man'ei film company, appearing in "romantic Japanese pictures," but went no further to explain their context or function. Implicitly critiquing Japan's empire building in his coverage of the movie star, Tajiri did remark in the *Pacific Citizen* that Japanese wartime censors eventually banned Yamaguchi's songs from *China Nights* because the officials were repulsed by the idea of intimacy between "foreigners" and Japanese.[61] Yamaguchi also raised this subject in her memoir. She added that, when she had visited Imperial Army troops at the front during the war, they still requested that she sing the forbidden tunes to help ease their hardships. This view suggested that she and the soldiers participated in creating other affective purposes from the songs, thus subverting the empire's bureaucratic rulings and intentions (104–106). But as Yamaguchi wrestled with her complicity in Japan's militarist endeavors, Japanese American papers mainly ignored this aspect of her career and its connotations of imperial dominance and destruction in Asia. Another reason to downplay these wartime associations may have been to prevent stirring prior suspicions about Issei and Nisei ties to Japan, which had been used to justify their mass confinement and other discriminatory actions against them. While these murkier histories might have linked the performer and her audience to feelings of guilt or shame derived from the Asia-Pacific War, Yamaguchi's appearances in postwar films and concerts in the United States settled the matter. Media coverage transformed them, respectively, into models of international alliance and of domestic citizenship.

In *Japanese War Bride,* however, wartime prejudices against Japan and Japanese Americans resurface when tensions erupt within the Sterling family over accepting Tae and the Hasagawa neighbors. When Tae becomes pregnant, the Sterlings fall for an anonymous "poison pen" letter (written by Jim's sister-in-law, Fran) accusing Tae of conceiving her child through an affair with Shiro Hasagawa. Although Jim believes his wife and not the rumor, the family pressure on Jim and Tae's marriage becomes too much to bear. Astonished at Tae's stoic countenance during this crisis, he shouts at her, in racially tinged frustration: "Don't you people ever cry?" Cruelly admonished, Tae does indeed break down and runs away with her child. Noticeably, she first turns to the Hasagawas and later to the Japanese American fishing community in Monterey for protection from the Sterlings' wrath and confusion. Part of becoming American for Tae is again enduring distrust and racism, which links her to the Japanese Americans who understand her position with the Sterlings and who thus provide her refuge.

As the film nears its conclusion, a restoration of race and gender hierarchies within the family and the neighborhood occurs when Fran's husband has enough of her bad behavior and slaps her to the ground. A liberal patriarchy, while hesitant throughout the story to establish its influence over recalcitrant white women, reasserts itself in this act of authoritative violence. The *Pacific Citizen* noted that this moment elicited cheers from the theater audience. Tajiri interpreted the crowd's reaction as a metaphorical strike against racism, particularly against the Japanese war bride and, more broadly, Japanese Americans. However, this brutality also reinstated men's power over headstrong women. Ironically, the scene recalls Tetsuo's slapping of the impetuous Keiran in *China Nights.* In each case, Keiran and Fran must acknowledge the limits of their own ignorance or prejudices as a result of this physical aggression. The violence instigates more enlightenment on Keiran's part or better conduct for Fran in their relations with supposedly benevolent men. This comparison applies as well, albeit in different contexts, to the dangers of impurity that both Yamaguchi and Maria Windsor, who played Fran, represented in their respective film careers. Windsor's notoriety stemmed from her femme fatale roles in crime dramas such as Richard Fleischer's *The Narrow Margin* (1952) and Stanley Kubrick's *The Killing* (1956). The character Fran in *Japanese War Bride* is a restless and conniving woman exposed to the corrupting taint of big city attractions, which acts as a foil to the Sterling family's simple rural life. Fran's debasing influence thus adds to her supposed need for rebuke to control the threat she represents.

In the end, Jim Sterling upbraids his family for its less-than-welcoming attitude toward his wife and sets out to find her. When he finds Tae (thanks to information from the Hasagawas), she is strolling along the rocky coastline in Monterey. Surprised and frightened, Tae runs away from him, contemplating suicide while looking at the watery depths below. But Jim catches up to her, and the couple embraces as the music swells and the end credits roll. What remains unclear about this finale is the reception that the lovers would receive upon returning to their home in Salinas. Would the Sterlings finally accept Tae into their lives, or would their still smoldering prejudices and resentments get the better of them? Meanwhile, after safeguarding Tae and her baby, the Hasagawas had only reluctantly given Jim the information about his wife's whereabouts, knowing full well that the Sterlings had mistreated her. The moment is full of uncertainty.

The contexts in which *Japanese War Bride* appeared explain some of this unresolved tension, since the outcome of the Korean War was still in doubt, and Americans were unsure about the loyalties of their new Japanese allies.[62] The film attempts to address this issue in its opening sequence. Viewers see a field at night, filled with dead American soldiers, and the word "Korea" emblazoned over the screen. A team of rescuers with flashlights searches for any wounded and come across Jim Sterling. The next sequence shows the lieutenant in a hospital bed in Japan with Tae tending to him. Jim tells Tae that he had been part of the occupation forces in Japan and had hated his experiences there, more because of his own loneliness than anything else. Then he went to Korea, and his appreciation for Japan blossomed. These sequences reveal the metaphorical ways in which a devoted and willing Japan would aid the United States in its fight against communism, regardless of American doubts and anxieties. Jim and Tae thus become the Adam and Eve of this new postwar world. Additionally, Shiro and Emma Hasagawa might reassure audiences that at least the Nisei would assimilate back into mainstream society, get past the hurts of their mass confinement, and forgive the Sterlings for their treatment of Tae.

Mainstream reviewers on both sides of the Pacific had varied reactions to *Japanese War Bride* that disclosed their broader take on U.S.-Japan relations. American and Japanese critics were pleased that the heroine did not die in the manner of Puccini's Madama Butterfly, a radical departure from U.S. films about Asians that appeared in the 1920s and 1930s.[63] But critics in the United States were lukewarm at best. Although many enjoyed Yamaguchi's performance, they found *Japanese War Bride* lacking in depth and complexity. The *New York Times* summed up what others saw: a film "without imagination despite [its] story that does make a perfectly valid plea for understanding."[64] Japanese columnists were also unimpressed with the production, remarking that it was made only to appease "Mr. and Mrs. America" in their simplistic views of the world. This assessment chided Americans' self-satisfaction and their desires for neat resolutions to racial problems. Other critics found the film clichéd and boring.[65] Yamaguchi herself remarked that reviewers in both nations took the film "to task for its inadequate portrayal of a Japanese woman married to an American" (281). Yet moviegoers in Japan and in the United States still appreciated Yamaguchi as a star performer. Japanese audiences saw the actor as an icon who sustained their national pride and evoked nostalgic visions of their past imperial glory, despite what they may have thought about the film itself. One writer even editorialized that Yamaguchi "occupied" the interests of Americans when in Hollywood, a play on words emphasizing her allure and influence on them while simultaneously poking fun at U.S. authority in Japan.[66]

The publicity about Yamaguchi's career shifted to a more personal level when she became acquainted with Isamu Noguchi, the Nisei sculptor and designer. Noguchi was the illegitimate son of the Japanese poet Yone Noguchi and the American writer and teacher Léonie Gilmour. Born in Los Angeles, Isamu came of age in Japan and then returned to the United States to finish his secondary education. But, as a mixed-race child, he had felt estranged from both nations because of his unusual background. By the 1930s, he had created a name for himself in New York City with his modern sculpture and his set designs for the dancer and choreographer Martha Graham. He never felt quite at home anywhere and sought exposure to different artistic styles when visiting Paris, Mexico City, Beijing, and Tokyo. Because he had lived in New York during the war, Noguchi was not considered part of the Japanese American population that required removal and confinement. He volunteered to go anyway, spending six months in the camp at Poston, Arizona, with the hopes of teaching art, creating a designed community, and sustaining democratic values among the imprisoned. After the war, Noguchi returned to Japan for a few years and met with young artists, whom he advised to fashion their own indigenous modern forms and styles, rather than mimicking Western ones. For him, the war's aftermath presented opportunities for new ways of seeing and producing art.[67]

The sculptor's romance with Yamaguchi came at a moment when each of them had developed a postwar fascination with the other's country and culture. They first met at a New York museum exhibit of kimonos in November 1950 and developed a relationship with the help of their mutual friends Ayako and Eitaro Ishigaki, the journalist and the painter, respectively.[68] What attracted Isamu and Yoshiko to each other were their cosmopolitan upbringings and sentiments. The two were, in Yamaguchi's words, "rootless souls" (267). Each understood the other's struggles fitting within and between different cultures and having their loyalties questioned because of their interstitial positions. As she noted, "In a spiritual sense, I was a mixed-race child between China and Japan, and he, in a literal sense, was a mixed-race child between Japan and the United States" (266). The Asia-Pacific War challenged their already fraught identities by alienating them from various populations and inspiring remorse about their homelands' treatment of other countries. Yamaguchi sympathized with China and what it suffered under occupation, even as she participated in Japanese propaganda about it. Noguchi became guilt-ridden when the B-29s dropped atomic bombs on Hiroshima and Nagasaki and wanted to contribute on some artistic level to reconcile with his father's land. But he still retained a complex relationship with Japan because of his mixed ancestry. In the United States, he sensed his estrangement from other Nisei upon entering the wartime camp at Poston. Noguchi was several years older than most of them, being closer in age to the Issei. As an accomplished and well-traveled artist, he did not share many of the Nisei's experiences or interests. His voluntary rather than compulsory confinement also made him suspect as a collaborator with the white camp administrators. The harsh Arizona climate and the lack of available art material added to his wish to leave early.[69] With such laden backgrounds, the movie star and the sculptor recognized their own worldliness and isolation in the other. During one of their first conversations, Yamaguchi was struck by Noguchi's empathy, when he observed that the war must have been difficult for her to endure, given her conflicted feelings for China and Japan. She realized that "he knew of what he spoke," with an attentiveness that eventually won her heart.[70]

In December 1951, the couple married in Japan. Their relationship attracted media attention, since both were celebrities. But to many observers, the romance between Noguchi and Yamaguchi also signified a broader postwar merging of Japanese and American interests.[71] That the two were transpacific bridge-builders came in literal and figurative forms. In June, while they were still dating, Noguchi visited Hiroshima, lured there "by a sense of guilt." As he further explained, "I wished somehow to add my own gesture of expiation" to the city's past and to its future well-being.[72] Because of Noguchi's notoriety, the renowned Japanese architect Tange Kenzo invited him to design the railings of two bridges (one symbolizing life, the other, death) that led into the proposed Hiroshima Peace Memorial Park.[73] In August, after touring the

Hiroshima site and meeting with Japanese officials and other architects, Noguchi flew to Los Angeles, where Yamaguchi was on a Hollywood set filming *Japanese War Bride.* Noguchi noted that he drew his initial bridge railing designs in her dressing room.[74] So while he was working on a project to help Japan memorialize its wartime destruction and postwar healing, Yamaguchi was performing the role of a war bride assimilating into American society and thus enacting a larger metaphor for a feminized, subordinate state to convince U.S. audiences that Japan was a dependable ally. In this emblematic moment, the couple came together to contribute to each nation's affective recovery from the Pacific War.

But even as the two figures came to epitomize a new partnership between their respective countries, strains emerged within this alliance from the ongoing American influence in Japan, from Japanese reactions to that presence, and from political developments in the United States. Problems related to these broader events lurked ahead for the celebrity pair. For Yamaguchi, the mixed responses in both nations to *Japanese War Bride* would continue with her second film, *House of Bamboo.* Also, amid the fervor of McCarthyism, she came under Federal Bureau of Investigation (FBI) suspicion as a communist sympathizer, just as her uncertain allegiances had attracted the notice of intelligence agencies during the war. Tensions with Noguchi arose as well, despite the couple's shared cosmopolitan sensibilities. Part of this friction came from growing anti-Americanism overseas, when some Japanese critics began tiring of Noguchi and his impact on their art scene. As the sculptor and the actor discovered, what they merged stylistically in their work did not come so easily in their marriage, or in their relations with each other's ancestral lands.

Trouble in Paradise

In her memoir, Yamaguchi noted with pride that she was the first Japanese performer working in postwar Hollywood (257). Stars from Japan, however, had pursued film careers in the United States beforehand. Sessue Hayakawa and his wife, Tsuru Aoki, appeared together in a series of silent films and founded their own movie production company in the early twentieth century.[75] Yet Yamaguchi's presence in Hollywood was still a major accomplishment, given how rare it was for Asian or Asian American actors to appear in U.S. films. When she first arrived in 1950, Yamaguchi was slated to appear in a Broadway musical, but the production never came to fruition. By then, she had taken the name "Shirley Yamaguchi." She later began socializing with such celebrities as Charlie Chaplin, Yul Brynner, and James Dean. She took acting lessons from Elia Kazan and met with Pearl S. Buck and Eleanor Roosevelt (263–265). But her success in the United States would be short lived. In 1955, the release of, and ensuing controversy over, *House of Bamboo* coincided with the end of her marriage to Isamu Noguchi.

House of Bamboo is Samuel Fuller's remake of another Twentieth Century–Fox motion picture, the film noir classic *The Street with No Name* (1948). Harry Kleiner served as the screenwriter for both films, which focus on an undercover agent who tries to infiltrate and destroy a criminal gang. *The Street with No Name* is the more conventional film noir production, with its black-and-white, tension-ridden scenes of a corrosive underworld lurking beneath the surface of postwar America. *House of Bamboo* is a hybrid, transitional work that combines elements of earlier film noir with those of later color-filled epics set in "exotic" lands. Shot in panoramic CinemaScope, *House of Bamboo* heralded the arrival of bright, lavish features set, and often filmed, in Asia, such as *The King and I* (1956), *The Teahouse of the August Moon* (1956), *Sayonara* (1957), and *South Pacific* (1958). *House of Bamboo* even helped to make *Sayonara* a reality, when Fuller gave Joshua Logan, the director for the latter production, his research on scouting locations in Japan as a professional courtesy.[76]

In *House of Bamboo,* Yamaguchi plays another war bride, Mariko Nagoya, who is secretly married to a U.S. Army veteran involved with a criminal organization composed of other former American occupation soldiers in Japan. Her war bride status is briefly noted when her GI husband, fatally wounded in a heist, is interrogated by investigators and reveals his unofficial marriage. He dies from his injuries, which include a bullet wound inflicted by his own gang, headed by the ruthless Sandy Dawson (Robert Ryan), meant to ensure silence about the group's activities. Mariko discovers her husband's life of crime only when the authorities contact her about his death. An Army investigator (Robert Stack) then appears, impersonating a hoodlum, Eddie Spanier, who wants to join Sandy's outfit. He tracks down Mariko and uses her as part of his cover to gain admittance to the group. Relations between Mariko and Eddie, initially tense and distrustful, evolve into a working partnership and eventually love, when she agrees to pose as his "kimono girl," the gang's jargon for female companions. Along the way, Mariko becomes alienated from the rest of Japanese society because of her association with Eddie. Thus, her assumed sexual and cultural "impurity" strengthens his trust in her, since she sacrifices her reputation for his goals. Eddie at this point reveals himself to Mariko as Sergeant Kenner and ultimately foils the crew of felons with the help of the American military and the Japanese police. As part of the grand finale, a dramatic shootout occurs on the roof of a Tokyo department store, complete with an amusement park, where the gang leader, Sandy, meets his end. The concluding long shots then show Kenner and Mariko walking in a city park on a sunlit day, intimating a longer romantic relationship to follow.

American critics admired the location shots of Japan and the Cinema-Scope color photography. Some reviewers noted that the film was part of a larger Hollywood strategy to incorporate exterior shots from the world over, including Europe and Hong Kong, that suggested American global predominance in cultural as well as in political developments. However, most reviewers, following the *Saturday Review,* called *House of Bamboo* a "routine cops-and-robbers story." One moviegoer was even troubled by the portrayal of criminal behavior, presuming that the United States would not want to export depictions of rogue Americans' antics to Japanese audiences.[77]

Overall, the film offered American movie patrons an opportunity to view Japan and its people through the imperial gaze of tourists who objectified and commodified what they saw.[78] This perspective coincided with travel writers' observations about postwar Japan. Lucy Herndon Crockett provided a tongue-in-cheek description of U.S. troops that revealed the masculine power Americans exerted on a feminized Japan and, in turn, Japan's transformative influence on those men. As she noted for *Travel* magazine in 1947: "So now a lumberman from Oregon, a cotton worker from a Louisiana shanty, a miner from Pennsylvania, all in khaki, can dine together to string music, are served by waitresses in colorful kimonos; they play at golf on the finest courses with Japanese girls to caddy for them, and lounge like Roman senators around marble hot sulphur [*sic*] pools."[79] In postwar Japan, soldiers from working-class backgrounds and from all parts of the country could convert themselves into something like imperial officials enjoying a luxurious life. Crockett also marks these levels of power and subservience through race and gender by emphasizing that the servants are all Japanese women, belittled here as "girls." Thus, instead of transforming imperial Japan into a postwar liberal state, democracy-loving Americans were changing into imperial occupiers—an idea that, on the surface, might generate anxiety about the U.S. overseas presence in the Pacific. But the breezy tone of the article assures readers that Japan is willing to serve and to follow Americans and their good intentions.

Miriam Troop also invested in orientalism as a tourist when reporting for *American Magazine* in 1955, the same year as *House of Bamboo*'s release. In her article's suggestive title, "I've Got a Yen for Japan," desire and spending power converge. In the essay itself, Troop remarked on "the crowds of doll-like, kimono-clad men and women," and on how Japanese shoppers on the Ginza "behaved . . . like the well-mannered chorus of a Gilbert and Sullivan operetta."[80] Describing Japan's men and women as diminutive and "kimono-clad" figures implies that both are nonthreatening and effeminate in the minds of Americans. Various observers from the United States packaged the Japanese in already familiar ways to consumers back home, who had acquired such constructed imagery from earlier Western productions about Asia. The author's reference to Gilbert and Sullivan, the late nineteenth-century English librettist and composer duo, and to their opera *The Mikado* (1885), recalls American tastes based on orientalist understandings developed from U.S. imperial involvements at the turn of the twentieth century.

House of Bamboo played into these touristic visions of Japan. Indeed, the amusement park scene at the film's conclusion serves as a broader metaphor for Japan as Hollywood's playground, which began with the occupation. Fuller prided himself on the location shots depicting the everyday populace in urban Japan. The film reveals multiple high-angle, "bird's-eye view" framings of the Tokyo streets taken from rooftops, with pedestrians negotiating the walkways, while traffic moves along the avenues. The cameras also capture the vibrant storefronts and colorful garb of passersby, adding to the "exotic" atmosphere. Other background shots include views of such tourist icons as Mount Fuji, the Great Buddha of Kamakura, and the exterior of the Imperial Hotel, designed by Frank Lloyd Wright. When Fuller reminisced about *House of Bamboo* in his autobiography, he resorted to the language of tourism when revealing sites for his production. "The light there is unique and wonderful," he remarked about Japan. "Colors come out looking postcard crisp."[81] In this sense, *House of Bamboo* itself was a series of postcards shown on film. But, as the *Saturday Review* noted, too much of the storyline can be "seen through only the camera's eye," when the film needed more character and narrative development.[82] Even so, most American critics were captivated by the Japanese scenery, which they associated with femininity. In *House of Bamboo,* according to *Newsweek,* "the shapes and colors of all the nonacting [*sic*] objects that fill the big screen . . . make a composition which has more than ordinary visual beauty." *Time* magazine's reviewer noted as well that the film was "enhanced by the petal-like beauty of the scenery." This description coincided with "Japan's picture-book beauty Shirley Yamaguchi . . . [who] has all the fluid rhythm of a ripple in a pond."[83] Here, "beauty" links the landscape and Yamaguchi's persona. Even though the film shows male Japanese detectives and police officers helping the American military capture the criminal gang, the character Mariko is the only developed representation of Japan, aside from the filmed scenery.

Fuller and the publicists at Twentieth Century–Fox were aware of the market potential of an interracial romance, emphasizing how *House of Bamboo* proceeded differently from conventional understandings of *Madame Butterfly* that presented a doomed relationship. Part of this focus arose from their realization of new Cold War alliances among former enemies and of the appearance of Japanese war brides in the United States. In the film's press book, the director observed: "In America, at least, people's thinking has been changed a great deal by the G.I. marriages to Japanese girls. Previously, we have been unable to go farther than 'Madame Butterfly,' in which lovers try but fail to clear the hurdle of tradition." That white men and Asian women could now bring their marriages to the United States, rather than simply keeping them abroad and away from a disapproving white mainstream, was for Fuller and others a significant advance in domestic race relations.[84]

Yet, even if interracial love endured in midcentury movies, variations of the Madame Butterfly image persisted in American expectations of Japanese women's subordination within a white patriarchy. Fuller later saw *House of Bamboo* less as a revision of *Madame Butterfly* than as a film noir story of betrayal. The key point for him is when Sandy and his second-in-command, Griff (Cameron Mitchell), develop a contentious relationship, when Eddie earns Sandy's trust at the expense of an increasingly jealous Griff. After an aborted heist, Sandy recognizes a police setup, and the criminals turn on one another over who is the betrayer among them. Sandy kills Griff under the mistaken assumption that Griff, rather than Eddie, was the informant who had alerted the authorities about the planned robbery. But Griff had been the loyal one all along.[85] Considering Mariko's sizeable screen presence in the storyline, loyalty, rather than betrayal, is the better premise by which to understand *House of Bamboo* because of her devotion to, and sacrifices for, Eddie. The Japanese war bride, who deceives the criminals through her role as a quick-thinking "kimono girl," becomes the heroine by overcoming her fears to help take down the outlaw gang. The *New York Times* caught the character of this dual narrative, describing the work as "a lean, hard-boiled, sharp detective thriller with just a light touch of 'Madame Butterfly.'"[86] As a Japanese woman and as a representative of Japan, Mariko is the perfect junior partner who, whatever her initial reservations, aids law-and-order-loving Americans in their quest to combat any subterfuge—an image that bolstered the idea of Japan evolving into a model ally.

Japanese critics, however, savaged *House of Bamboo,* disclosing the larger simmering tensions between the United States and Japan. Part of their outrage came when *The Blackboard Jungle* (1955), a movie about inner-city juvenile delinquency, upset Japanese parents with its overwrought violence. It also happened to appear in Japan in the same year as *House of Bamboo.* Concerns about the latter film centered on developments that occurred both on-screen and off. Reviewers noted that *House of Bamboo* shamelessly misrepresented aspects of Japanese culture. Although location shots of Tokyo street life were essential to the production, the interiors filmed in the United States looked too wide open, and thus fake, to audiences. Others complained about the errors in the traditional and modern costumes worn by the actors. A larger issue focused on movie distribution in Japan, where theater owners felt compelled by American studios to show disliked features. One of Japan's largest newspapers, *Asahi*

Shimbun, called the situation "a national disgrace" because of the U.S. film industry's power to determine what to offer Japanese theaters. This practice had started during the occupation, but remained in place afterward, bothering those who pressed for self-determination in cultural as well as political decisions. The president of a theater owners association suggested more collaboration with U.S. companies, noting that the group would otherwise "consider barring all American movies from movie houses and theaters" to protest their nation's lack of choice in selecting films to run. As the *Christian Science Monitor* summarized the prevailing mood in Japan for American readers, *House of Bamboo* had become the flashpoint for these overseas resentments and "has been scorned and attacked by all Japanese reviewers."[87]

Given this overseas turmoil, Japanese American reviewers were divided about the film's importance regarding domestic race relations and their roles as transpacific brokers. Some Nisei critics were quick to praise Yamaguchi's presence and performance in the film. Tajiri noted in the *Pacific Citizen* how, similar to *Japanese War Bride, House of Bamboo* portrayed an interracial relationship in a better light than previous works that followed the Madame Butterfly narrative, in which the Asian woman must sacrifice her life as the only alternative to her lover's rejection. Tajiri also praised Fuller for tackling the issue of racial prejudice, as seen in his earlier work, *The Steel Helmet* (1951), showing Nisei and African American soldiers fighting alongside their white counterparts in Korea. Significant also for Tajiri, *The Steel Helmet* and *House of Bamboo* employed minority actors of Asian ancestry, giving them a rare opportunity to work in Hollywood. Fuller would later do so again for *The Crimson Kimono* (1959), a crime story set in Los Angeles, in which a Nisei detective romances a white woman.[88]

Yet the *Pacific Citizen*'s Tokyo correspondent, Tamotsu Murayama, warned of Hollywood's impact on Japanese audiences, which might also adversely affect the Nisei living in Japan. He reported that Japanese reviewers dismissed *Blackboard Jungle* especially because it showcased a Nisei character as one of the juvenile delinquents, which the reviewer feared would undermine the model status of Japanese Americans. Another article in the *Pacific Citizen* noted that Japanese audiences "jeered" at the cultural inaccuracies in *House of Bamboo,* while also reporting how one newspaper in Japan "urged Japanese not to cooperate in making . . . such pictures." Most critical to Murayama, the tensions derived from such troubling Hollywood productions made the Nisei's job at building better relations between the United States and Japan more difficult, since they would be caught up in the anti-American sentiments brewing abroad. Despite their shared ancestry with those in Japan, Murayama intimated, their U.S. citizenship would associate them with the power of the occupation and with whatever Hollywood invented about Japan.[89]

Yamaguchi offered her own insights about appearing in American films to Japanese readers—a strategy likely intended to deflect criticism of her involvement in making them. The actor noted in the *Japan Times* that once she signed a contract, she could not change anything in her role, "no matter how awkward it appeared" to her. She knew how wrong the impression of Japanese culture *House of Bamboo* gave, also realizing that the film catered to American expectations. Although she did not mention Samuel Fuller by name, Yamaguchi complained that U.S. directors desired that she play only "the part of a Japanese girl that the American movie goers like to see on the screen."[90] It was thus another aspect of her "becoming Japanese," but from a Hollywood perspective. Twentieth Century–Fox's promotional material for *House of Bamboo* revealed as much in a movie ad tagline: "In Japan, a woman is taught from childhood to please a man!"[91] Mariko recites this statement to Eddie to explain why she treats him so well, as she draws his bath, cooks his breakfast, and massages his back. These behaviors became part of the Hollywood rendition of what American audiences expected from Japanese women, that they cater to male needs and desires. That Japan was the land of submissive Madame Butterflies coming to sexual maturity solely for white men's pleasure also played into broader perceptions of a U.S. empire that allowed for overseas miscegenation as a part of that imperial project. As *House of Bamboo* ends, we see Sergeant Kenner, as a representative of that American martial presence abroad, now dressed in his military uniform, walking with the kimono-clad Mariko as the epitome of a successfully wooed Japan.

Such was not the case when Yamaguchi's marriage to Noguchi began unraveling. The couple's global travels and separate work schedules meant that out of their four years of marriage, they were together for about half that time. When he was scouting a project in Europe, she was working on a film in Japan. When he conferred with artists in Japan, she performed in concerts in the United States. Seen as a hopeful melding of two cultures, these prominent figures also personified the unresolved frictions emerging between their respective countries.

Trouble for Noguchi began when he was designing his bridge railings for the Hiroshima Memorial Peace Park. Tange asked him to also create a model for the cenotaph that would memorialize the atomic bomb deaths in the city. Noguchi's remarkable and haunting design consisted of a large, thick, black arch, with its legs rooted deep underground, visible in a subterranean room containing the names of the dead. The city's planning committee, however, rejected Noguchi's model. The decision was based not so much on the abstract design itself. Instead, the issue concerned Noguchi's being an American (and, more particularly, a Nisei of mixed ancestry) involved with building a monument about Japanese identity and suffering. One critic made the point clear: "In Isamu Noguchi's blood there is [a] mixed half which is from overseas." "Coming to occupied Japan where *Nisei* have clout," the writer continued, Noguchi "spread the idea . . . that he, of all people, was the most suitable person to make the monument."[92] The Japanese detractor critiqued not only Noguchi's foreignness and inferior racial status but also his apparent feelings of superiority over the Japanese because of his U.S. citizenship. Noguchi appeared as a Nisei getting his way in Japan because of the American half of his ancestry, one associated with the power of the U.S. occupation. The point recalls worries Murayama expressed in the *Pacific Citizen* about the impact of disparaged Hollywood films on the Nisei working in Japan. Although Noguchi himself had felt distant from the Nisei in the United States, the logic coming from his Japanese critics was that even if the artist was not quite American, he was also not quite Japanese.[93]

The reaction against Noguchi coincided with feelings of anti-Americanism in Japan that arose from the peace treaty ending its postwar occupation. Many voiced discontent long afterward with the ongoing U.S. military presence in their country that the treaty ensured.[94] These larger events affected how the Japanese saw Noguchi as an American interloper in their arts scene. Noguchi became angry and frustrated when learning of his rejected work and responded the only way he could, as a cosmopolitan. "I was opposed by the people of Hiroshima because I am an American," he explained. "Certainly, I am an American, but my heart is that of a Japanese."[95] The project was not just a matter of ancestry for him. Noguchi saw himself as a by-product of two cultures that wished to offer recompense for a human tragedy. What the nuclear destruction of Hiroshima and his cenotaph design represented, he argued, was meant not just for Japan, but also for the world at large. A few Japanese writers concurred with Noguchi on this issue, suggesting that his art transcended boundaries and that his participation conferred international significance on Hiroshima. These more expansive beliefs, however, fractured against the planning committee's views of Japanese nationalism and victimhood that developed after the war. As a result, Noguchi's memorial cenotaph was never built.[96]

Meanwhile, Yamaguchi had her own problems with American authorities, developments that became layered with irony. After her work in *Japanese War Bride,* she returned to Japan in 1953 to work on several film projects there. But later, when she tried to reenter the United States to rejoin her husband in New York, the State Department denied her a visa because officials considered her a security risk. Earlier, the FBI placed the actor under surveillance while she was filming *Japanese War Bride.* The agency thought that she might have been a spy working for various factions, including the communists, in Manchuria during the war. Alongside this presumed past, her different stage names and multilingual skills only added to these distrustful inclinations. The FBI also targeted Yamaguchi because agents suspected that she was a "fellow traveler" when socializing with the Ishigakis, the couple that introduced her to Noguchi. Eitaro Ishigaki's leftist leanings in particular resulted in government threats to deport him as a subversive, but he left for Japan in 1951 (joined voluntarily by his wife Ayako), before legal proceedings could begin. Noguchi, frantic because of these developments, used his political contacts in Washington, D.C., to seek information about why his wife could not enter the United States. But neither he nor Yamaguchi ever learned the reason for her denial of entry, although they assumed correctly that the issue revolved around charges of communist affiliations. In 1954, after a year of trying, Yamaguchi obtained a visa after Noguchi's persistent calls to U.S. congressmen and other highly placed officials (273–277).[97] By this time, McCarthyism's hold on the nation was weakening, as the junior senator from Wisconsin began accusing the U.S. Army of harboring communists, an overreach that would spell his political demise. Studio publicists for the upcoming *House of Bamboo* could then depict its star as a refugee from communism, while the film itself presented Yamaguchi as a Japanese war bride and a model ally conforming to U.S. Cold War aims.

The messy mix of art and politics was not the only obstacle in front of Noguchi and Yamaguchi. Noguchi proved demanding of himself as an artist, but he also made life difficult for those around him. He appeared controlling to Yamaguchi, offering takes on her appearance and clothing that recall Lieutenant Pinkerton's dictates to Cho-Cho-San. Noguchi forbade his wife from cutting her hair. He wanted both of them to wear kimonos of his design and straw slippers that hurt her feet. On another front, Noguchi was unwilling to entertain her friends and guests, appearing bored and detached from them, even though she accommodated his acquaintances. In the end, as their separate work schedules and personal disagreements created spatial and emotional distance between them, Yamaguchi realized how "Japanese" she was and how "American" Noguchi was, despite their cosmopolitan ways (280–281).[98] Signs of trouble rooted in their national identities appeared from the start. When registering the couple's marriage in Japan, a U.S. official asked Yamaguchi if she wanted to pledge her allegiance to the United States. She answered in the negative: "Even though I married an American, I had no wish to become an American myself." For her, "becoming American" was reserved for her on-screen roles. As she elaborated, memories of the Asia-Pacific War made her resist the idea of having dual citizenship (274). Posing as a Chinese national with divided loyalties during the war had resulted in traumas and hardships, including the threat of execution for treason. Yamaguchi knew firsthand the dangers associated with merging national loyalties, and she did not want to imperil herself again by identifying with another occupying power. By the mid-1950s, with the divorce from Noguchi, living as a rootless, worldly celebrity seemed no longer possible for her.

Postscript

In 1958, Yamaguchi retired from the movie business. She appeared in a few Japanese productions and in a brief nonstarring role in one last American film, the small-scale comedy *Navy Wife* (1956), before resuming her life in Japan. She also gained passing notice when Hollywood studios began filming *Sayonara* (1957), an eventual blockbuster about a white American officer wooing a Japanese woman during the Korean War. The narrative displayed all the trappings of a postwar Madame Butterfly melodrama, with its romantic tensions set amid color-filled settings in Japan and a happy ending that called for racial tolerance. The story was based on James A. Michener's bestselling novel of the same title, which appeared in 1954. The *Los Angeles Times* reported that "the noted Japanese actress" Shirley Yamaguchi "was practically signed" to play Hana-ogi, the Japanese dancer courted by Major Lloyd Gruver (Marlon Brando). Industry executives, however, decided instead to give the Hana-ogi role to Miiko Taka, a young Nisei woman whom a talent agent had spotted in a parade celebrating Nisei Week in Los Angeles.[99]

Yet, even as Yamaguchi's postwar film career came to a close, she managed to create new public identities. In the year that she retired from movie making, Yamaguchi married the Japanese diplomat Otaka Hiroshi. She hosted a television show throughout the 1960s and 1970s, reporting from such political hot spots as Vietnam and the Middle East. What attracted her to these locales, and particularly to sympathizing with the Palestinian cause, were her own memories of growing up in occupied China and the brutalities enacted by the Japanese. She then translated these journalistic interests into more formal political engagements. In 1974, Yamaguchi won a seat in the Japanese Diet as a member of the ruling Liberal Democratic Party, serving for eighteen years. Her public expressions of remorse for her complicity in Japanese imperialism during the 1930s and 1940s reemerged during this time, when the former "traitor" to China became a cultural diplomat amid Japan and China's efforts at reconciliation. She attended several delegations on goodwill visits to China and later served as the vice president of the Asian Women's Fund, an organization that sought acknowledgment of, and compensation for, the "comfort women" exploited by the Japanese military. During the 1980s and 1990s, Yamaguchi's love songs recorded during the war gained new listeners when re-releases appeared on the Chinese and Hong Kong markets. Her contributions to aiding peaceful exchanges between the two nations also stirred interest in dramatizing her life story. A Japanese musical, *Li Xianglan* (1991), and a four-part television show, *Sayonara Ri Koran* (1989), played to audiences throughout East Asia. In this manner, Yamaguchi's involvement in these later Sino-Japanese relations called for selectively forgetting and redefining her prior entertainment-as-propaganda ventures—moves that helped renew her star appeal.[100]

The interlude of the early Cold War years also revealed Yamaguchi in stages of celebrity transformation—from a Chinese/Japanese to a Japanese/American to a Japanese entertainer—designed to surmount national borders and expectations. Indeed, her performances indicated a series of interactions with Americans that differed from, and overlapped with, her associations with China and Japan. Despite the advent of her postwar "Japanese" persona, she played along the solidus of a Japanese/American identity for her publicity in Hollywood productions. "Becoming Japanese" as Yamaguchi Yoshiko in her public and private lives took precedence in these years. But on the screen and in the press, she participated in broader transpacific exchanges that embodied both the achievements and the frictions within U.S.-Japan relations. These moves highlighted her Japanese/American marriage to Isamu Noguchi, how Japanese audiences resisted American influence in their nation, and her film star image that attracted Issei and Nisei audiences. Her war bride roles and other appearances, however momentary or problematic, served to incorporate Japanese Americans in a process of postwar healing and public recognition. In this sense, Yamaguchi's visit to the United States played a brief but important role in her far-ranging journeys in the arts and politics of the postwar era and beyond.

3

Beyond Confinement

The Racialized Cosmopolitan Style of Henry Sugimoto

IN 1981, the Issei artist Henry Sugimoto appeared before the Commission on Wartime Relocation and Internment of Civilians, a federal entity designed to assess the effects of the mass confinement on Japanese Americans. Sugimoto and his family were incarcerated at the Fresno Assembly Center in California in May 1942, and then several months later at the Jerome and Rohwer camps in Arkansas, where they remained until the war's end in August 1945. During this time, he and other artists rendered scenes of their trying circumstances, from the harsh and distant landscapes to everyday life within the barracks and barbed wire. Now, decades later, Sugimoto bore witness to this injustice as part of the larger efforts to attain redress. He even brought some of his paintings to his testimony, hoping to accentuate for the committee the distressing impact of the wartime imprisonment. "Forgive me if I should at times sound emotional," he began. "On this occasion I am recalling the bitter experiences of all the 110,000 Japanese in this country who suffered at the outbreak of . . . World War II." The commission's findings from such evidence eventually led to the Civil Liberties Act of 1988, which offered reparations of $20,000 to each living survivor. It also included apologies from federal officials, with a formal statement from President George H. W. Bush when the first redress checks were allocated in 1990 (the year of Sugimoto's death). These events sharpened public awareness about not only the ordeal of confinement but also Sugimoto and his paintings. In 1987, a sampling of his work appeared in the Smithsonian Institution's National Museum of American History exhibit *A More Perfect Union: Japanese Americans and the U.S.*

Constitution. In 2001, the Japanese American National Museum (JANM) in Los Angeles assembled the largest retrospective showing of Sugimoto's art, gaining him further nationwide attention.[1]

This commemorative endpoint arose from a long and uneven career spanning prewar renown to postwar disregard to renewed appreciation. In the 1930s, Sugimoto was a promising, internationally recognized artist, with exhibitions of his impressionist-inspired landscapes and still lifes occurring in the United States and abroad. But the war disrupted his further development as a professional painter, and he struggled to regain his reputation afterward, having been almost forgotten. Once released from the camps, Sugimoto and his family relocated to New York City, where he worked for textile design companies, among other jobs, to make ends meet. He also began revising his realist versions of camp life throughout the 1950s to the 1970s, often resorting to bigger canvases and brighter color schemes. Important as well, the artist broadened his range of interests by exploring the pre- and postwar presence of Japanese Americans in the United States. Despite his near obscurity in these later decades, Sugimoto managed to show several pieces in small exhibits. Few galleries, however, wanted to display his paintings on the mass imprisonment, selecting instead his scenes of the French countryside or of New York City street life.[2] But a shift in sentiment was underway. The late 1960s and early 1970s saw the rising interest in Asian American studies amid ongoing civil rights activism and new ethnic minority-centered programs in colleges and universities. In 1972, the California Historical Society sponsored an exhibit, *Months of Waiting, 1942–1945,* which featured the wartime works of six Japanese American artists, Sugimoto's among them. Community advocates such as the Japanese American Citizens League, U.S. congressmen of Japanese ancestry, as well as other groups, individuals, and institutions, also began pushing for further recognition of, and recompense for, the wartime incarceration. This drive to confront the legacies of confinement led to the establishment of the federal commission before which Sugimoto appeared, placing him and other Japanese Americans back in the public spotlight.[3]

This chapter examines the war years to the mid-1960s as a noteworthy period in the development of Sugimoto's work on the mass imprisonment and on related Japanese American topics. Similar to other artists confined in the camps, such as Miné Okubo, Chiura Obata, Hisako Hibi, Tokio Ueyama, Gene Sogioka, and many more, he left an important visual record of the incarceration and an account of his alienation, adaptation, resistance, and survival. Yet no other painter of Japanese ancestry matched Sugimoto's sizeable body of work (with more than one hundred extant pieces) or the decades-long time span in which he continued to depict these themes.[4] Most Japanese American artists either stopped painting after the war, or they moved into abstract art when it became the predominant style of the 1950s cultural scene in New York. Sugimoto, however, kept refining his realist images of the mass detention over the ensuing decades. Thus, despite national and communal efforts to forget a wartime past in which Japanese Americans endured imprisonment without just cause, he persisted in resuscitating it with renewed vigor and imagination. The postwar era reveals as well the evolving breadth of his creativity, from which he produced an epic vision of Japanese American life throughout the twentieth century. As Sugimoto grappled with the tormenting aftereffects of his own incarceration, he also gazed beyond national borders to consider the histories of Japanese emigration to the United States, the Pacific War, and the mass confinement as intertwined events. By the mid-1960s, for example, the artist implicitly linked immigration and incarceration in a series of large-scale works, in which human figures not only traversed the Pacific but also were blocked from entering the United States, or were contained within the country by mass confinement and other acts of racial prejudice. His three-year imprisonment in the camps consequently stirred a more expansive imagining of the spatial and temporal experiences of Japanese Americans, ones shaped by the racial tensions within the United States and in U.S.-Japan relations.

Sugimoto interpreted this Japanese American history through a cosmopolitan aesthetic that relied on French Postimpressionist and Mexican muralist influences, along with social realist and folk art elements. Attracted to Western styles since his student days in the late 1920s, he adapted these approaches to create a new wartime and postwar sensibility in his paintings. Although he conveyed little prewar interest in Japanese American subjects (aside from occasional portraits of family members), the camp populace and the surrounding landscapes dominated his work throughout his incarceration. After the war, his desire to connect the historical developments of the Japanese presence in the United States to a transpacific point of view took strong hold in his work, in which muralist forms and methods are readily apparent. What fascinated him was how the Mexican muralists emphasized human figures on a monumental scale with flattened perspectives to present larger, multipart narratives. His coopting of modern European and Mexican styles when rendering accounts of Japanese American life lent a distinct visual quality to his work that transformed over time. Yet the art still revealed a consistent urgency to illuminate sweeping events and their impact on an ethnic community.

I consider Sugimoto's achievements and circumstances within the broader outline of a "Japanese/American" formation, which changed in meaning and intent from the time of his early career to the period of the war and its aftermath. This framing helps to mark the transitions in his sentiments and identity as an artist, in his portrayals of Japanese American history, and in the public reception of his work. Here, the relationships between "Japanese" and "American" indicate three different processes that expose the fluctuating interactions between the signifiers: his prewar reliance on Japanese and Japanese American support for his art, a wartime separation and confinement of people enacted by a state suspicious of anything Japanese, and, finally, a resuturing and a redefining of relations between "Japanese" and "American" in his postwar identity, when a comprehensive shift occurred in U.S.-Japan affairs that enlarged his artistic views.

In the 1930s, Sugimoto was a Japanese national who literally pictured himself as a cosmopolitan artist in the western European mode, as seen in his self-portraits and photographs. We see in these works the ideal of a well-traveled citizen of the world who exuded curiosity about other cultures and places without being wholly defined by them.[5] Sugimoto, a Japanese national living in the United States and studying in France and Mexico, fit this mold, and as such he hoped to transcend political ideologies, racial barriers, and state boundaries. But, in doing so, he submerged himself specifically in western European notions of art, fashion, enlightenment, and worldliness. Still, he relied on the Japanese American community in California and on Japanese expatriate contacts in France and Mexico in order to create, exhibit, and sell his art. His embodying of cosmopolitan ideals and the worldwide attention he received for his work was thus made possible by the financial and structural support from these two groups, even though the still lifes and landscapes he sketched and painted at this time had little to do with Japanese or Japanese American subjects. Sugimoto's embrace of a Eurocentric version of cosmopolitanism to frame his identity and his art, however, was challenged during his wartime confinement, when Japanese Americans became his central thematic focus.

During the war, Sugimoto became in the eyes of the United States an "enemy alien" whose sympathies were assumed to align with imperial Japan. Regardless of their nationality or their feelings of loyalty to the United States, the Issei and Nisei were considered "Japanese, not American." The federal government placed those on the West Coast into prison camps as an apparent military exigency, a condition arising from a distrust of their loyalties and from longstanding white racial prejudice. Nevertheless, the artist contested these sentiments, composing scenes of incarcerated families and communities who asserted their own ideas about being or becoming Americans. In this light, we can regard him as a "racialized cosmopolitan" once the Pacific War erupted and derailed his plans to become a full-time professional artist.[6] Retaining the ideal of cosmopolitanism, Sugimoto aspired to create forms of modern representational art that defied rootedness in particular approaches or places, a longing that remained with him throughout his life. He did so by positioning himself above any partisan fray, when chronicling his subjects' emotive responses to the mass confinement as an aesthetic choice. But this stance emerged from, and was shaped by, the realities of the wartime incarceration that defined him as an enemy alien through a constructed racial Otherness. Concerning his style then, the phrase "racialized cosmopolitan" also captures the tensions between the artistic possibilities he sought and the structural pressures he negotiated in his work. In response to such demanding circumstances, the artist began with a much-traveled outsider's perspective looking in, painting scenes of the camp terrain and a displaced people's imprint on it. He portrayed this Japanese American presence through a transnational aesthetic crafted from Postimpressionist and muralist modes of painting to record, as well as to confront, the injustice of confinement. Seeing Sugimoto as a cosmopolitan in this way highlights how he not only created a new style while in the camps and afterward but also countered his own racialization by the state, even as he navigated around it in order to produce and gain notice for his paintings. He was able to secure white liberal patronage, for instance, to exhibit some works at Hendrix College in Conway, Arkansas, and elsewhere while he was still imprisoned in the camps, small recompense for a career that he feared had ended.

After the war, Sugimoto moved with his family to New York City, which had become the modern art capital of the postwar world. He also became a U.S. citizen as a result of the McCarran-Walter Act of 1952, which allowed foreign-born Asians to apply for naturalization. This period reveals his interest in depicting the transpacific movements of Japanese coming to the United States and in connecting these migrations through a succession of works about the discrimination and legal restrictions encountered, which eventually led to mass incarceration in World War II. But these pieces, together with his wartime art depicting the camps, never attracted much public attention until the 1970s and 1980s, when mounting institutional recognition of the Issei and Nisei's prior sufferings began in earnest.

Assessing Sugimoto's works portraying prewar immigration and wartime confinement from a postwar perspective reveals that he was not simply rendering "American" experiences of loyalty or citizenship. Several observers have claimed that Sugimoto's travails in the camps made him more appreciative of his civil rights and of the cherished principles of freedom and democracy that contributed to his developing an American mind-set.[7] Indeed, many of his portrayals of camp life disclose the patriotism and patience of Japanese Americans that suggest them as unjustly maligned model minorities. He often played on this status not only to combat their dehumanization by the state but also to garner white support for his art. Sugimoto's desires for being known as a cosmopolitan artist, however, coexisted in tension with these notions of national belonging. Although Sugimoto became a U.S. citizen in 1953, he attained a sense of artistic renewal when he returned to Japan in 1964 and during further trips there in the years to come. The initial visit made him realize how American he was by then, noting the tremendous changes to his birthplace since he had left more than four decades before.[8] But the recurring journeys across the ocean also helped foster his epic vision of Japanese Americans in a transpacific context. Given these events, his was not quite a unilateral "immigrant to American" success story of overcoming obstacles, achieving recognition, and becoming assimilated. It was instead something more intricate and developed that arose in part from reconnecting with his ancestral land. Sugimoto's artistic sensibilities altered to the extent that his worldliness became informed by a growing awareness of the larger structural workings of white racism and the history of Japanese movements across the Pacific. For him, then, becoming an American—as a citizen and as a painter—also meant revisiting and embracing his Japanese past.[9]

Sugimoto's efforts were validated throughout the 1970s and 1980s in interviews and other news coverage that reconsidered his body of work, during which he expressed hope in his publicity notes that his art "would be able to contribute to both Jap[anese] & Ame[rican] culture."[10] This sentiment emerged from the renewed attention he received in not only the United States but Japan as well. The city hall in Wakayama, Sugimoto's hometown, wanted to acknowledge his artistic feats by commissioning a mural from him, which he completed in 1978. Measuring almost thirty feet in length and seven feet in height, the work displayed part of the New York City skyline that focused on Washington Heights, featuring the Cloisters and the George Washington Bridge. Sugimoto's choice of subject was telling, in that he claimed himself as "a native son" of Wakayama and as an adopted New Yorker, using the visual prominence of the bridge as a metaphor for his life and for his relations to both cities.[11] Other opportunities in Japan soon followed. In 1980, the newspaper *Yomiuri Shimbun* sponsored an overview exhibit of his work since the 1930s. Sugimoto also self-published a collection of his art for Japanese audiences, *Hokubei Nihonjin no shuyojo: kiroku kaiga* (1981), from which he produced an English version, *North American Japanese People in Relocation Camps* (1983). In the book's introduction, the art critic and educator Kubo Sadajiro observed: "I surely believe that Henry Sugimoto will leave his name . . . on Japanese art history as [a] camp scene artist. On these works were carved into history . . . the sufferings of the Japanese people." Kubo regarded Sugimoto as part of a larger diaspora of Japanese artists, including Kitakawa Tamiji, Eitaro Ishigaki, and Yasuo Kuniyoshi, who were linked by their transpacific migrations and by the sorrowful memories and reverberations of World War II. For each of these figures, art as a cosmopolitan practice and as a human endeavor transcended national loyalties and boundaries, as seen through their merging of genres and other cultural components in their work.[12]

But even as Sugimoto took heart in the changing relations between his ancestral and adopted homelands, he refused to recoil from depicting the wartime frictions that had placed the Issei and Nisei in such dire straits. This is not to say that he surrendered his dream of becoming a renowned artist invested in illustrating the more urbane aspects of the human condition or the beauty he found in nature. Sugimoto continued to paint still lifes, landscapes, and portraits until the end of his life. But he admitted from the hindsight of a 1986 interview that his work on the wartime imprisonment and its relation to the broader issues regarding Japanese Americans was his central legacy—"My major achievement as an artist," as he put it.[13] As such, his work depicting scenes from Japanese American history represents an ambitious and unrivaled rendering of war, immigration, and incarceration through a racialized cosmopolitan style.

A Prewar Art Career

Yuzuru "Henry" Sugimoto was born in 1900 in Wakayama, Japan, where he spent most of his youth until immigrating to the United States in 1919. His father moved to the Central Valley farming community of Hanford, California, when Henry was still an infant. His mother then left for Hanford in 1909 to join her husband, later giving birth to two sons. The Sugimoto parents made their living through farm work and managing a boarding house for other Japanese laborers. In the meantime, Henry and a younger brother were left in the care of his maternal grandparents in Japan. During this period of his childhood, he began drawing by mimicking Japanese scroll paintings, with his grandfather's encouragement. When he and his brother reunited with their parents and the other siblings in Hanford after years of separation, Sugimoto recalled how he initially felt distant from a patriarch of whom he had no recollection, but how he promptly embraced his still recognizable mother. He later enrolled in the local high school, improving his English and converting to Christianity along the way. He then went to the University of California at Berkeley but realized that pursuing an initial interest in medical studies there did not suit him. Following a friend's advice, Sugimoto decided to attend the California School of Arts and Crafts in Oakland, where he developed a passion for oil painting. The young man became enthralled with the Postimpressionists, studied the works of Cézanne, Van Gogh, and Millet, among other favorites, and adapted their styles and approaches when depicting still lifes and the California landscape. The atmosphere at the school also proved exhilarating for him because he could paint alongside other students from different parts of the country and the world who were committed to their art. He graduated with honors in 1928 and then enrolled in several classes at the

California School of Fine Arts in San Francisco in 1929 to continue honing his skills.[14]

Sugimoto's education was noteworthy in that the arts scene in California at that time remained more open to accepting an Asian presence than other organizations in the state. Although some Asian students attended segregated schools in certain communities, art institutions in particular, such as the ones Sugimoto attended, admitted anyone with potential talent regardless of their ethnic background. Places to exhibit their pieces were also readily available. The Painters and Sculptors Annual Exhibitions in Los Angeles, the Los Angeles Oriental Artists Group, and the San Francisco Museum of Art Annuals, for example, presented several venues, even for beginning artists, to show their work.[15] The Bay Area also offered an array of exhibitions for Sugimoto to visit, especially the California Palace of the Legion of Honor and the M. H. de Young Memorial Museum, both in San Francisco. Yet, as much as these sites provided new artistic avenues to explore, Sugimoto felt the need to see and learn firsthand from the European masters and other influences.[16]

Significant to the artist's development were his travels abroad in the 1930s, first to France and then to Mexico. Arriving in Paris in 1930 with no particular plan in mind, Sugimoto made contacts with already settled Japanese expatriate artists, who housed and fed him and guided him to museums. He later ventured into the countryside to sketch and paint landscapes. The artist Fujioka Noboru, who had lived in New York City, and the journalist Inoue Isao, who, like Sugimoto, came from California, were some of his closest associates in appreciating what France had to offer. Sugimoto also attended the Académie Colarossi in Paris to refine his abilities and took language classes at the Alliance Française to improve his French. That same year, he submitted work to the prestigious annual exhibit the Salon d'Automne, but was rejected. In 1931, still feeling distraught over this setback, he followed his colleagues' suggestion to revisit the French countryside, where he befriended and stayed with the Japanese artist Ogi Moto, who lived in Voulangis, a village near Paris. The two spent their time painting the local landscape and conversing about their art, a relationship that proved fruitful to Sugimoto's development. Later that year, he learned that the Salon d'Automne selected a different landscape painting of his for exhibition, a major breakthrough for the young artist.[17]

Throughout this period, Sugimoto began accruing international renown for his landscapes and still lifes by adapting the style of the French Postimpressionists, with Maurice de Vlaminck and André Dunoyer de Segonzac as his foremost influences. Vlaminck in particular had started his career painting scenes in the Fauvist mode, resorting to unnatural, bright colors and an expressionist approach in his work at the turn of the twentieth century. In the following decades, especially after World War I, he shifted to impressionist-

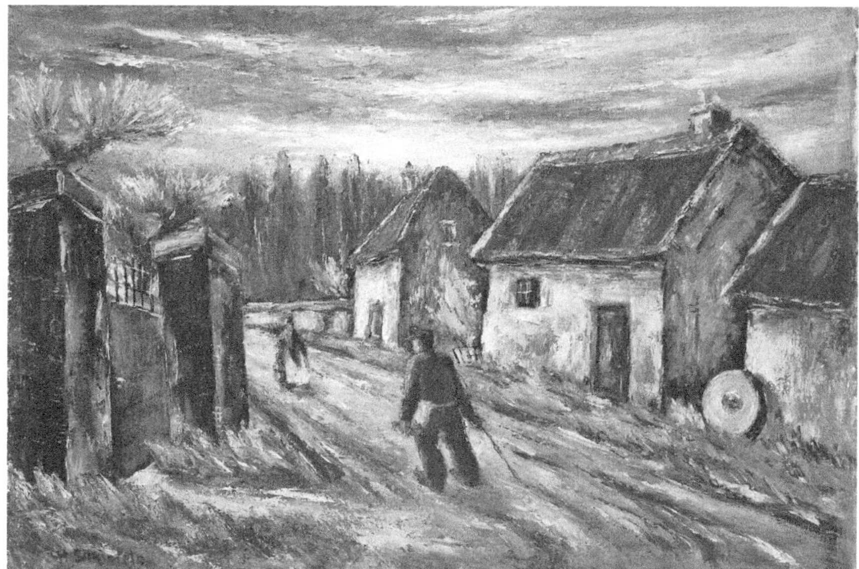

Henry Sugimoto, *Village of Villiers* (1930). (Japanese American National Museum
[Gift of Madeleine Sugimoto and Naomi Tagawa, Japanese American National Museum,
92.97.76].)

style landscapes that sought to capture a darker, more isolated mood.[18] His
impact is evident in not only Sugimoto's early pieces portraying French fields
and villages but also the later works of wartime camp buildings and landscapes, many showing a similar mixing of blues, greens, and browns applied
freely with quick and broad brush strokes. We see, for example, how Sugimoto
adapted the perspectives and forms of Postimpressionism from Vlaminck's
winter village scene *Saint-Maurice-Les-Charencey* (1928) in his own depiction,
Village of Villiers (1930). Here, farm dwellings and other structures occupy
both sides of the canvas, with a row of buildings on the right extending at
an upward angle from the lower corner into the painting's center. A central
dirt road between the edifices starts from the bottom foreground and continues in a parallel rising slant into the picture's middle horizon. A few small
human figures also appear, as they do in Vlaminck's work, walking on the
road into the background. This scene has a lonely feel to it, heightened by
the dark coloring and the overcast skies. But Sugimoto offered a different
take on Vlaminck's style, one that was contemplative, rather than gloomy, as
the Issei artist embraced a more extensive palette. Visualizing the landscape
through Postimpressionist eyes would then provide Sugimoto with a useful
artistic vocabulary, reappearing in slightly different ways in his renderings of
the wartime camps.

Also during his time in France, Sugimoto cultivated a more self-conscious cosmopolitan persona that originated from his art school days in California. In 1931, a self-portrait and photographs reveal his adherence to cosmopolitanism as a universal concept derived from modern European culture, where intellectually minded persons, as citizens of the world, desired to engage humanity in its wholeness and to detach themselves from specific loyalties, locales, and other limitations. In these pictorial forms, Sugimoto wears his signature black beret, which evokes his identification not only as an artist but specifically with Paris and its standing as the cultural capital of Western society. In the realist-mode portrait, Sugimoto sits before a blank canvas to his left, as he looks off slightly to his right beyond the viewer, a somber and somewhat enigmatic expression on his face. The background behind him is also bare, with only the unadorned wall and a small black stove in sight. His spare use of colors, with reds, browns, and yellows the most apparent, heightens the simplicity of the scene. The resulting depiction gives the impression of an artist at the beginning of his professional promise, the blank canvas signifying the possibilities yet to be discovered and rendered. A photograph of Sugimoto and his friend Ogi, however, offers a different outlook. The two artists, dapper in their berets and white shirts with dark neckties, pose outdoors in front of a French farm building, each with a palette and a brush in hand. Sugimoto stands, and Ogi crouches alongside their impressionist village scenes, the canvases leaning on easels that face toward the viewer. Ogi sports a slight smile, already confident in his well-being. In contrast, Sugimoto's upright posture, serious demeanor, and finished product (unlike the blank canvas in the self-portrait) suggest an artist growing in assurance and accomplishment.

By 1932, however, the Great Depression took tighter hold of the world, and Sugimoto's parents beckoned him home to help the family. Back in California, the artist applied what he learned in France to works depicting the local landscape—from the rivers and mountains in Yosemite Valley to ocean views and mission scenes in Carmel—that gained the notice of several art dealers and museums.[19] The California Palace of the Legion of Honor offered him his first solo exhibition in June 1933, describing the young man as a "rising artist, whose achievements are the results of unceasing endeavor, strong will power, and perseverance."[20] Other gallery invitations from Oakland, San Francisco, Los Angeles, and San Diego followed. One even came from the Museum of Modern Art in New York City. But Sugimoto thought that, because he had already committed to other gallery showings in California, he had to decline the request from the esteemed institution. He later lamented this decision, when realizing the greater potential impact the New York exhibition would have had on his career.[21]

Nonetheless, the Japanese American press in California was especially

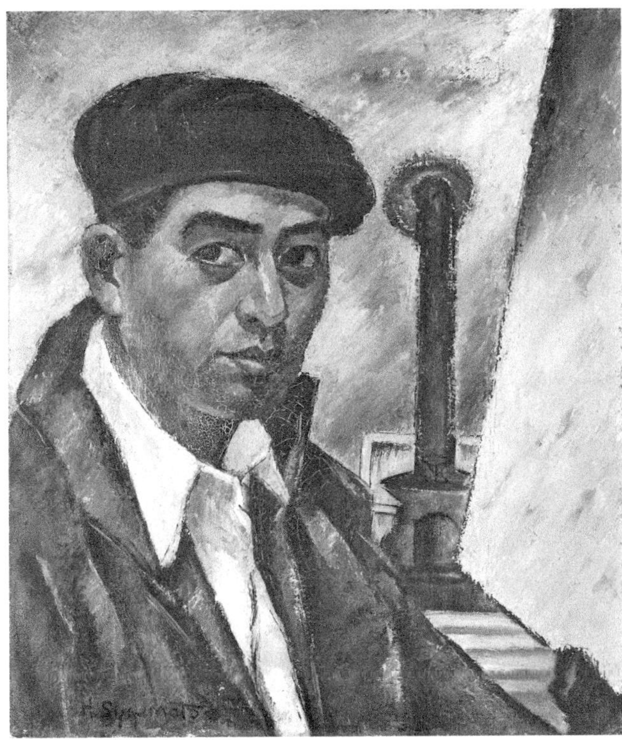

Henry Sugimoto, *Self-Portrait* (1931). (Japanese American National Museum [Gift of Madeleine Sugimoto and Naomi Tagawa, Japanese American National Museum, 92.97.106].)

keen on promoting his exhibitions, touting Sugimoto and other Issei and Nisei artists as new "Oriental" talent that deserved more public attention. Among the four hundred paintings shown at the San Francisco Art Association, as the *Kashu Mainichi* noted in January 1935, seventeen of them were by "Japanese artists" that, along with Sugimoto, included Takeo Edward Terada, Koichi Nomiyama, and Miki Hayakawa. In April 1934, the paper emphasized on its front page how the "First Oriental Art exhibition" at the Western Foundation of Art in Los Angeles "is expected to give an impetus to a new trend in art," with Sugimoto's works displayed beside those of Benji Okubo, Hideo Date, and Tokio Ueyama. *Rafu Shimpo* in the same year also promoted on its front page an exhibit of paintings by the "well known San Francisco artist" Henry Sugimoto at the Wilshire Art Gallery in Los Angeles, citing that "special care has been taken to make the art display . . . one of the [most] outstanding." These news items did not specify what constituted the Japanese American painters' styles or their unique contributions to the art world. The variety of these artists' approaches made it almost impossible to find any unifying theme, since the works ranged from surrealist portraits to realist urban scenes to impressionist landscapes. But the media coverage intimated that showcasing this talent, however cosmopolitan in its methods, training, or impact, was an affair rooted in ethnic pride and thus worthy of support from local Japanese communities.[22]

Amid these artistic successes, Sugimoto married Susie Tagawa in April 1934. The two had dated since their high school days in Hanford and managed to maintain their relationship throughout Henry's lengthy travels and the months and years apart from one another. The Tagawa elders had immigrated to the United States at the turn of the twentieth century, around the same time that Sugimoto's parents arrived, and established a laundry business. In 1910, Susie was born, and ten years later came a younger sister, Naomi. Henry and Susie married at the local Japanese Presbyterian Church and moved to the Bay Area after their wedding. But they relocated back to Hanford and to their extended families when a daughter, Madeleine Sumile, arrived in 1936. To better support themselves, the Sugimotos lived with the Tagawas, and Henry worked at the laundry and various other jobs while continuing to focus on his art.[23] Susie proved an essential figure in the development of Henry's aspirations by not only encouraging his continued travels and time spent abroad but also providing through her labors the financial stability in their lives, the housekeeping, and the childrearing. As Henry later recalled about her contributions, Susie "made it possible for me to do what I wanted to do and [provided] the time to do it."[24]

This acknowledgment pertained as well to other women of Japanese ancestry whom Sugimoto encountered in the United States and abroad. When he visited Carmel to paint the landscape there, he met an Issei couple, Mr. and Mrs. Kodani, who offered him living quarters in a cabin near their house. Sugimoto reminisced that "Mrs. Kodani even made me all my meals, breakfast, lunch, and dinner . . . so I was able to work on many more sketches." While in France, the artist gave not only Ogi but also his wife credit for their generous accommodations. "Mrs. Ogi," he noted, "cooked three meals a day for me along with the rest of her family." "When I went out to sketch in the mornings," he continued, "Mrs. Ogi would even pack a lunch for me, so I could sketch the scenery wherever I wanted to until evening without having to take a break."[25] This pattern of feeding and housing the proverbial starving artist in these Japanese immigrant and expatriate families allowed Sugimoto the precious time and quiet to paint and sketch, providing a more communal look at how he was able to produce his work across continents.

Sugimoto's reliance on the diaspora of other Japanese contacts helped his further travels and studies. In 1939, he had the opportunity to visit Mexico for a few months through the auspices of several Japanese businessmen. Dwight Takashi Uchida, the father of Yoshiko Uchida (discussed in Chapter 4), worked for the Mitsui Company's branch office in San Francisco and, being acquainted with Sugimoto, recommended the artist to the trading firm's network in Mexico City.[26] There, Sugimoto was moved by the works of three major muralists—Diego Rivera, David Alfaro Siqueiros, and José Clemente Orozco—when visiting museums and other exhibition venues. Unlike his experiences in France, where he focused on impressionist landscapes, in Mexico Sugimoto sketched and painted ordinary human figures, along with street scenes of Mexico City. His association with Mitsui presented the opportunity for him to display several paintings in the company offices, where employees then purchased several of the pieces. The chance to show and sell his work to Japanese clients made him consider staying in Mexico for several more months, but an illness caused him to return home earlier than expected.[27]

More significant for Sugimoto's artistic development, his interest in human figures that developed during this period in Mexico later became evident in his art depicting Japanese American life in the wartime prison camps, where such figures dominate his most notable compositions. Although in several works he rendered in impressionist fashion the barracks, guard towers, and landscapes of the camps, it was the imprisoned bodies themselves, in their rounded and blocklike forms that followed muralist and social realist sensibilities, that gave his paintings of Japanese Americans a unique and compelling look. Sugimoto never painted any murals, or resorted to a muralist style, during the 1930s. He instead emphasized what other visiting artists from the United States had done while in Mexico in the 1910s to the 1940s: portraying the idealized rural simplicity of the landscape and its peoples. In this framing, painters ignored the modernizing forces emerging in Mexico, with its industrial factories and railway lines, its large and lively urban centers, and its other developed aspects, since these traits would spoil their nostalgic vision of what the country was supposed to look like.[28] For instance, the studies that Sugimoto created while in Mexico were of conventional, even stereotypical, scenes. One consists of a farmer plowing the land, another of a woman selling her wares in a village market, each invoking the simple, noble life of the peasantry.

But the Mexican muralist and realist styles, with their themes regarding social injustice, would become more pronounced in Sugimoto's aesthetic approach during the war, when his own displacement and incarceration transformed his artistic vision into sharper commentary. The muralists' coloring techniques, outlining of bodily shapes and postures, and focus on laborers and the poor as central subjects of Mexican modernity were influential in this regard. Noticeable as well, Rivera, Siqueiros, and Orozco highlighted in their works the presence and influence of indigenous populations in Mexico and of ethnic minorities in the United States. These subjects and stylistic elements offered attractive models for African American muralists, such as Hale Woodruff, Charles White, and John Wilson, for tracing the past degradations of slavery and the struggles toward a more hopeful future.[29] Sugimoto likewise paid attention when considering the plight of Japanese Americans. Chances for him to see Rivera's work were not limited to Mexico but extended to the Bay Area as well. *Allegory of California* (1931) in the City Club of San Francisco and *The Making of a Fresco Showing the Building of a City* (1931) at the San Francisco Art Institute would have caught Sugimoto's notice in the years after his return from Paris. In contrast to the Mexican and African American artists' concerns about engaging in revolution and social reform, however, Sugimoto avoided overt political tones in his own work. Yet, after the war, he continued to rely on muralist methods to portray the broader aspects of Japanese American history, capturing its range and vitality through coinciding scenes and figures.[30]

Sugimoto's life and work in the 1930s thus disclose a cosmopolitan life already formed, from which he was able to navigate different facets of the art world in the United States and abroad. He gained the attention of American, European, and Japanese patrons and critics, exhibited his paintings across the hemispheres, discussed work with fellow Japanese artists and French masters while studying in Europe, and enjoyed the support of Japanese American communities in California. Although Sugimoto thought of himself as an artist who won acclaim from working primarily in the impressionist mode, he was a man of the world in a broader sense, given the mix of his experiences within several nations, his contacts across different classes and ethnicities, and his own background as an Issei. As Karen Higa observes, these social and professional circles in which Sugimoto participated add a different tinge to the conventional portraits we have of Japanese immigrants in the United States as field laborers and shopkeepers living in segregated ethnic communities during the early twentieth century. Because Sugimoto belonged in part to privileged groups and traveled widely, his career did not appear adversely affected by the rampant discrimination that other Japanese encountered. But his talents and his circumstances would be sorely tried, given the looming war with Japan and what it portended for Japanese Americans as a whole.[31]

Cartographies of Confinement: Wartime Camp Life

The wartime incarceration left its brutal mark on a broad range of Japanese Americans. To cope with the grueling environment of the camps, they produced an impressive array of art, from photography and sketches to craft arts and paintings, with many of these pieces offering important social critiques on the confinement. Among the Issei and Nisei were professional artists who had their own studios before the war and who, like Sugimoto, offered to teach classes in the camps. Conditions, however, were challenging. Much of what the instructors and their students could create while behind barbed wire was limited due to lack of resources. Art materials were often scarce, and people had to be inventive with what was available. Sugimoto resorted to using mattress covers, pillowcases, canvas wrappings that had been employed to transport belongings, and other found material on which to paint. He and others also began sketching, painting, or photographing their surroundings in secret, since the Wartime Civilian Control Administration, run by the U.S. Army, forbade them to document what was occurring inside the assembly centers. Once the War Relocation Authority (WRA) took over the supervision of inmates and confined them further inland, officials allowed them to paint scenes of the prison camps. Through these efforts, Japanese Americans left an immense, yet underappreciated, artistic record of their experiences, revealing the extent of their ingenuity and craftsmanship.[32]

Other important visual artifacts came from established photographers, such as Dorothea Lange and Ansel Adams, who captured the process of forced removal and life in specific camp locations. Lange shot scenes of Japanese Americans before and during the removal process in California and visited various incarceration sites. Adams took his camera to record the camp life at Manzanar, located in Owens Valley in California, and published the results in *Born Free and Equal: The Story of Loyal Japanese-Americans* (1944). Both Lange and Adams were sympathetic to the difficulties facing their subjects. Adams's collection sought to convey the heroic endurance of the Issei and Nisei amid the transformative natural environment that they inhabited. At the same time, he reinforced predominant stereotypes about Asian passivity, picturing them as part of the western landscape itself, and did not challenge the racial reasons for the Japanese American imprisonment.[33] Lange in particular worked under the auspices of the WRA's Information Division and often had her photos censored to prevent unfavorable images of confinement from circulating in public. The WRA hired white photographers to detail the removal and detention process to emphasize how Japanese Americans were being well treated, even as their confinement required justification, whether the photographers agreed with this institutional intent or not.[34] As Jasmine Alinder notes about the broader effects of this documenting work, "the camera served as a kind of visual gatekeeper that determined who was fit to be a part of the body politic and who should be cast out."[35] Starting with the creation of Asian immigration credentials in the late nineteenth century, photography became an instrument by which federal authorities could record and reinforce their message about who was suitable for citizenship, who was loyal or disloyal, and whose presence was tolerable, if not welcome, within the nation. The origins of documenting and imagining alien or exotic Others in this manner had deep roots in American popular culture and in U.S. imperial ventures in Asia: photographers exhibited these subjects for the purposes of both science and entertainment. But the framing process that warranted the confinement of Japanese Americans, two-thirds of whom were U.S. citizens, was rife with internal contradictions. The resulting photographs and their supplementary captions portrayed the Issei and Nisei as quiet and dignified in their comportment during the removal. Some of the younger subjects even smiled at the camera, visual evidence for white viewers of Asian civility and good-natured compliance, characteristics that tended to support their assimilation and acceptance. Yet the federal government categorized these men, women, and children as enemy aliens and thus a threat to the nation's security.[36]

By creating different or little-known scenes of their tribulations, Sugimoto and other Japanese Americans offered counternarratives that modified, if not contested or complicated, the WRA-sponsored versions of the camp experiences that served to promote the government's benevolence. Individuals like the professional photographer Toyo Miyatake and others snuck in camera parts and took their own photographs from makeshift devices, or even made home movies. These visual recordings, including paintings, sketches, and illustrations, varied in their levels of discernible protest or critique, depending on the intentions, perspective, or tone of each. As examined below, such disparities occurred within Sugimoto's own body of work, in which he explored the possible range of his subjects' sentiments and attempted to grasp what he observed and faced in the camps.[37]

All through his career, however, Sugimoto denied any political intentions in his work, seeing himself instead as a worldly artist who was merely "documenting" life as he saw it. He intimated by this statement that to document meant to record in an emotionally truthful manner, conveying through his art a lasting aesthetic experience. Sugimoto wanted to focus on recounting the circumstances and feelings of Japanese Americans during the war, rather than on criticizing the federal government for its actions against them. Several reasons explain this stance regarding the function of his work. First and foremost, being detached from political motives fit his ideal of a cosmopolitan figure unconfined by borders, styles, or expectations when pursuing artistic aims. As Sugimoto explained in an interview in the 1980s: "Art is essentially a means of expression designed to give aesthetic pleasure." This ideal remained as true for him while in art school during the 1920s as it did six decades later.[38]

But there may have been underlying, yet unexpressed, motives as to why Sugimoto avoided addressing issues in such a way that others could interpret as attacks on the government, or why he did not want to see his past experiences and his art defined in this manner. The wartime incarceration itself proved how state power could adversely affect entire populations that it considered a threat. Japanese Americans for the most part remained quiet for years afterward about their lives in the camps, many having been shamed or traumatized into silence. The ensuing Cold War climate, in which anyone who criticized national ideals or institutions fell under suspicion as a communist or a sympathizer, also contributed to repressing dissent and the voicing of grievances. People's lives and careers at the time could come to quick ruin merely on the basis of innuendo or rumor. That Japanese Americans suffered charges of disloyalty due to their ancestral background even before their mass imprisonment made them all the more careful in the probing glare of McCarthyism.[39] From another angle, Sugimoto may have adopted a noncommittal view on sensitive or controversial topics simply to safeguard his prospects when attempting to gain favor from patrons in the United States. Even then, showing the nation's racial prejudice against Japanese Americans in his work misaligned with art galleries' preferences for exhibitions and sales. These desires coincided with the broader directives of the federal government during the Cold War, when U.S. officials sought to counter Soviet propaganda on the shortcomings of American democracy. Not until the 1980s did Sugimoto acknowledge in interviews the racial discrimination he and his family members faced in the United States. He recalled his student days, when he could not practice with his white teammates on the high school swim team at other institutions' pools. He also noted that his brother Ralph, despite serving in the U.S. Army, could not get a haircut at a local barbershop because of his ethnic background. These later reminiscences highlight how Sugimoto may have dealt with earlier personal traumas, or how his generation addressed such racial instances: by keeping silent about them as they occurred. Despite these hindrances, however, it is important to remember that he continued to paint scenes of wartime camp life.[40]

At the same time, the artistic ideas espoused by the Mexican muralists shadowed Sugimoto's labors as he adapted their politically charged styles that included narratives about revolution and social injustice.[41] This point became more apparent to art critics in the post–civil rights era. As one reporter noted in the 1980s, Sugimoto's "documentary works combined the brooding Expressionist styles he grew up with, with the political literalness of an editorial cartoonist and the sentiment of a magazine illustrator." A reviewer of the 2001 retrospective exhibit at the JANM went further, writing that "the tone and mood of Sugimoto's pieces [were] driven by political activism," wherein his pieces "from the mid-'40s on . . . converse with activist-based works that began to emerge again in the '70s."[42] In this case, the assumption that his documenting events were political acts (and not just aesthetic practices) suggests that he was participating in, or setting the foundations for, other artistic critiques of social issues regarding ethnic minorities. Although Sugimoto would have demurred at describing his art as "activist," his reliance on particular styles and the interpretations of his art by different audiences over the years reveal the charged dynamics of the work, given his selection of subject matter and perspective. The war- and immigration-related compositions were thus not as timeless, objective, or apolitical as they appeared, especially when viewed from the vantage point of Asian American political engagements that lent his work renewed public visibility in the 1970s and 1980s.

Considering Sugimoto's own artistic process, the affective power of his art on the mass confinement stemmed from his feelings of fear and doubt during that moment and from his need to keep reconceiving those sentiments in new and different ways. His tone in, and approach to, recording occurrences in the camps and during prewar migrations, then, were more fluid and open, since he kept revising many of the paintings over the course of decades. For example, we can see the transformations in two variations of a similarly titled scene, *My Papa* (circa 1942; circa 1965). In each of these renderings, an FBI agent takes away a farmer dressed in blue overalls from his plowing, located on the left side of the frame, the horse and farm buildings on the right-center, as his wife and two children helplessly watch in the lower right corner. The incident in the painting occurs after the bombing of Pearl Harbor and the rounding up of Japanese heads of households begins. Religious themes often permeated Sugimoto's work, and here, the mother and baby are reminiscent of a Madonna and Christ child, the woman with a white head covering seen in profile from the back and left side, the infant facing the viewer. In this scene, an unjust state power intrudes on a now separated family's innocence and sanctity of home. The little girl in the lower-middle foreground of the picture chases after her father as he looks to his right, back at her (in the later adaptation), bolstering the affective power of the scene. The first version (circa 1942), measuring eighteen by twenty-two inches, discloses a less sentimental perspective. The father glances to his left, away from his family, perhaps because he cannot bear the pain of seeing their aggrieved countenances. The held baby in the lower right places its hand on the mother's cheek as small comfort. This depiction shows hurried, heavy brushwork with few colors in the composition, a reflection of the Sugimotos' rush to pack a few possessions before their removal to the detention center in Fresno. Browns and blues predominate, with the figures revealing a naïve, folk art look that matches the simple, yet powerful, emotions of seeing a Japanese American family disrupted in this manner. By 1965, the artist revisited *My Papa* with a bigger canvas (fifty-two by sixty-five inches), softer brushwork, and brighter colors. He also began painting

FACING PAGE, TOP: Henry Sugimoto, *My Papa* (circa 1942). (Japanese American National Museum [Gift of Madeleine Sugimoto and Naomi Tagawa, Japanese American National Museum, 92.97.91].)

FACING PAGE, BOTTOM: Henry Sugimoto, *My Papa* (circa 1965). (Japanese American National Museum [Gift of Madeleine Sugimoto and Naomi Tagawa, Japanese American National Museum, 92.97.139].)

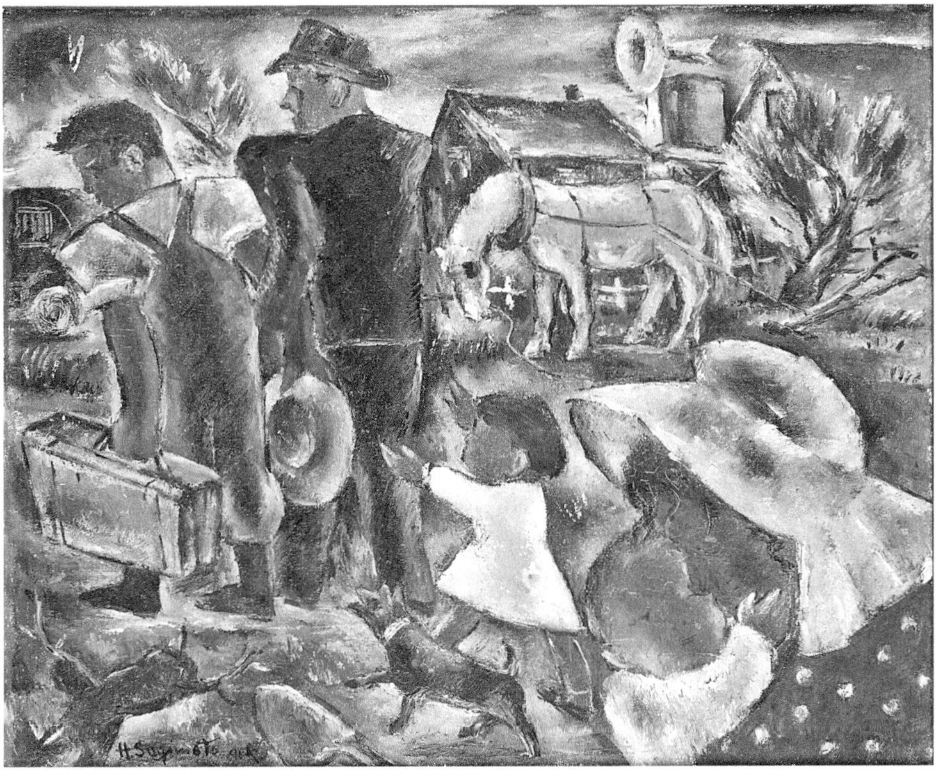

H Sugimoto

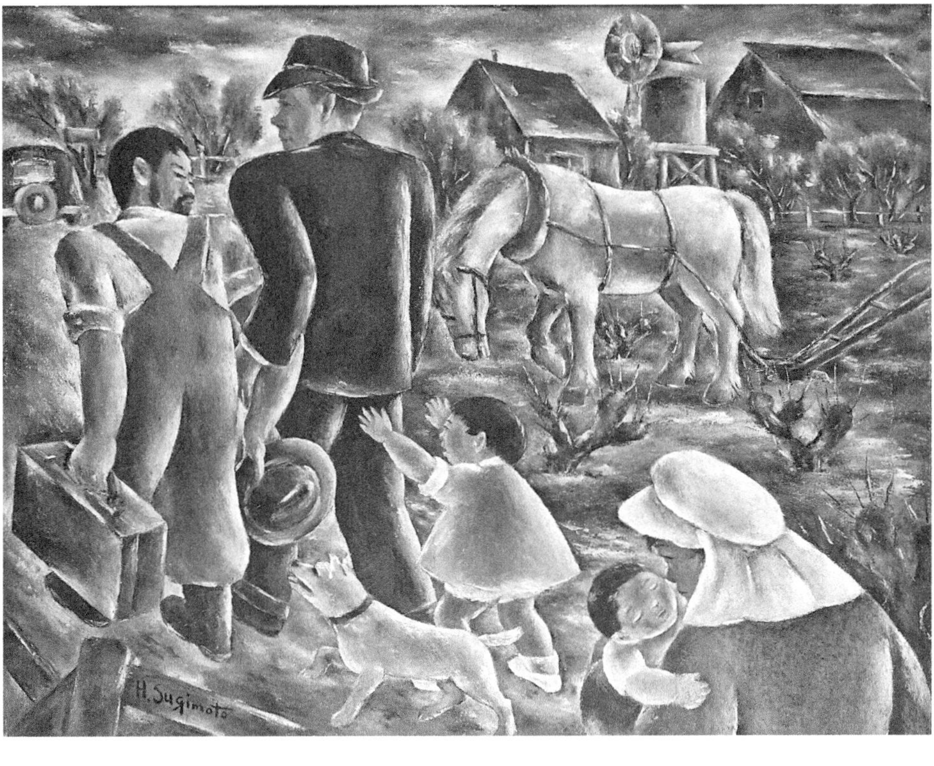

H. Sugimoto

scenes of prewar Japanese immigration at this time, with a comparable array of hues and on large-sized canvases. We can then appreciate Sugimoto's body of work as an evolving series of social critiques ingrained in the racially laden experiences of Japanese Americans throughout the twentieth century. In this framework, the Pacific War was a major turning point for him that clarified his and others' inferior, racialized status, as decreed by the United States.

These matters became more evident to Sugimoto once the federal government declared war on Japan on December 8, 1941, a day after the attack on Pearl Harbor, and the FBI began arresting Japanese nationals with any suspicious ties to their homeland. Sugimoto worried about his own safety after some of his colleagues at a Japanese-language school, where he also worked as a part-time instructor, were held for questioning about their connections to Japan. Gripped by panic, the artist went to the school and buried the textbooks over the next few days, hoping to destroy any signs of disloyalty or acts of purveying Japanese culture on his part. He then waited with his family in fear of what might develop. But somehow, to his relief, the agents never came for him.[43] Several weeks passed, with hardly any calls for a mass removal. However, pressure on the federal government from local political leaders and white farming interests that wanted to rid themselves of Japanese competition on the West Coast increased. Growing fears of the Japanese functioning as a fifth column within the United States and early victories by Japan's imperial forces in the Pacific also began to change people's sentiments against the Issei and Nisei. President Roosevelt's signing of Executive Order 9066 in February 1942 activated an array of actions that held ominous import for Japanese Americans across the West Coast. In April, the U.S. Army alerted them about their impending removal from their homes and neighborhoods to temporary holding areas.[44] The Sugimoto family, which then included Henry and Susie, their six-year-old daughter Madeleine, and Henry's parents and brothers, were assigned in early May to the Fresno Assembly Center, a former fairground located near Hanford, California. The detention facility held more than five thousand people, who had had only a few days to bundle their belongings, or sell what they could not carry, before being transported there on buses under armed guard. Amid this rush of activity, Sugimoto gave about one hundred paintings to a San Francisco art dealer for safekeeping while he was away. But to his dismay at what he learned afterward, the dealer went out of business and the work went missing, presumably auctioned off to unknown clients. Sugimoto was never able to recover these pieces or any profits from them, which he valued at over ten thousand dollars at the time.[45]

Adding insult to injury, the arrivals at Fresno met with other unanticipated adversities. For one, they were housed in buildings that had served as horse stalls; the artist recounted later how the smell of animals still pervaded their quarters. The dismalness of the situation, however, failed to diminish Sugimoto's desire to continue making art. "We were allowed [a] limited amount of personal belongings—bare necessities," he recalled about the move, "but being an artist I snuck in art materials like [a] few tubes of pigment, three brushes and a small bottle of turpentine."[46] This lack of supplies and the conditions under which they were made gave his early paintings of the scenes around him a rough and hurried look. We saw this method in *My Papa* (circa 1942), where his stylistic touches and dark coloring schemes lent such works a pervasive mood of despair and uncertainty amid the hasty dislocation of civilians.

When transported in a secondary move from Fresno to the Jerome camp in southeastern Arkansas in October 1942, Sugimoto recalled the cross-country train ride as a long and arduous journey. The railway cars were old and uncomfortable, having been out of service for years, as they rattled, screeched, and plodded toward their destination. The windows were draped with black shades, so the passengers could not see out and thus had no idea where they were. The lavatory in the Sugimotos' compartment flooded, filling the aisle with water and soaking the luggage. Sleep came in fits and starts. Amid these conditions, Sugimoto was able to create small, four-by-six-inch sketches of the southwestern surroundings on rest stops along the way. Some of these captured farm and village landscapes, while others depicted Japanese Americans moving their suitcases, waiting in stations, and one with his wife and daughter leaning against each other on a train seat.[47]

By the time the Sugimoto family and thousands of others reached the camp at Jerome, what they saw disheartened them further. The site was located amid swampy woodlands, where snakes and mosquitos thrived. The barracks were still unfinished, so the new arrivals had to sleep in warehouses, with blankets covering the floor. Once assigned to their quarters, the inmates then discovered that the WRA officials had failed to supply them with tables, shelves, or chairs, so they had to build their own furniture, taking any excess lumber from the camp construction to do so. Although fatigued and anxious at this point, Sugimoto was determined to continue painting. As he recounted, "If I can make my art still, I am feeling not so bitter." Once the camp populace established mess halls, schools, clinics, and other civic facilities, Sugimoto began teaching art at the high school and night classes for adults, where his salary was nineteen dollars a month. This position allowed him to collect more art supplies, both for his students and for himself. We can observe the changes in his style by 1943, with the wider range of color schemes, the increased precision in brushwork, and the experimentation in forms. Despite his feelings of uncertainty and the hardships encountered, Sugimoto was able to produce a new and different genre of art from his prewar work as a way to survive, even to flourish, when doing what he loved.[48]

Painting scenes of the camp landscape initially proved difficult for the artist. Recollecting his first impressions of the surroundings in Arkansas, he noted that, compared to the French countryside, there was "nothing good . . . just barracks" to depict on his makeshift canvases.[49] Yet, when rendering this environment in Postimpressionist fashion, he was more than able to reconfigure the desolation around him into visions of pensive beauty to offset the severity of his circumstances. In several variations of the landscape, such as *Jerome, Ark.* (circa 1942), *Jerome Camp from Swamp* (circa 1942), or *Near the Jerome Camp* (circa 1943), we recognize Sugimoto's earlier shadings, strong brush strokes, and vantage points developed from his prewar efforts in France. Most of these later depictions also reveal similar cloud-streaked skies, this time over rows of gray barracks, low wire fences, and guard towers set amid the fields and forests of Arkansas. A tiny figure or two often ambles along a road in front or alongside of the barracks. But Sugimoto moved beyond a partiality for Postimpressionism as an aesthetic style and created what he called a "documentary record" of what he saw and experienced in the camps.[50]

One of the more suggestive portrayals is the winter scene *Sunrise—Jerome* (1943). The camp is discerned in the distance, a row of barracks and other structures occupying the middle horizon of the canvas. Below them is a grassy field that dominates the right and middle foreground. A path and a ditch with walkways over it run parallel in a diagonal slant from the immediate middle foreground to the left side of the frame. Sugimoto renders much of this winter atmosphere in blues, whites, and grays, heightening the sense of dreariness and seclusion that engulfs the camp. Unlike his other prison landscapes, no human figure is present. What captures the viewer's attention amid this overall bleakness is the crimson orb that emerges above the barracks, its presence faintly tinting the surrounding sky in wispy pinks. We notice, too, the signs of human activity in the barracks, with some of the tiny windows aglow in yellow-orange light and the smoke curling up from the chimneys. As this particular day begins, which will renew itself in following sunrises, we detect the artist's small, glimmering hope in these specks of bright colors, that despite the isolation and despair pervading the camp, life still continues. Furthermore, the painting presents the rising red sun, the symbol of Japan, as conveying

FACING PAGE, TOP: Henry Sugimoto, *Jerome, Ark.* (circa 1942). (Japanese American National Museum [Gift of Madeleine Sugimoto and Naomi Tagawa, Japanese American National Museum, 92.97.31].)

FACING PAGE, BOTTOM: Henry Sugimoto, *Sunrise—Jerome* (1943). (Japanese American National Museum [Gift of Madeleine Sugimoto and Naomi Tagawa, Japanese American National Museum, 92.97.14].)

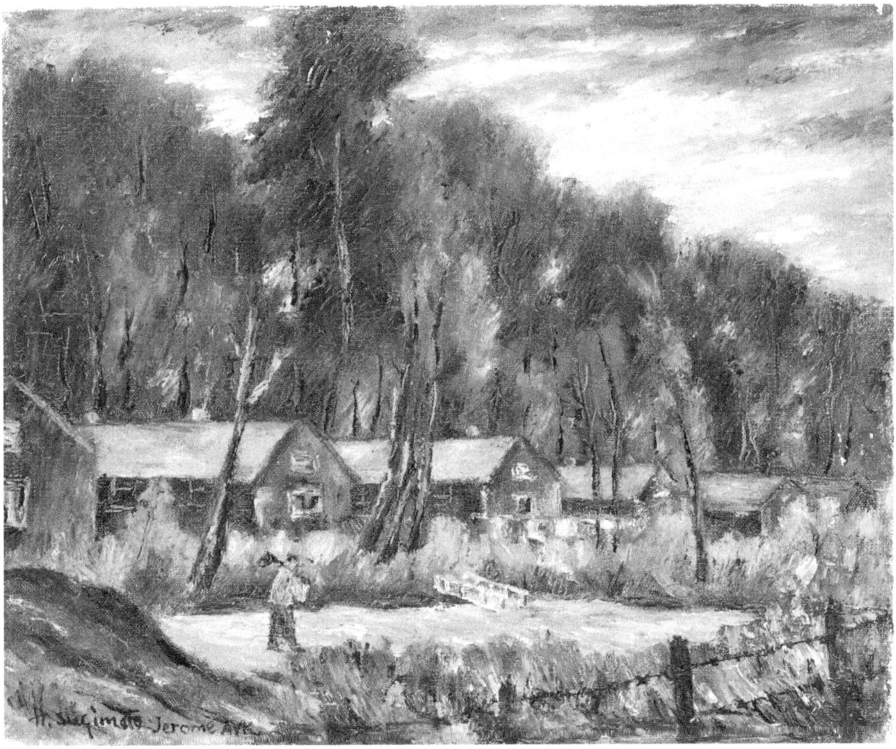

H. Sugimoto Jerome Ark.

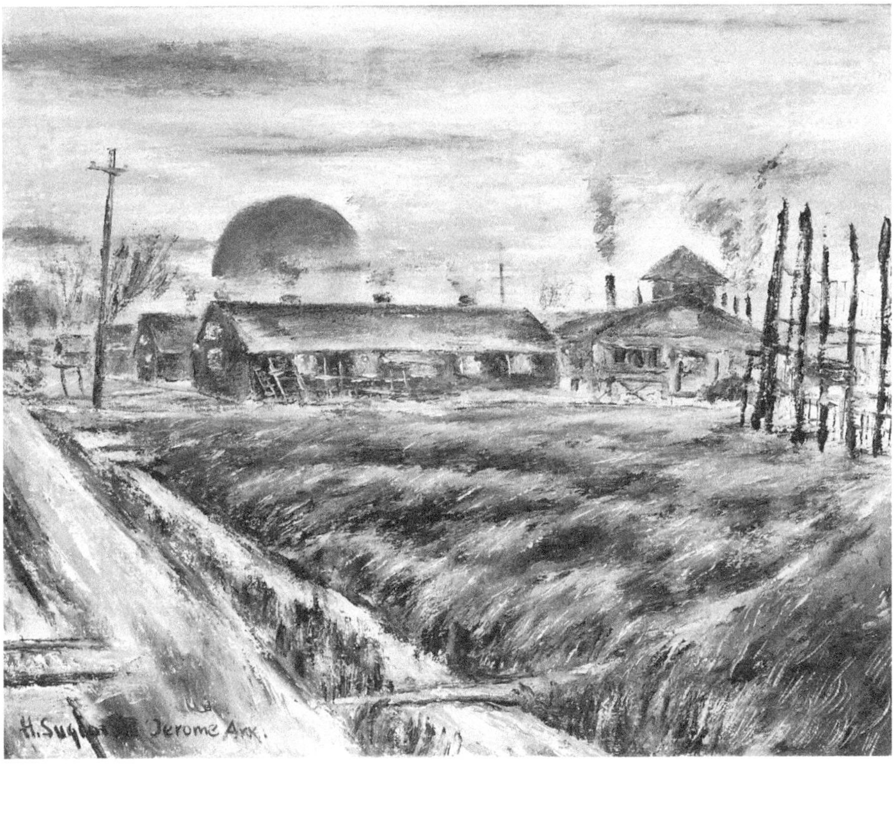

H. Sugimoto Jerome Ark.

something other than its associations with imperial desires and destructiveness. Instead, it suggests a more measured sense of ethnic pride and peaceable endurance located within the Japanese diaspora. Considered a domestic racial threat by the U.S. government, Sugimoto countered this charge in subtle and diverse ways throughout his work. He did so in transnational styles that also at times evoked transnational movements in his muralist compositions. But here, Sugimoto offered a new twist along these lines to his Postimpressionist training. *Sunrise—Jerome* implies, through the camp landscape, that a migratory people in their ordinary pursuits (including the painter himself), and not the imperial state across the Pacific, better represents the traditions, spirit, and cosmopolitan yearnings of Japan.

Much of Sugimoto's artistic and affective power came from his adaptations of muralist and social realist approaches to create his own style when rendering the everyday lives of incarcerated Japanese Americans. Although he avoided expressing any developed political ideology, his work reflected the tenets of social realism, with its concerns for the poor and working classes that intensified in the 1930s amid the Great Depression and the rise of fascism across the globe. Many of Sugimoto's views stemmed from his own past experiences of the rural poverty of Japanese American farming communities in Hanford. He also realized that Issei farmers could not own property due to the alien land laws that prevented such opportunities. These acts developed from other restrictive measures, such as denying them the right to become naturalized citizens, thus sustaining their alien status and inability to purchase land, among other disallowed privileges. As a result, their choices in a small community like Hanford were limited to establishing their own small businesses (restaurants, vegetable stands, watch repairing), laying iron tracks for the railroad companies, or working for white agricultural interests as sharecroppers. These conditions made Sugimoto later sympathize with the plight of impoverished African Americans he saw near the camps and around the towns in Arkansas, since they reminded him of his own generation's and forebears' struggles in California.[51]

Thus, even as Sugimoto became a world-traveling professional artist, he was attracted to rural settings and themes and to the presence of laboring classes, in part because of his awareness of the social and racial conditions that Japanese Americans endured in the United States. In many of his paintings, for example, he included male subjects toiling in overalls. Indeed, this figure became for him a central archetype—the man in blue overalls—depicted as a farmer or a manual laborer, often with a family, modeled in the two adaptations of *My Papa* that I have discussed. In this way, Sugimoto's artwork fits within the broader American tradition of celebrating the nation's democratic ideals, as rooted in the populace at large, through this type of protagonist. A familiar and similarly clothed person appears in American art throughout the 1930s and beyond that paid homage to the rural and urban traits of the nation. We see him in the works of American regionalists, such as Thomas Hart Benton's *The Engineer's Dream* (1931) and *Arts of the West* (1932). The figure even achieves iconic status in Grant Wood's *American Gothic* (1930). Documentary photographs emphasized this representative persona, including Walker Evans's portraits of Floyd Burroughs in Hale County, Alabama (1936) and Charles C. Ebbets's New York City construction workers in *Lunch atop a Skyscraper* (1932). But Sugimoto's art also functioned in visual dialogue with works that extended the meaning of "American" beyond the white national mainstream or its regional counterparts, engaging with other U.S. ethnic minority artists or with those from Latin America. Mexican and African American muralists, Diego Rivera and Hale Woodruff among them, referenced as well the sufferings and the nobility of common people through the image of working men in overalls. Rivera's *Detroit Industry Murals* (1932–1933) and Woodruff's *The Building of Savery Library* (1942), a part of his series at Talladega College in Alabama, illustrate this theme. By including Japanese Americans in this genre, Sugimoto conversed in figurative terms with preceding and coinciding artwork through a racialized cosmopolitan style that exposed the trans-American state of minority families and communities. Although disenfranchised, they yet endured.

Laboring characters appear across the decades in Sugimoto's art, from the 1940s to the 1970s. What aligns his work more with the concerns of social realists, such as Diego Rivera, than with regionalists or others is the impending danger or injustice that this figure in overalls and his family encounters. Although Sugimoto was cognizant of working people's economic struggles, he focused more on the racial prejudice that Japanese Americans confronted in the United States. He may have found that overcoming matters of race were more pertinent to his own self-perception as a cosmopolitan artist who had already gained cultural capital from his professional training and early critical reception. As mentioned previously, however, race and class concerns were apparent and interconnected in Sugimoto's work and memories since he empathized with the Issei farmers in California and with the segregated African American populace in Arkansas. Yet the artist shunned a militant tone, even as he conveyed the innocence of civilians smarting under institutional authority, as represented by the U.S. soldiers and FBI agents who detained them as alien offenders. He otherwise relied on affective approaches of valorizing ordinary families, portraying them as peaceable, hard-working figures facing national pressures that molded them into racial threats.

The main idea that captures the variety of Sugimoto's works during this period is how Japanese American communities adapted to trying circumstances, while also revealing their humanity in everyday tasks and occurrences. His paintings of the removal process to Fresno and life in Arkansas, including his own family's arrival in Jerome, recall realist imagery from the 1930s regarding the themes of migration and displacement. We can see in the wartime pieces the beginnings of a racialized cosmopolitan style, wherein the artist engaged with Mexican muralist and social realist influences that focused on the dislocation and disempowerment, as well as the heroism and endurance, of Japanese Americans. Indeed, Sugimoto's compositions fit within the broader, trans-American grain of realist art, alongside the works of Lange and Rivera, that depicts families threatened by transition and uncertainty.

Sugimoto's work, as a set of cultural narratives that portrayed a population anxious about their displacement, aligns with earlier documentary photographs of poor whites during the Great Depression, as captured by Lange. The famous photographs in her *Migrant Mother* series (1936) establish the difficult conditions faced by these individuals through a haggard mother and her children waiting among other pea pickers in the fields of Nipomo, California. Lange began working for the Resettlement Administration in 1935, which then became the Farm Security Administration. As part of Roosevelt's New Deal programs, the purpose of these organizations was to record the dire circumstances of the poor in order to justify their need for federal assistance. The photographs that Lange took of Florence Thompson and some of her young children in various poses were widely distributed and have become part of American iconography. In Lange's framing, the mother becomes a secularized Madonna figure, with the baby replacing the Christ child and the other offspring acting as surrounding cherubs. But unlike earlier religious imagery, the parent and older children look uncertain and fearful about the future. In one particular composition (no. 5 in the series), the mother holds her sleeping infant, while an elder child stands slightly behind her, leaning a tired head on her left shoulder and looking off-camera in a dazed stare. A canvas sheet held up by a wooden pole serves as not only a makeshift tent but also the backdrop for this family portrait. A suitcase with an empty tin plate perched on top is evident in the immediate left foreground, accentuating a not-so-bountiful future of itinerancy and hunger. As Wendy Kozol suggests, these pictures of women and children became intentional symbols of helplessness and innocence, designed to stir empathy for their plight among urban, middle-class audiences. The strategy appeared to work, as a selection of Lange's images caught the American imagination, a vision of life during the Depression that survives to this day.[52]

Sugimoto's art challenges these purposes and contexts, while providing a similar mood of doubt and despair. In an untitled 1942 work, he shows a Japanese American migrant mother tending to her children and in compa-

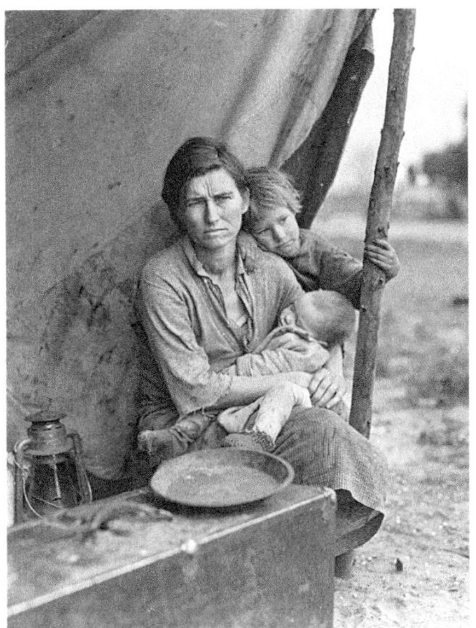

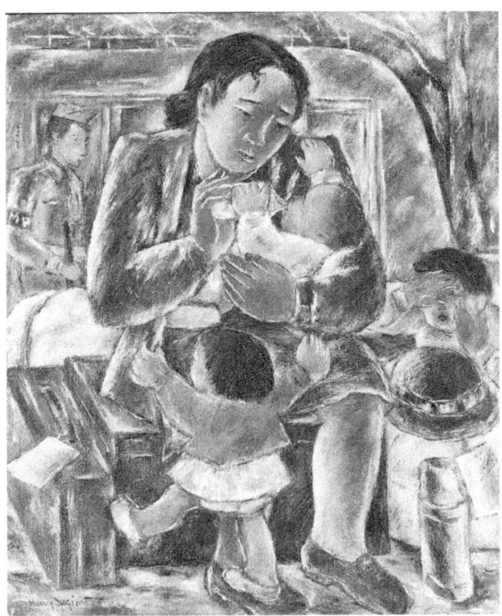

ABOVE LEFT: Dorothea Lange, *Migrant Mother* (no. 5, 1936). (Library of Congress [LC-USF34- 009095-C].)

ABOVE RIGHT: Henry Sugimoto, untitled (circa 1942). (Japanese American National Museum [Gift of Madeleine Sugimoto and Naomi Tagawa, Japanese American National Museum, 92.97.69].)

rable distress to Florence Thompson and her offspring. Likewise, the painting discloses poses similar to those seen in Lange's *Migrant Mother*. In Sugimoto's rendering, suitcases also occupy the foreground, while the mother, with an exhausted and concerned countenance, sits while bottle-feeding her infant in the same position as Lange's migrant mother when holding her sleeping child. Yet, in the Japanese American case, two other tired young children beg for the mother's attention, one standing in front with her arms up, waiting for a comforting embrace, while another off to the side cries in anguish, hands on his face. The scene, unlike the repose and quiet desperation of the mother and children in Lange's 1936 photograph, instead invokes the physical motions and aural turbulence of the unhappy children, heightening the affective impact of the composition. While Lange's mother gazes to the viewer's right into the middle distance, Sugimoto's looks at her baby, caught in the immediacy of the distressing moment, as she feeds the infant. Shades of brown, applied heavily and quickly, prevail in the mother's clothes, the luggage, the background, and the family's skin tone. Also notably different in Sugimoto's portrait of the Japanese American Madonna, aside from the racial makeup of the family, is the squared back end of a bus, which acts as the backdrop (replacing the canvas tent in Lange's formulation), waiting to convey the family to a detention center. An Army MP, identified by his light-brown uniform and armband, also stands in the left background, visible over the mother's shoulder, ensuring an obedient transport with his presence and his rifle.

In Lange's and Sugimoto's renderings of a migrant mother, a male head of household is missing. This lack of a patriarchal presence suggests the disruptiveness of economic depression and war, which disorders family and gender hierarchies. As in the numerous religious depictions of the Madonna and Christ child throughout history (wherein the unseen God replaces Joseph as the father), these modern, secularized versions also supply a substitution, if not an explanation, for the vanished patriarch. As Robert Hariman and John Louis Lucaites contend about Lange's migrant mother, the viewing public itself takes the place of the father figure as part of the photograph's appeal to help her condition, one caused by larger, unseen forces beyond her control. This collective empathy and call for reform would then be expressed through the liberal state and even become embodied in President Roosevelt as the symbolic replacement father.[53]

In Sugimoto's 1942 portrayal of Japanese American displacement, the dynamics are altered because the government itself is the cause of the mother and her children's woeful situation. As Colleen Lye argues, the intentions behind New Deal liberalism went hand in hand with the mass removal and incarceration of Japanese Americans. The link becomes clear, she notes, when we see how the Roosevelt administration and associated American writers and intellectuals, such as Carey McWilliams, viewed the camps as "experiments in cooperative living," a directive that aligned with broader ideas about rural reform and Asian assimilation.[54] Concerns in the West over rising property costs, more efficient land use, irrigation methods, and the racial presence of Asian laborers had been evident since the Progressive Era and intensified in the 1930s. Federal projects involving land reclamation and overseen by the Farm Security Administration, the Works Progress Administration, and the Civilian Conservation Corps served as models for establishing the War Relocation Authority. That WRA officials also had backgrounds working in federal agricultural agencies was no accident. Thus, by wartime, these earlier matters of land and labor management coincided in varying degrees with revised Asian exclusion and removal policies. In this new system, Japanese Americans in the distant and desolate camps could reclaim underutilized acreage and become self-sufficient through their farming and other manual labor, while later dispersing and integrating themselves among the general populace.[55]

Sugimoto's untitled painting makes the structural and political reasons for displacement clear: the federal government's presence, embodied in the U.S. soldier, is the power behind the removal because of the nation's fearful attitude toward Japanese Americans as a wartime threat. Thus, the Army MP becomes the symbolic figure and force of the patriarchal liberal state. The previously discussed *My Papa* (circa 1942), when read alongside the untitled work of the Japanese American migrant mother created around the same time, then explains this lack of a father figure. The FBI agent detaining the Japanese American farmer replayed Sugimoto's own fears and memories of detention, wherein we can surmise from a broader representational sense how that mother in the untitled work might be left alone with her children, as they wait for their transportation to a detention facility. Both the untitled work of the Japanese American migrant mother and *My Papa* can also be viewed as outgrowths of a transnational style that originated from Sugimoto's Mexican travels, when he portrayed a farmer plowing the land in a 1939 composition. But the benign brown skin of the Mexican farmer in this earlier work becomes a sign of racialized endangerment for the similarly brown-skinned Japanese Americans. In *My Papa,* as in the untitled work, the tone—both of color and of emotion—undermines any notions of government benevolence because we see the state's force enacted against ordinary civilians.

When portraying his own family's arrival at the Jerome camp, Sugimoto adapted the human forms and poses from a lithograph by Diego Rivera, *El Sueño* (The Dream, 1932). Rivera's depiction is a detail from a larger mural, *La Noche de los Pobres* (The Night of the Poor, 1928), which Sugimoto may have seen while visiting Mexico City. The applicability of this work is apparent in *Arrival in Camp Jerome* (1942), with Sugimoto's focus on the tired and vulnerable bodies of his displaced family. The father figures in Rivera's and Sugimoto's pieces mirror one another, the former's facing right, the latter's facing left, with their heads resting on their arms, elbows akimbo. Meanwhile, the mother and child pairings are replicated in parallel ways, with the parents' sitting bodies tilted toward the right and their children leaning into them toward the left. Sugimoto worked on several versions of *Arrival in Camp Jerome,* among other specific scenes from their incarcerated lives. The first rendition of this piece, for instance, was painted when the Sugimotos initially came to Jerome. We should recall that the artist lacked his usual array of brushes and paint colors, so the rough, sketch-like quality of this family portrait is noticeable. But even as he drew from Rivera's work, Sugimoto did not follow the muralist's Marxist leanings about the proletariat's class struggles and the revolutionary transformations required to reform society at large. Instead, Sugimoto relied on his Christian faith and references to religious themes, both indirect and explicit, for his multiple versions of camp experiences. *Arrival in Camp Jerome* shows how a family's forced removal and homeless, unwelcome status in the United States evokes depictions of Joseph and Mary with the Christ child, wherein the three figures suffer from perse-

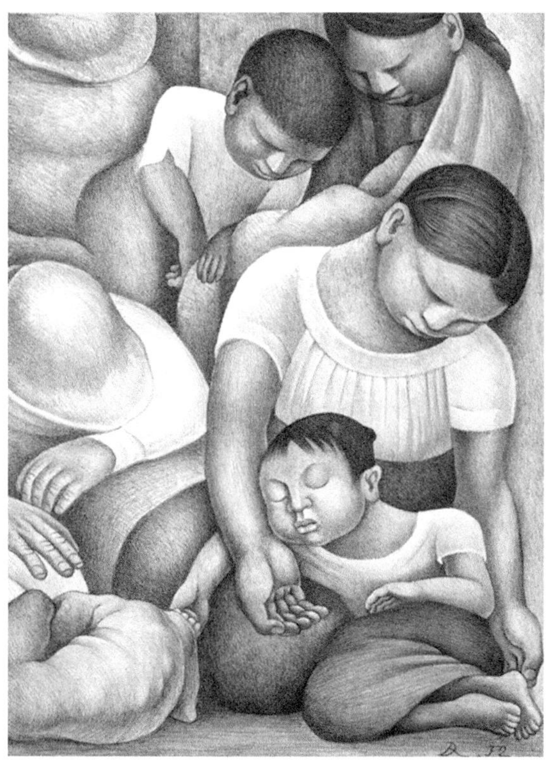

LEFT: Diego Rivera, *El Sueño* (1932). (© 2018 Banco de México Diego Rivera Frida Kahlo Museums Trust, Mexico, D.F. / Artists Rights Society [ARS], New York.)

BELOW: Henry Sugimoto, *Arrival in Camp Jerome* (1942). (Wakayama Civic Library, Wakayama, Japan.)

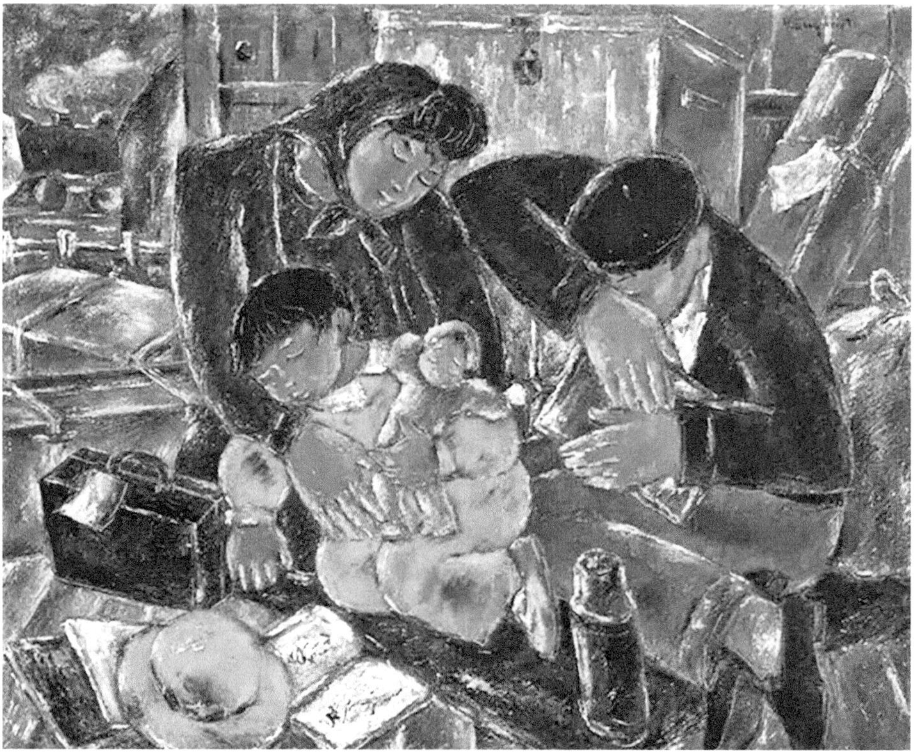

cution while finding temporary shelter. Yet no discernible imagery appears to explain the institutional causes behind their situation, since Sugimoto seemed intent on producing an immediate emotional and spiritual impression rather than one that called for political action.

The artist, however, was no mere mimic when appropriating styles and compositional perspectives. The circumstances of the war, and what he and his family endured, pushed him into new modes of originality. Sugimoto frequently relied on family members, especially his wife, Susie, and his daughter, Madeleine, as his models to advance the boundaries of his art. One memorable moment that the artist rendered during the initial removal process to the detention facility at Fresno focused on his daughter. After the family finished a packed meal of rice balls, she asked her mother when they could go home, thinking that the outing was a temporary picnic, rather than the beginning of a long-term exile. Sugimoto depicted several adaptations of mother and daughter in this heartrending instant. One of the best-known versions is *When Can We Go Home?* (1943), in which Sugimoto transposes the incident at the Fresno Assembly Center to the camps in Arkansas. Here, we see the mother in a frontal view holding forth her arms to embrace and comfort her child, the daughter with her back slightly to the observer and facing her parent. While doing so, Madeleine points left in the direction of home, signified by the buildings and bridges of the Bay Area in the background. The artist portrays both figures through muralist influences on a monumental scale with truncated perspectives, the mother in a yellow dress and the daughter in red. Perhaps making a statement about the visibility of their race, Sugimoto renders their skin tone in dark brown (even darker than in some of his earlier Japanese American subjects), a noticeable trait, given his access to a more varied palette at this later time. Multiple and overlapping Cubist shapes and images surround them: on the left, the aforementioned sights in California, while the prison camp towers stand on the right, together with local flora and fauna from Arkansas that curve into the foreground. These include a sunflower and a rattlesnake, the latter a threatening presence to the two central subjects. What appears as a translucent lightning bolt flashes in zigzag fashion across the middle of the composition, fracturing the painting into different panels, though each remain as part of the larger whole. This method recalls how, in the 1920s and 1930s, artists such as the precisionist Charles Demuth and the African American muralist Aaron Douglas employed background lines and shapes in similar ways, when splitting and forming compositional space. Starting in the lower-left corner of *When Can We Go Home?* the bolt shears upward toward the right across the two figures and then continues its path toward the upper left corner, suggesting the sudden and intense rupture of a family and a community from their established

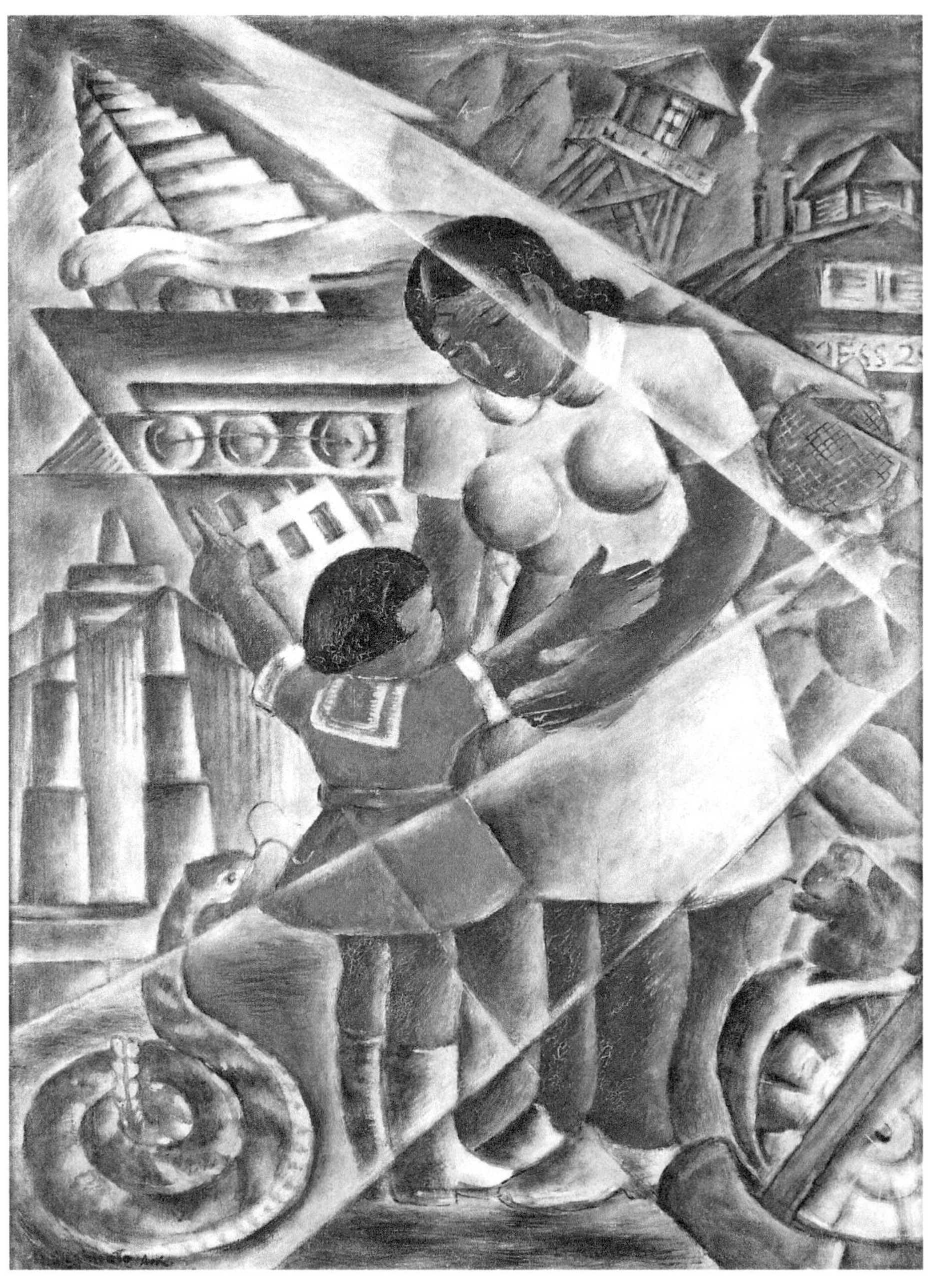

Henry Sugimoto, *When Can We Go Home?* (1943). (Japanese American National Museum [Gift of Madeleine Sugimoto and Naomi Tagawa, Japanese American National Museum, 92.97.3].)

moorings. Given this mix of elements and styles, the painting is one of Sugimoto's most original and provocative pieces from the war.

The artist's other scenes of families and communities adapting to hardships with little complaint both reinforce and undermine the idea of Japanese Americans as a model minority. In a host of portrayals, the subjects appear to build sustainable lives through common chores (bathing, laundry duties, gathering wood for fuel), social get-togethers (playing board games, eating at the mess hall), or displays of patriotism with the American flag (family portraits, Nisei soldiers in the U.S. Army leaving the camp to fight overseas). Although these depictions of supposed ordinariness under unusual circumstances lend a sense of stability to the populace's uncertain future, they also offer counterimages to those supplied by the federal government. When Sugimoto first began painting in his quarters so as not to be discovered, a U.S. Army film crew arrived at his door to record aspects of daily camp life to show the good treatment of Japanese Americans. Sugimoto recollected how the men instructed him and Susie to continue their activities so that these scenes could be documented. We see at the start of filming Sugimoto sitting at an easel in his barracks, looking toward the camera, when a director's clapboard appears and snaps, and he turns back to the canvas and begins to paint. He then repeats the painting sequence when standing outdoors with his work.[56] As Sugimoto recounted, the production team also filmed the mess hall with an abundance of provided food, but he noted that the camp population never ate so well as at that moment when posing for the cameras. Sugimoto understood that these acts of documenting on the part of the government, capturing the apparent everyday normality of incarcerated Japanese American lives, served the purpose of propaganda. In response, he worked within and around the filming process, due in part to the government's nonchalance about what it considered as recreational matters. "They don't care. So I was free to paint," he later told an interviewer. Sugimoto knew in this instance that he would be able to produce art as he wished, often in ways that challenged what the films recorded.[57]

As one example, Sugimoto painted several variations of a scene at the mess hall, in contrast to what was shot by the government crew. *Our Mess Hall* (1942) shows in flattened perspective a long table of eight people, four to each side, ranging from small children to a grandmother figure. A man in blue overalls sits in the bottom middle foreground scooping rice from a bowl into his mouth. A mother across the table from him tries to feed her child, as the boy resists her attempts with his hands up in protest. Others are engaged in various stages of their meal. Another rendition of this scene, *Mess Hall* (circa 1943), reveals additional details resulting from Sugimoto's more exact outlining practices and enlarged palette of colors. In both composi-

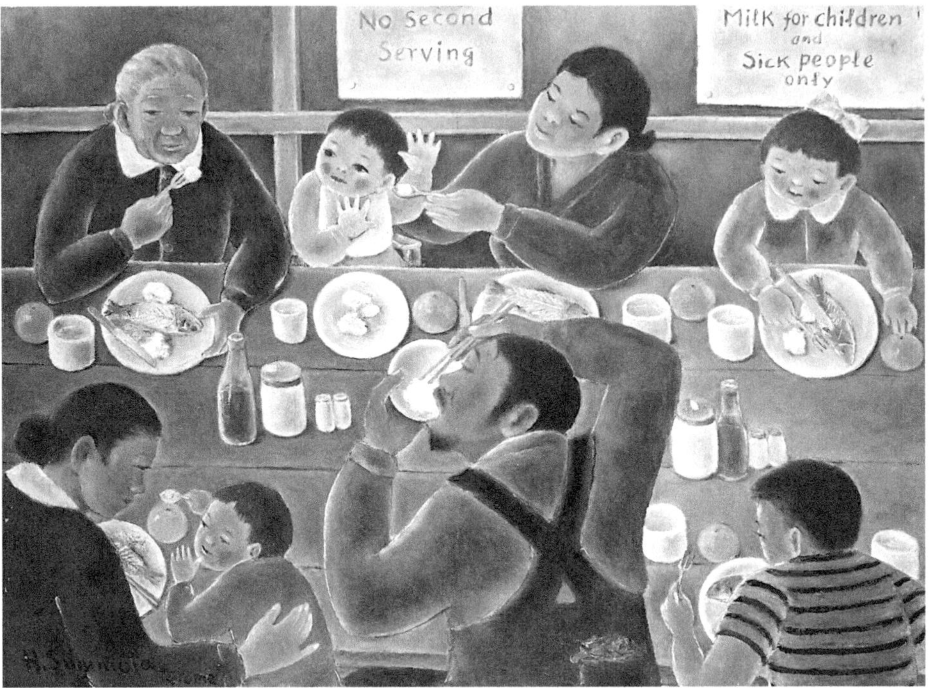

Henry Sugimoto, *No Second Serving* (circa 1970). (Japanese American National Museum [Gift of Madeleine Sugimoto and Naomi Tagawa, Japanese American National Museum, 92.97.113].)

tions, signs on the background wall read, "No Second Serving" and "Milk for children and Sick people only." Seen in the context of what Sugimoto recollected about the film crew at the mess hall with its excess of food, these paintings suggest more than mere documenting of an event, in fact disclosing the actual rationing of provisions. In this way, the artist challenged the government's narrative of benevolence, taking advantage of the institutional indifference toward his art and creating opportunities from that unconcern to record and to contest what occurred in the camps. We even perceive how Sugimoto's tone changed when he revisited the mess hall scene decades later with brighter colors and softer brushwork that establishes a buoyant atmosphere. The title, *No Second Serving* (circa 1970), which repeats the cautionary message on the wall, destabilizes this mood by emphasizing how people's sustenance was curbed. But the vibrancy of colors demonstrates a still lively community that endured despite the imposed shortages.[58]

Sugimoto's more direct statements about the psychological costs of confining civilians reveal themselves in other depictions. These images capture the unspoken or unseen traumas and humiliations experienced by Japanese

Americans. The titles of the works make certain that viewers understand the consequences of an incarceration without just cause. Some scenes reveal the affective toll that incarceration takes on the camp populace, others present circumstances laced with ironic commentary, while others do both. We perceive in them Sugimoto's adaptation of muralist styles and folk art sensibilities, with the paintings' truncated perspectives and proportions, their naïve appearance, and their themes of communal suffering from social injustice. Although it is unclear how Sugimoto became interested in folk art elements, he followed in the tradition of other modern artists, including the Postimpressionist Henri Rousseau, the Mexican muralists, and painters in the Harlem Renaissance, among others, who were attracted to primitive forms. *Am I an American Citizen?* (circa 1943) shows two men, broad, blocklike, and angled in posture, taking a break from chopping wood for fuel in the Arkansas forest. The figure on the right sits with his head in his hands, feelings of despair sapping his form. The other stands and looks at his companion in sympathy, the unanswered question of citizenship hanging over them. *Our Bus* (circa 1943) reveals the open backs of two trucks next to one another, which play on the Mexican muralists' penchant for pairing images for didactic purposes. The truck on the right carries Japanese Americans to some unspecified destination, perhaps to resettle elsewhere or to the Rohwer camp. The other on the left transports livestock, with a mother cow and her calf visible, corresponding to the human cargo, with parents standing behind their children. In the provocatively titled *Nisei Babies in Concentration Camp* (circa 1943), we see several infants clothed only in diapers, their white blanket that they inhabit presenting a perspective so flattened that it tilts up like a wall behind them. Meanwhile, an armed guard stands nearby to the left. Sugimoto adds a playful sense of irony when depicting one baby saluting, while another waves an American flag. But they do so out of view of the Army MP, each perhaps teasing the authority invested in the soldier, the conventional symbol of the nation's wartime sacrifices. Here, Sugimoto's blameless young figures and disturbing compositions highlight the government's dehumanizing cruelties, even as the uprooted populations assert their humanity through irony and emotion, and disrupt white mainstream definitions of what it means to be an "American."

One prevalent topic among Sugimoto's depictions of camp life focused on the Nisei men who volunteered from the camps to fight for the U.S. military in the segregated 442nd Regimental Combat Team in its European campaigns. A variety of scenes show them taking leave of their families, thus portraying the sacrifices of a model minority. In these cases, even with the federal government's power to confine their friends and families, they still proceed to fight for the nation's ideals on distant battlefields. This perspective

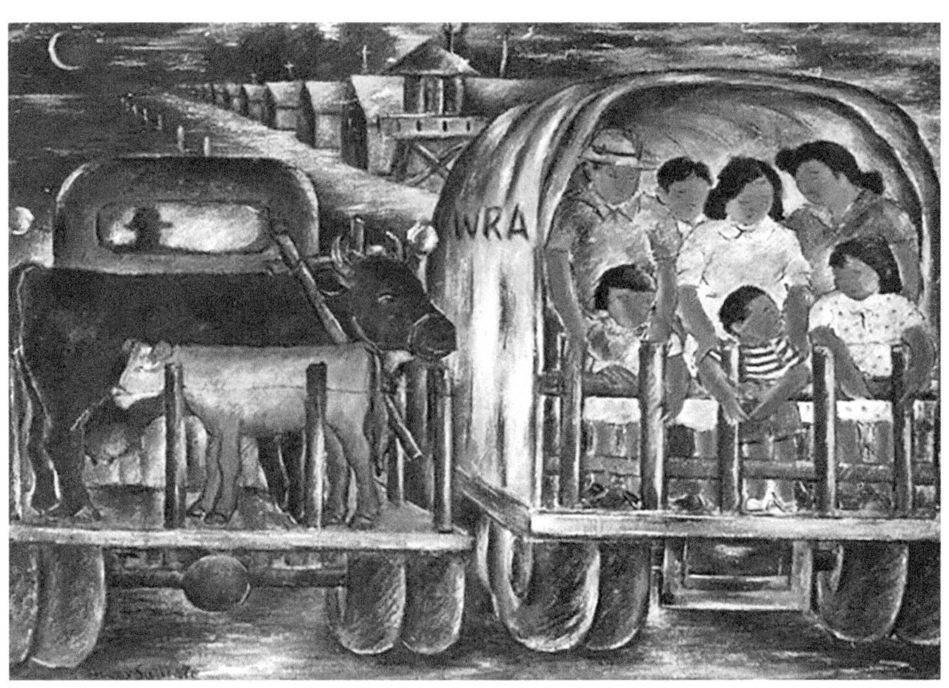

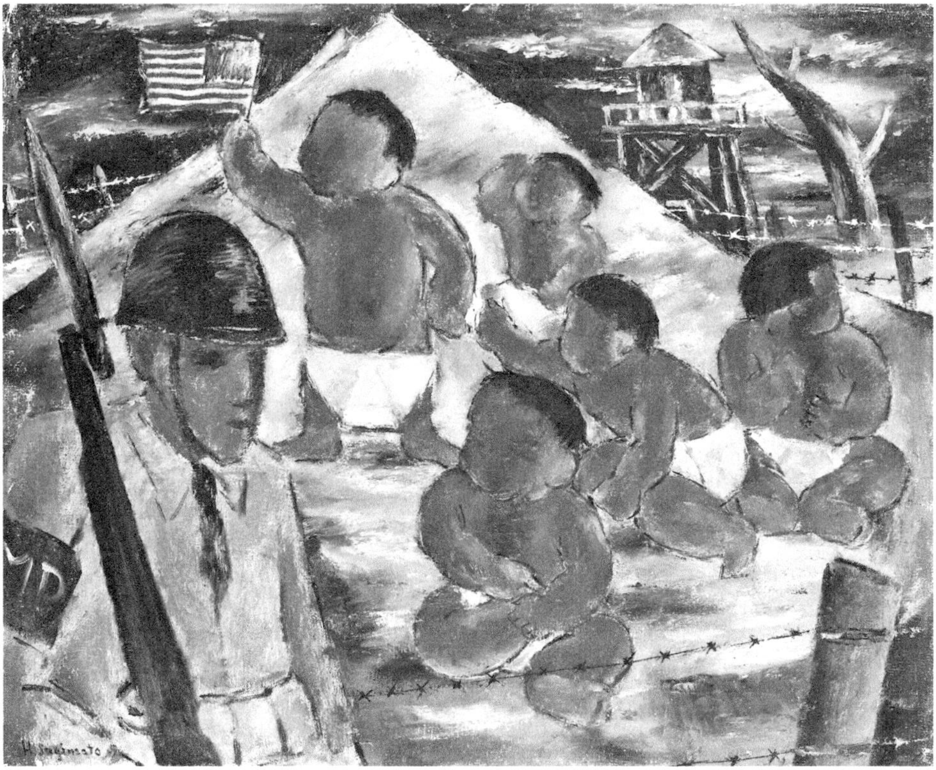

had personal ramifications for Sugimoto, his younger brother Ralph having served in the unit, for which he received a Purple Heart. Many of these portrayals also reflect the artist's Christian faith, in which the soldiers' sacrifices for the nation parallel Christ's sufferings for humankind. The departures from parents, wives, and children in the camps then reveal the broader impact on, and the more intimate moments within, Japanese American communities at large. But Sugimoto later recounted in interviews how the military's call to arms aroused mixed emotions among the camp populace at Jerome, since many resented their treatment by the government. More than a few realized the hypocrisy of fighting for a nation that imprisoned them and their families, while disregarding their rights. Others, however, felt compelled to fulfill their duty. Regarding the choices before the Nisei, Sugimoto noted that, "Some said to act according to justice while the others proposed to act on conscience but no one . . . showed them [any] definite way to follow" as to whether the young men should enlist or resist. Thus, in his scenes of the recruits' leave-taking from camp, Sugimoto engaged in no plain or easy patriotism.[59]

In one image, *Send Off Husband at Jerome Camp* (1943), a Nisei soldier leaves the confines of camp to fight for his country, while a ghastly, white-faced guard and a "STOP" sign block his wife and two children from proceeding further to say their farewells. The contrast between the Nisei soldier's sacrifices and the state's ability to detain civilians is apparent. The little girl's waving of the American flag symbolizes the hopes and values of the nation and partially covers the "S" on the literal sign of state authority. The word "STOP" then reads "TOP," reinforcing our attention on the top figure, the Nisei soldier, who is associated with the flag. This figure, in turn, embodies the American principles of freedom and democracy and of fighting for those ideals, in opposition to the surrounding signs representing repressive government authority. The painting can then be read as a development from *My Papa,* in which the FBI agent leads away the Japanese American farmer, as his family watches with unease. The soldier in *Send Off Husband at Jerome Camp* now goes off to war for a country that initially detained him, again with anxious family members left behind as observers. The families in each painting heighten the sense of disruption that results from these departures, the first due to the husband/father/farmer's questioned innocence and the second because of

FACING PAGE, TOP: Henry Sugimoto, *Our Bus* (circa 1943). (Wakayama Civic Library, Wakayama, Japan.)

FACING PAGE, BOTTOM: Henry Sugimoto, *Nisei Babies in Concentration Camp* (circa 1943). (Japanese American National Museum [Gift of Madeleine Sugimoto and Naomi Tagawa, Japanese American National Museum, 92.97.130].)

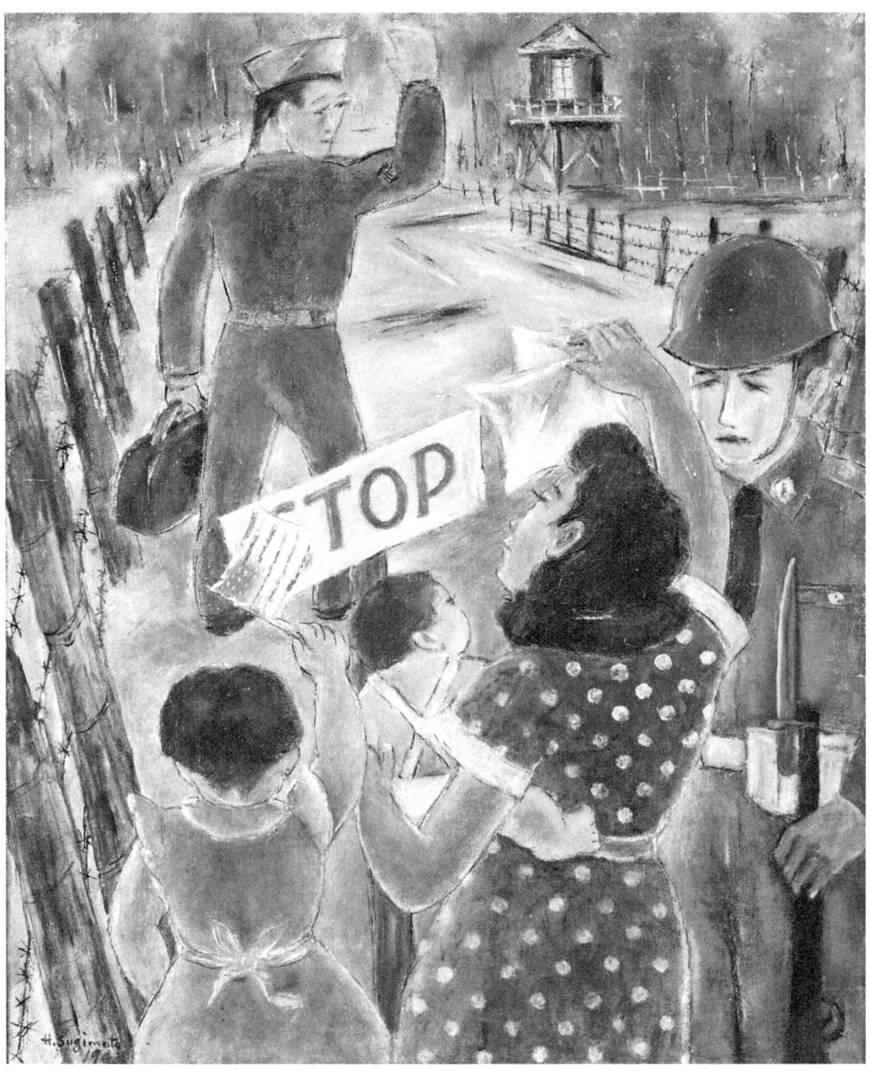

Henry Sugimoto, *Send Off Husband at Jerome Camp* (1943). (Japanese American National Museum [Gift of Madeleine Sugimoto and Naomi Tagawa, Japanese American National Museum, 92.97.1].)

the husband/father/soldier's impending sacrifices, with each set of mothers and children still placed in uncertain straits. The government's oppression thus functions in manifold ways when enacted against its own civilians, first envisioned as a farmer in blue overalls with a family. This institutional power then reconfigures itself to recruit the Nisei into military service, supposedly in order to uphold the nation's ideals of freedom and democracy when fighting overseas, a position that, as Sugimoto acknowledged, created more friction than consent among the camp population.[60]

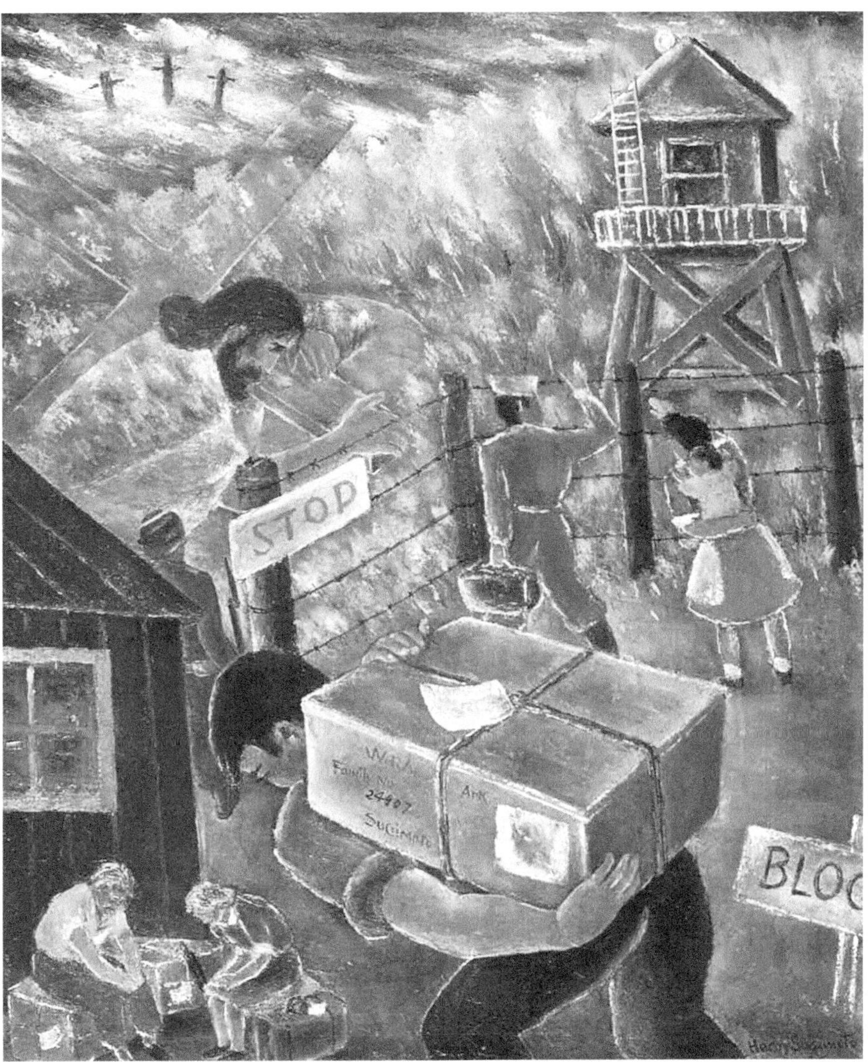

Henry Sugimoto, *Carrying Heavy Burden* (circa 1943). (Wakayama Civic Library, Wakayama, Japan.)

In other renderings of the camps, Sugimoto displayed a developing artistic and political sensibility by combining several different images into one larger narrative, framing them within national and Christian ideals. This practice becomes apparent in *Carrying Heavy Burden* (circa 1943), in which the artist displays three types of encumbrances endured by the imprisoned population. The first two burdens are borne by the two generations of Issei and Nisei family members. In the lower-left corner, a sitting Issei couple prays for the safety of their Nisei son, who, at the top right, leaves his wife and child to fight. This section comprises earlier individual studies, such as *Send Off Husband at*

Jerome Camp. The Issei parents appear in *Prayer for Safety* (circa 1943), which shows them in similar meditative poses with heads bowed, regarding their uncertain future once they have arrived at Jerome, and in *Old Parents Thinking about Their Son on the Battlefield* (circa 1944), in which a bust-like image of a young man in uniform appears as a vision between the two worried parents. In the middle space of *Carrying Heavy Burden* is the third load assumed by Christians in the camp. We see a man bent over by a large package on his back, a posture that faces and mirrors Christ carrying the cross, positioned slightly to the left above the man. Sugimoto included this image from another study, *Thinking about Christ* (1943). The artist's merging of these multiple images follows the methods of muralists, which later became an important element in his postwar pieces, in which he situated Japanese Americans in a larger epic of immigration, war, and confinement. In *Carrying Heavy Burden,* we again see evidence of not only Sugimoto's faith and how Japanese Americans replay the travails of Christ but also how the camp woes connect to one another. The three crosses at the painting's top left recall not only the crucifixion scene at Golgotha but also the sacrifices of Issei parents lending their sons to battle and the impending martyrdom of these Nisei soldiers, all intended for the benefit of humankind. In other versions of this painting, the three crosses become the numerous crosses in a cemetery, marking the gravesites of the Nisei soldiers who died for their country.

In another vein, Sugimoto wrestled with his status as a racialized cosmopolitan, as evidenced in his wartime self-portraits. A 1943 depiction captures one of his responses to confinement, a work developed from, but also proceeding beyond, his earlier depictions of himself. In contrast to the 1931 self-portrait examined earlier, the wartime likeness discloses a more mature artist, in that he surrounds himself with paintings already completed. We see in the background a still life and a few landscapes done in impressionist fashion. Although Sugimoto again wears his black beret, he sits in front of a canvas in the process of completion on the left, his signature noticeable on the bottom-right corner. His right hand holds a palette that generates a wider arrangement of colors on the whole of the self-portrait than seen in his prewar depiction. We also discern several artistic influences, with not only the impressionist landscapes and still lifes but also elements of Cubism noticeable on his left shirt shoulder and sleeve facing the viewer, with its sharp creases and angular forms. Sugimoto thus presents himself as a cosmopolitan in the conventional sense, in that his concerns are aesthetic, worldly, and apolitical. More noteworthy, he avoids any evidence of camp life, even in the shown paintings, suggesting a man who lives simply for art and who desires to transcend the everyday realities of his incarceration. In this way, Sugimoto defied

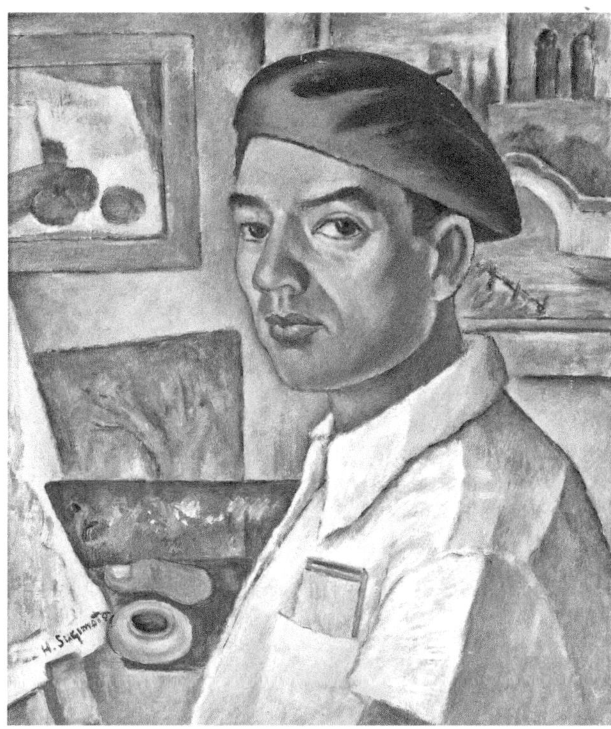

Henry Sugimoto, *Self-Portrait in Camp* (1943). (Japanese American National Museum [Gift of Madeleine Sugimoto and Naomi Tagawa, Japanese American National Museum, 92.97.5].)

his racialization by the state through a painting that appeared as if it could have been done anywhere, free from any institutional confines.

Sugimoto's talents eventually drew the notice of local artists and writers. H. Louis Freund, a resident artist and professor at Hendrix College in Conway, Arkansas, visited the Jerome camp and, after surveying Sugimoto's work, invited him to exhibit some pieces at the school. Once the WRA officials approved the event, other members of the college community soon became involved. The curator of art, Floy Katherine Hanson, organized the show, which opened in February 1944. Paul Faris, an English professor, wrote the news release for it, noting that Sugimoto's works "contain no suggestion of bitterness and are marked by tenderness and occasional humor." He concluded that the artist "and his family are loyal Americans and members of the Presbyterian [Church]." By emphasizing the Sugimotos' loyalty, Christianity, lack of bitter feelings, and willingness to show humor, Faris established them as a nonthreatening model minority for public consumption.[61] Hendrix College officials reasoned that they needed to position Sugimoto in this manner, given that the exhibition opened at the time when the federal government released a report about Japanese imperial forces abusing American prisoners of war during the Philippines campaigns at Bataan and Corregidor in 1942. The exhibit curators thus wanted to distance the Sugimotos from the potential anger from white audiences that might associate the painter with these overseas atrocities.[62] At the same time, Sugimoto relied on his respectable conduct to gain favors from WRA administrators and white benefactors, such as obtaining art materials to teach classes in the camps, or accepting the chance to show his work beyond the guard towers and barbed wire. For a cosmopolitan who lived for his art, this model of belief and behavior was not merely posturing on his part: it was the way his persona functioned and how he framed his worldview. He needed to negotiate opportunities to keep producing, exhibiting, and selling his work.

Invited to attend the Hendrix College exhibition's opening, Sugimoto and his wife, Susie, obtained permission from the WRA to journey outside of Jerome. These ventures were not uncommon, given that Japanese Americans roamed in and out of the nearby towns and other vicinities for work or shopping expeditions. One WRA official, Eudora Akin, even accompanied Sugimoto to New Orleans in 1944, when he tried to find employment there but was unsuccessful. Although other artists might not have had the same freedom of movement to appear at exhibitions as the Sugimotos did at Hendrix College, they were still able to display their works through the sponsorship of various art associations and civic groups.[63] Venues in the Bay Area exhibited paintings by students of Chiura Obata who were housed at the detention facility at Tanforan in San Bruno, California, and at the camp at Topaz, Utah. One show in Cambridge, Massachusetts, entitled *Relocation Center Art Exhibition,* included pieces by Japanese Americans from all ten camps and drew nationwide notice. Some of Sugimoto's works also toured throughout the United States for two years in an exhibition sponsored by the California Watercolor Society. As Gordon H. Chang observes, these art shows not only served aesthetic purposes but also gained Japanese Americans a degree of visibility that humanized them to the white mainstream of society. The traveling artwork in this way challenged other graphic depictions of Asians that resorted to racial caricatures as war propaganda, especially against Japan.[64]

Yet Sugimoto could not escape the enduring racism and suspicions against him, despite his standing as a respected artist. When journeying with Susie to Hendrix College via Little Rock, he recalled the tense atmosphere along the way. *At Little Rock Station* (1944) records the mixed reactions the couple receives from white passengers. The artist captures an ambiguous moment in southern segregation, wherein public areas such as bus stations and train platforms implied not strict separation but racial intermingling.[65] We discern the curious, if not sympathetic, look of the black porter on the bottom left, counterbalanced by the white racist cab driver on the bottom right, who ges-

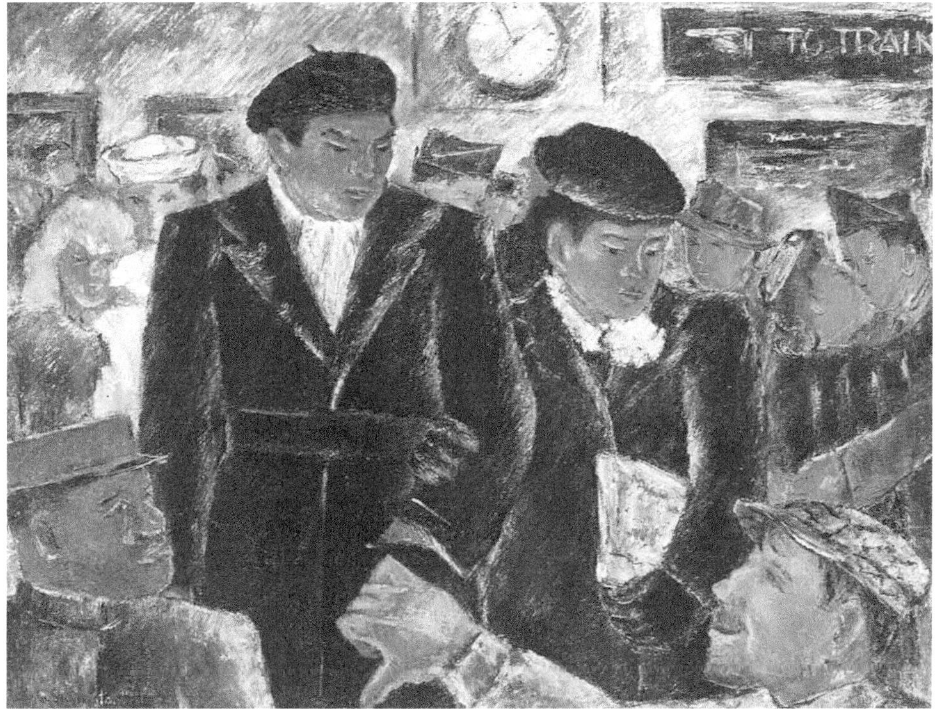

Henry Sugimoto, *At Little Rock Station* (1944). (Wakayama Civic Library, Wakayama, Japan.)

tures his "thumbs down" disapproval of the Sugimotos. The couple occupies the middle space of the composition, suggesting that Japanese Americans were caught between, but also challenged, the categories of "black" and "white" in the Jim Crow South.[66] Indeed, the artist renders the skin tone of the Sugimotos a light brown, a shifting marker of race located somewhere between the porter's darker brown skin and the lighter tan face of the cabbie. Sugimoto realized the extent of this improvised and indeterminate racial status of Asians in Arkansas and later recounted in a 1982 interview his own confusion about where to sit on the bus. Considering the dictates of segregation and of his own racialization at this moment, the artist assumed that he should proceed to the "colored" section but was told to place himself in the "white people's place." This more privileged position, however, only conjured for him prewar memories of racial oppression against the Issei in California. Reflecting on the treatment of African Americans in the South, he noted that "colored people [were] living so poor and I'm so pity, like Japanese immigrants [who] came to [the] United States." As he acknowledged from these entangled instances, issues of race, class, and region came under the rule and resolve of white supremacy.[67]

In the painting *At Little Rock Station,* the racial hostility expressed toward Henry and Susie Sugimoto is palpable, but more complicated than at first imagined, even with their newfound "white" positioning. Here, the target of the white figure's disgust includes not only the couple's same racial makeup as the Japanese enemy but also their cosmopolitan presence. Their clothing, signified by the artist's beret and his wife's fashionable hat, and their long winter coats, implies a certain amount of class privilege and sophistication that reinforces their foreignness. Surrounded by servicemen going off to war, they stand among, but also above, the emblems of southern working-class life: that is, the white cabbie with his flat cap and the black porter with his signifying hat. Sugimoto, then, discloses a fraught moment in his artistic imaginings of race, class, and region. Occupying the middle space of the composition, he is reminded by others that the racialized cosmopolitan couple does not belong anywhere. This state of instability and itinerancy would reoccur in June 1944, when the family endured their third move, this time to the Rohwer camp near McGehee, Arkansas (about thirty miles from Jerome), where they would remain for over a year until the war's end.

Cartographies of Containment: Postwar Paintings

After their release from Rohwer in early August 1945, a few days before the official surrender of Japan, the Sugimotos and their relatives had to decide where to go. The extended family members eventually dispersed to different parts of the country, with Susie's parents moving back to Hanford, while Henry's relocated with his brother Ralph to Cleveland, Ohio. Rather than return to their prewar location in California, Sugimoto wanted to expand his artistic opportunities, thinking that New York City would provide better exposure and contacts for his talents. Susie readily agreed. Once they arrived, other Japanese immigrant families who had already relocated there helped them with finding an apartment, some used furniture, and other necessities for starting life anew in their Harlem neighborhood. A visiting minister from their Hanford days relied on his community sources and found Susie a job as a typist for the local Baptist church. But Henry's artistic ambitions would be disappointed. Dealers and galleries were not interested in paintings on the mass confinement, let alone works done in a social realist manner, especially when the New York market preferred abstract expressionists in the immediate postwar years. To help with the family finances, Sugimoto found employment designing textile fabrics for several companies, illustrating children's books (including one for Yoshiko Uchida), and writing Japanese captions for English-language films sent to Japan. Meanwhile, he continued to paint in his spare time, reworking the wartime compositions and adding scenes of New York City street life to his repertoire.[68]

Perhaps because of these pressures to establish new living arrangements in another environment, Sugimoto did not produce much art during the period between 1945 and 1960. The few paintings completed at this time, however, reveal how he began to revise his wartime work and to extend his awareness of the immigrant Japanese presence in the United States. One piece, *To Find a Job* (circa 1950), is one of his first on migrants, which shows a lone Japanese laborer walking along railroad tracks and following the sign toward Hanford in search of work. He carries a suitcase in hand as well as a bundle on his back with various cooking utensils hanging from it. The man also wears a hat and a suit, both bluish-gray in color, with a blue shirt underneath. Bulky in build and sporting a beard, this figure recalls both earlier and later renditions of the man in blue overalls, often portrayed with a similar bewhiskered mien and blue shirt. *To Find a Job*, then, may have been a way for Sugimoto not only to think about Japanese migrants but also to trace the origins of this archetypal character and his ensuing family life, which began with the artist's prior wartime compositions, such as *My Papa* (circa 1942).

Then there is an intriguing scene from the Fresno to Arkansas trip that Sugimoto distinctly recollected, which consisted of a stop to let the civilians out to stretch and get some fresh air. These moments usually occurred in some desolate place, he noted, with the military police guards cordoning off an area and pointing their weapons at the passengers to ensure no escape.[69] In *Take Fresh Air* (1957), the signs of state power enacted on civilians proved a powerful, emotive way not only to record the tragedy of the mass removal and imprisonment but to highlight the absurdity of it as well. The style of the work does not fit any particular impressionist or muralist approach that Sugimoto used in other paintings. Instead, *Take Fresh Air* appears to disclose an experiment in folk art forms, with its flattened perspective and the naïve look of the composition and its figures. The Japanese Americans, in their numerous stances and wondrous array of colorful clothing, occupy much of the painting's center, positing a lively and enduring community. Their small, almost indistinguishable figures stretch out, converse or play catch with one another, and care for children. Life for them continues as much as it can, given the circumstances. But the artist encloses this populace between the train in the background and the larger-sized, stiffly postured soldiers forming a half-circle from the immediate right foreground to the whole left side of the canvas, these mechanical and human barriers rendered mainly in browns and grays. Sugimoto even makes viewers complicit in the federal government's dark actions when locating them in the same line of sight that the U.S. Army troops

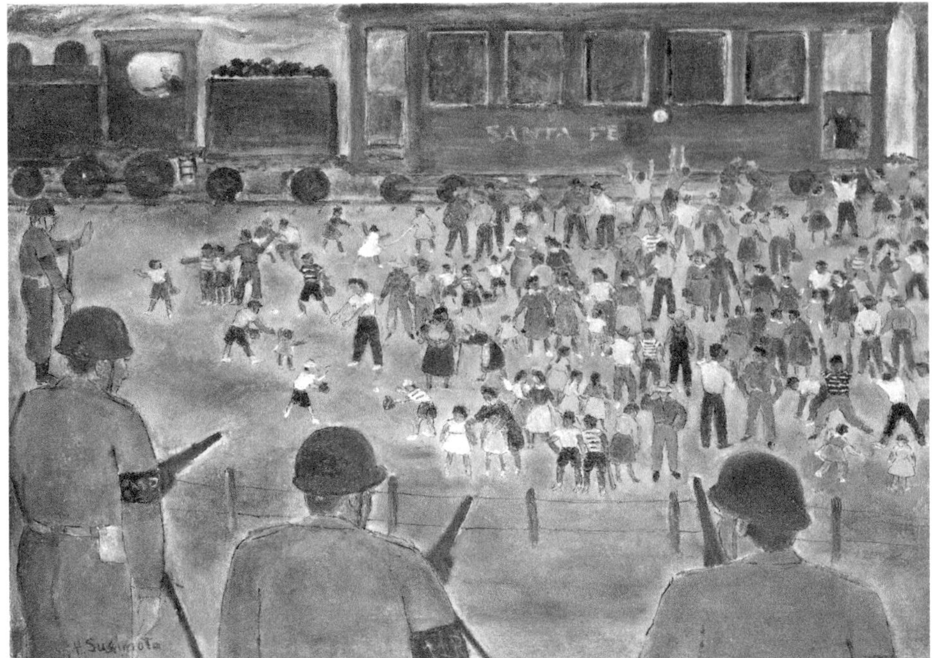

Henry Sugimoto, *Take Fresh Air* (1957). (Japanese American National Museum [Gift of Madeleine Sugimoto and Naomi Tagawa, Japanese American National Museum, 92.97.55].)

have of their Japanese American charges. One literally looks over the MPs' backs and shoulders and down the barrels of their machine guns at the scene they are responsible for controlling. Thus, the overall portrayal of the rest stop has an awakening effect on the spectator. Sugimoto alerts us through our implicated gaze to remember the removal and racial segregation of civilians who had posed no threat to the nation at large. Given the social and political expectations of the Cold War years in which he produced the piece, however, one can imagine why it would not find a venue or an audience.

Yet, by 1965, Sugimoto had completed an impressive array of work reconceiving the wartime incarceration and the prewar history of Japanese immigration. Much of this art retraces episodes of his camp life from the 1940s, both in paintings and in woodblock prints.[70] Other compositions veer toward new muralist directions that disclose the artist's larger, epic vision of Japanese Americans that explored the interwoven themes of migration, war, and confinement. Thus, when viewed as a series, we see how the early twentieth-century Japanese migrations connect to the wartime incarceration and to the dropping of atomic bombs on Japan.

Much of this new course that Sugimoto took in his artwork developed from his postwar travels abroad. In 1962, he retired from the textile design company for which he had worked during the prior several years. He then traveled to France and Japan, believing that these trips were his final chance to have an impact with his paintings. The two countries held great significance for him, the former offering his first major opportunities to make his name in art, the latter because he had not visited since he had left over forty years before. In interviews from the 1980s, Sugimoto did not offer much detail about his two-year stay in Paris, aside from revealing that he did some painting and sketching. As his biographer, Kristine Kim, suggests, "The scenery no longer held the same magical charm" that it had during his initial visit in the 1930s. Attempting to recapture this youthful moment was complicated not only by the transformations within France since his travels there three decades before but also by the wartime incarceration that had kindled new desires and directions in his art.[71] This changed feeling toward his work was expressed in the fact that he did not paint many camp landscapes in impressionist fashion during the postwar years. Sugimoto's travels to Japan in 1964, and especially to his hometown of Wakayama, made a greater lasting imprint on his artistic focus. The painter basked in renewed relations with his extended family and involvement in the Japanese art scene. At one point, Sugimoto was invited to exhibit some of his work as part of an annual art collective, the Nikakai. The members discouraged him from presenting any of his wartime camp pieces, since they felt that the public still wanted to avoid reminders of anything associated with the Pacific War. The trip, however, proved a success. Sugimoto noted that the paintings he had brought with him sold for a much greater sum than he usually earned from American sales of his work. It was a pleasing moment that recalled his earlier successes in the 1930s, when he relied on Japanese patronage of his art.[72]

Sugimoto's lack of success in the postwar years in the United States was due in part to how abstract expressionism began to rule the art market, dominated by the likes of Willem de Kooning, Jackson Pollock, Barnett Newman, and Mark Rothko, among others. Even though the public initially remained indifferent at best, or surly at worst, toward the new style, postwar expressionism and other varieties of abstract art became the predominant symbol of American freedom and originality.[73] The federal government, through the State Department and the CIA, even sponsored overseas tours of American modernist art as a Cold War strategy to advertise the types of liberality allowed in the United States. At the same time, as other studies suggest, abstract expressionism in particular became a mode of political resistance to McCarthyism and to the suffocating demands of the Cold War.[74] Sugimoto, unlike other Japanese American artists, such as Hideo Date, Miné Okubo, and Hisako Hibi, never considered abstract art a possible avenue to explore.

He intimated in a later interview that it did not appeal to his tastes, since the style was too much a matter of "anything goes."[75] Then again, his reliance on aspects of social realism made it more difficult for him to gain acceptance in the postwar art world, given its decline in popularity. That his works also addressed a taboo subject, the wartime confinement, only added to his inability to garner more critical or public notice.

Yet Sugimoto's continued adherence to muralist and social realist elements suggest that these methods still proved effective for him, especially for addressing the topics of Japanese American confinement and prewar Japanese immigration. In this sense, he was not too different from the African American artists who also engaged in social realism long after its heyday in the 1930s and early 1940s.[76] For example, we can compare Sugimoto's career trajectory with that of Hale Woodruff's. During the war, Woodruff explored similar issues of racial discrimination, painting allegorical views of African American history when based in Atlanta. This is not to say that Sugimoto and Woodruff influenced one another stylistically, or that enduring black poverty and degradation were similar to what Japanese Americans faced in the United States. The artists' careers and interests, however, ran on parallel tracks that reveal similar cosmopolitan ways of envisioning their subjects. Both began painting with an admiration for the French Postimpressionists. Both traveled to Mexico in the 1930s and learned from the work of muralists (Woodruff even studied under Rivera). Both also relocated to New York City to continue their work from the 1940s onward.[77]

But here the similarities end. Unlike the postwar African American muralists, many of whom were steeped in the radical leftist politics of earlier decades, Sugimoto disclosed only muted sensibilities, even going out of his way to claim that he was apolitical. Furthermore, what aided African American artists in sustaining their work were the historically black colleges, small businesses, and community centers that provided them sites on which to paint murals. Throughout the early Cold War, Mexico City also became a safe haven for expatriate African Americans and others to create a variety of art without the burdens of anticommunist harassment that they encountered in the United States. Art collectives, such as the Taller de Gráfica Popular, provided African American artists with a collaborative atmosphere in which to produce work alongside their Mexican brethren, forming in the process a transnational aesthetic through shared techniques, themes, and audiences.[78] Sugimoto had no such institutional support. Nor was he able to attract much public notice for his art until the 1970s and beyond, when critics, curators, and activists saw its artistic as well as political and historical value that spoke to their contemporary concerns regarding the unjust exercise of authority and the resistance to it.

Woodruff and others who depicted large, multipart narratives in their murals, however, corresponded with Sugimoto's broad view of Japanese American history that connected migrants who came to the United States in the early twentieth century to what occurred during the Pacific War. We see in Woodruff's *Amistad Murals* (1938) and *The Negro in California History— Settlement and Development* (1949) how the artist traced the long-reaching impact of Africans and African Americans on the United States and its history. His mentor Rivera and other Mexican muralists indicated through their art how the past as allegory could be used as political commentary on continuing social injustices and as a call for reform, if not revolution.[79] Sugimoto expressed no developed intent to render the oppressive conditions of Japanese Americans into a critique of liberalism or of its institutional failures, even though such views are evident in his artwork and in his later interviews. But his scenes of immigration and prewar settlement that connected to his previous work on the wartime confinement aligned with these other artists' objectives: charting the racial prejudice encountered and their subjects' persistence in shaping their own lives and in asserting their humanity. Through the representative man in blue overalls, Sugimoto delved further into the past, using his working-class protagonist as a chronic marker of the Japanese presence in American and transpacific history. It is through this recurring figure, then, by which the artist could depict and relate the themes of immigration, incarceration, and war as parts of a larger, epic whole.

By the 1960s and onward, Sugimoto not only painted on larger canvases but also paired several of them in ways that, when viewed together, linked the historical movements of war and immigration across the Pacific. Central to these works are Japanese American figures that, in their migrations across the Pacific, occupied ambivalent and exposed positions that played on the shifting definitions of "Japanese" and "American." The artist continued to adapt his postwar style, turning to more precise outlining and brighter, oil-based color schemes. Compared to the wartime works, these newer renderings are also greater in scale to match the significance and enormity of the topics presented, with canvases measuring on average fifty-five inches by forty inches. Thus, despite the setbacks in his artistic goals, the postwar years were some of the most creative in Sugimoto's career, building on a hybrid style that merged his formal training with muralist and folk art sensibilities.

One pair of Sugimoto's paintings focuses on the migration of Japanese picture brides to the United States and the legal restrictions limiting their entry. Each portrayal has a truncated geographical perspective, from which the viewer discerns both Japan and the United States across a minimized Pacific Ocean, with Japanese populations inhabiting each shore. The first work, *Picture Bride* (circa 1965), draws on the muralist strategy of collapsing space

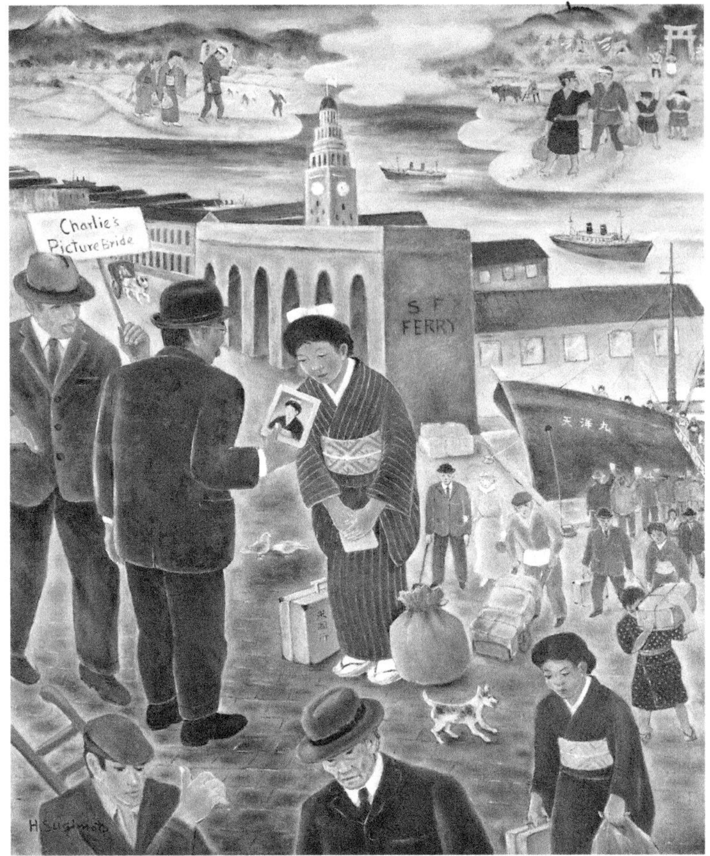

Henry Sugimoto, *Picture Bride* (circa 1965). (Japanese American National Museum [Gift of Madeleine Sugimoto and Naomi Tagawa, Japanese American National Museum, 92.97.108].)

and time in one frame or composition, showing the vastness of Japanese immigration. At the top of the canvas is Japan, where we perceive Mount Fuji as well as farming villages positioned in the background, with men leaving their homes and families earlier in the nineteenth century. Meanwhile, modern steamships traverse the ocean. The arrival of picture brides at a San Francisco pier in the early twentieth century occupies most of the foreground, with a few Japanese men in Western clothes looking at photographs to match with the faces of the incoming women. The new arrivals walk from right to left at an upward angle, from the docked ships toward the viewer, lending a sense of momentum and promise to the scene. By situating Japanese immigration as a transpacific process that incorporates ancestral and adopted homelands from the nineteenth century onward, Sugimoto provides a geographic and chronological grandeur to this history.

The second work, an untitled piece featuring the words "STOP PICTURE BRIDE" (circa 1965), recalls the 1924 immigration restrictions that further

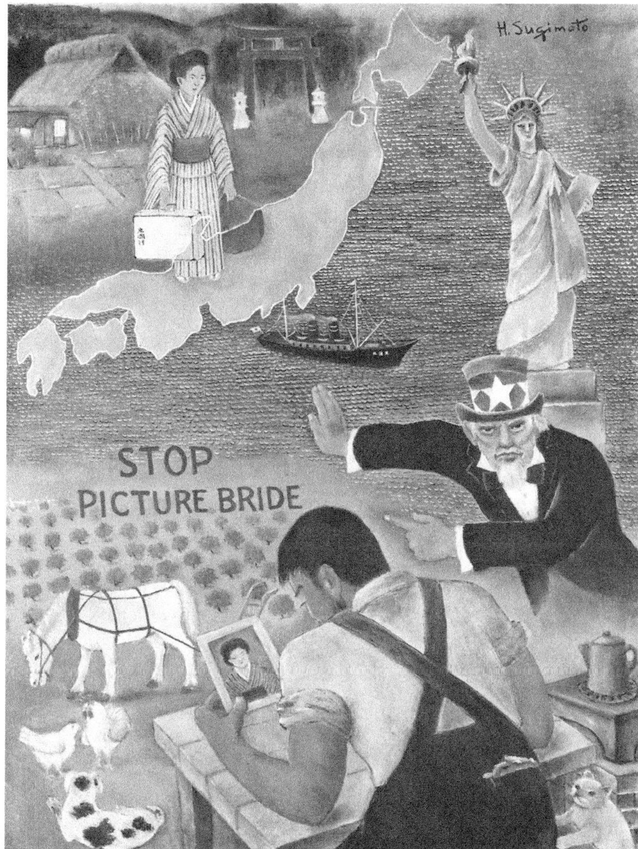

Henry Sugimoto, untitled (circa 1965), featuring the words "STOP PICTURE BRIDE."(Japanese American National Museum [Gift of Madeleine Sugimoto and Naomi Tagawa, Japanese American National Museum, 92.97.121].)

curtailed migrants from Asia, along with those from southern and eastern Europe, to the United States. In a telling comparison of American ideals and the U.S. government's practices, Sugimoto positions on the right side of the canvas the Statue of Liberty above Uncle Sam. In the top left of the painting, the picture bride wears a kimono and stands on a map of Japan. She also holds her baggage near a ship ready to cross the ocean to the United States. Her placement is almost parallel with the Statue of Liberty. Uncle Sam appears in the lower-right frame, looking sternly at a bearded man in blue overalls located in the immediate foreground. In turn, this Japanese farmer sits at a kitchen table surrounded by his crops and livestock on the American side of the ocean and looks at a picture of his intended bride. Meanwhile, glaring at the farmer, Uncle Sam holds his right arm and hand in the halt position directed toward the picture bride above him. As he points at the red words "STOP PICTURE BRIDE" with his left hand, his extended arms divide the picture horizontally.

In this rendering, the disparities between American ideals and practices appear in gendered and racialized forms. Uncle Sam's motion to stop the picture bride replays the Army MP's actions in the earlier wartime camp scenes. The "STOP" sign in *Send Off Husband at Jerome Camp* that halts the mother and her children from proceeding further from the camp confines when the Nisei soldier departs, for instance, implies the unfair exercise of institutional power, as it does in the untitled work representing the immigration restrictions against picture brides. Sugimoto associates Uncle Sam, like the Army MP, with legal and martial might. Depicted as an angry and aggressive white patriarch of the nation, Uncle Sam replays a version of his classic "I Want You" face and finger-pointing image used as a World War I recruiting poster beckoning Americans to make the world safe for democracy. But the artist transforms this figure's message and body posture to the more exclusionary "I Don't Want You" directed at Asian immigrants. The corresponding female figures of the picture bride and the Statue of Liberty in their side-by-side stances, however, suggest representations of the nation's more fully embodied ideals. The migrant woman's ability to help build families and communities supports the efforts of the man in blue overalls, who appears amid the signs of domestic stability. Adding to this scene, the statue's symbolic power of freedom and equality aligns with the nation's principles of color blindness, marking the contradictions between Uncle Sam's government policies and Lady Liberty's values. That the Statue of Liberty is "colored" as blue, in line with the ocean's hue, serves to transform both Asians and southern and eastern Europeans, groups seen by the nation's mainstream as not "white," into acceptable immigrants.[80] That the statue also appears on the West Coast signifies its importance beyond its actual location on the East Coast and its applicability to Ellis Island, where the southern and eastern Europeans arrived. Liberty's embrace now includes Asians in the West too. The painting thus implies a level of racial consciousness and immigrant solidarity that applies to the Japanese in particular and perhaps to Asian migrants and others in general, their presence contesting the domain of "whiteness." From this perspective, the Statue of Liberty itself is a racialized cosmopolitan, a welcoming, inclusive, colored symbol to the world, even as it must acquiesce in this principle to the overriding state power and racial restrictions represented by Uncle Sam.

A work that proceeds forward in chronology from the picture bride paintings, although completed around the same time, is an untitled piece featuring the partially obscured words "NO JAPS WANTED" (circa 1965). This picture reflects the prewar prejudices faced by Japanese American communities, as depicted through the bearded man in blue overalls and his family. The husband, wife, and two children are outdoors, perhaps in an orchard, given the low wooden fence and the trees in the background, in front of which is a large

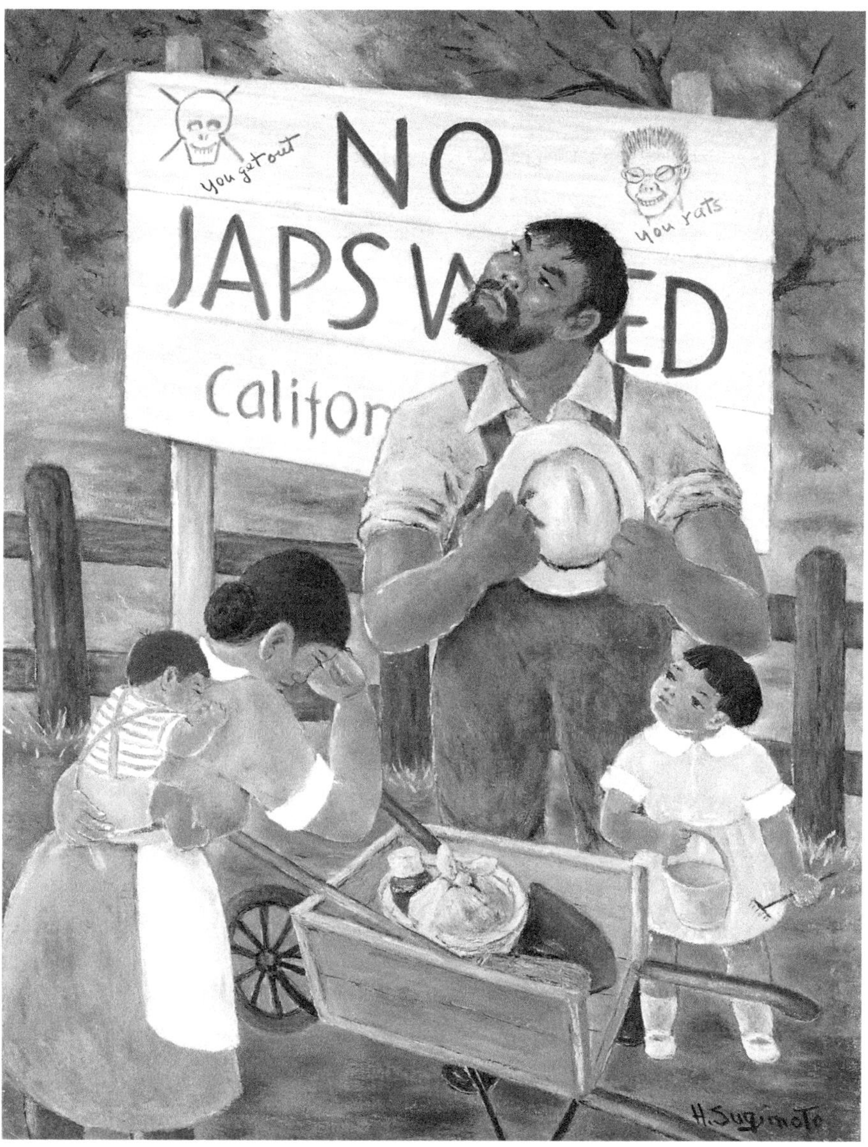

Henry Sugimoto, untitled (circa 1965), featuring the partially obscured words "NO JAPS WANTED." (Japanese American National Museum [Gift of Madeleine Sugimoto and Naomi Tagawa, Japanese American National Museum, 92.97.122].)

makeshift sign with the message "NO JAPS WANTED." Smaller illustrations appear in the top corners: a skull and crossbones with the phrase "you get out" on the left, and a caricatured head of an Asian man with slanted eyes with "you rats" printed underneath it on the right. The man in blue overalls stands before the sign, partially blocking the word "California," indicating the location of this incident, his body facing the viewer, but with his head tilted back toward the threatening message. His facial expression reveals concern, if not anger, as he grips his straw hat in both hands. The wife stands in the lower-left foreground, a baby carried on her back, as she lowers her head and cries into her hands. The puzzled young daughter stands to the right by her father, her head also angled in parallel fashion toward the sign to see what is upsetting him. We again discern the artist's reliance on social realist sensibilities, as he shows the figures in muscular, blocky forms. Sugimoto positions the family within a triangular formation, in which the father's head acts as the apex, while the bodies of the other members establish the sides and the two lower vertices. A wheelbarrow in front of them adds to part of the base. The father's two arms holding his hat upward toward his chest form a smaller, concentric triangle within the larger framing. Yet, within this geometric signal of supposed order within a family hierarchy, its fleeting stability cannot sustain or protect itself against a society's eruption of undue racism and the resulting anguish it causes.

This work becomes part of the larger narrative Sugimoto was creating about Japanese Americans. Read in sequence, what occurs in the painting with the "NO JAPS WANTED" sign follows from *To Find a Job,* with the initial arrival of the bearded man, and then *Picture Bride* and the untitled piece with the phrase "STOP PICTURE BRIDE" on it, with some of the Japanese migrant women able to enter the United States while others are denied. The reappearance of the man in blue overalls in these works points to the continuing racist obstacles and threats against the unwanted presence of Japanese on the West Coast. But families soon develop, despite the legislative hurdles. Furthermore, the untitled painting featuring the "NO JAPS WANTED" sign anticipates what will occur in the two renderings of *My Papa,* when the FBI agent comes for the man in blue overalls after the attack on Pearl Harbor. Sugimoto even painted the family figures in the later version of *My Papa* (circa 1965) in the same clothing colors as those worn by the family standing in front of the "NO JAPS WANTED" sign, the parents in blue and the young daughter in a lime-green dress. Although not necessarily the same clan, its members become a constant marker of the racial prejudice and the social transformations that Japanese Americans endure. The postwar paintings in this way connect the prior individual studies that Sugimoto completed during the war, with his scenes of camp life, into a broader overview of ethnic minority experiences that he began tracing in the 1950s and 1960s.

Another pair of paintings presents Sugimoto's most expansive and significant statement about the Pacific War and its effects on Japanese Americans. In two mural-like narratives, he framed the onset and the end of U.S. involvement in World War II through the attack on Pearl Harbor in December 1941 and the bombings of Hiroshima and Nagasaki in August 1945, with Japanese Americans caught between the destruction in both epochal moments. Each portrayal focuses on their reactions to these historical events, causing great concern to the figures involved. Sugimoto situates the bombing scenes in the upper-left and upper-right-hand corners of his two paintings. In the first (circa 1965), which is untitled and features the newspaper headline "Japanese Planes Bombed Pearl Harbor," we see the Japanese aircraft destroying the U.S. battleships, with plumes of flame and smoke rising amid their towers, an image made familiar from news photographs that remain prominent in American collective memory. In the second, *Bombing of Relatives Homeland, 1945* (circa 1965), the mushroom cloud of an atomic blast emerges over the destruction unleashed on a Japanese city, with a tiny shadow of an American B-29 flying away after dropping its payload. Sugimoto locates each scene in the two paintings within corresponding scalloped, cloud-like forms floating above the main Japanese American figures. In this way, the outlines of the upper-corner sections of the artwork, when positioned side by side, mimic the shape of theater curtains pulled back to reveal the central characters as part of a larger historical drama.

As its main focus, the untitled work presents a three-member Japanese American family in their kitchen. The parents sit at the table with a radio, listening with concern to the news of the Japanese attack. A newspaper with the headline "Japanese Planes Bombed Pearl Harbor" lies nearby on the floor in the lower left-hand corner. The little boy stands with his back to the viewer, looking out the window and watching a bird fly away. This image recalls Sugimoto's work *Freedom Day Came* (1945), a painting made while he was still in the camp at Rohwer. This earlier piece shows a young man sitting with elbows on a table, chin resting on hands, pondering a bird in an opened-door cage, with a map of the United States framing them in the background. The man, like the bird, considers where he might resettle once released from his confinement. In the 1965 untitled piece, however, the bird in flight is a portent of dangers to come. That is, the boy sees his youth, his promise, and his freedom flitting away from him. But since his back is turned from his parents, he also fails to see their worried countenances and thus cannot fully process what is happening at that instant. The parents listen to the radio with worried expressions, an image developed from a previous work, *Attacked Pearl Harber* [*sic*] *(Attacked Pearl Harbor Hawaii)* (1947). In the later rendition, Sugimoto locates the family in Hanford, California, as the local school pennant hanging on the wall suggests. Symbols of Americanism also decorate the room, with a portrait of Abraham Lincoln and an American flag positioned alongside the pennant. But none of these signifiers of loyalty and patriotism

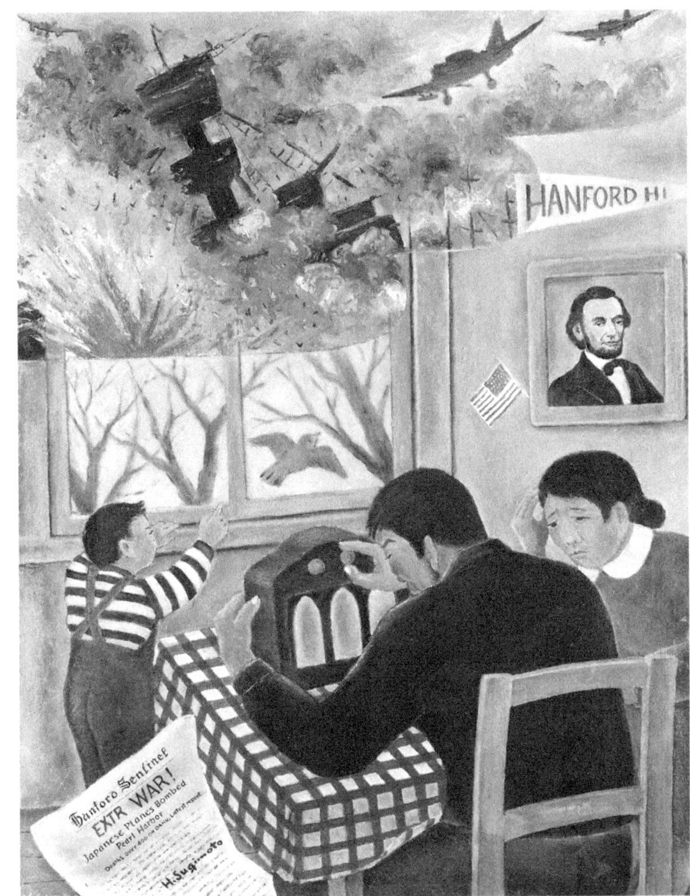

Henry Sugimoto, untitled (circa 1965), featuring the newspaper headline "Japanese Planes Bombed Pearl Harbor." (Japanese American National Museum [Gift of Madeleine Sugimoto and Naomi Tagawa, Japanese American National Museum, 92.97.104].)

will save them from the upcoming removal and imprisonment, since their Japanese ancestry will render moot their lives as Americans.

Bombing of Relatives Homeland focuses on Japanese American figures standing on the grounds of the Rohwer camp, learning of the nuclear destruction in Japan that ends the war. In this composition, we perceive how Sugimoto reused his wartime images of the camp structures, with the barracks, a mess hall, a guard tower, and the American flag in the background, as seen in *Mess Hall Jerome Camp (Our Mess Hall Documentary)* (circa 1942). Two male figures in the foreground, one clothed in blue overalls, discuss the event, with the other holding a camp bulletin while pointing to the upper-right corner of the far-removed scene of the bombing. A third figure in the lower-right foreground reads a sheet and scratches his head, trying to come to grips with what has happened. Further in the background are groupings of other figures, one with three women and a child, two of the adults hold-

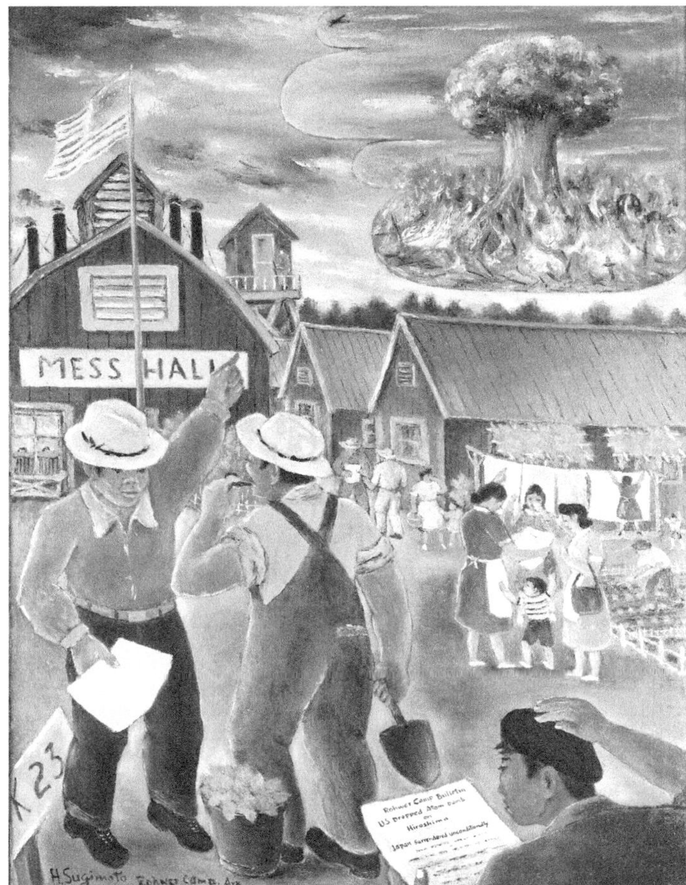

Henry Sugimoto, *Bombing of Relatives Homeland*, 1945 (circa 1965). (Japanese American National Museum [Gift of Madeleine Sugimoto and Naomi Tagawa, Japanese American National Museum, 92.97.8].)

ing handkerchiefs to wipe their tears, while the third reads from the distributed newsletter. The dual tragedy here encompasses Japanese Americans who are still incarcerated, while their extended families overseas suffer from the atomic explosion, as the painting's title suggests. Read in concert, the untitled painting about the family's reaction to the Pearl Harbor attack and *Bombing of Relatives Homeland* convey the dangers inherent in being part of a transpacific, interstitial community, when caught in the expectations of, and the violence enacted by, two warring empires.

Moreover, these visual bookends of the conflict coincide with, yet challenge, what Tom Engelhardt calls the "end of victory culture" in the American popular mind-set. At the close of World War II, as he observes, the United States experienced great ambivalence in the aftermath of dropping atomic bombs on Hiroshima and Nagasaki. Although these acts broke imperial Japan's ability and willingness to continue the war, the destruction also released unforeseen consequences as to how the United States understood itself as a nation. Before and during the conflict with Japan, the dominant cultural narrative consisted of the "war story." This account's basic theme consisted of imagining a few brave souls who fought against superior numbers of the attacking foe, usually peoples of color. Mexicans at the Alamo, Native Americans at Custer's last stand, or the Japanese at Pearl Harbor filled the role of alien enemies that required subjugation. This plotline had framed the American popular consciousness since the nation's colonial origins, when English settlers fought against native peoples. But it also disguised the historical reality that white Americans were often themselves the invaders, especially when claiming the western continental frontier or overseas colonies and client states in the Pacific. The "war story" served to mask this part of the nation's past, assuring its white citizens that, despite initial defeat, they would eventually achieve total victory as vengeance against the racial Other. In the Pacific War, these were the sentiments after the bombing of Pearl Harbor, and many in the United States saw the destruction of Hiroshima and Nagasaki as acts of retaliatory justice.[81]

In the postwar world, however, the annihilating powers of nuclear weaponry reduced the ability to attain complete victory. If future conflicts between atomic-minded nations promised mutual all-out destruction, no one would survive to bear the outcome. Triumphing over the enemy would cost as much for the victors as for the defeated. Even so, conventional warfare on the Asian continent proved hazardous for Americans as well. Particularly unnerving for the U.S. public to learn about were American and other United Nations units in Korea being swarmed by massive numbers of communist Chinese and North Korean troops in the early 1950s. This drama would replay itself with further disastrous consequences in Vietnam only a few years later. Poverty-ridden, nonindustrialized Third World nations supported by the Soviet Union and communist China appeared to outfight a technologically superior United States and its allied forces. Thus, a "question mark," a sense of unknowingness, informed postwar Americans' thoughts about how they could advance their interests and values in the world, when other nations appeared disinterested in, if not combative against, such an objective.[82]

Positioning Sugimoto's and other Japanese Americans' paintings within, but also against, Engelhardt's idea of the war story narrative offers a more complicated, transpacific understanding of not only Japanese Americans within the nation but also the resultant nuclear blasts on the Japanese populace. For instance, Benji Okubo's surrealist *Atom Bomb* (1945) renders the mushroom cloud in white, skull-like formations that emerge from the mouth of a monster-shaped cloud of blackish-gray smoke, which itself arises from flashes of orange fire at ground level. Eitaro Ishigaki's *Disaster by Atomic Bomb* (1946) presents a Dantesque vision of hell, with its heavy brushwork treatment of dark browns, oranges, and reds to show naked, vulnerable masses dying amid, or streaming from, a city in flames. Chiura Obata's watercolor trilogy *Devastation* (1945), *Prayer* (1946), and *Harmony* (1946) conveys the emptiness, hope, and resolve of two small human figures—a postwar Adam and Eve—surviving on a barren landscape that transforms itself over time. As charted in the three works, the terrain both shapes and reflects human emotions, moving from the blacks, browns, and reds of scorched ruin and personal despair to nature's reviving rains and resurgent greenery. These intense artistic responses as a whole avoided nationalist visions of American triumph or Japanese defeat, focusing instead on the philosophical and affective considerations of what humanity lost, and what it could regain, from such destructiveness.

Sugimoto's paired works provide a view of Japanese Americans as an indeterminate and contested presence, a "question mark" in their own right regarding their racial Otherness within the United States and their familial ties to Japan. What makes Sugimoto's postwar art on the bombings at Pearl Harbor and on imperial Japan innovative is his placement of this minority populace in each instance, challenging the dominant victory narrative manufactured about the war. Rather than a footnote to the broader history of global conflict, theirs was the central, ambivalent drama of his concern, in which they carefully negotiated between their "Japanese" and "American" identities during those transformative moments. Sugimoto conveyed this combination of conflicting sentiments and sprawling events in ways that no other artist did. As a result, the overall series of his postwar paintings regarding early immigration, prewar prejudice, mass confinement, and the war's atomic finale reveals the most developed artistic vision we have of a multifaceted Japanese American past.

Reclamation

In the end, Henry Sugimoto still thought of himself as a cosmopolitan artist who simply wanted to paint scenes of the world around him. But he got and gave more in return. Were it not for the churning ferocity of World War II, his reputation as a celebrated, rising artist of Japanese ancestry in the 1930s might have survived into better days. Instead, the conflict between the United States and Japan, and his ensuing imprisonment in the camps with his family, shortened this promising trajectory. The price he paid was exacting, with anxieties suffered, a professional career lost, and public inattention to what he was producing in the following decades. Even so, he remained undaunted in his painterly pursuits, converting into compelling art the wartime experiences of Japanese Americans and their earlier history of immigration.

When Sugimoto and others testified before Congress during the redress movement in the 1980s this action helped his visibility and accelerated a national rediscovery of the artist and his work that began in the previous decade. Building on the social activism of the civil rights era, Japanese Americans and like-minded others influenced how the United States could more fully realize and redeem its wartime actions through the stories and presence of the once incarcerated. In this manner, the new social and political environment also promoted occasions, such as the JANM retrospective exhibit, to reevaluate Sugimoto's body of work, even as the artist himself avoided any political framing of it. Yet the significance of his art emerged from a broader and more complex history, given how his worldly sentiments in the 1930s transformed into the subtle political protest of a racialized cosmopolitan during and after the war. The transpacific migrations of Japanese that affected Sugimoto's own life, and the aesthetic ideas and social circumstances that informed his work and worldview, thus oblige us to examine his achievements in more nuanced fashion. From this viewpoint, we can perceive an artist in various states of transition, who enlarged his creative capacities in trying conditions and in extraordinary ways.

Teach Your Children Well

The Postwar Tales of Yoshiko Uchida

Yoshiko Uchida was just beginning her career as a children's author when she wrote with excitement to her parents in 1950. A year earlier, the New York–based publisher Harcourt, Brace and Company released her first book, *The Dancing Kettle and Other Japanese Folk Tales* (1949). The work contained stories that Uchida had heard as a child, and she adapted them for young American readers, hoping the collection would contribute to building better cultural relations between the United States and Japan after World War II. Yet the book was not the main topic Uchida discussed in her letter. Instead, she told her mother and father about meeting with a *New Yorker* magazine editor who encouraged her to create adult short fiction about the wartime confinement of Japanese Americans. The editor suggested that Uchida provide accounts based on her family's experiences to edify the periodical's subscribers. Thus inspired, Uchida confessed to her parents, "I've had the whole evacuation story inside of me for so long—just waiting to be written. I certainly hope I can be successful in this venture."[1] The possibilities for making her mark on the literary world at this time and in this fashion appeared promising indeed.

A prolific author of essays, short stories, and more than thirty books, Uchida was a major figure in American culture, with a career spanning the late 1940s to the early 1990s. Her range of topics was impressive: children's books on Japanese folktales, essays on Japanese folk traditions, young adult stories with characters from Japan and the United States befriending one another, children's and adult fiction and memoirs about the wartime incarceration of Japanese Americans, and narratives with historical and modern-day Japanese protagonists. To the general public, Uchida was a beloved, award-winning writer who displayed a nuanced sympathy for her characters that appealed to all ages. That many of her books still appear in print attests to her continued popularity. Despite this profound influence in the United States, Uchida's body of work has attracted only slight critical attention. Especially lacking are studies on her texts produced in the early Cold War era. It was during this time that the author developed not only her understanding of cultural relations between the United States and Japan but also the themes, characters, and narrative strategies she would later apply to her works on the wartime confinement of Japanese Americans.

Although the breadth of topics Uchida covered was extensive, her legacy rests on her writings about the incarceration period.[2] More than any other author, Uchida conveyed to generations of young readers the fraught history of a nation that valorized the ideals of liberty and democracy while denying basic rights and privileges to Japanese Americans before, during, and after World War II. As early as 1950, however, she focused on writing for adult audiences about this matter. Uchida sent drafts of short stories to the top periodicals of the day, including the *New Yorker,* the *Atlantic Monthly, Harper's, Mademoiselle, Woman's Day, Esquire,* and others. Yet many of these pieces went unpublished, as she collected reams of rejection letters from these esteemed journals. At the same time, the declined work revealed her ambition to reach mainstream consumers.[3] These compositions were also crucial to developing Uchida's thinking on the mass confinement and were published in revised form during the 1970s, two decades after she initially expressed enthusiasm for the subject when corresponding with her parents. *Journey to Topaz* (1971) and *Journey Home* (1978) were her first and most familiar young adult books about the imprisonment and its aftermath. The texts fictionalized many of her family's grueling experiences at the Tanforan Assembly Center, a former racetrack in California; then at Topaz, a War Relocation Center in the Utah desert; and finally, on their return home to California after the war. She produced two memoirs as well: one for adult readers, *Desert Exile: The Uprooting of a Japanese-American Family* (1982), and another for adolescents, *The Invisible Thread* (1991). The wartime incarceration also appeared as a plot device in the novel *Picture Bride* (1987) and in a children's illustrated book, *The Bracelet* (1993). The reasons for Uchida's success with these publications, and for the scholarly interest they attract, are not hard to fathom, considering the historical and cultural contexts from which they emerged. By the 1970s and onward, the civil rights movement, the Japanese American reparations movement, and the growing attention to multicultural literature created a more amenable environment to address the consequences of this tragedy.[4]

Reviewers, publicists, and Uchida herself consequently portrayed her lifework as one that started with adapting Japanese folktales and creating young adult fiction about Japan for an American readership. This focus made sense in light of the new alliance and cultural interest emerging between the United States and Japan. Only later in her career, as this conventional understanding goes, did she emphasize the wartime confinement of Japanese Americans. Uchida, however, was a more complex and wide-ranging author than this image presents. Although she failed to publish work on the mass incarceration in the early Cold War era, she still thought deeply about it, disclosing a simultaneous interest in Japanese American experiences and in U.S.-Japan relations that persisted throughout her body of work.

In this context, Uchida presents an aspect of the "Japanese/American" dynamic in which the opposing and overlapping relations between each signifier changed over the course of her life. When coming of age before the Pacific War, Uchida showed little interest in U.S.-Japan relations, considering herself thoroughly American. She tried to remain distant from her Japanese ancestry, seeing it as an unwelcome, though always present, attribute that emphasized her foreignness within the United States. But this desired separation from her ancestry and her longing to participate in white society without racial stigma was impossible, given the nation's broader history of excluding people of Asian descent from the American mainstream. Uchida realized this conundrum with more clarity as she matured. Although she wanted to be "American, not Japanese," the federal government marked her family and community as "Japanese, not American," resulting in their wartime incarceration. The bloody conflict between her native and ancestral lands proved a major turning point, pressing her to reflect on how both parts of this Japanese/American configuration informed, developed, and complicated one another through their mutual histories. By the late 1940s, Uchida embraced what Japan and its culture offered, positioning herself through her writings as a cosmopolitan mediator, as she extended her views of the world and of her own American life.

This transition in Uchida's thinking began with the attack on Pearl Harbor and the signing of Executive Order 9066. Daunting as confinement was, it also fostered Uchida's appreciation of her Japanese ancestry, a reaction that most Japanese Americans did not share. At the war's outbreak, many responded with shock and disbelief at the news from Pearl Harbor. The Issei and Nisei knew racial prejudice firsthand and sought to disassociate themselves from their ethnic background as a survival strategy. To eviscerate any trace of their ties to Japan, they destroyed or hid letters, books, artwork, clothes, and other artifacts that would link them to the enemy. This purging, however, could not stop their looming displacement. Yet, for Uchida, the forced removal and life in the camps awakened, rather than repressed, her interest in

Japanese culture. What she endured throughout the war prompted a growing valuation of her family background. In retrospect, Uchida acknowledged to a fuller extent her parents' travails during this time, and realizing what they taught her contributed to a strengthened desire to tell their stories as well as her own. The improved postwar relations between the United States and Japan also inspired her to appreciate her ancestral heritage. Her research and writing about a rich folk tradition arose from these new perspectives.

Uchida's curiosity about Japan and her work on folktales likewise encouraged, rather than overshadowed, her desire to write about the confinement of Japanese Americans. She initially expressed her thoughts and observations in a wartime diary and a scrapbook, later reworking these compositions into short story drafts. After the war, she addressed these experiences in other media, including press interviews for her folktales, undeveloped fictional sketches, autobiographical pieces, and correspondence with editors, friends, and family members. The early Cold War era in this way proved vital to developing Uchida's fiction and memoir writing on the mass imprisonment, aided by her interest in Japanese folktales and in postwar Japan. For her, teaching children to appreciate a common humanity and its different cultures lessened the chances for global conflicts and for racially discriminatory acts, such as the uprooting and imprisoning of Japanese Americans, from occurring again. Thus, rather than seeing her texts on the mass imprisonment as simply a product of late-twentieth-century national developments that centered on the civil rights movement, we can find their origins in earlier efforts that aligned with her international interests stemming from the postwar period. Examining the temporal and topical range of Uchida's work through her entwined interests in Japan and Japanese Americans from the late 1940s onward can then enrich our thinking about how she confronted the legacies of war and confinement through a transpacific cultural framework.

A Family Uprooted

The main source that inspired Uchida to write about Japanese culture and about the wartime confinement was her Issei parents. Dwight Takashi Uchida emigrated from Japan to Hawaiʻi in 1903, when he was nineteen years old. He worked on the islands as a Japanese-language teacher before moving to San Francisco three years later. He then relocated to Seattle to live with his mother and one of his sisters, who had previously moved there from Japan. During these perambulations, the young man had ambitions of attending Yale medical school, but the plan never materialized since he felt financially obligated to help bring his other sisters to the United States. He found work in Seattle at a general merchandise store for a year and managed another in Portland for nine years. In 1917, Mitsui and Company, a Japanese trading firm, admired his management skills and hired him to work for its San Francisco branch office. Dwight Uchida also married Iku Umegaki that year. Dwight and Iku had never met before, but they had shared the same professors at Doshisha University, a Christian institution in Kyoto, Japan. The two also came from similar backgrounds: their fathers had been samurai who then moved into the professional class after the Meiji Restoration. Both patriarchs died young, leaving their families to fend for themselves. As adolescents working at menial jobs and sometimes living with relatives, Dwight and Iku became resourceful and empathized with others who struggled. The Doshisha professors, sensing kindred spirits in their former students, suggested that Dwight and Iku correspond with one another. The pair did so for a year, exchanging letters and photographs before Iku came to the United States as a picture bride to join her intended husband.[5]

Settling in the Bay Area, Dwight and Iku raised Yoshiko and her elder sister Keiko (or Kay) there. In her memoirs, the author depicted her parents as polar opposites in personalities: he with his good-natured garrulousness, business acumen, and pragmatism, she with a quieter, more artistic sensibility. Iku, however, was open and generous in her own way. While attending Doshisha University, she studied British literature and taught English to Kyoto factory workers. Yoshiko often wondered at her mother's courage when coming to the United States at a young age, without friends or family, to start a new life with a husband who already had associates and his mother and sisters with him. Because of their father's professional status, Yoshiko and her sister enjoyed a childhood spent in relatively stable material comfort, despite the hardships of the Great Depression and the housing restrictions on Japanese Americans in Oakland and Berkeley, where the family rented dwellings. The Uchidas also maintained social contacts across the Pacific, hosting Japanese visitors—ministers, students, businessmen, and others—who luxuriated in the household's food, the opportunities for conversation, and other kindnesses. Yoshiko remembered a satisfying and romanticized childhood while portraying in a lighthearted manner the usual resentments when growing up. Her sister Kay, four years older, relished bossing the younger sibling around. The Japanese visitors presented another problem as an ever-present intrusion that Yoshiko felt took parental attention away from her. She complained that the Japanese-language church services that the family attended were too lengthy and onerous. Her parents' socializing and organizing with other congregants afterward only prolonged her boredom and misery (6–16).

As Uchida matured, she became more aware of the prejudices that Japanese Americans encountered and endured. The family had to call ahead to see if swimming facilities or hair stylists in town would accept them to avoid the humiliation of being turned away in person. She expressed the desire to date white students but was never asked out by them; it was her belief that her ethnicity prevented such romantic pairings. These circumstances led her to examine the contradictory status of being an American citizen of Japanese ancestry, given its opportunities and its limitations. What readers gain from the author's memories of her early years is a well-crafted depiction of a middle-class Japanese American family in the 1930s. This background, understood in all its joys and its indignities, provided important material from which Uchida constructed many of her characters and stories about Japanese culture and about the mass confinement.

The coming war with Japan only intensified Uchida's feelings of alienation and endangerment. When the attack on Pearl Harbor occurred, she was studying for final exams as a senior at the University of California at Berkeley. Like other Japanese American families, the Uchidas waited anxiously to see what would happen next. Within hours, the FBI began detaining the male heads of Japanese American households for questioning. The agents eventually appeared at the Uchida home, taking Dwight into custody because of his employment with Mitsui. The three women were left wondering about his whereabouts for several weeks. They later learned that the FBI had moved Dwight to San Francisco for initial screening and then to a Justice Department detention center in Missoula, Montana, with other Japanese men. Although he posed no threat, authorities held him for five months and censored his correspondence to the family.[6]

In February 1942, President Roosevelt's Executive Order 9066 mandated the forced removal of Japanese Americans from the West Coast. By late April, the Uchida women received word from federal authorities to pack up or sell their belongings within ten days. They were then evicted from their Berkeley home and escorted by the U.S. Army to waiting buses (52–68). Yoshiko noted in her wartime diary: "I remember . . . the tears we had to fight back on seeing armed guards at every door way . . . [when] climbing onto the bus, and driving past our home, not knowing when we would ever return."[7] On May 1, they arrived at the Tanforan Assembly Center, a former racetrack in San Bruno, California, to live with eight thousand other Japanese Americans in converted horse stalls that still reeked of manure. Other hardships made their new lives challenging. The soldiers who guarded them were a constant and ominous presence. People waited in long lines for meals, to do laundry, and for almost everything else. The bathrooms had few walls inside them to ensure privacy. The food initially consisted of bland bread and canned sausages. Yoshiko was troubled by a litany of ailments, induced by the meager diet and by the stressful circumstances. But some good news appeared a week after their arrival. Dwight Uchida, released from the Missoula detention center and looking worn and slimmer from the strain, joined his family at Tanforan after those months of separation and anxiety.

In September 1942, the War Relocation Authority moved the Uchidas and several thousand others on crowded railway cars to the Topaz Relocation Center in Utah. Located in the desert, this camp delivered another tormenting experience for its Japanese American inmates. Barbed-wire fences surrounded the area, while armed guards in watchtowers kept vigil over it. Similar to conditions at Tanforan, the wooden barracks were shoddy, the food was tasteless, people rushed through their washing before the hot water ran out, and no one had any privacy. The weather itself became a determined foe, with its extreme daytime heat and nighttime cold. Further misery came from the punishing dust storms that arrived with sudden ferocity, whipping people's bodies and unsettling their minds (102–120).[8] Uchida wanted to record every aspect of what she saw and endured, writing fervently in her diary with posterity in mind. In an entry dated September 27, 1942, she wondered at the distressing circumstances under which Japanese Americans lived and how they had reached such a point. "We are at Topaz as I write these recollections," she remarked. "I need not write them down, for they have been stamped indellibly [*sic*] in my mind . . . but the mind fails, and someday . . . sometime . . . some other[s] may want to read this . . . these notes of an event which has never before happened in the history of this country, and which I hope cannot and will not ever happen again to any other group of people."[9]

Even at this moment, Uchida longed to give narrative shape to how this catastrophe for Japanese Americans and for the nation would be remembered. The scale of such a tragedy demanded it. Yet her diary at this point revealed uncertainty about the future: "What lies ahead of us no one know[s]."[10] She realized, too, that the processes of memory, both her own and the nation's, were unreliable and constantly shifting over time. How could she then translate this stark past into something redemptive? "Evacuation . . . what fear and dread that single word caused," she mused while still behind barbed wire, "what heart-ache and anxiety, no one will ever know. No one except those who actually lived through those terrible months as an alien enemy, or a descendent of one."[11] Uchida's concerns about what might be ignored or forgotten, or remembered in ways that failed to elucidate wartime sufferings, affected much of her imprisonment writings. That the mass confinement might become unknowable to future generations also compelled her to write professionally, informing her children's books and other works decades later.

As seen in Uchida's early efforts, the wartime dislocation and the ensuing concerns affected not only her physical health but also her sense of self, challenging her prior notions of what it meant to be an American of Japanese ancestry. Thus the author's desire to foster cultural understanding among different populations framed her stories for young readers, beginning in the late 1940s and lasting throughout her career. She achieved this goal by focusing on several related themes in her works for children: the power of Japanese folk culture to increase global understanding, the search for purpose in postwar Japan, and the documenting of ethnic diversity in the United States. These three topics corresponded with one final matter that emerged from the postwar era: Uchida's longing to convey her memories of the wartime imprisonment.

Japanese Folktales and Cold War Cosmopolitanism

Throughout the postwar era, Uchida made a name for herself as an author of folktales and young adult fiction with modern-day Japanese and Japanese American protagonists. Well before the advent of mainstream interest in multicultural literature, she offered U.S. audiences a look into the distinct yet overlapping worlds of Japanese and American cultures. Her adaptations of Japanese folktales and her other works for children gained prominence in part because of the broader contexts of the early Cold War. As the United States sought to secure anticommunist partners in the Pacific, foreign policy makers, social critics, and cultural producers wanted to educate the American public about the importance of accepting overseas Asians as capable and loyal allies. To achieve this objective, Hollywood films, popular fiction, magazine coverage, and Broadway musicals portrayed Asians as people who shared the same desires and interests as Americans. Venues in popular culture served to create sentimental bonds between American audiences and Asian subjects to produce mutual understanding intended to overcome the political differences among diverse populations across the globe. At the same time, these attempts at establishing cultural connections coincided with U.S. efforts to consolidate access to overseas markets and resources.[12]

Uchida's children's books and other writings from the late 1940s to early 1960s were part of this larger movement to assist Americans in comprehending their new relations to other regions and peoples. The Japanese folktales revealed her espousal of a Cold War cosmopolitanism to combat discrimination and to advocate for democratic ideals throughout the wider world. Sensing the postwar possibilities for both the United States and Japan, Uchida wanted her tales to convey the shared joys and yearnings of children everywhere in the hopes of decreasing future hates and misunderstandings among them. But Uchida rejected the idea of inflicting American mainstream views on other nations or cultures in a one-sided manner, knowing how material self-interest and racism in the United States played a major part in her incarceration. Instead, she encouraged a multilateral approach, in which peoples would learn from one another in a more wide-ranging, cosmopolitan manner. Japan itself would be a vital resource to help American children understand other societies and to broaden their global sensibilities. In turn, as the Japanese attempted to adopt liberal democratic reforms, Uchida argued that they needed to develop their own versions of social restructuring that suited their specific purposes. The author thus espoused the tenets of liberalism (democracy, individualism, multiculturalism, representative governing), but without the authority of the United States to enact them. On a deeper level, she did not or could not articulate an alternative vision of what a more cosmopolitan world would look like without liberal ideals reinforcing it, or having the problematic power of a liberal state to guide it. This message of acceptance and understanding, however limited, became evident in her young adult novels set in postwar Japan that she composed after traveling there in the early 1950s. As later shown, the visit contributed to her shifting views of both American and Japanese cultures and to her emergence as a cosmopolitan writer.

Two of Uchida's earliest publications, *The Dancing Kettle and Other Japanese Folk Tales* (1949) and *The Magic Listening Cap: More Folk Tales from Japan* (1955), are collections of traditional stories she adapted for American consumption. In the wake of the war's destruction, she felt that the younger generation had to develop an appreciation for, rather than a fear of, cultural and ethnic differences. The central message she wanted to impart in these works, then, was twofold: that all children share the same interest in reading a good story, and that they should embrace the diversity of peoples and cultures delineated within her narratives. The Japanese folktales became an appropriate medium through which to accomplish these goals.

Although Uchida hoped that her tales would have wide appeal because of their commonality with other stories from around the world, she also acknowledged that they were not fixed in content or in meaning. As Jack Zipes notes, the supposed universality of folktales "has more to do with the specific manner in which they were constructed historically as mythic constellations than with common psychic processes of a collective unconscious." These stories, he continues, "are constantly rearranged and transformed to suit changes in tastes and values" instead of remaining as unchanged universal truths.[13] Uchida was cognizant of the pliable nature and transmission of folktales, even as she embraced the notion that her stories had universal appeal. In the preface for *The Dancing Kettle,* she admitted: "I have retold [these tales] in my own words, and have taken the liberty of adapting them so they would be more meaningful to the children of America."[14] Uchida thus positioned herself as a cultural broker between the United States and Japan to help acquaint American readers with various peoples and societies to embolden cooperation rather than conflict. But she offered insights that served another purpose. On the domestic front, publicizing the folktales and the intention to create more tolerance allowed her to talk about her family's experiences of racial discrimination and the wartime confinement.

Book reviewers recognized the historical and cultural significance of Uchida's publications. As the *Saturday Review of Literature* remarked in 1949, most books that translated Japanese folktales into English were out of print in the postwar era, thus making Uchida's efforts in *The Dancing Kettle* "an important work."[15] This new availability led other critics to broader conclusions about the folktales' relationship to the unsteady state of international affairs. Also reviewing *The Dancing Kettle,* the *New York Herald Tribune* noticed about Uchida's aspirations: "In the author's hope that these tales will help [us move] toward 'one world,' she joins Dr. [F.S.C.] Northrop's theory of the possible meeting of East and West through mutual understanding of cultural heritages."[16] Here, the columnist refers to the Yale philosophy professor who published *The Meeting of East and West: An Inquiry Concerning World Understanding* (1946). Northrop's thesis focused on how the shared cultural systems within nations, as opposed to divisive political ideologies, could foster a more peaceful age. For U.S. audiences, the importance of Asia to American interests could enhance cultural sympathies to curtail worldwide wars. "The time is here when we must understand the Orient if we would understand ourselves," Northrop wrote, "and when we must learn how to combine Oriental and Occidental values if further tragedy, bitterness, and bloodshed are not to ensue."[17] No evidence suggests that Uchida read, or was familiar with, Northrop's writings. Reviewers of her work, however, saw in it similarities with the general patterns of thought that pervaded postwar American culture about creating international goodwill through cultural understanding, despite whatever differences remained. This point applied to not only the world in general but also children's literature in particular. As the *San Francisco Chronicle* noted about *The Magic Listening Cap* in 1955, "Increasing interest in world affairs in our day makes it easy to see that now a knowledge of other lands, peoples and customs have [*sic*] become a basic essential of education."[18]

These lessons of acceptance in children's books paralleled the growing interest in Japanese culture in the United States, particularly in the 1950s. Uchida's works corresponded with others that highlighted the comparable experiences that American and Japanese children shared, as well as their unique cultural traditions. Around the time Uchida published her two books on Japanese folktales, Taro Yashima's *The Village Tree* (1953), *Plenty to Watch* (1954), and his Caldecott Honor–winning *Crow Boy* (1955) also encouraged interest in Japanese culture. Yashima was born in Japan and spent his early adulthood there developing his skills as an artist. He and his wife later migrated to the United States as political refugees who opposed the militarists in imperial Japan. Yashima worked for the American government during the war and then made his living as a writer and artist in New York City.[19] Both *The Village Tree* and *Plenty to Watch* arose from his daughter's questions about his own youthful days in Japan. The former work begins with some queries for the reader: "Do you know a country far, far to the east, that we call Japan? Do you know, there too we have many children like you?"[20] The "you" here carries a double meaning, with collective applications. Initially, it refers to Yashima's daughter, the original audience for the book. The children of Japan, the author implies, are similar to her in ethnic ancestry and in racial appearance. Yet, since *The Village Tree* was also intended for American children of all ethnic backgrounds, the "you" also applies to them, especially when Yashima describes the common joys of playing outside amid the wonders of nature.

Reviewers in the United States appreciated Yashima's works, as they did Uchida's, for their portrayals of childhood and of Japanese culture. One book critic declared that Yashima's drawings in *The Village Tree* were "more than likely to evoke self-identification whether the reader be in Tappan, N.Y., or Buntok, Borneo."[21] A reviewer for the *Washington Post* made a related comment about *Plenty to Watch,* which depicts the sights, sounds, and curiosities of street life that a boy observes as he walks to school. This text, she remarked, would provide American children with "an understanding of Japanese life and an awareness that everywhere people have similar needs which they meet in accordance with their own resources and desires."[22] Children in the United States or in Asia, in metropolitan areas or in small villages, would recognize the joys and marvels of outdoor adventures, freed from any adult presence. Yet the critic also considered each locale and each population's specific needs that defied universal standards. The desire for understanding also meant that differences required acceptance, no matter what the circumstances. *Crow Boy* offers an example of embracing each person's individuality. The title character, a shy and quirky boy named Chibi, is at first alienated from his classmates because of his peculiar behavior. As the book progresses, however, they learn to value Chibi's manners, especially when he displays a remarkable talent for imitating the sounds of crows. Guided by an understanding teacher, Chibi's acceptance by his now impressed classmates marks the triumph of a cosmopolitan worldview, as demonstrated for American readers by the book's Japanese schoolchildren.

In Uchida's case, the publicity for her children's works on Japanese folk culture provided her a platform not only to promote *The Dancing Kettle* and *The Magic Listening Cap* but also to talk about the forced removal of Japanese

Americans. Indeed, the memories of World War II and of her confinement influenced her to write children's books about Japan in the first place. Uchida recounted for newspapers across the nation the story of how she and her family became targeted as enemy aliens because of the racial hostility directed against Japanese Americans. The details of her comments to the press followed the same pattern. She told of the prewar discrimination in housing when she lived in Berkeley. She recounted how Japanese Americans had to form their own social outlets while attending the university there. She relayed the anger she felt when receiving her college diploma while she was behind barbed wire at the Tanforan Assembly Center. As Uchida observed in a 1955 interview in the *Oakland Tribune* to publicize *The Magic Listening Cap,* "My diploma was delivered to me by mail. Of course that really did not matter—but I minded. O yes, indeed, I minded!" That she received her diploma in the mail was not the main issue; this event "really did not matter." It was what the act represented that kindled her resentment. Even though she was a U.S. citizen, that status was endangered because of her race and ancestry. Uchida emphasized the purpose for connecting her past imprisonment with adapting Japanese folktales. "If I could write in such a way as to build a bridge across the differences in customs and ways of living," then children could recognize the shared humanity among others and refrain from prejudicial actions against what they considered foreign, strange, and threatening.[23] The implication was clear to anyone purchasing her books or reading what she said about them with regard to her past spent at Tanforan and Topaz. The texts were to educate younger generations to appreciate ethnic differences and, more specifically, to ensure that the imprisonment of Japanese Americans or any other minority group would never happen again in the United States. As developed in Uchida's later books on the wartime confinement, her critique was not so much against mainstream society, of which she longed to be a part, or against the liberal state, but the pervasive racism ingrained within them.

Many of the stories in *The Dancing Kettle* and *The Magic Listening Cap* chart the commonalities among diverse peoples by providing lessons that are prevalent in other cultures' folkways. One critic pointed out as much for *The Dancing Kettle:* "Most of the familiar characters common to fairy tales the world around are found in this collection."[24] In both *The Dancing Kettle* and *The Magic Listening Cap,* inanimate objects, trees, and animals take on anthropomorphic qualities. The works also contain otherworldly stories occupied by princes and princesses, beneficial and malcontent gods, witches and soothsayers, and other characters found in folktales around the world. In their interactions with one another and with human protagonists, these characters highlight acts of generosity and gratitude, or greed, trickery, and shortsightedness. Circumstances that involve good or ill fortune also emerge. The title stories from each book, for instance, center on magical objects: a teakettle that sings and dances, and a cap that helps its wearer understand the thoughts of nature. Each item benefits poor yet sincere elderly men. These characters, described as "a good and generous man" in *The Dancing Kettle* and "an honest old man who was kind and good" in *The Magic Listening Cap,* profit materially from their associations with these objects.[25] The dancing kettle brings its owner riches from the entertainment it offers to the villagers, while the listening cap helps its wearer learn from birds and trees how to heal a dying wealthy man, who then rewards the poor one with gold coins. Yet these unanticipated turn of events never instigate greed. Instead, the aged protagonists express their gratitude toward spiritual leaders or beings, content with the more comfortable life they now have.

Other tales in Uchida's collections depict incidents of trickery, with the weak taking advantage of the strong, or the trickster getting its comeuppance for deceiving others. These stories hardly differ from those in *Aesop's Fables, Grimm's Fairy Tales,* or African and African American folklore that portray morality tales through animals. In *The Dancing Kettle,* the tale "The Rabbit and the Crocodile" is reminiscent of the Brer Rabbit character in African American folk tradition. In Uchida's version, a white rabbit on an outer isle hopes to visit Japan's main island. He accomplishes this wish by tricking a crocodile and its friends to form a bridge with their bodies so the rabbit can cross over the water. Yet, instead of gratitude, the rabbit boasts of its mastery over the crocodile's gullibility. The latter, however, enacts its revenge by capturing the rabbit and tearing off all its fur. Only when a kindly god restores the rabbit's white coat does the animal realize the errors of its ways. In *The Magic Listening Cap,* "The Fox and the Bear" tells the story of the fox tricking the bear into growing food for them both. Yet once the bear realizes this duplicity, he has the last laugh, getting a horse to drag away the fox by its tail.

Responding with enthusiasm, elementary school teachers and their students across the United States composed volumes of correspondence to Uchida about her folktales. Classes often focused on Japan as part of learning sequences on international issues, with children writing appreciative notes to Uchida about what they discovered. One boy from Wichita, Kansas, exclaimed to the author in 1959: "I thought I would tell you that I think your books *The Magic Listening Cap* and *The Dancing Kettle* are the best books I ever read."[26] Administrators expressed their appreciation as well. A supervisor of public elementary schools in Springfield, Massachusetts, saw the value of *The Dancing Kettle* for her students. At the book's release in 1949, she wrote to Uchida, "The preservation of the best of the Japanese stories is a great service to the people of Japan and a real gift to our children."[27] In her responses, Uchida never missed a chance to reiterate her main objective by noting the similarities among cultures and the need to appreciate their differences. Replying to a teacher from Springdale, Arkansas, in 1952, Uchida remarked, "I was glad to learn that you were using [*The Dancing Kettle*] in connection with your study of Japan. I think that teaching children about the ways of people in other lands is one of the best ways to bring about the 'one world' which we all seek so desperately these days."[28]

Uchida's folktales appealed to Japanese American critics and audiences too, when they recognized her contributions as a Nisei writer. Surveying the literary landscape in 1949, the San Francisco–based *Nichi Bei Times* saw *The Dancing Kettle* as part of a growing body of nationally recognized work by Japanese American authors from the East Bay Area. The paper noted that Toshio Mori's short story collection, *Yokohama, California,* appeared shortly after Uchida's folktales and that Miné Okubo's *Citizen 13660* had been released three years earlier. In the reviewer's mind, a golden age of Nisei writing appeared forthcoming in the aftermath of the war's degradation of Japanese Americans. The *Pacific Citizen* took another approach, declaring Uchida's work an important global resource. The adapted stories in *The Dancing Kettle,* the periodical observed, "have humor, action and a host of characters that deserve an international reputation and should . . . become part of the folk literature of the world." The reviewer hoped as well that Nisei parents would confer these tales onto their Sansei children. The book would then foster or continue an interest in Japanese culture for future generations of Japanese American youth. Implied in this point was that these children would appreciate their ancestral heritage. Yet learning from these tales would also combat the shame associated with this background, spurred by World War II and by the racial discrimination that their communities endured in the United States.[29]

Just as Uchida wanted her folktales to broaden American children's attitudes, she aimed to extend her appeal to Japan as well. Writing to her editor, Margaret McElderry, Uchida asked, "Do you think there is any possibility of having [*The Dancing Kettle*] approved by the AMG [American Military Government] and used in Japanese grade schools as supplementary English readers?" She also inquired of McElderry in 1953 if the publishing company could distribute the book to U.S. Army post exchanges in Japan for American schoolchildren there.[30] By promoting her work, Uchida acknowledged a desire to advance democratic reforms in Japan and to strengthen alliances with it. Indeed, Japanese readers valued her efforts at rebuilding relations across the Pacific. One correspondent in Tokyo lavished praise on *The Dancing Kettle* in 1949, noting "A book like that . . . can be enjoyed by everyone, regardless of age. . . . [I]t can do much in furthering international understanding and good will."[31] A fan from Nagano wrote in 1955 about *The Magic Listening Cap,* "I believe . . . your gentleness and kindness for humankind . . . in your work will be . . . gifts to children of all the world. . . . [T]hank you . . . [for being] a represent[ative] of your mother land Japan."[32] Both Japanese and Japanese Americans took pride in Uchida's accomplishments, viewing her as an important cultural broker within a transpacific community founded on a common ancestry. But they also understood the broader issues at stake. By adapting aspects of Japanese culture in her American works, Uchida participated in larger efforts to encourage worldwide friendship that attempted to offset the past sufferings from the Pacific War and the new tensions of the Cold War.

Reorienting Postwar Japan

Uchida's interest in Japanese culture was not particularly robust during her childhood. She notes in her memoirs that, when growing up in Berkeley in the 1920s and 1930s, the Uchida family ate Japanese food, worshipped at a Christian church with services conducted in Japanese, and observed Japanese holidays and traditions. This ancestral culture was for the young girl part of a daily ingrained ritual but also something she reluctantly endured. Often it challenged her sense of being an American, something she considered herself to be first and foremost. But she inherently knew and acknowledged later that the overlapping worlds of the Issei and Nisei contributed to shaping her attitudes, beliefs, and values. In her memoir for young readers, *The Invisible Thread,* Uchida reveals her initial longing for the power, attractiveness, and greater social ease that whiteness could grant her. "How wonderful it would be, I used to think, if I had blond hair and blue eyes . . . [o]r a name like Mary Anne Brown or Betty Johnson."[33] As in other ethnic autobiographies, Uchida recounts the difficulties of coming of age segregated from, but also living within, the white American mainstream. Although she avoids a more developed interiority or a more pronounced rebuke of white supremacy in her work, she still discloses the resentments and insecurities of being marked as alien, while negotiating between the nation's predominant values and behaviors and her parents' influences.[34]

At one point, Uchida recalls resisting her mother's desires that she and her sister learn to read and write Japanese to communicate with extended family across the Pacific. "We wanted to be *Americans,* not Japanese!" she exclaims. Language itself, and a "foreign" one at that, would only serve to estrange her further from her attempts to assimilate or to become invisible (15). Uchida expands on how this feeling of not belonging led her to distance herself from her parents, who embodied the "alien" presence of the Japanese in the United States. In *Desert Exile,* she notes: "Many of us Nisei tried to reject our own Japaneseness and the Japanese ways of our parents" (42). The Issei's clothes, habits, food, and inability to speak English fluently presented a burden and a betrayal to their progeny. The behavior of Uchida's mother was especially bothersome. When meeting Japanese friends in public, Mrs. Uchida would bow incessantly, proving a source of constant embarrassment for the Nisei daughter. Iku Uchida made evident what Yoshiko sought to escape: the "peculiar" customs of the Issei that she feared would accentuate her own foreignness by association.

This dual identity would become more complicated when Uchida traveled as a child with her family to Japan to visit relatives in the 1930s. She reminisces in *The Invisible Thread* how she felt caught between two worlds. On the one hand, Uchida enjoyed the adventure of meeting her parents' extended families, of visiting temples and shrines, and of enjoying other new experiences. She also felt relieved that she could fit into the wider Japanese population. "Here, at least, I looked like everyone else," she writes. "Here, I blended in and wasn't always the one who was different" (52). On the other hand, she could not escape her own alienation in Japan. Although she understood Japanese when spoken to, she could not read the language and spoke it haltingly. Uchida and her sister also dressed and acted differently from their peers and elders. Asserting her sense of American identity, she admits homesickness: "I missed my own language and the casual banter with friends. I longed for hot dogs and chocolate sodas and bathrooms with plumbing." Despite this yearning for home, Uchida realized the difficult position in which she found herself: "The sad truth was, in America, too, I was perceived as a foreigner" (52). Not only was she caught between two worlds; she felt that she belonged to neither.

These sentiments were no mere self-pity on her part. The outbreak of World War II brought Uchida's feelings of estrangement to full-fledged tragedy for her and other Japanese Americans in the United States. But the youthful complacency she displayed toward her ethnic ancestry began to dissolve in the cauldron of her wartime experiences. What the American nation suspected as a sign of disloyalty among the Issei and Nisei now offered something she could embrace afterward to challenge racial prejudice at home and to help develop better transpacific relations between two erstwhile enemies.

A significant moment for Uchida's budding career came in 1952, when she won a Ford Foundation fellowship to study the arts in Japan. This visit offered opportunities to develop her appreciation of Japanese culture as well as to see friends and relatives. Even so, she continued to struggle to see how she fit between two cultures, reflecting on how her American citizenship presented possibilities and privileges in Japan that the Japanese themselves did not have, even as she shared in their racial ancestry. For Uchida, Japan in the postwar years was both wasteland and wonderland. She began recording her travels and experiences there in stereotypical American ways. The author saw the nation as backward, dirty, and lacking in the modern necessities that she was used to back home. Material deprivation among the populace was still rampant, and this state of want made her appreciate her life back in the United States all the more. At the same time, Uchida remarked on how visiting Japan gave her the chance not only to study its cultural forms but also to deepen her own understanding of the United States. She was already familiar with racism before the war and during the mass imprisonment of Japanese Americans. But seeing how the U.S. occupiers implemented democracy in Japan also made her more reflective about both the ideal's promises and its limitations when applied to other lands. Uchida certainly supported American attempts to democratize Japan. Yet she also warned her Japanese readers and listeners against embracing too much of Western culture. She advised instead that Japan develop its own styles of democratic living that harmonized with its ancient traditions. Thus Uchida's overseas interactions complicated her views of each nation, and she acquired a more cosmopolitan outlook that led her to advocate for multilateral exchanges that served more than just American interests.

Arriving in Tokyo in October 1952, Uchida wrote to inform her parents in Oakland about the family and friends she visited, the wonderful food she ate, and the sites she saw. Ambling throughout the city, however, Uchida still described Japan as "primitive and crude" or "a poor country with so many problems."[35] When touring a public park (once the Imperial Gardens) with relatives in Shinjuku, a ward of Tokyo, Uchida particularly enjoyed the chrysanthemum beds. But she also compared the plants there to the populace of Japan. "All [of the gardens] were very formal and shaped to certain molds," she noted to family members back in California, "and I thought they were just like the Japanese people." "Instead of growing freely and naturally," she continued, "they are molded and shaped and constantly disciplined all their lives, and so are very unnatural in their behavior."[36] With this characterization she sought to explain how the Japanese could have followed an emperor, and especially the militarists, during the war. Also evident was her hope that liberal democratic reforms would help them to grow "freely and naturally" to align more with American values and interests.

When Uchida landed in Kyoto a month later, however, shifts occurred in her thinking about the country. Part of this change in mind-set started with her thoughts about being an American of Japanese ancestry in Japan. She noticed the opportunities that her U.S. citizenship provided, a status that did little to offset the detriments of being a Japanese American in the United States during the war. The U.S. occupation, although officially ended by the time of her visit, remained a part of how she negotiated the country. The American military presence in and around Kyoto allowed her special admittance to tourist sites and archives. She also gained entrance to guarded venues, such as the Imperial Palace grounds, that no ordinary Japanese person could access. On the one hand, "to have a Japanese face brings no special privileges," she noted about herself and about the native populace. On the other hand, having Japanese features but also "an American passport is often a ticket of admission to many interesting places."[37] Uchida realized the benefits of being an American citizen to her travels and her work. Yet occupying this position was also a humbling experience that complicated her transpacific sensibilities. The privileges she enjoyed made her more attentive to the social inequalities she saw between white Americans in Japan, with whom she identified as a U.S. citizen, and a Japanese population that looked like her.

Uchida thus amended her earlier understanding of Japan, just as she recalibrated her outlook on the United States. In January 1953, she wrote home, "Right now, America seems to me a smooth, shiny, brassy, efficient machine." Indeed, she elaborated, "American life seems very shallow as I look at it from over here—and too preoccupied with physical ease and comfort." Japan, however, is "a rather old and soiled tea cup made of clay, simple, but with much depth."[38] Living in postwar Japan accentuated Uchida's thinking about the limits of American culture and modernity, including their effects on people's attitudes, while her appreciation of Japanese values and traditions continued to grow. From this vantage point, she critiqued the degree to which American democracy and mass consumerism could benefit other peoples and nations. Instead, she valorized a sense of authenticity about Japan, which affected her desire to see and experience it in part, ironically, as an American tourist and consumer.

The author admitted her enthrallment with Japan and the limits of American influence on it in a March 1953 interview for the *Mainichi,* a major Tokyo-based newspaper. Uchida's personal education developed alongside her realization that Japan, with "its poverty, its unsanitary conditions, its low standard of living . . . differed from American life." Yet, after having spent five months there, Uchida confessed, "Those purely physical aspects of Japan have become increasingly unimportant to me." "I have come to understand and respect Japanese culture," she continued, "and have found much to admire in the serenity and beauty of its many art forms." In Uchida's mind, American materialism and individualism posed a great danger to Japan, and she felt that they should not indiscriminately adopt all U.S. tenets and practices. As she cautioned her Japanese readers, parts of U.S. culture "are only very superficial aspects of American life, and yet, they seem to be incorporated into Japanese life as a part of 'democracy.'"[39] She did not desire to see

Japan develop into a miniature version of the United States. Rather, she urged the Japanese to selectively approach how they would fit American ideals and values into their own culture.

Uchida's two books for young adults set in postwar Japan reflect this position: *Takao and Grandfather's Sword* (1958) and *The Full Circle* (1957). Her storytelling took new directions, revealing to American readers the folk culture of modern Japan in the former work and, in the latter, how the Pacific War and the U.S. occupation affected Japanese youths' sense of their social responsibilities.

Takao and Grandfather's Sword is a fictional tale about a young Japanese boy in Kyoto who desires to help his father in the pottery business. In this celebration of folk culture, Uchida elaborates on the tensions between tradition and modernity, with Japanese culture consisting of both. *Arrietty's Notes,* a publicity vehicle for the book's issuer, Harcourt, Brace and Company, suggested about the author, "This talented young Japanese-American has a special gift for interpreting the ancient and modern ways of Japan to American children."[40] Uchida wanted her American readers to know that, despite the U.S. occupation, Japan was no ordinary developing nation. It already had a proud sense of modernity that coexisted with its ancient traditions. In this way, Uchida shared a view advanced by another Cold War cosmopolitan, the University of Chicago anthropologist Robert Redfield. Redfield argued that a society's particular traditions were vital to guiding and shaping its modernization process. Although they accepted the premises of Western liberalism, both the children's author and the anthropologist believed that the universal values binding humans together still depended on appreciating the cultural differences expressed through localized customs.[41]

Uchida's interest in Japan's artistic traditions coincided with her portrayals of its innovations. Part of her strategy when writing about Japanese folk culture was to display the roots of an already existing democratic practice to American audiences. Describing the influences that went into composing *Takao and Grandfather's Sword,* Uchida noted her attraction to *mingei* (folk arts). An idea advanced through the Folk Arts Movement by three of its main artists—Yanagi Soetsu, Kawai Kanjiro, and Yamada Shoji—*mingei* captured Japanese interest in the late 1920s and continued throughout the 1930s and into the war.[42] For Uchida, the lure of *mingei* was its artists' appreciation of ordinary material used by ordinary people. Yanagi, Kawai, and Yamada, she wrote in 1955 for the magazine *Craft Horizons,* "expressed a common desire to tell the world how they had uncovered objects of uncommon beauty among the ordinary articles used by the rural folk of Japan in their everyday lives."[43] Uchida's embrace of folk culture was vital to understanding the version of Japan that she wanted to transmit to American readers. She made the connection clear when dedicating *Takao and Grandfather's Sword* to her friends in the Folk Arts Movement. But, as she stressed, postwar Japan would still have to chart its own course within this broader rubric. Unlike the United States, as Uchida continued in the *Craft Horizons* piece, "Japan . . . is one of the few industrialized countries of the world [that] maintains a fairly healthy balance between machine and handmade articles."[44]

In *Takao and Grandfather's Sword,* the boy Takao and his family struggle to make a living through folk crafts. The demands of modern production and consumerism do not so much threaten as pressure those who participate in the ancient ways of making pottery. Takao's father is financially dependent on Mr. Kato, an unscrupulous middleman, and the network of local shop owners who sell the wares. Manufacturing demands are made clear through Mr. Kato, who also has associations with buyers in the United States, marking how global exchanges are connected to consumer desires. Mr. Kato tells Takao's father that one purchaser sailing for America needs twenty-five tea sets within the next three weeks. Mass production and consumerism link Mr. Kato and his client to the demands of efficiency, with little appreciation for how a more traditional society creates finer wares. Takao's father initially resists such a request, noting the difficulties in mass-producing handicrafts in short order. "It is not wise to hurry the making of a beautiful thing," he cautions.[45] But he relents to keep his business solvent. Takao in response likens the predatory and materialistic Mr. Kato to an old dragon, with the smoke pluming from a pipe held between his gold teeth. Increasing the family's ire, Mr. Kato also covets Takao's samurai sword, a valuable relic bestowed on the boy by his deceased grandfather.

The plot develops around Takao's guilt when a series of consequences arise from his mistakes and immaturity, especially when the family workshop and pottery catch fire from his negligence. Strengthened by strong winds, the flames destroy his father's work in progress. The boy offers to compensate for the family's loss by selling his grandfather's sword and giving the profits to his father to begin crafting again. An old and mysterious gentleman, Mr. Yamaka, buys the sword. But, touched by Takao's concern for his family's business, Mr. Yamaka agrees to finance the new production of ceramic wares. He then chastises Mr. Kato, revealing himself as the owner of the local shops on which the middleman relies. Mr. Yamaka returns the sword to Takao, realizing that its value extends beyond any monetary worth, and thanks the boy for befriending him. In this way, Uchida suggested how market forces should not overly determine personal relationships, which she feared would happen if Japan followed the path the United States wanted it to take. Yet she still maintained a selective amount of faith in these same liberal foundations on which she thought modern societies should be established.

The Full Circle focuses on one family's experiences in imperial and occupied Japan, based on the real life of Umeko Kagawa, the daughter of the prominent Christian leader Dr. Toyohiko Kagawa. Published by Friendship Press, an organ of the National Council of Churches, *The Full Circle* intended to show American readers Umeko's "hopes and dilemmas . . . shared by teenagers the world over." More specifically, Uchida wanted to disclose her subject's "problems in adjusting to a postwar world similar to those that confront many young people in Japan."[46] Thus, in one sense, the book is similar to Uchida's other works, in that she employs a Cold War cosmopolitan framing of friendship to show how to bridge the cultural gaps between the United States and Japan. At the same time, Uchida delves into the wartime and postwar history of Japan to offer more complex and humane portraits of its people. The second goal, however, reinforces the first: all peoples and nations suffered during the war, but Japan still needed to rebuild on its own terms.

The book's title refers to how Umeko Kagawa initially resists the legacy of her famous father's work in Japan, but then comes "full circle"—that is, to understanding and embracing this legacy—and realizing its larger social value. As young girls, Umeko and her friend Kazu desire independence from their families and from Japan's cultural traditions. Umeko wants to be a writer or an actress rather than enter an occupation that, like her father's, requires personal sacrificing for the good of the community. Indeed, this service to others has a price. As Uchida writes, "Father was always so busy with his work, sometimes Umeko felt that she really did not know him very well" (13). But Umeko is also oblivious to the broader implications of living in a militarist state, barely absorbing the concerns of her parents. As a twelve-year-old in 1941, Umeko cannot fathom the ensuing horrors that her family and her nation will endure once the United States enters the Pacific War.

Not until the attack on Pearl Harbor does Umeko realize what is coming, when Dr. Kagawa and his friends become suspects of the Japanese government because of their Christian pacifist beliefs. Although Umeko fails to comprehend the whole of these developments, the text also delineates the elders' worries about their inability to stop the militarists. Hearing the news about Pearl Harbor, Umeko thinks to herself, "She couldn't suddenly hate America as an enemy country. So many of the missionaries who had come to work in Japan were Americans. How could she possibly hate them?" (28). *The Full Circle* in this manner highlights through the Kagawa family the antimilitarist tendencies that certain parts of the Japanese population advocated. This portrayal would then give hope to Americans that Japan could reject its imperial past and sympathize with U.S. interests. *The Full Circle* also emphasizes the opportunities for Christian conversions in postwar Japan, with these issues coming together in Umeko's mind. During the hardships of war and defeat, she then acknowledges the value of her father's labors on behalf of a wider spiritual community and his work as a postwar mediator between occupied Japan and the American forces.

Uchida admired Dr. Kagawa's Christian pacifist beliefs, but she also suggested that a pluralist democracy would offer a better foundation on which to construct Japan's future. She trusted that the nation's prospects would include Christian elements. Yet the Japanese needed to encompass other beliefs too. Uchida raised this point in her 1953 interview with the *Mainichi,* when she expressed a desire to see postwar Japan adopt more democratic practices without hewing toward the crass materialism they engendered. She also hoped that Japan would retain many of its traditions, including non-Christian ones. This idea is evident in *Takao and Grandfather's Sword,* in which the community practices Buddhism. Uchida at one point even admitted to the allure of Buddhism when meeting Kawai Kanjiro, one of the master artists of the Folk Arts Movement. Kawai, she wrote in *The Invisible Thread,* "introduced Zen Buddhist thought into my consciousness. . . . I was growing and reaching, and that felt good." This experience, she continued, was part of what "I admired and loved about Japan" (131). Although considering herself a Christian, Uchida was drawn to Buddhism as another way to attain spiritual peace. But she also saw the belief system as part of a longer ancestral history that a diverse and democratic Japan could still nurture.

Thus, even as *The Full Circle* traces Umeko's moral development when she accepts her social obligations, the work also urges the Japanese to adopt the best of what their nation and the United States offered, while rejecting each of their ills. The character Miss Tanaka, Umeko's music teacher, voices what Uchida herself told the Japanese newspapers: "You young people want to make everything black and white, but everything Japanese isn't necessarily bad and everything Western isn't always good." As Miss Tanaka elaborates: "You've got to be discriminating and choose the good from both" (122). Uchida in this way positioned herself as a cosmopolitan writer who refused to accept the unilateral enacting of American ideals and practices onto Japan. As a Japanese/American writer, she legitimized her opinions on the basis of having lived in both nations and seeing the opportunities and limitations of each. Readers acknowledged her position as a cultural broker. In one letter to Uchida, a close friend pinpointed the author's intent after finishing *The Full Circle*: "Now what country do you belong to? Both, of course, and to the whole world."[47]

Balancing different cultures, however, tests Umeko's maturity and willingness to serve others when her friend Kazu starts dating an American GI during the occupation. For Kazu, the relationship offers the hope of a more independent life from her traditional parents. But Kazu's family denounces the affair and arranges a marriage for her to an impoverished Japanese merchant. Umeko learns after the wedding that her friend lives in a poverty-stricken area in town. Kazu's submission to her family's more traditional ways curbs her sense of self-determination, one awakened by fraternizing with the American soldier. This development offers a counterargument to the warnings that the music teacher Miss Tanaka and Uchida herself imparted about Japan embracing all things Western. That is, tradition itself can be burdensome. Both Umeko and Kazu denounce the unfairness of elders who can decide the direction of their young lives. Yet Kazu's arranged marriage and ensuing hardships are the key moments that cement Umeko's commitment to helping her friend and others like her. Thus Umeko comes "full circle" when rejecting her idealized sense of independence that borders on selfishness and instead follows in her father's footsteps of performing socially conscious work for the less fortunate.

The Full Circle's significance is also apparent in ways that may have affected Uchida's later writings. Reading this text in light of her works from the 1970s and beyond, when her books on the wartime confinement appeared, reveals similarities in how, leading up to the Pacific War, the United States and Japan confined or terrorized populations that maintained overseas connections. In *The Full Circle,* Uchida details the effects of a militarized society on families and their extended relations. The wartime experiences of the Kagawas from this perspective correspond with Uchida's dramatizing some of her own family's hardships in *Journey to Topaz* and *Journey Home.* In *The Full Circle,* Dr. Kagawa draws the notice of the military police because of his Christian pacifism. At one point, they even take him into custody for interrogation. This incident recalls Uchida's chronicling of the FBI detaining her father after the attack on Pearl Harbor. *Journey to Topaz* begins with the roundup of Japanese men, which frightens the main character, Yuki Sakane, a preteen girl like Umeko Kagawa, when Yuki's father is arrested. Also disruptive to family life in imperial Japan and in the United States is how both nations forced their minority populaces to take self-protective measures against impending suspicions and seizures. In *The Full Circle,* the music teacher Miss Tanaka burns her notes and papers, fearing that they might implicate her in the crime of appreciating Western classical compositions. Other friends of the Kagawas who are Japanese Christians are questioned about their relationships with the West and its missionaries. Likewise, when hearing reports from Pearl Harbor, Japanese Americans destroyed artifacts, documents, and other material objects that linked them by association to Japan before their removal and confinement. For Umeko Kagawa and Yuki Sakane, then, the wartime and postwar eras provide corresponding backdrops for their moral development and coming of age in challenging times.

Evident as well in *The Full Circle* and in Uchida's later texts on the confinement are the costs of military service on young men in imperial Japan and the United States. Toshio, the adopted elder brother of Umeko, joins the Imperial Army in a fit of patriotism. Afterward, he becomes disillusioned by his combat experiences in the Pacific and suffers from feelings of dishonor for surviving the war as a prisoner of the Americans. Once returned home, he ignores his bewildered family and joins the communists and black marketeers to vent his frustrations against the uncertainties of the new world order. Umeko and Dr. Kagawa can only hope that Toshio will return to the family's Christian fold. But Toshio is representative of the larger unease that both Japanese Christians and Americans had about the discontent and chaos brewing in Japan, which bore the imprint of communist agitation. Likewise, Uchida creates in *Journey to Topaz* and *Journey Home* the character Ken Sakane, Yuki's elder brother. Joining other Nisei soldiers of the 442nd Regiment, Ken returns in a frazzled state of mind, suffering a survivor's guilt since his best friend is killed in action. Like Toshio in *The Full Circle,* Ken is terse and uptight: both veterans display damaged psyches from the war. For Umeko, "something was wrong" when she sees Toshio "thin and unshaven" (86), with "the rims of his eyes . . . strangely red against the paleness of his cheeks" (88). For Yuki, "something was different" with Ken. "There were creases fanning out from the corners of his eyes now, and he was so thin she could see his pale skin stretched taut over the bones of his cheeks and his jaw."[48] Here, Uchida reprocessed the language of wartime trauma when describing how returning soldiers adapted to the changes in postwar Japan and in the United States. In such parallel scenes, the parents of these Japanese and Japanese American veterans can only urge patience and understanding from Umeko and Yuki, respectively, when living among young men with tortured souls.

Uchida's comparison of the actions of imperial Japan and the United States during the war does not suggest that she saw them in the same way. She did not believe that a militarist regime with an emperor was on par with a democratic government. Especially during the postwar occupation, the reconstruction of Japan presented many challenges, both for its populace and for its occupiers, as the United States became a dominant world power. In *The Full Circle,* Toshio never recovers from his postwar disenchantment, despite Umeko's pleadings for him to return to school. The Kagawa family can do nothing to stop him from joining the communists, and he eventually disappears from their lives. In *Journey Home,* Ken never questions the rationale for the United States going to war, or his decision to volunteer from the camps to prove his patriotism. Similar to the model behavior of other Nisei soldiers, he demonstrates his loyalty to the cause. His only problem is that he cannot forgive himself for his inability to prevent his friend's death. But Ken's mental state improves when he resolves to continue his education to become a physician. Despite these differences, Uchida's larger intention was to delineate the common bonds that linked families across the Pacific in their desires for peace. She also charted the adjustments that civilians and former soldiers had to make in postwar societies. Uchida thus presented to her predominantly white American readers how World War II affected the humanity of both Japanese and Japanese Americans. Uchida's young adult texts on this level emphasized the need to create more compassion and understanding between the two nations in light of their sacrifices and sufferings during that time.

On another front, not until years afterward did the language in *The Full Circle* become more apparent in Uchida's thinking as applied to her own experiences regarding Japanese American confinement. Like Umeko Kagawa, Uchida revealed her own coming "full circle" in her life when she realized the importance of Japanese culture to her identity during and after World War II. In the epilogue to her memoir, *Desert Exile,* Uchida documented how her travels throughout Japan in the 1950s were "as positive and restorative as the evacuation had been negative and depleting" (152). In this assertion, the sentiments stirred from remembering her wartime experiences in the United States required addressing. Visiting postwar Japan was for her a significant source of healing, from which she could assuage and confront the traumas of her confinement as an American citizen. Uchida also gained a new appreciation for a family ancestry that she never fully acknowledged when growing up. By early adulthood, however, "the circle was complete" (152). Likewise, when concluding *The Invisible Thread,* the author admitted, "In my eagerness to be accepted as an American during my youth, I had been pushing my Japaneseness aside. Now at last, I appreciated it and was proud of it. I had finally come full circle" (131).

Uchida's travels in postwar Japan, her visits with folk arts craftsmen, and her work on Umeko Kagawa's life story arose from a revitalized interest in the exchanges between American and Japanese cultures. In *Takao and Grandfather's Sword,* she delineated the need to balance modern and traditional ways of thinking in Japan after the U.S. occupation. *The Full Circle* shared this theme, as both works provided American readers a sympathetic glimpse into the experiences of a former enemy population. But Uchida's embrace of cosmopolitan ideals had a larger thematic and chronological reach. As developed in her later work on the Japanese American confinement, she applied an earlier postwar vocabulary of realization and acceptance to express her maturation, assessing in more nuanced fashion a cultural heritage that she had once rejected as alien and threatening.

Creating a Multiethnic America

Uchida's strategy to enhance American understanding of other nations and cultures is also evident in her books that showcased multiethnic relationships within the United States. While working on the Japanese folktales and on stories about postwar Japan, she also published books for young readers that depicted friendships among white American, Japanese American, and Japanese characters. *New Friends for Susan* (1951), *The Promised Year* (1959), and *Mik and the Prowler* (1960) offered models of behavior for getting along with others, with Japanese and Japanese American protagonists often at the center of attention. In these novels, Uchida crafted utopian worlds that transcended the complicated geopolitical forces exerted on children's lives, such as those described in *The Full Circle*. Indeed, she was well aware of the three books' propaganda value for advertising the American way of life to international readers, especially in Japan. Yet, when presenting examples of cosmopolitan friendships, Uchida avoided addressing the wartime imprisonment in these texts, even though they featured Japanese Americans as main characters. As in her folktales, Uchida instead emphasized the more saleable theme of enhancing cultural understanding at home and abroad to diminish racial discrimination and future conflicts.

At first glance, *New Friends for Susan* would gain little notice nowadays. Uchida based the work on her own childhood memories of growing up in the Bay Area during the 1930s. The plot is fairly conventional, revolving around nine-year-old girls who befriend one another, host and attend parties, participate in after-school activities, and enjoy the love and support of their parents. Yet what is striking about the text, given its release during the early Cold War years, is that it presents children of different ethnic backgrounds developing close relationships with one another. Susan, the Nisei protagonist, brings together her newfound friends, one from white middle-class America and the other from Japan. The value of *New Friends for Susan,* then, is in its demonstration of a Japanese American household as a negotiated space, wherein mainstream American aspirations and the less familiar world of Japanese culture meet and influence one another.

Susan becomes an intermediary between these two worlds. When Susan and her white friends participate in a festival celebrating different cultures across the globe, she dresses in a kimono to emphasize her ancestry. She also invites her classmates to her home to show them her Japanese doll collection to coincide with Japan's Doll Festival. In these instances, readers see how children from diverse upbringings appreciate and learn from one another's cultural differences. Susan also receives a visit from a Japanese girl, Sumiko. The visual and aural proximity of Susan's name with Sumiko's suggests an ancestral kinship between the two characters. Their names thus reconnect a world separated by the Japanese diaspora. Yet, unlike what happened in World War II, when Japanese Americans were suspected of sympathizing with the enemy solely on the basis of ethnicity, *New Friends for Susan* embraces, rather than hides or denies, this cultural link. Sumiko becomes a popular student at Susan's school, sitting as a model for an art class, in which the curious and welcoming students want to paint the visitor's portrait. As the book concludes, Susan looks forward to future interactions with Sumiko as she sees her new friend off at the San Francisco pier. Susan imagines herself in Sumiko's place as the young Japanese girl sails for home, creating a transpacific sensibility connected by personal ties between the United States and Japan. The text closes on a hopeful note, emphasizing again Uchida's internationalist approach to writing children's literature. "The whole world felt so good just then," the author writes, "so friendly and complete and full of promise."[49] In Susan's mind, her ability to make friends not only in other neighborhoods but also across the ocean encourages her self-confidence and her broadening views of the outside world.

Although *New Friends for Susan* never mentions the wartime confinement, its promotional material did emphasize the incarceration as part of the author's background. In a form letter to potential reviewers, Alice Dalgliesh, the editor of "Books for Younger Readers" at Charles Scribner's Sons, remarked on the normality of the main character's experiences. *New Friends for Susan,* she wrote, is "the first picture of a Japanese-American child growing up normally and happily in this country, and having the home and school experiences of any child." Susan, that is, was like other children in the United States, despite her potential to disrupt notions of what constituted an "American" through her racial Otherness. Dalgliesh wanted reviewers to know, however, that "Miss Uchida was one of the 'Moved-Outers'—Japanese Americans sent to camps during the war." The editor also mentioned that Henry Sugimoto (analyzed in Chapter 3) was the illustrator for the book and had spent time in the prison camps as well. The text's dust jacket included a short biography of Uchida, noting that she received her college diploma while imprisoned at Tanforan. Although the book publicity brought attention to Uchida's confinement, it also highlighted how she and other Japanese Americans triumphed over this past adversity. Dalgliesh even categorized *New Friends for Susan* as "quiet and unassuming," terms used by the mainstream press to portray Japanese Americans as model citizens. In these accounts, Uchida became associated with the forgiving ethnic minority who achieved success despite the disadvantages of her once maligned ancestry.[50]

This information only underscores the lack of discussion of the confinement in *New Friends for Susan.* No mention of it appears in the text, since the plot occurs in the 1930s, before Japanese Americans were uprooted and imprisoned. But the children's literature critic for the *New York Times,* Gladys Grofoot Castor, noticed upon the book's release the incongruity between the book's cheerful storyline and its missing references to the mass imprisonment. "The wartime experiences of the Japanese-Americans on the West Coast," she remarked, "are not touched upon, nor is there the faintest plea for racial tolerance."[51] Although Castor did not develop her critique beyond this statement, the point was clear. She was looking for something in *New Friends for Susan* that would indicate the author's willingness to teach American children about racial and ethnic differences and about the tolerance required for a diverse society to function in the postwar era. Despite this caveat, Castor praised the novel, finding it an enjoyable read. Reviews of *New Friends for Susan* in Japanese American newspapers, such as *Rafu Shimpo, Nichi Bei Times,* and *Hokubei Shimpo,* quoted Castor's fleeting yet significant remark about the absence of addressing racial tolerance and the tragedy of confinement. At the same time, these critics avoided developing or commenting on her statement. None offered more pointed assessments, suggestions, or options of approach.[52] Perhaps like Castor, they too realized the limits of what Uchida could accomplish in a book designed for young children. Yet Japanese American reviewers took pride in Uchida's achievements, which had garnered national attention, and may have wanted to evade criticism of a Nisei who wrote about multiethnic friendships among children.

What also must be considered is Uchida's early writing experiences and prior career as an elementary school teacher in the camps and afterward. At Topaz, she was in charge of the first- through third-grade students. In June 1943, Uchida had the opportunity to leave Topaz, having been accepted into the graduate program in education at Smith College. During this time, she also taught at a public school in western Massachusetts. She then graduated in 1944 and accepted a teaching position for first and second graders at the Frankford Friends School, a Quaker institution in Philadelphia.[53] Given her experiences with these early elementary schoolchildren, Uchida may have found it too difficult to convey the experiences and thought processes of characters in confinement in fictional form. She also may have felt that the topic was not appropriate for a novel that Charles Scribner's Sons marketed to seven-to-nine-year-old readers.[54]

Earlier children's works from other authors did emerge about the wartime confinement. Florence Crannell Means's *The Moved-Outers* (1945), a Newbery Honor award winner, presents one example of young adult fiction that incorporated the forced removal and incarceration of Japanese Americans as a major theme. This novel, however, was intended for higher grade–level readers, with its teenage main protagonists, Kim and Sue Ohara, a brother and a sister, respectively. Means took care to research her topic, interviewing Japanese Americans who had been incarcerated at Amache, the prison camp in Colorado. In this story, the Ohara family tries to make the best of their difficult situation. Kim over time begins to question his place in the United States, while Sue sustains her faith in the American Dream. Means privileges the protagonists' model status as a clean-cut, middle-class family to heighten her point about the injustice of imprisoning such law-abiding citizens. The high-school-age central characters also speak with the optimism and innocence of their youth. But Means refused to shy away from the complexities of camp life, depicting the Japanese Americans at Amache as diverse and divided in opinion about their present and future circumstances.

As discussed earlier, Uchida was often upfront when talking about racial prejudice in the Bay Area and about her confinement experiences when promoting her Japanese folktales. Yet her evasion of the incarceration in *New Friends for Susan* was consistent with her other public statements about her broader purpose in writing children's books. As she noted for the *Nichi Bei Times* in 1951, "What I want most from this book is to have children who read it somehow realize that all children are basically alike no matter what their racial backgrounds may be."[55] Both domestic and international relationships, she emphasized, required a level of mutual understanding to avoid the pitfalls of prejudice, oppression, and violence. To suggest that the book contained little in the way of pleading for racial tolerance, then, misses the intentions and actions of Susan and her friends. Uchida urged children to be more accepting, based on the model of her protagonists' behaviors toward one another. Playing on the ideals of Cold War cosmopolitanism while eyeing potential sales, the author wanted to focus on the similarities and shared interests among children of different backgrounds. Her aim in *New Friends for Susan* was to create a utopian vision of a multiethnic American childhood that reflected her hopes for peace and understanding in the early 1950s.

The appeal of *New Friends for Susan* contributed to the advancement of American priorities in the Cold War. The U.S. Army found the text useful, incorporating it into its reorientation program in occupied Japan. To acclimate the Japanese to democratic ideals, the Army established libraries with films, books, and magazines that encouraged American liberal values and the possibilities they could offer Japan. This goal had larger geopolitical aims and consequences. By "bringing the peoples of occupied areas into the mainstream of democratic life," as the program's 1950 annual report noted, the United States will "make friends who will uphold democracy against totalitarian ideologies and similar forms of government."[56] As its title suggests, *New Friends for Susan* suited this purpose. As one officer wrote to an assistant editor at Charles Scribner's Sons in October 1951, "The book is a delightful picture of little girls—Japanese, American, and Japanese-American—and will be highly suitable for the Reorientation Program that the Army is carrying out in its Information Centers in Japan."[57] The novel's multiethnic characters and the lessons of getting along matched the objectives of the United States to show the workings of a diverse and tolerant democracy to Japanese audiences that, in turn, could help contain communism.

That Uchida avoided the theme of wartime confinement in *New Friends for Susan* increased its attraction for the reorientation program since the U.S. Army wanted to promote democracy's benefits, as opposed to its failings, to young readers in Japan. Her work thus accommodated U.S. overseas objectives within a Cold War liberal framing to contain communism and to integrate regions into market and military alliances. But Uchida's efforts require further consideration within a wider chronological context. In 1965, more than a decade after *New Friends for Susan*'s release, one reporter for the *Saturday Review of Literature* noted how the majority of children's books still included only white protagonists. This lack of ethnic diversity had global implications. "There seems little chance of developing the humility so urgently needed for world cooperation, instead of world conflict, as long as our children are brought up on gentle doses of racism through their books," she declared.[58] What Uchida accomplished in her children's tales through multicultural themes and characters cannot be undervalued, given the restrictive circumstances of the Cold War. Yet even as her works enlarged possibilities for global understanding, they also presented boundaries on addressing past tragedies.

However limiting Uchida's strategy to avoid the wartime incarceration as a topic was, this evasion proved successful for her early career. The central grouping of white American, Japanese American, and Japanese characters in *New Friends for Susan* found its way into her later children's novels. *The Promised Year* (1959) and *Mik and the Prowler* (1960) offer similar structures in which three different types of characters befriend one another. Yet the plots occur explicitly in the postwar world, as opposed to the earlier context of *New Friends for Susan*. In *The Promised Year,* a young Japanese girl travels to the United States to stay with her aunt and uncle in the Bay Area and befriends a white American boy. *Mik and the Prowler* focuses on a Sansei youth who, with the help of his white friend and a visiting Japanese girl, solves the mystery of a neighborhood burglary. Both texts, like *New Friends for Susan,* avoid mentioning the incarceration of Japanese Americans. Instead, Uchida offers a romanticized version of a multiethnic postwar nation that could move beyond prior hurts and grievances.

The Promised Year presents young audiences with a version of the United States from the perspective of a Japanese girl. Readers see the world through ten-year-old Keiko's eyes, and all sorts of mysteries and adult concerns appear to lie beyond the child's comprehension. But the text provides a more complicated vision than *New Friends for Susan,* accentuating the transnational connections retained by Japanese families after the war. The story focuses on Keiko's visit with her Aunt Emi and Uncle Henry in California. Aunt Emi knows the hardships her extended family in Japan face and writes Keiko's mother to invite one of the children to visit family in the United States for a year. Aunt Emi's letter vaguely references past wartime sufferings in Japan and the postwar abundance in the United States. "Your family is now without a father and you have many mouths to feed," she writes to Keiko's mother. "We have no children, and milk and butter are plentiful in California."[59] Keiko's father is dead, presumably a casualty of the Asia-Pacific War. The other unmentioned background story concerns Aunt Emi and Uncle Henry, who were part of the imprisoned Japanese American population from California and who returned to a level of normalcy after the war. Uchida gives neither the wartime plight of the Japanese nor the Japanese Americans much depth here. But these omissions are not surprising, given the author's evasions of still-controversial topics in her children's books at this time. Instead, Uchida focuses on the postwar reunion of once-separated family members: Keiko can at least enjoy the good life with her relatives in the United States.

If the postwar hardships in Japan establish the reason for Keiko's traveling to the United States, another reference explains the relationship between Keiko and her elders. Aunt Emi and Uncle Henry are Issei, she originally from Kyoto and he from Osaka. When Uncle Henry returns from working at his Bay Area flower business, the three sit together in the kitchen drinking tea and eating cookies. Keiko favors these moments when her uncle is more reflective, even nostalgic, about his earlier years in Japan and the United States. As Uchida writes, "The tired lines of worry would ease away from his face, he would lean back and smoke his pipe, and a softness would come into his voice. Then he would ask Keiko about Tokyo and remember about his home in Osaka and tell how different things had been before the war" (132). This brief but notable reference to World War II and its destructive consequences frames Uncle Henry's sense of nostalgia and loss. Although immigrants to the United States, he and Aunt Emi maintain familial ties to Japan that conjure more pleasant memories of their own youthful times. Aunt Emi recounts when she and Keiko's mother were adolescents and how they would explore the forests around Kyoto to enjoy the "springtime when the rice fields were green and the blossoms of the . . . plants looked like scattered gold" (133). Nature evokes the elder characters' sense of promise and rejuvenation. That these figures retain such thoughts of Japan links them to Keiko in a deeper sense. They value their ancestral homeland for its comforting memories, just as the United States offers Keiko a chance at a more comfortable future life.

Mik and the Prowler aligns more with the structure and expectations of *New Friends for Susan,* in that the main protagonist befriends both white American and Japanese children. A Sansei boy, Mikitaro Watanabe (or simply Mik), desires to prove to his parents that he is ready and responsible for adult tasks. An elderly neighbor, Mrs. Whipple, hires Mik to look after her home when she leaves town. Yet all sorts of troubles and obstacles arise that compound the boy's obligations. An intruder breaks into another neighbor's house. A Japanese girl, Tamiko, comes to visit, which at first disappoints Mik because he hoped Tamiko would be a boy. Uchida once again offers synonymous sounding and looking names for her protagonists, suggesting, as in *New Friends for Susan,* a cultural connection between Japanese and Japanese Americans. As in Uchida's other previous works, such as *Takao and Grandfather's Sword,* the text also traces Mik's maturation. He adjusts to changes in his life, allowing him to appreciate tasks and situations that were initially not to his liking.

Uchida's creation of young Japanese American characters corresponds with Beverly Cleary's volumes of children's literature that also began appearing in the 1950s. Cleary framed her books around the everyday adventures and concerns of her well-known protagonists Henry Huggins and the sisters Beezus and Ramona Quimby. Like Mik Watanabe, these characters live in a postwar consumer society with understanding parents and single-family suburban homes. The characters own or desire pets and engage, sometimes testily and sometimes warmly, with children and adults in their neighborhoods. Cleary had a better ear for the rhythms of children's banter than Uchida did. In *Henry Huggins* (1950) and *Beezus and Ramona* (1955), Cleary includes the teasing, faultfinding, and evasions that children display toward one another. Uchida, however, depicts her child protagonists, especially the Japanese American ones, as rarely getting into arguments with one another. Although not without faults, her characters are pleasant, hardly revealing the insecurities and latent concerns of children, as she builds on the ideal of a model minority. But even though Uchida never acquired the same level of popularity as Cleary did, she offered a more varied world with her ethnic minority characters. This point speaks to both the radical and moderate temperament of Uchida's works for children in the postwar era. While the author gives voice to Japanese and Japanese American characters, she also avoids having their lives associated with racial prejudice or with memories of the wartime confinement.

Reviews of *Mik and the Prowler* were mixed but revealed critics' expectations of Uchida's stories. The children's book reviewer for the *San Francisco Sunday Chronicle* noted that Uchida "builds a very comic suspense story laced with affectionate understanding of life in big families, whether they be of

Japanese ancestry or any other."[60] Here the critic acknowledged Uchida's desire to create family portraits that defied national borders and expectations. But the reviewer for the *New York Times Book Review* admitted that she "missed the special charm of [Uchida's] previous books," referring to *The Promised Year* and *Takao and Grandfather's Sword*. "Mik is so Americanized," the critic continued, "that there is no place for the expressive oriental flavor which Miss Uchida can impart so skillfully."[61] The reviewer's phrasing of "oriental flavor" marks how U.S. mass consumption highlights the exoticism of Japanese culture. But it also points to the perils of wanting to assimilate into mainstream American culture. Indeed, what makes Mik or Uchida's other characters noteworthy is their Asian ancestry. That Mik is "too Americanized" translates into him being "too white." He cannot belong in the United States without the badge of Otherness, since audiences expect that his racial features come with other ethnic trappings. This observation highlights what Ellen Wu and others have argued about the problematic positioning of Asian Americans as "assimilating Others" when attaining model minority status.[62] Mik cannot fully integrate into the white mainstream because he is not white, even though he lacks any hint of being Asian, aside from his physical appearance. Yet, if he embraces Japanese cultural traits, then this action would serve only to emphasize his Otherness. Making him appear like any other child in the United States thus presented limitations on what critics and readers alike expected from Japanese American authors and their work.

When beginning the project, Uchida explained her intention to Margaret McElderry, the editor of children's books at Harcourt, Brace and Company, that Mik should represent "any American child." Uchida further wrote, "There are no peculiarly Japanese touches within the family because these no longer exist in most *nisei* [*sic*] homes."[63] The author wanted to remark in her book on the assimilation of the Nisei and Sansei generations by the early 1960s. She did not intend to submerge or deny any cultural traits of Japanese Americans so much as she wanted to record what was happening to their families in the postwar United States. Yet McElderry, like the *New York Times* book reviewer, sensed that something was missing. *Mik and the Prowler,* she responded to Uchida, "does not in some ways have the body of Takao and Grandfather's Sword or of The Promised Year."[64] The editor still hoped that, despite *Mik and the Prowler*'s lack of emphasis on Japanese cultural traits, the work would attract an audience that identified with the assimilation of Japanese Americans.

As in *New Friends for Susan, The Promised Year* and *Mik and the Prowler* disclose Uchida's concern for creating increased global understanding amid U.S. material abundance in middle-class suburbia. That these three novels offer a distinct set of characters that embody variations of American and

Japanese identities reveals Uchida's skill at recognizing the importance of intercultural contacts. The works coincide with her Japanese folktales, in which she strove to appeal to audiences through the stories' embracing of universal characteristics and cultural differences. In her telling, a postwar future that stressed the shared qualities among societies trumped a more complicated history of war and confinement that offered an unclear path on how to redress grievances. Uchida desired a future inhabited by more peaceful-minded generations exposed to, and tolerant of, peoples from other lands and cultures. She hoped to contribute to this realization, not by recounting past wrongs, but by envisioning a utopian society filled with the possibilities of cultural exchange.

Remembering the Wartime Confinement

In September 1944, Uchida was ready to start a new chapter in her life. She graduated from Smith College and began teaching at the Frankford Friends School. In that same month, her father and mother joined her in Philadelphia after their release from Topaz, so that most of the family was together again. Educating first and second graders was enjoyable for Uchida, but the long hours of preparation and its physical demands took a toll on her already fragile health. More significantly, time engaged in the classroom prevented her from writing as a professional author, which became her most desired goal. After a year in Philadelphia, Uchida and her parents relocated to New York City, where her elder sister Kay was working, also as a schoolteacher. While in New York, Uchida worked as an office administrator for several Christian and charity organizations. By 1947, she had more time to focus on her writing and began composing her collection of Japanese folktales. It was also when she started giving voice to her imprisonment experiences.[65]

Despite the success of her first children's books, Uchida felt the need to hone her writing skills for adult readers, the target audience for her wartime tales. In 1952, shortly before traveling to Japan as a Ford Foundation fellow, she enrolled in a creative writing class at Columbia University. One of her assignments was a ten-page autobiography, from which some material later appeared in her memoirs, *Desert Exile* and *The Invisible Thread*. Readers see in this early sketch and in other writings Uchida's attempts to place the personal and historical events of her life into focus, albeit in very brief and undeveloped form. The creative work based on her confinement experiences she then sent to major periodicals. As Uchida admitted, however, "I can't quite seem to get over the hump" of getting them published.[66] Although periodicals rejected these fictional pieces, she constantly returned to them in the late 1960s to early 1970s and beyond, revising earlier themes, plots, characters, and vocabularies formed in the postwar years, to ensure that future generations of readers would appreciate the importance of this tragedy. Her children's works that appeared in the late 1940s to early 1960s provided a way to think through the issues and strategies to write about the mass incarceration. Uchida already had been recounting her wartime experiences in her diary when teaching children at Tanforan and Topaz, in postwar publicity material for the Japanese folktales, and even in *The Full Circle,* however indirectly. We can then consider these works in part as literary experiments that provided the means by which to convey her memories about the removal and confinement.

The main premise that connects many of Uchida's short stories is that, because of the suffering, endurance, and alienation of the Issei, the Nisei owe a debt to this older generation. Uchida's obligation to her parents originated when she left Topaz in 1943 to continue her education at Smith College. "My parents had been caring and compassionate people before they were uprooted," she wrote in *The Invisible Thread,* "and they still were." Her sadness and guilt at leaving them behind clarified her appreciation for what they accomplished and how they comported themselves under extreme duress. But this sentiment developed in hindsight. "I understood all this only many years after the war was over," she continued. "On that warm, dusty day" when she and her sister were released from Topaz, "my thoughts were still too muddled for me to be properly grateful" (121). This postwar expression of gratitude suggests that her emerging cosmopolitan ideals applied to embracing not only other cultures but also other generations that embodied those different cultures. As previously mentioned, Uchida tried to distance herself from the practices, beliefs, and language of her parents to assert her own sense of being an American. Supportive as they were, Dwight and Iku Uchida were still a disruptive presence in their daughter's childhood. She feared that their status as Japanese nationals and their cultural differences would wrench her from what she considered "normal" when attempting to fit into the white mainstream. But Uchida's growing awareness of Japanese culture and her travels to Japan widened her knowledge and acceptance of what was both familiar and foreign, as embodied in her parents. She not only wanted mainstream Americans to indulge their curiosity about other cultures but also urged the Nisei to appreciate the ancestral traits and treasures offered by their Issei parents. This was the dual basis on which she grounded her initial wartime memories and stories.

One of Uchida's first publications on this topic, "Courage of the Issei," appeared in the New York–based *Hokubei Shimpo* in 1949, the same year that *The Dancing Kettle* was released. She also intended the essay for the U.S. Army's reorientation program in Japan. In this piece, Uchida paid homage to the sacrifices of her parents' generation, describing the Issei in terms similar to those used by mainstream publications to portray the Nisei as model citizens after the war. This message served several purposes. Since Uchida wrote the article partly for overseas Japanese readers, she only briefly mentioned the confinement period and avoided discussing other instances of racial prejudice that Japanese Americans encountered in the United States. The Army employed the essay to show the promising aspects of democratic life in America, assuring the Japanese that the Issei persisted and succeeded as immigrants "despite the handicaps of racial discrimination." Uchida's other audience was the Nisei, who "could learn from their [parents'] perseverance, their capacity for hard work, and their courage and determination to create fine homes and families in a country once strange and foreign to them."[67] In this sense, "Courage of the Issei" was a tribute to Uchida's own mother and father, whom she came to cherish and respect as she matured. Last, the article reassured white Americans, including the Army editors, that Japanese Americans would forgive and recover from their wartime incarceration. That Uchida neither blamed the federal government at this time nor delved into the structural reasons for confinement reveals her awareness of how she had to negotiate around diverse audiences' expectations.

Among the fictional tales that Uchida composed in the early 1950s that address the confinement or its aftereffects, two of the most significant include "Saturday Visit" and "Crepe Paper Flowers." "Saturday Visit" was Uchida's only short story to appear in print in the 1950s. Published by *Woman's Day* for its October 1952 issue, the tale focuses on a young Nisei female narrator who visits an elderly Issei couple at their New York City apartment. The story indicates that the aged husband and wife had been incarcerated during the war and that they relocated afterward to the East Coast rather than return to the West, having lost their California farm. The tale's power stems not from portrayals of camp life but from the Issei couple's nostalgic remembrances of times before the war and the reality of their subsequent living conditions. The main character finds only the elderly wife at home, the husband having not yet returned from work. The two women pass the time poring over old photographs and reminiscing about life in California. In their recollections of earlier days, Uchida conjures the American pastoral ideal, in which farming the western lands presents a utopian portrait of self-sustaining livelihood. The Nisei narrator also recalls her own childhood innocence when she had visited the couple's farm, enjoying daytime picnics and nighttime stargazing. But these events were no longer possible once the war began.

Significant in this story, as in Uchida's other pieces, is the absent indictment of liberal state power or of the racial prejudice that influenced the process of mass confinement. Given its publication venue, the lack of outrage is unsurprising. Uchida instead develops a prevailing tone of nostalgia and loss. When evening descends and the Nisei narrator feels obliged to leave for another social engagement, she regrets not having more time to spend with the elder woman, especially since the husband's return is imminent. As the narrator leaves the apartment, she spots the Issei gentleman on the crowded sidewalk, going to his home. But she does not approach him, feeling that his tired and defeated posture hints at his desire to be left alone. No amount of memories from a more heartening prewar period in California can revive what has already been lost. Such were the consequences of the wartime dislocation and postwar alienation.[68]

The most noteworthy of the unpublished fictional tales from this period is "Crepe Paper Flowers," likely written around 1952.[69] The story's title refers to a real-life incident, in which the women at Topaz created the funeral decorations for a sixty-three-year-old Issei bachelor, James Hatsuki Wakasa, who was killed by a watchtower guard. Wakasa apparently had strolled too close to the barbed-wire fence and did not hear the guard's warning, which then prompted the deadly response. No one, aside from the shooter, witnessed the event. Yet troubling inconsistencies arose from the investigation by camp officials. The guard maintained that Wakasa was trying to crawl underneath the fence to escape. Wakasa's body, however, was found three feet inside the perimeter. Forensics also suggested that he was shot while facing the guard. The Topaz inmates responded with shock, distress, and anger.[70] As Uchida noted in her wartime diary on April 12, 1943, the day after the shooting, "It could easily be one of our friends or family next if this sort of thing continues. . . . [There's] more fuss now, as everyone's all stirred up about it."[71]

The incident created such controversy that it was referenced in various art forms by those incarcerated at Topaz. Miné Okubo devoted attention to it in her illustrated book *Citizen 13660* (1946). Rather than depicting Wakasa's death, she focuses instead on the effects it had on the wider Japanese American community. In the two text-and-drawing panels that commemorate the Issei bachelor, Okubo includes herself as participant and spectator. The first illustration shows a large gathering of mourners, with the casket displayed on a stage in the far background. Many of the people in the foreground, including Okubo, reveal faces that are saddened by, and resentful of, Wakasa's manner of dying. The text briefly notes how three different responses emerge. The camp administrators, she recounts, never provided an adequate explanation as to what actually happened. Among the inmates, the reactions are varied. On one side, the "pro-Japanese" leaders call for increased protests against their overall treatment. On the other, calls for "protection against soldiers with guns" arise, and the guards are eventually removed to a farther distance from the populace. These points of view not only undermine the government's stance of holding Japanese Americans in protective custody but also disclose the fractures and tensions within the inmate community, created from their confinement. The second panel is composed of a few women, Okubo again included, who quietly fashion the paper floral wreaths that will decorate Wakasa's grave. In this rendering, the women make up part of the extended camp family of Wakasa, who will carry on his memory.[72]

The painter Chiura Obata's Asian-inspired black-and-white watercolor offers another perspective. *Hatsuki Wakasa Shot by M.P.* (1943) centers on the moment of Wakasa's death as the Issei falls to the ground from the tower guard's deadly aim. The figure is bent toward a dog he was about to pet, which was Obata's explanation of what had occurred, when the soldier perhaps mistook this kindly deed as part of an attempt to escape the prison camp. But the bullet, having already entered Wakasa's body, makes him lurch forward in agony, his angled back and hips forming the apex of a triangle. His head and limbs make up the sides, and his hands and feet the points of the base. The dog, startled by the sound of the shot and Wakasa's moment of death, appears as part of the triangular extension of the dropping body as its arms reach toward the animal. The geometric shapes in the painting lend an ironic stability to this violent act. In the background, the horizontal lines created from the Utah mountains, the thin clouds overhead, and the barbed-wire fence suggest an eerie sense of permanence in the desert, against which we see the falling figure of Wakasa. The composition achieves a simple yet powerful tone that conveys how an Issei's affectionate gesture to overcome his alienation results in tragedy.

In Uchida's "Crepe Paper Flowers," the plot involves not a bachelor but an elderly couple, Mr. and Mrs. Takata, who are in the midst of removal to a camp in Utah. Unlike their friends, they initially have other options. Their estranged daughter, Mary, lives with her white husband in Nevada, outside of the restricted areas of the West Coast. To avoid the hardships of camp life, the aged parents move in with her. But Mr. and Mrs. Takata face all sorts of difficulties. As immigrants, they speak English poorly. Mary's husband's business suffers because of his known harboring of his Japanese in-laws. Mrs. Takata also tells her husband of enduring the severe glances and mutterings of the local townspeople as she goes shopping. Always awkward around their daughter anyway, the couple resolves to be with their friends and to move to the camp at Topaz.

Uchida frames the story through the eyes of Mrs. Takata, allowing the author to provide a sense of depth to the shooting victim—that is, her husband—that few in the camps knew about the real-life James Wakasa. This strategy offers both a personal and a social background for Wakasa and his fictional counterpart, Mr. Takata. The decisions Mr. and Mrs. Takata make,

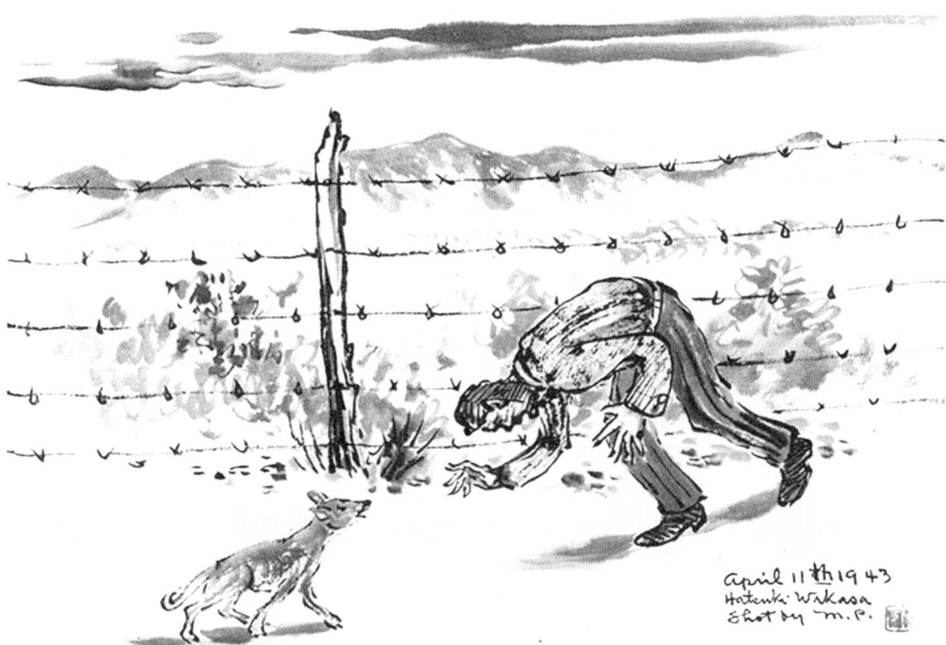

Chiura Obata, *Hatsuki Wakasa Shot by M.P.* (1943). Armed Forces History Division, National Museum of American History, Smithsonian Institution.

and the difficulties they suffer, were similar to those encountered by many Japanese Americans. Uchida in this way wanted to dramatize the collective inner torments faced during the mass imprisonment. The tale opens at the camp hospital, where Mrs. Takata is in a shocked state of mind. Having just viewed the body of her husband, she notices that "he appeared to be made of soft, crinkled tissue paper."[73] This description of his countenance parallels the story's conclusion, in which paper floral wreaths, made by the camp women from that same "soft, crinkled tissue paper," will decorate his grave.

Attempting to remember the events that had brought them to this end, Mrs. Takata blames herself for her husband's death. He had wanted to stay with their daughter. Mrs. Takata desired to be with their friends in camp. Readers see how the old couple occupies a difficult position of choosing between two unappealing options, even as Uchida again avoids critiquing the federal government that placed them in this situation. Once at Topaz, a desert with its swirling, choking dust storms, Mr. Takata becomes morose. But he soon adapts and begins collecting Indian arrowheads he finds on the ground. This is the explanation Uchida provided to explain the shooting: Mr. Takata discovered a piece for his collection near the fence, bent down to gather it, and was shot by the guard. The day after the funeral, Mrs. Takata looks out beyond the fence to where her husband's grave is located, fretting that she cannot leave him in this horrific place. Yet the paper flowers by this time are gone, like Mr. Takata's spirit, the winds having carried them over the seemingly endless desert.

Uchida's literary agent, Harriet Wolf, recognized the value of "Crepe Paper Flowers," calling it "a beautiful story."[74] This tale, however, like nearly all of Uchida's other short fiction during this early period, faced an endless stream of rejection letters. Although most editors did not specify the reasons for their decisions, one actually did. Similar to Harriet Wolf's reaction, the editor at *Charm* magazine called "Crepe Paper Flowers" beautiful. But, he insisted, the tale was "so tragic that I'm afraid we can't use it."[75] The public, he felt, was simply not ready for it. This may have been the reason for the other rebuffs that Uchida received for her other writings on the confinement. They were all too despairing for general consumption in the 1950s.

The story, of course, does not end here. The Wakasa incident, as it became known, reappeared in other versions throughout Uchida's later writings. She included the scene in her two memoirs of Japanese American confinement, *Desert Exile* and *The Invisible Thread*. But the disparities in how Uchida approaches and contextualizes the consequences of the Issei's death in these works are noteworthy. Designed for adult audiences, *Desert Exile* gives the Wakasa incident only brief mention. As Miné Okubo had done in *Citizen 13660*, Uchida links the turmoil caused by the shooting to the eruption of "pro-Japan agitators" who "became increasingly threatening" (140). Uchida's portrayal, however, carries more personal ramifications. In their anger, members of the pro-Japan faction target Japanese Americans, whom they see as collaborators with the camp authorities. The accused group included Dwight Uchida, leading to his and Iku's release in 1944 because of fears for their safety. Yet this version of events simplifies the class and cultural divisions among Japanese Americans in the camps and why some of them protested in the first place.[76] *The Invisible Thread*, a book for young adults published almost ten years after *Desert Exile*, reveals a more poignant experience for the author that avoids the internal dissensions within the inmate community. As Uchida writes, "It seemed a cruel irony that [Wakasa] could finally get beyond the barbed-wire fence only because he had died" (109). *The Invisible Thread* conveys a pointed personal tone directed more at the condition of the inmates' lives at Topaz than at anything else. Perhaps by the 1990s Uchida was more willing to forgive Japanese Americans for the conflicts that had jeopardized her parents and to censure the federal government for placing them all in such a trying position. Instead of tracing the social consequences of Wakasa's death, Uchida writes about her decision to leave the confines of imprisonment in the desert. "The bleakness of Topaz was now seeping deep inside me," she wrote. "I felt as though I couldn't bear being locked up one more day. I wanted to go out into the world and live a real life" (110).

Uchida also felt the continual need to fictionalize Wakasa's killing, as if it kept haunting her to replay it for different generations of readers. She adapted elements of "Crepe Paper Flowers" in *Journey to Topaz* and then again in *Picture Bride.* To heighten the emotional impact of the shooting, Uchida resurrects the Issei victim as a family man, with a wife, children, grandchildren, and friends and admirers. *Journey to Topaz* devotes a whole chapter to develop the tragedy. It starts with the foreboding attempts to plant trees in the desert. Mr. Kurihara, the fictional stand-in for James Wakasa, frowns on such efforts, thinking that the trees will soon perish because of the soil's lack of nourishment. This point parallels Uchida's own desire "to go out into the world and live a real life." Only death lingered in the desert, literally for Wakasa and the trees, metaphorically for Uchida and the Japanese American community. Later, no one, including the main protagonist, Yuki Sakane, believes the news of Mr. Kurihara's death by the barbed-wire fence. The event strikes her all the more, since her closest friend, Emi, is Mr. Kurihara's granddaughter. But Yuki is the source of more optimistic thoughts. She rationalizes to herself that Mr. Kurihara would not have minded his burial beyond the camp fences, since he "had grown quite fond of the desert." Indeed, "its vastness had fascinated him even as the ocean did."[77] Yet, upon seeing Mrs. Kurihara's grief, Yuki is at a loss for words to comfort any of the suffering family.

Picture Bride concludes with the slaying, one that follows the closest to "Crepe Paper Flowers." The novel depicts the trials and tribulations of an Issei woman, from her immigration to the United States at the turn of the century to her wartime incarceration. Hana Takeda, like the similarly named Mrs. Takata in the short story, endures the trauma of her husband's death while at Topaz. Yet, unlike *Journey to Topaz* and *Desert Exile,* writings that developed in the late 1960s and early 1970s, *Picture Bride* recaptures the forlorn finales of Uchida's early short stories. Although hope and endurance are themes that still resonate in her Issei characters, the harsh environment at Topaz always threatens to engulf and endanger them. The novel's last line reveals as much when Hana and her friends leave her husband's funeral: "They did not know that by the time they walked to Hana's barrack at the opposite end of camp, another dust storm would be coursing over the desert sands, enveloping all of Topaz in its white fury."[78] The intense and unresolved quality of the conclusion, in which the "white fury" of nature evokes the power of white racism enacted against Japanese Americans, is akin to Uchida's feelings expressed in *The Invisible Thread.* In both of these later works, she discloses a more pronounced frustration and sadness when remembering her encounters with racial prejudice and the wartime incarceration than she had done in *Journey to Topaz* and *Desert Exile.* In this sense, Uchida came "full circle" when conveying the despondency from her first unpublished works in the 1950s in her last books on the mass confinement appearing in the late 1980s and early 1990s.

Uchida's reverence for the Issei, her embrace of Japanese culture, and the stories she told about Tanforan and Topaz had deep roots in the postwar period. These emerged from an appreciation of her parents, who initially entertained her with Japanese folktales, established models of behavior in the face of life's challenges, and provided material for her works on Japanese immigrants and the wartime confinement. The early Cold War era, then, was not so much a blurry transition from the more clearly defined epochs of the mass incarceration to the later activist movements for redress that began in the late 1960s. Instead, the late 1940s to early 1960s were a crucial moment during which Uchida combined her interests in Japanese culture and in rendering scenes from World War II that would make her name in popular literature. Ironically, Uchida continued to write about Japan and its folktales until her death in 1992. But these works remained in the shadows of those that focused on Japanese American imprisonment once she began publishing them in the 1970s. What gets lost here is the complex postwar environment that initially framed her dual interests. Thus, if we are to appreciate the depths and concerns of such an author, we must acknowledge the intimate and historical connections each topic had in her ever-creative mind.

Conclusion

I N *Transpacific Studies: Framing an Emerging Field* (2014), the editors Janet Hoskins and Viet Thanh Nguyen introduce this collection of essays by highlighting a basic tension in how scholars consider the complex relations among peoples, cultures, and nations across the Pacific. On the one hand, the history of these interactions divulges a series of "conquest, colonialism, and conflict" in Asia, exacted by not only the United States and western Europe but also Japan, China, and other nations. On the other hand, such contacts show how marginalized populations create "collaborations, alliances, and friendships" through counternarratives and social movements that challenge the hegemony of regional powers.[1] We should note, too, how both antagonisms and agreements among colonizers, collaborators, and the subjugated change over time. This span of reactions even occurred simultaneously in the case of the United States and Japan throughout the Cold War. Yesterday's enemy can become tomorrow's ally, but not without misunderstandings and residual resentments that contribute to uneasy political, economic, military, and cultural attachments. These relationships among once and future imperial states also affect more vulnerable communities and territories caught up in the currents of transpacific engagements, to which they then have to adjust or respond accordingly. From these myriad exchanges among friends, foes, and the nonaligned arise shifting hierarchies of power within and between nations, as well as opportunities to contest these institutions within more localized populaces and places.[2]

The artists and writers examined in *From Confinement to Containment*—Hanama Tasaki, Yamaguchi Yoshiko, Henry Sugimoto, and Yoshiko Uchida—offer suggestive instances of how performing cultural work was particularly difficult and compromised because they functioned within the broader frictions between two powerful nation-states before and during World War II and in the ensuing alliance afterward. In one creative form or another, the four figures revealed cosmopolitan sensibilities that were aspirational in reaching across cultural and national borders, even as they accepted in varying degrees the dominant values of a liberal nation that policed and invaded such borders. As the United States extended its influence throughout the world, it also wanted to avoid having its actions seen as new versions of European colonialism by showcasing itself as a multiethnic democracy that appreciated all cultures and populations. Yet more than a few American officials, intellectuals, and cultural producers insisted that their allies and developing countries follow the U.S. lead in endorsing liberal principles to combat the spread of communism. The use of violence, as manifested in the wars in Korea and Vietnam, was one way to achieve this aim. These four Japanese/American artists and writers opposed introducing specific structures or ideologies to other lands by force, especially given their own terrifying wartime experiences of Japanese imperialism (for Tasaki and Yamaguchi) and of the Japanese American confinement (for Sugimoto and Uchida). Yet they did not necessarily question how democratic and capitalist systems coincided with overseas military involvements and internal restrictions against minority populations, thinking instead that these governing measures had been misapplied. For these artists and authors, their views of domestic and international affairs became influenced by the imposing power of Cold War liberalism, which appeared to them as the norm, especially since they worked within the Western cultural environment and sought approval from mainstream American audiences.

We then see how these Japanese/Americans could not simply resist the expectations and demands of U.S. Cold War culture. Hanama Tasaki warned postwar Americans through his novels about the dangers of following imperial Japan's path when occupying other nations. He also valorized liberal individualism and the multiethnic democracy of Hawai'i as models for societal possibilities. But to advance these positions, he had to remake his past and ignore the racial slights he endured as a Nisei that contributed to his voluntary service in the Imperial Army. Yamaguchi Yoshiko enjoyed the plurality of cultures encouraged in Japanese-occupied Manchuria, just as she was a willing participant in the empire's propaganda machine that urged moviegoers to accept Japan's dominance. Similarly, she desired stardom in Hollywood films, only to discern how the United States relied on orientalist images of her ancestral land to underscore American supremacy. Henry Sugimoto embraced cosmopolitan aesthetics in his art, while realizing the hazards of being a Japanese national during his wartime confinement. Even then, in later interviews he evaded criticizing his adopted country's racism against ethnic minorities, despite what his paintings revealed, leaving this task up to younger generations of Asian American activists to reframe the significance of his work. As a youth, Yoshiko Uchida sought acceptance from the white mainstream to escape the racial stigma associated with her Japanese background. She was able to find new avenues of healing and creativity from her ancestral culture after the trauma of her wartime incarceration. At the same time, the children's author argued that postwar Japan should create its own version of a tolerant, middle-class society when mixing its traditions with liberal modernity. From these evolving viewpoints, the artists and writers tried to formulate through their affective work visions of more peaceful societies. But these outlooks also revealed ambivalent, if not contradictory or unstated, feelings toward the American Cold War state's impact on its citizenry and on the rest of the world.

Assessing the dimensions of transpacific subjectivities as an alternative or a supplement to nation-based ethnic studies thus requires careful contextualizing of such identities and works within specific historical, political, and cultural developments. For instance, cosmopolitanism as an analytical category or as a description of experiences may present alluring possibilities, freeing individuals from parochial limits and expectations and allowing them to welcome and learn from societal differences across the globe, even if they have localized perspectives.[3] Yet, following Lisa Lowe and Anthony Pagden's cautionary arguments, we should consider the historical and structural roots of cosmopolitanism, ones entangled with those of liberalism and imperialism. Western narratives of freedom, progress, and individualism have often justified liberal states' bureaucratic penchant for generating hierarchies through racism, exploitation, violence, and empire building, within which universal rights are reserved for some, rather than applied to all.[4] In this light, scholars working in transnational studies are rethinking past approaches, as seen in such works as Hoskins and Nguyen's *Transpacific Studies*. Theorists of cosmopolitanism have expanded the term's connotations beyond the traditional understanding of privileged men from the West who traverse the globe to construct a "citizen of the world" persona. Critics recognize how naturalized "cosmopolitanism" has become in its supposed universality as they more closely examine its modern formations amid the shadows of empires. Calls now arise for including immigrants, servants, refugees, and other types of stateless persons, displaced or otherwise, as part of this new and more intricate universe.[5] In their efforts to contest or to move beyond what nations could dictate or destroy, however, the four Japanese/American writers and artists discussed here demonstrate the challenges of working as transpacific cosmopolitans, negotiating around the powers and paradoxes of the liberal state to create artistic possibilities.

Indeed, these matters resonate in current political events, in which new forms of Cold War struggles and debates are occurring over U.S. immigration policies, the integration and control of global markets, the confinement and deportation of "subversives," the demonization of political opponents, and the nation's ongoing military engagements throughout the world. This study has emphasized how Japanese/American artists and writers rendered more visible, and how they could thus critique, the interrelatedness of domestic and overseas affairs. Fears of Asian immigrants from the late nineteenth century onward, as Henry Sugimoto traced in his paintings, affected how the nation later incarcerated Japanese Americans, viewing them as threatening racial Others. We likewise see, in a different context, the worries in the United States over Islamic influence and calls for detaining Muslims that have developed from U.S. interventions in the Middle East. These past and present subjects have even converged, when the Japanese American confinement became a cited precedent for banning and containing peoples of Middle Eastern ancestry. In response, those who suffered through the wartime mass imprisonment and their descendants, including Madeleine Sugimoto (Henry's daughter), have joined civic protests against such executive orders, because they understand the consequences of this prejudicial treatment.[6] Yet "America First" intentions and internal restrictions persist alongside U.S. overseas involvements, both having evolved in a post-9/11 environment. Commentators from a variety of fields have criticized the impact of the American military in Iraq and Afghanistan, as well as in other interventions (with the support of authoritarian client states) that have encouraged political instability, terrorism, and ethnic chauvinism.[7] Many of these U.S. commitments have contributed to producing "unwanted" immigrants and refugees in the name of safeguarding national security and of spreading freedom and democracy around the world. Another replay of Cold War hostilities—albeit with different principals, purposes, and technological capabilities—has also emerged from these quandaries. As enduring geopolitical rivals, Russia and China have disclosed desires similar to those of the United States to sway events in the Middle East, Central Asia, and on the Korean peninsula. Adopting a critical transnational stance from the perspectives of redefined, subaltern cosmopolitans may then broaden and deepen interrogations into the extensive reach and ruinous practices of global powers. Studies have considered, for example, the adaptations made within and against these shifting, competing authorities by marginalized peoples, whose ability to survive and to create cultural forms appears as modes of resistance.

Such inquiries are evident in Asian American studies, where scholars have established how artistic, literary, social, and legal formations offer sites of cultural critique of American power and Asian atrocities within late twentieth- and early twenty-first-century transpacific locations. Several works have examined the Cold War's cultural legacies on U.S.-Asia relations and on the battles within Asia through such "outsiders" as orphans, mixed-race populations, expatriates, "comfort women," and refugees who yearn not only to achieve recognition and recovery but also to attain justice.[8] My study shows a different kind of positioning that artists and writers occupied through their work in the pre-1965 era of the Cold War. The irony here is that most of these figures became known in post-1965 national and activist frameworks, in which Asian Americanists deemed Sugimoto and Uchida as relevant voices opposing their wartime confinement, and Asian Studies scholars assessed Yamaguchi and Tasaki through the prism of Japanese war guilt and anti-militarism.[9] Yet, when placed within larger geopolitical settings, the four individuals' diverse postures suggest not only how war, empire building, immigration, confinement, and occupation were intertwined. They also tell us how various communities across state boundaries coped and healed in the aftermath of such disruptive events, through which struggles over power, definitions of race and place, and avowals of humanity in the face of subordination become apparent. However compromised, the artists and writers' lives and labors during the early Cold War made these connections clear, with creative interests springing from their hindsight, hope, and resolve to belong in the wider world.

Notes

INTRODUCTION

1. Lawrence E. Davies, "Japanese Premier Hailed on Arrival," *New York Times,* September 3, 1951, 3. See also Philip Potter, "Yoshida Sees Pact Success on Schedule," *Baltimore Sun,* September 3, 1951, 1; Chesly Manly, "Yoshida Picks Vital Date to Reach Parley," *Chicago Daily Tribune,* September 3, 1951, 6.

2. "Yoshida Credits Nisei Troops with Change of U.S. Attitude," *Rafu Shimpo,* September 6, 1951, 1.

3. John W. Dower, *War without Mercy: Race and Power in the Pacific War* (New York: Pantheon, 1986), 34–36, 78–93; Frank Ninkovich, "History and Memory in Postwar U.S.-Japanese Relations," in *The Unpredictability of the Past: Memories of the Asia-Pacific War in U.S.–East Asian Relations,* ed. Marc Gallicchio (Durham, N.C.: Duke University Press, 2007), 91–92.

4. A sampling of scholarship on the wartime confinement of Japanese Americans includes Roger Daniels, *Concentration Camps USA: Japanese Americans and World War II* (New York: Holt, Rinehart and Winston, 1972); Michi Nishiura Weglyn, *Years of Infamy: The Untold Story of America's Concentration Camps,* updated ed. (Seattle: University of Washington Press, 1996); Tetsuden Kashima, *Judgment without Trial: Japanese American Imprisonment during World War II* (Seattle: University of Washington Press, 2003); Brian Masaru Hayashi, *Democratizing the Enemy: The Japanese American Internment* (Princeton, N.J.: Princeton University Press, 2004); Greg Robinson, *A Tragedy of Democracy: Japanese Confinement in North America* (New York: Columbia University Press, 2009). Other works address Japanese American literature, art, photography, and oral histories from the period. Some of this scholarship includes Deborah Gesensway and Mindy Roseman, *Beyond Words: Images from America's Concentration Camps* (Ithaca, N.Y.: Cornell University Press, 1987); Lawson Fusao Inada, ed., *Only What They Could Carry: The Japanese American Internment Experience* (Berkeley, Calif.: Heyday, 2000); Linda Gordon and Gary Y. Okihiro, eds., *Impounded: Dorothea Lange and the Censored Images of Japanese American Internment* (New York: Norton, 2006).

5. Davies, "Japanese Premier Hailed on Arrival," 3.

6. T. Fujitani, *Race for Empire: Koreans as Japanese and Japanese as Americans during World War II* (Berkeley: University of California Press, 2011), 206–236; Scott Kurashige, *The Shifting Grounds of Race: Black and Japanese Americans in the Making of Multiethnic Los Angeles* (Princeton, N.J.: Princeton University Press, 2008), 186–204.

7. Ellen D. Wu, *The Color of Success: Asian Americans and the Origins of the Model Minority* (Princeton, N.J.: Princeton University Press, 2014); Cindy I-Fen Cheng, *Citizens of Asian America: Democracy and Race during the Cold War* (New York: New York University Press, 2013); Madeline Y. Hsu, *The Good Immigrants: How the Yellow Peril Became the Model Minority* (Princeton, N.J.: Princeton University Press, 2015). See also Thy Phu, *Picturing Model Citizens: Civility in Asian American Visual Culture* (Philadelphia: Temple University Press, 2011).

8. John W. Dower, *Embracing Defeat: Japan in the Wake of World War II* (New York: Norton, 1999); Yukiko Koshiro, *Trans-Pacific Racisms and the U.S. Occupation of Japan* (New York: Columbia University Press, 1999); Naoko Shibusawa, *America's Geisha Ally: Reimagining the Japanese Enemy* (Cambridge, Mass.: Harvard University Press, 2006); Bruce Cumings, *Parallax Visions: Making Sense of American–East Asian Relations at the End of the Century* (Durham, N.C.: Duke University Press, 1999), 212.

9. Pearl S. Buck, *My Several Worlds: A Personal Record* (New York: John Day, 1954), 406–407; James A. Michener, *The Voice of Asia* (New York: Random House, 1951), 327. When describing the United States as a postwar empire, Michael S. Sherry summed it up best when writing: "In . . . the riches generated for the imperial center, in the universalist claims for American ideals, in the racial or gendered language used to describe nonwhite peoples, in the resentments it aroused, and above all in the reach of its military power, the United States after World War II achieved much of the reality and many of the trappings of empire. Precisely how much seems a matter only for quibbling." Sherry, *In the Shadow of War: The United States since the 1930s* (New Haven, Conn.: Yale University Press, 1995), 126. Paul A. Kramer similarly notes about U.S. power in the world, and about empires more generally, that "the imperial refers to a dimension of power in which asymmetries in the scale of political action, regimes of spatial ordering, and modes of exceptionalizing difference enable and produce relations of hierarchy, discipline, dispossession, extraction, and exploitation." Kramer, "Power and Connection: Imperial Histories of the United States in the World," *American Historical Review* 116 (December 2011): 1349. For a broad view of U.S. imperialism throughout the twentieth century, see Michael H. Hunt and Steven I. Levine, *Arc of Empire: America's Wars in Asia from the Philippines to Vietnam* (Chapel Hill: University of North Carolina Press, 2012).

10. Mary L. Dudziak, *Cold War Civil Rights: Race and the Image of American Democracy* (Princeton, N.J.: Princeton University Press, 2000). See also Thomas Borstelmann, *The Cold War and the Color Line: American Race Relations in the Global Arena* (Cambridge, Mass.: Harvard University Press, 2001); Robert Vitalis, *White World Order, Black Power Politics: The Birth of American International Relations* (Ithaca, N.Y.: Cornell University Press, 2015); Christina Klein, *Cold War Orientalism: Asia in the Middlebrow Imagination, 1945–1961* (Berkeley: University of California Press, 2003); Penny M. Von Eschen, *Satchmo Blows Up the World: Jazz Ambassadors Play the Cold War* (Cambridge, Mass.: Harvard University Press, 2004); Laura A. Belmonte, *Selling the American Way: U.S. Propaganda and the Cold War* (Philadelphia: University of Pennsylvania Press, 2010).

11. Dower, *War without Mercy*, 293–318; Shibusawa, *America's Geisha Ally*.

12. "Second Chance in Asia," *Commonweal*, June 29, 1951, 277; "Japan: A 'Greater Asia' Deal with the Reds?," *Newsweek*, February 15, 1951, 38; Edwin O. Reischauer, "To Make Japan an Asset to Democracy," *New York Times Magazine*, August 26, 1956, 23.

13. Dower, *Embracing Defeat*, 87–200, 271–227; Douglas H. Mendel, Jr., "Japan Reviews Her American Alliance," *Public Opinion Quarterly* 30, no. 1 (Spring 1966): 7. See also Michael Schaller, *The American Occupation of Japan: The Origins of the Cold War in Asia* (New York: Oxford University Press, 1985); Akira Iriye and Warren I. Cohen, eds., *The United States and Japan in the Postwar World* (Lexington: University Press of Kentucky, 1989). A useful evaluation of scholarship on the occupation is Laura Hein, "Revisiting America's Occupation of Japan," *Cold War History* 11, no. 4 (November 2011): 579–599.

14. Caroline Chung Simpson, *An Absent Presence: Japanese Americans in Postwar American Culture, 1945–1960* (Durham, N.C.: Duke University Press, 2001). Simpson draws from Marita Sturken, "Absent Images of Memory: Remembering and Reenacting the Japanese Internment," *positions* 5 (1997): 687–707.

15. Kurashige, *The Shifting Grounds of Race,* 195–198; Greg Robinson, *After Camp: Portraits in Midcentury Japanese American Life and Politics* (Berkeley: University of California Press, 2012); Brian Komei Dempster, ed., *Making Home from War: Stories of Japanese American Exile and Resettlement* (Berkeley, Calif.: Heyday, 2011).

16. Peter Ota, quoted in Studs Terkel, *"The Good War:" An Oral History of World War II* (New York: New Press, 1984), 32; Yoshita Wayne Osaki, quoted in Dempster, *Making Home from War,* 111. See also Tetsuden Kashima, "Japanese American Internees Return, 1945–1955: Readjustment and Social Amnesia," *Phylon* 42, no. 2 (Summer 1980): 107–115.

17. For works on Asian American activism in the 1960s and 1970s, refer to Daryl J. Maeda, *Chains of Babylon: The Rise of Asian America* (Minneapolis: University of Minnesota Press, 2009); Maeda, *Rethinking the Asian American Movement* (New York: Routledge, 2011); Steven G. Louie and Glenn K. Omatsu, eds., *Asian Americans: The Movement and the Moment* (Los Angeles: UCLA Asian American Studies Center Press, 2001); William Wei, *The Asian American Movement* (Philadelphia: Temple University Press, 1993); Diane C. Fujino, *Heartbeat of Struggle: The Revolutionary Life of Yuri Kochiyama* (Minneapolis: University of Minnesota Press, 2005). See also Judy Tzu-Chun Wu, *Radicals on the Road: Internationalism, Orientalism, and Feminism during the Vietnam Era* (Ithaca, N.Y.: Cornell University Press, 2013).

18. Recent studies have examined Asian American literature and its critique of the Cold War in intriguing ways, but have focused mainly on works from the 1980s and 1990s to assess the legacies of military involvement in Asia. See Jodi Kim, *Ends of Empire: Asian American Critique and the Cold War* (Minneapolis: University of Minnesota Press, 2010); Josephine Nock-Hee Park, *Cold War Friendships: Korea, Vietnam, and Asian American Literature* (New York: Oxford University Press, 2016). An interesting work that examines Japanese culture during the Cold War is Ann Sherif, *Japan's Cold War: Media, Law, and Literature* (New York: Columbia University Press, 2009).

19. David Palumbo-Liu, *Asian/American: Historical Crossings of a Racial Frontier* (Stanford, Calif.: Stanford University Press, 1999), 1.

20. I refer to "Japanese/American" to describe a theoretical process, distinguishing it from my use of "Japanese American" to denote the ethnic group. I realize each category is a construction that overlaps with the other as far as histories and political intentions, but I make this distinction to avoid confusion.

21. Alan Nadel, *Containment Culture: American Narratives, Postmodernism, and the Atomic Age* (Durham, N.C.: Duke University Press, 1995), 4.

22. Sample titles include Elaine Tyler May, *Homeward Bound: American Families in the Cold War Era,* updated ed. (New York: Basic, 2008); K.A. Cuordileone, *Manhood and American Political Culture in the Cold War* (New York: Routledge, 2004); David K. Johnson, *The Lavender Scare: The Cold War Persecution of Gays and Lesbians in the Federal Government*

(Chicago: University of Chicago Press, 2004); Tyler T. Schmidt, *Desegregating Desire: Race and Sexuality in Cold War American Literature* (Jackson: University Press of Mississippi, 2013); Shelton Stromquist, ed., *Labor's Cold War: Local Politics in a Global Context* (Urbana: University of Illinois Press, 2008); Colleen Doody, *Detroit's Cold War: The Origins of Postwar Conservatism* (Urbana: University of Illinois Press, 2012); William Inboden III, *Religion and American Foreign Policy, 1945–1960: The Soul of Containment* (Cambridge: Cambridge University Press, 2010); Dianne Kirby, ed., *Religion and the Cold War* (New York: Palgrave, 2013); Kari Frederickson, *Cold War Dixie: Militarization and Modernization in the American South* (Athens: University of Georgia Press, 2013); Kevin J. Fernlund, ed., *The Cold War American West* (Albuquerque: University of New Mexico Press, 1998).

23. Andrea Friedman, *Citizenship in Cold War America: The National Security State and the Possibilities of Dissent* (Amherst: University of Massachusetts Press, 2014); Andrew J. Falk, *Upstaging the Cold War: American Dissent and Cultural Diplomacy, 1940–1960* (Amherst: University of Massachusetts Press, 2010); Thomas Doherty, *Cold War, Cool Medium: Television, McCarthyism, and American Culture* (New York: Columbia University Press, 2003); Rebecca Schreiber, *Cold War Exiles in Mexico: U.S. Dissidents and the Culture of Critical Resistance* (Minneapolis: University of Minnesota Press, 2008).

24. Scholars (especially historians) have lately focused on cosmopolitan figures and institutions that challenged hardline Cold War sentiments. See Nicole Sackley, "Cosmopolitanism and the Uses of Tradition: Robert Redfield and Alternative Visions of Modernization during the Cold War," *Modern Intellectual History* 9, no. 3 (November 2012): 565–595; Julia Horne, "The Cosmopolitan Life of Alice Erh-Soon Tay," *Journal of World History* 21, no. 3 (September 2010): 419–445; Glenda Sluga, "UNESCO and the (One) World of Julian Huxley," *Journal of World History* 21, no. 3 (September 2010): 393–418; Antoinette Burton, "Cold War Cosmopolitanism: The Education of Santha Rama Rau in the Age of Bandung, 1945–1954," *Radical History Review* 95 (Spring 2006): 149–172; Michael R. Auslin, *Pacific Cosmopolitans: A Cultural History of U.S.-Japan Relations* (Cambridge, Mass.: Harvard University Press, 2011), 169–217.

25. Lisa Lowe traces this global development since the eighteenth century, when liberalism emerged as a powerful ideology, one that also encouraged racism, imperialism, and exploitation. See Lowe, *The Intimacies of Four Continents* (Durham, N.C.: Duke University Press, 2015).

26. As the following chapters show, the four artists and writers did not adhere to one specific definition of, or approach to, their interactions with the world. Some works that trace the multiplicity of these relations and classifications include Pheng Cheah and Bruce Robbins, eds., *Cosmopolitics: Thinking and Feeling beyond the Nation* (Minneapolis: University of Minnesota Press, 1999); Sheldon Pollock, Homi K. Bhabha, Carol A. Breckenridge, and Dipesh Chakrabarty, "Cosmopolitanisms," *Public Culture* 12, no. 3 (Fall 2000): 577–589; Glenda Sluga and Julia Horne, "Cosmopolitanism: Its Pasts and Practices," *Journal of World History* 21, no. 3 (September 2010): 369–373; Cyrus R. K. Patell, *Emergent U.S. Literatures: From Multiculturalism to Cosmopolitanism in the Late Twentieth Century* (New York: New York University Press, 2014); Bruce Robbins and Paulo Lemos Horta, eds., *Cosmopolitanisms* (New York: New York University Press, 2017).

27. Fujitani, *Race for Empire*, 206–236; Kurashige, *The Shifting Grounds of Race*, 186–204.

28. Wu, *The Color of Success*; Cheng, *Citizens of Asian America*; Hsu, *The Good Immigrants*.

29. Klein, *Cold War Orientalism*; Shibusawa, *America's Geisha Ally*.

30. Viet Nguyen, *Race and Resistance: Literature and Politics in Asian America* (New York: Oxford University Press, 2002), 4–7. See also Jinqi Ling, *Narrating Nationalisms: Ideology and Form in Asian American Literature* (New York: Oxford University Press, 1998).

31. Sample works that place Japanese Americans within a broader transpacific context include Eiichiro Azuma, *Between Two Empires: Race, History, and Transnationalism in Japanese America* (New York: Oxford University Press, 2005); Rumi Yasutake, *Transnational Women's Activism: The United States, Japan, and Japanese Immigrant Communities in California, 1859–1920* (New York: New York University Press, 2004); T. T. Fujitani, Geoffrey M. White, and Lisa Yoneyama, eds., *Perilous Memories: The Asia-Pacific War(s)* (Durham, N.C.: Duke University Press, 2001); Michael Jin, "Beyond Two Homelands: Migration and Transnationalism of Japanese Americans in the Pacific, 1930–1955" (Ph.D. diss., University of California, Santa Cruz, 2013); Christine Yano, *Airborne Dreams: "Nisei" Stewardesses and Pan American World Airways* (Durham, N.C.: Duke University Press, 2011).

CHAPTER 1

1. John A. Rademaker, *These Are Americans: The Japanese Americans in Hawaii in World War II* (Palo Alto, Calif.: Pacific Books, 1951), 29–35; "Okinawa: Levittown-on-the-Pacific," *Time,* August 15, 1955, 20.

2. Ellen D. Wu, *The Color of Success: Asian Americans and the Origins of the Model Minority* (Princeton, N.J.: Princeton University Press, 2014), 222–223.

3. "The Nisei in the Occupation," *Pacific Citizen,* May 31, 1952, 4; Mike Masaoka, "Nisei—and New Japan," *Pacific Citizen,* December 31, 1954, 2. See also Kelli Y. Nakamura, "'They Are Our Human Secret Weapons': The Military Intelligence Service and the Role of Japanese-Americans in the Pacific War and in the Occupation of Japan," *The Historian* 70 (Spring 2008): 54–74.

4. Edward Tang, "Reorienting Empires: Hanama Tasaki's *Long the Imperial Way* and Postwar American Culture," *Journal of Asian American Studies* 17, no. 1 (February 2014): 31–59.

5. John J. Stephan, *Hawaii under the Rising Sun: Japan's Plans for Conquest after Pearl Harbor* (Honolulu: University of Hawai'i Press, 1984), 36; John Shy, "Hanama Tasaki and His Contemporaries" (unpublished manuscript), 2; "MCC Takes in 16 Members: Neophytes in Citizenship Club Are Active Students," *Nippon Jiji,* October 11, 1930, 1.

6. Takashi Oka, "Two Novels That Tell about People," *Christian Science Monitor,* August 12, 1950, WM7. The author thanks Greg Robinson for the information on Tasaki's English translation of the Imperial Rescript.

7. Ray Falk, "The Machine Was Cruel," *New York Times,* August 13, 1950, BR3; Harvey Breit, "Talk with Mr. Tasaki," *New York Times,* August 20, 1950, 176; Merle Miller, "'All Quiet' of the Eastern Front," *Saturday Review,* August 12, 1950, 8.

8. "A List of 275 Outstanding Books of the Year," *New York Times,* December 3, 1950, BR32; "Ten Books of the Year—As Chosen by Tribune Reviewers," *Chicago Daily Tribune,* December 3, 1950, F4; Edmund Fuller, "War, as Seen thru Eyes of Jap Private," *Chicago Daily Tribune,* August 20, 1950, H5; Miller, "'All Quiet' of the Eastern Front," 9; Harold Strauss, "A Japanese Conscript," *The Nation,* August 19, 1950, 171.

9. A. LaVonne Brown Ruoff and Jerry W. Ward Jr., eds., *Redefining American Literary History* (New York: Modern Language Association of America, 1990), 361; Amy Ling, "Whose America Is It?" *Weber Studies* 12, no. 1 (1995): 27–35; Stephen Hong Sohn, Paul Lai, and Donald C. Goellnicht, "Introduction: Theorizing Asian American Fiction," *Modern Fiction Studies* 56 (Spring 2010): 6.

10. On transnational approaches to Asian American literature, see Sau-ling C. Wong, "Denationalization Reconsidered: Asian American Cultural Criticism at a Theoretical Crossroads," *Amerasia Journal* 21 (1995): 1–27; Pin-chia Feng, "Re-Mapping Asian American Literature: The Case of *Fu Sang*," *American Studies International* 38 (February 2000):

61–71; Wen Jin, "Transnational Criticism and Asian Immigrant Literature in the U.S.: Reading Yan Geling's *Fusang* and Its English Translation," *Contemporary Literature* 47 (Winter 2006): 570–600; Shelley Fisher Fishkin, "Asian Crossroads/Transnational American Studies," *Japanese Journal of American Studies* 17 (2006): 5–52; Richard Jean So, "Collaboration and Translation: Lin Yutang and the Archive of Asian American Literature," *Modern Fiction Studies* 56 (Spring 2010): 40–62.

11. Stephen Hong Sohn discusses the variances among Asian American authors and the subject matter in their work, which may not conform to their specific ethnic backgrounds or perspectives. He traces this development in contemporary fiction published in the "postrace era" (or, after 2000). I would argue that this phenomenon appears much earlier, albeit in different forms, contexts, and purposes. Tasaki's novels, for instance, do not address Asian American themes, characters, or concerns. See Stephen Hong Sohn, *Racial Asymmetries: Asian American Fictional Worlds* (New York: New York University Press, 2014).

12. The scholarly neglect of *Long the Imperial Way* extends to cultural historians and literary critics who have examined the collective memories of wars between the United States and East Asia, as well as conflicts among Asian nations. These works include T. T. Fujitani, Geoffrey M. White, and Lisa Yoneyama, eds., *Perilous Memories: The Asia-Pacific War(s)* (Durham, N.C.: Duke University Press, 2001); Marlene J. Mayo, J. Thomas Rimer, and H. Eleanor Kerham, eds., *War, Occupation, and Creativity: Japan and East Asia, 1920–1960* (Honolulu: University of Hawai'i Press, 2001); Marc Gallicchio, ed., *The Unpredictability of the Past: Memories of the Asia-Pacific War in U.S.–East Asian Relations* (Durham, N.C.: Duke University Press, 2007); Sharalyn Orbaugh, *Japanese Fiction of the Allied Occupation: Vision, Embodiment, Identity* (Leiden, Netherlands: Brill, 2007); Michael S. Molasky, *The American Occupation of Japan and Okinawa: Literature and Memory* (New York: Routledge, 1999).

13. Susan Koshy, "Minority Cosmopolitanism," *PMLA* 126 (May 2011): 593.

14. Ibid., 594. See also David Palumbo-Liu, *Asian/American: Historical Crossings of a Racial Frontier* (Stanford, Calif.: Stanford University Press, 1999); Mae M. Ngai, "Asian American History—Reflections on the De-centering of the Field," *Journal of American Ethnic History* 25 (Summer 2006): 97–108.

15. Breit, "Talk with Mr. Tasaki," 176.

16. Hanama Tasaki, *Long the Imperial Way* (Boston: Houghton Mifflin, 1950), dust jacket. Page citations from this edition appear parenthetically in this essay.

17. A useful interpretive survey on imperialism in U.S. and world history is Paul A. Kramer's "Power and Connection: Imperial Histories of the United States in the World," *American Historical Review* 116 (December 2011): 1348–1391.

18. The author thanks Eiichiro Azuma for suggesting this concept's application to Hanama Tasaki and his novel.

19. Stephan, *Hawaii under the Rising Sun*, 23–54; John J. Stephan, "Hijacked by Utopia: American Nikkei in Manchuria," *Amerasia Journal* 23 (Winter 1997–1998): 1–42; Michael Jin, "Beyond Two Homelands: Migration and Transnationalism of Japanese Americans in the Pacific, 1930–1955," (Ph.D. diss., University of California, Santa Cruz, 2013), 19–70.

20. Mae M. Ngai, *Impossible Subjects: Illegal Aliens and the Making of Modern America* (Princeton, N.J.: Princeton University Press, 2005), 170–174. See also Eiichiro Azuma, *Between Two Empires: Race, History, and Transnationalism in Japanese America* (New York: Oxford University Press, 2005), 111–186; Jin, "Beyond Two Homelands," 19–110.

21. Masayo Umezawa Duus, *Unlikely Liberators: The Men of the 100th and 442nd* (Honolulu: University of Hawai'i Press, 1987); Robert Asahina, *Just Americans: How Japa-*

nese Americans Won a War at Home and Abroad (New York: Gotham, 2006); Alice Yang Murray, *Historical Memories of the Japanese American Internment and the Struggle for Redress* (Stanford, Calif.: Stanford University Press, 2008), 99–116, 368–369; *Personal Justice Denied: Report of the Commission on Wartime Relocation and Internment of Civilians,* foreword by Tetsuden Kashima (Washington, D.C.: Civil Liberties Public Education Fund; Seattle: University of Washington Press, 1997), 258.

22. Monica Sone, *Nisei Daughter* (Seattle: University of Washington Press, 1979), 201.

23. Greg Robinson, *A Tragedy of Democracy: Japanese Confinement in North America* (New York: Columbia University Press, 2009), 109–113; Yang Murray, *Historical Memories of the Japanese American Internment,* 426–429.

24. "442nd Reunion" *Pacific Citizen,* June 5, 1953, 2.

25. Wu, *Color of Success,* 72–110.

26. Albert Q. Maisel, "The Japanese among Us," *Reader's Digest,* January 1956, 192.

27. Bradford Smith, "Test of American Democracy," *Saturday Review of Literature,* June 7, 1947, 20, 21.

28. Christopher Rand, "A Reporter at Large," *New Yorker,* November 16, 1957, 135.

29. For discussions on *Go for Broke!* as a postwar artifact, see T. Fujitani, *Race for Empire: Koreans as Japanese and Japanese as Americans during World War II* (Berkeley: University of California Press, 2011), 206–234; Edward Tang, "From Internment to Containment: Cold War Imaginings of Japanese Americans in *Go for Broke,*" *Columbia Journal of American Studies* 9 (Fall 2009): 84–112.

30. Dore Schary, undated note, Box 39, Folder 10, Dore Schary Papers, Wisconsin Historical Society/Wisconsin Center for Film and Theater Research.

31. Larry Tajiri, "Vagaries: Meets Dore Schary for the First Time," *Pacific Citizen,* July 29, 1955, 1.

32. Dore Schary to Joseph Yorvin, July 13, 1951; William Gordon to Dore Schary, May 14, 1951, Box 39, Folder 8, Dore Schary Papers, Wisconsin Historical Society/Wisconsin Center for Film and Theater Research.

33. "Yoshida Credits Nisei Troops with Change of U.S. Attitude," *Rafu Shimpo,* September 6, 1951, 1. See also "Premier Yoshida Hails Role of Nisei during Last War; Notes Changes in Attitude," *Pacific Citizen,* September 8, 1951, 1; "Yoshida Hails Ex-Foes: Japanese Premier Pays Visit to Cemetery in Hawaii," *New York Times,* September 2, 1951, 6.

34. "Japanese Fete Nisei Veterans at Tokyo Party," *Pacific Citizen,* April 22, 1950, 1; "Japan Official Hails Loyalty of Nisei to U.S.," *Pacific Citizen,* October 6, 1951, 2.

35. "The Nisei in the Occupation," *Pacific Citizen,* May 31, 1952, 4.

36. The occupation of Japan also revealed the challenges in assuming that Nisei servicemen would be fitting cultural brokers between the two countries. Difficulties arose when they tried to negotiate their standing as disparaged racial minorities in the United States and as American military personnel in Japan. The former called for the Nisei to sympathize with Japanese nationals because of their shared racial features and ancestry. On the other hand, more than a few Nisei soldiers exercised their power and status as U.S. citizens over the subordinated in Japan in oppressive ways, reinforcing American imperial might. See Eiichiro Azuma, "Brokering Race, Culture, and Citizenship: Japanese Americans in Occupied Japan and Postwar National Inclusion," *Journal of American–East Asian Relations* 16, no. 3 (Fall 2009): 183–211; Azuma, "The Lure of Military Imperialism: Race, Martial Citizenship, and Minority American Transnationalism during the Cold War," *Journal of American Ethnic History* 36, no. 2 (Winter 2017): 72–82. See also Susan L. Carruthers, *The Good Occupation: American Soldiers and the Hazards of Peace* (Cambridge, Mass.: Harvard University Press, 2016).

37. John J. Stephan, e-mail communication with the author, June 24, 2013.

38. Stephan, *Hawaii under the Rising Sun*, 36. See also Gary Okihiro, *Cane Fires: The Anti-Japanese Movement in Hawaii, 1865–1945* (Philadelphia: Temple University Press, 1991); Franklin Odo, *No Sword to Bury: Japanese Americans in Hawai'i during World War II* (Philadelphia: Temple University Press, 2004).

39. Stephan, e-mail communication.

40. Shy, "Hanama Tasaki and His Contemporaries," 3–4, 26; Stephan, *Hawaii under the Rising Sun*, 43. Although Tasaki worked as a correspondent before becoming a novelist, the level of his Japanese-language skills in reading and writing are unknown. He did seek help in translating *Long the Imperial Way* for a Japanese edition. This version, however, did not receive much critical or commercial notice.

41. Fuller, "War, as Seen thru Eyes of Jap Private," H5.

42. Cindy I-Fen Cheng, *Citizens of Asian America: Democracy and Race during the Cold War* (New York: New York University Press, 2013), 10–11.

43. Greg Robinson, *After Camp: Portraits in Midcentury Japanese American Life and Politics* (Berkeley: University of California Press, 2012), 85–101.

44. Larry Tajiri, "The Nisei and the Novel," *Pacific Citizen*, August 2, 1952, 4.

45. Naoko Shibusawa, *America's Geisha Ally: Reimagining the Japanese Enemy* (Cambridge, Mass.: Harvard University Press, 2006), 163–166.

46. Bill Hosokawa, "'Long the Imperial Way': The Story of a Nippon Soldier," *Pacific Citizen*, August 26, 1950, 5.

47. Azuma, *Between Two Empires*, 181–182, 211, 213; Ngai, *Impossible Subjects*, 173.

48. See, for example, Weldon James, "Main Street Moves to Japan," *Collier's*, June 14, 1947, 16–17+; "Who Picks the 'Democracy' for Japan?" *Saturday Evening Post*, April 10, 1948, 156; Edwin O. Reischauer, "It's Time We Encouraged the Japanese to Build a Democracy of Their Own," *Saturday Evening Post*, April 23, 1949, 12; Helen Mears, "Japan: Challenge to Our Prestige," *Harper's*, July 1950, 73–78; Eric Johnston, "Japan: Partner or Problem?" *Look*, April 5, 1955, 104; "Self-Government on Trial in Japan," *Life*, November 28, 1960, 118–126.

49. "Japan, Reborn, Can Be Our Ally," *Collier's*, May 7, 1949, 82; Deputy Under Secretary [Robert Daniel] Murphy, "America, Japan, and the Future of the Pacific," *Department of State Bulletin*, March 22, 1954, 431.

50. Peter Kalischer, "Japan," *Collier's*, March 2, 1956, 58. See also Demaree Bess, "The Japs Have Us on the Griddle Now," *Saturday Evening Post*, April 4, 1953, 24–25, 68, 70–71.

51. Kalischer, "Japan," 59.

52. John W. Dower, *Embracing Defeat: Japan in the Wake of World War II* (New York: Norton, 1999), 33–64; Shibusawa, *America's Geisha Ally*, 133–135. Dower discusses American and Japanese racial depictions of each other during World War II in *War without Mercy: Race and Power in the Pacific War* (New York: Pantheon, 1986). Sandra Wilson, however, notes that later in the 1950s, Japanese veterans became less reviled in the minds of the populace. Instead, former soldiers involved themselves in politics and became cultural heroes, contesting the nation's sense of pacifism and war guilt. See Wilson, "War, Soldier and Nation in 1950s Japan," *International Journal of Asian Studies* 5 (2008): 187–218.

53. "Japanese Farmer," *Life*, December 24, 1945, 67, 70.

54. Darrell Berrigan, "Japan's Hope and Despair: Her Veterans," *Saturday Evening Post*, August 9, 1947, 24.

55. James A. Michener, *The Voice of Asia* (New York: Random House, 1951), 23, 26.

56. Ibid., 27.

57. Ibid., 28.

58. Michener concluded his collection of essays with this thought about U.S. intentions in Asia: "America has an honorable place in Asia, not as the new imperialist . . . but as a co-operating friend working on problems of mutual concern and no doubt mutual profit." Yet the Japanese veteran Masao Watanabe prodded Michener to consider how U.S. involvement in Korea might be based on intentions similar to those of imperial Japan; it was all the same to Watanabe. This opinion Michener considered as too absurd, even as it made him uncomfortable about U.S.-Japan relations. Michener, *The Voice of Asia,* 327.

59. Dower, *Embracing Defeat,* 204–213. Scholarship on the U.S. occupation of Japan is voluminous. For a recent assessment, see Laura Hein, "Revisiting America's Occupation of Japan," *Cold War History* 11 (November 2011): 579–599. Additional key works include Michael Schaller, *The American Occupation of Japan: The Origins of the Cold War in Asia* (New York: Oxford University Press, 1985); Yukiko Koshiro, *Trans-Pacific Racisms and the U.S. Occupation of Japan* (New York: Columbia University Press, 1999); John Swenson-Wright, *Unequal Allies? United States Security and Alliance Policy toward Japan, 1945–1960* (Stanford, Calif.: Stanford University Press, 2005); Shibusawa, *America's Geisha Ally.*

60. Stewart Alsop, "Matter of Fact: American Japan," *Washington Post,* April 25, 1949, 6; Helen Mears, "The Russians are Making the Most of Our 'Imperialist Rule' in Japan," *Saturday Evening Post,* April 29, 1950, 12.

61. Demaree Bess, "Those American Towns in Japan," *Saturday Evening Post,* August 23, 1952, 96; Robert Sherrod, "How Can Japan Survive?" *Saturday Evening Post,* October 9, 1954, 33.

62. Stephen H. Sumida, *And the View from the Shore: Literary Traditions of Hawai'i* (Seattle: University of Washington Press, 1991); Christine Skwiot, *The Purposes of Paradise: U.S. Tourism and Empire in Cuba and Hawai'i* (Philadelphia: University of Pennsylvania Press, 2010).

63. Work problematizing Japanese American wartime and postwar loyalties within a transpacific context includes Yuji Ichioka, "The Meaning of Loyalty: The Case of Kazumaro Buddy Uno," *Amerasia Journal* 23 (Winter 1997–1998): 44–71; Naoko Shibusawa, "'The Artist Belongs to the People': The Odyssey of Taro Yashima," *Journal of Asian American Studies* 8 (October 2005): 257–275; Jin, "Beyond Two Homelands," 211–269.

64. Gary Y. Okihiro, *Cane Fires: The Anti-Japanese Movement in Hawaii, 1865–1945* (Philadelphia: Temple University Press, 1991), 98–105, 118–128, 225–252. See also Beth Bailey and David Farber, *The First Strange Place: The Alchemy of Race and Sex in World War II Hawaii* (New York: Free Press, 1992).

65. Mary L. Dudziak, *Cold War Civil Rights: Race and the Image of American Democracy* (Princeton, N.J.: Princeton University Press, 2000); Thomas Borstelmann, *The Cold War and the Color Line: American Race Relations in the Global Arena* (Cambridge, Mass.: Harvard University Press, 2001); Christina Klein, *Cold War Orientalism: Asia in the Middlebrow Imagination, 1945–1961* (Berkeley: University of California Press, 2003); Penny M. Von Eschen, *Satchmo Blows Up the World: Jazz Ambassadors Play the Cold War* (Cambridge, Mass.: Harvard University Press, 2004).

66. "Hawaii—A Bridge to Asia," *Business Week,* May 13, 1950, 128; "The 49th State," *Collier's,* April 8, 1950, 74; "Statehood Blocked by Racial Issues," *Christian Century,* November 29, 1950, 1413.

67. Gretchen Heefner, "'A Symbol of the New Frontier': Hawaiian Statehood, Anti-colonialism, and Winning the Cold War," *Pacific Historical Review* 74 (November 2005): 562. See also John Whitehead, "Alaska and Hawai'i: The Cold War States," in *The Cold War American West, 1945–1989,* ed. Kevin J. Fernlund (Albuquerque: University of New Mexico Press, 1998), 189–210.

68. Rademaker, *These Are Americans,* 1.

69. Other postwar histories of Japanese Americans in Hawai'i offered a similar take on the model minority narrative. See Andrew W. Lind, *Hawaii's Japanese: An Experiment in Democracy* (Princeton, N.J.: Princeton University Press, 1946).

70. Shelley Ayame Nishimura Ota, *Upon Their Shoulders* (New York: Exposition Press, 1951), 253; Kazuo Miyamoto, *Hawaii: End of the Rainbow* (Rutland, Vt.: Charles E. Tuttle, 1964), 396–397.

71. Miller, "'All Quiet' of the Eastern Front," 8. The novel's dust jacket carries this same quote.

72. Dower, *Embracing Defeat,* 30.

73. Breit, "Talk with Mr. Tasaki," 176; Miller, "'All Quiet' of the Eastern Front," 8; Falk, "The Machine Was Cruel," BR3.

74. Klein, *Cold War Orientalism,* 79–81; Robert Frazier, "Kennan, 'Universalism,' and the Truman Doctrine," *Journal of Cold War Studies* 11 (Spring 2009): 3–34. See also David C. Engerman, Nils Gilman, Mark H. Haefele, and Michael E. Latham, eds., *Staging Growth: Modernization, Development, and the Global Cold War* (Amherst: University of Massachusetts Press, 2003); Nils Gilman, *Mandarins of the Future: Modernization Theory in Cold War America* (Baltimore, Md.: Johns Hopkins University Press, 2003).

75. Breit, "Talk with Mr. Tasaki," 176.

76. Ibid.

77. On the invisibility of American empire, see Michael Sherry, *In the Shadow of War: The United States since the 1930s* (New Haven, Conn.: Yale University Press, 1995); Michael H. Hunt and Steven I. Levine, *Arc of Empire: America's Wars in Asia from the Philippines to Vietnam* (Chapel Hill: University of North Carolina Press, 2012); Kramer, "Power and Connection," 1358–1359.

78. Breit, "Talk with Mr. Tasaki," 176.

79. Monroe Engel, "The Enemies," *Commentary,* September 1950, 299.

80. Miller, "'All Quiet' of the Eastern Front," 8.

81. Strauss, "A Japanese Conscript," 171; Falk, "The Machine Was Cruel," BR3; Edith Weigle, "An Intense, Moving Novel of Japan Today," *Chicago Daily Tribune,* August 3, 1952, B3.

82. Yoshikuni Igarashi, *Bodies of Memory: Narratives of War in Postwar Japanese Culture, 1945–1970* (Princeton, N.J.: Princeton University Press, 2000), 13.

83. Orville Prescott, "Books of the Times," *New York Times,* August 14, 1950, 27; Oka, "Two Novels That Tell about People," WM7; Lee Grove, "Life (or Less) in the Jap Army," *Washington Post,* August 20, 1950, B6.

84. Prescott, "Books of the Times," 27.

85. Grove, "Life (or Less) in the Jap Army," B6.

86. Hanama Tasaki, *The Mountains Remain* (Boston: Houghton Mifflin, 1952), 173, 314–315.

87. Tamura Taijiro, quoted in Douglas N. Slaymaker, *The Body in Postwar Japanese Fiction* (New York: Routledge Curzon, 2004), 3.

88. Slaymaker, *The Body in Postwar Japanese Fiction,* 4–5; Igarashi, *Bodies of Memory,* 55–61. Slaymaker notes that the flesh writers were all male, and in their postwar sexual anxieties exacerbated by the U.S. occupation, they supported returning to a prewar domination of women. This perspective relocated the despised imperial state's activities of exploring, conquering, and regulating onto Japanese female bodies.

89. David C. Stahl, *The Burdens of Survival: Ooka Shohei's Writings on the Pacific War* (Honolulu: University of Hawai'i Press, 2003), 8.

90. Oka, "Two Novels That Tell about People," WM7; Prescott, "Books of the Times," 27.

91. Orville Prescott, "Books of the Times," *New York Times,* May 7, 1948, 21.

92. Dower, *Embracing Defeat,* 198–199.

93. "Spokesman of Japan," *Sydney Morning Herald,* June 13, 1953, 8; Peter Russo, "View of the Jap Soul (Before Democratised)," *The (Australian) Argus,* May 12, 1951, 16.

94. Paul Kramer notes the ironic similarities among the "latecomers to empire"—the United States, the Soviet Union, and Japan—regarding how "the national components of their empires became fundamental to their exceptionalist self-conceptions as anti-empires." Kramer, "Power and Connection," 1369.

95. John Osbourne, "Report from The Orient: Guns Are Not Enough," *Life,* August 21, 1950, 77; "Betraying the American Ideal," *Christian Century,* January 24, 1951, 102.

96. Miller, "'All Quiet' of the Eastern Front," 8.

97. "The Quarter's Polls," ed. Mildred Strunk, *The Public Opinion Quarterly* 15 (Spring 1951): 171; Edward A. Suchman, Rose K. Goldsen and Robin M. Williams, Jr., "Attitudes toward the Korean War," *Public Opinion Quarterly* 17 (Summer 1953): 171.

CHAPTER 2

1. General biographical information comes from Yamaguchi Yoshiko and Fujiwara Sakuya, *Fragrant Orchid: The Story of My Early Life,* translated and with an introduction by Chia-ning Chang (Honolulu: University of Hawai'i Press, 2015). Hereafter, page citations from this work appear parenthetically in the text. Although Yamaguchi published several versions of her life story, I rely on *Fragrant Orchid* as the most recent scholarly edition.

2. The exact number of war brides coming from Japan to the United States is difficult to determine. Elfrieda Berthiaume Shukert and Barbara Smith Scibetta place the number of marriages between GIs and Japanese women as high as 100,000, but these included unions that ended when soldiers returned to the United States without their wives. In 1957, Mike Masaoka, a spokesman for the Japanese American Citizens League, estimated that around 26,000 war brides were in the United States, making up one-sixth of the overall Japanese American population. Elfrieda Berthiaume Shukert and Barbara Smith Scibetta, *War Brides of World War II* (Novato, Calif.: Presidio Press, 1988), 208; "26,000 Japanese War Brides in U.S. Group Told," *Pacific Citizen,* June 7, 1957, 1.

3. Shukert and Scibetta, *War Brides of World War II,* 193–194; Susan Zeiger, *Entangling Alliances: Foreign War Brides and American Soldiers in the Twentieth Century* (New York: New York University Press, 2010), 188–189; Mire Koikari, "Gender, Power, and U.S. Imperialism: The Occupation of Japan, 1945–1952," in *Bodies in Contact: Rethinking Colonial Encounters in World History,* ed. Tony Ballantyne and Antoinette Burton (Durham, N.C.: Duke University Press, 2005), 356–357; Akaya Yoshimizu, "'Hello, War Brides': Heteroglossia, Counter-Memory, and the Auto/biographical Work of Japanese War Brides," *Meridians* 10, no. 1 (2010): 115–116.

4. Zeiger, *Entangling Alliances,* 163–202; Shukert and Scibetta, *War Brides of World War II,* 197–205.

5. Ann Laura Stoler, ed., *Haunted by Empire: Geographies of Intimacy in North American History* (Durham, N.C.: Duke University Press, 2006). See also Frederick Cooper and Ann Laura Stoler, eds., *Tensions of Empire: Colonial Cultures in a Bourgeois World* (Berkeley: University of California Press, 1997).

6. Antoinette Burton, *The Trouble with Empire: Challenges to Modern British Imperialism* (New York: Oxford University Press, 2015); Tony Ballantyne and Antoinette Burton, eds., *Moving Subjects: Gender, Mobility, and Intimacy in an Age of Global Empire* (Urbana:

University of Illinois Press, 2009); Heonik Kwon, "The Transpacific Cold War," in *Transpacific Studies: Framing an Emerging Field,* ed. Janet Hoskins and Viet Thanh Nguyen (Honolulu: University of Hawai'i Press, 2014), 64–84.

7. Laura Hein, "Revisiting America's Occupation of Japan," *Cold War History* 11, no. 4 (November 2011): 587–589; John W. Dower, *Ways of Forgetting, Ways of Remembering: Japan in the Modern World* (New York: New Press, 2012), 126–129.

8. Paul A. Kramer, "Power and Connection: Imperial Histories of the United States in the World," *American Historical Review* 116 (December 2011): 1352.

9. Ibid., 1368–1369.

10. T. Fujitani, *Race for Empire: Koreans as Japanese and Japanese as Americans during World War II* (Berkeley: University of California Press, 2011); Yukiko Koshiro, *Trans-Pacific Racisms and the U.S. Occupation of Japan* (New York: Columbia University Press, 1999).

11. Michael Baskett, *The Attractive Empire: Transnational Film Culture in Imperial Japan* (Honolulu: University of Hawai'i Press, 2008), 142–145; Shelley Stephenson, "A Star by Any Other Name: The (After) Lives of Li Xianglan," *Quarterly Review of Film and Video* 19 (2002): 9; Yiman Wang, "Affective Politics and the Legend of Yamaguchi Yoshiko/Li Xianglan," in *Sino-Japanese Transculturation: From the Late Nineteenth Century to the End of the Pacific War,* ed. Richard King, Cody Poulton, and Katsuhiko Endo (Lanham, Md.: Lexington Books, 2012), 152–156.

12. Baskett, *The Attractive Empire,* 135–142; Wang, "Affective Politics and the Legend of Yamaguchi Yoshiko/Li Xianglan," 147–153.

13. Naoko Shibusawa, *America's Geisha Ally: Reimagining the Japanese Enemy* (Cambridge, Mass.: Harvard University Press, 2006); Traise Yamamoto, *Masking Selves, Making Subjects: Japanese American Women, Identity, and the Body* (Berkeley: University of California Press, 1999), 9–61.

14. Lori Watt, *When Empire Comes Home: Repatriation and Reintegration in Postwar Japan* (Cambridge, Mass.: Harvard University Asia Center, 2009), 2–3, 38–39.

15. Louise Young, *Japan's Total Empire: Manchuria and the Culture of Wartime Imperialism* (Berkeley: University of California Press, 1998). See also Stephen R. MacKinnon, Diana Lary, and Ezra F. Vogel, eds., *China at War: Regions of China, 1937–1945* (Stanford, Calif.: Stanford University Press, 2007); Peter Duus, Ramon H. Myers, and Mark R. Peattie, eds., *The Japanese Wartime Empire, 1931–1945* (Princeton, N.J.: Princeton University Press, 2010).

16. Dower, *Ways of Forgetting, Ways of Remembering,* 66–75.

17. Kyoko Hirano, *Mr. Smith Goes to Tokyo: Japanese Cinema under the American Occupation, 1945–1952* (Washington, D.C.: Smithsonian Institution Press, 1992), 206–207.

18. For background on the film industry in imperial Japan, see Baskett, *The Attractive Empire*; Peter G. High, *The Imperial Screen: Japanese Film Culture in the Fifteen Years' War, 1931–1945* (Madison: University of Wisconsin Press, 2003); David Desser, "From the Opium War to the Pacific War: Japanese Propaganda Films of World War II," *Film History* 7, no. 1 (Spring 1995): 32–48.

19. Stephenson, "A Star by Any Other Name," 7–8; Wang, "Affective Politics and the Legend of Yamaguchi Yoshiko/Li Xianglan," 151.

20. Shelley Stephenson, "'Her Traces Are Found Everywhere': Shanghai, Li Xianglan, and the 'Greater East Asia Film Sphere,'" in *Cinema and Urban Culture in Shanghai, 1922–1943,* ed. Yingjin Zhang (Stanford, Calif.: Stanford University Press, 1999), 222–245; Yiman Wang, "Between the National and the Transnational: Li Xianglan/Yamaguchi Yoshiko and Pan-Asianism," *IIAS Newsletter* 38 (September 2005): 7.

21. Watt, *When Empire Comes Home,* 56–97.

22. Jennifer Coates, "The Shape-Shifting Diva: Yamaguchi Yoshiko and the National Body," *Journal of Japanese and Korean Cinema* 6, no. 1 (2014): 30.

23. Coates, "The Shape-Shifting Diva," 30; High, *The Imperial Screen*, 237–238, 241; Kim Brandt, "'There Was No East or West When Their Lips Met': A Movie Poster for *Japanese War Bride* as Transnational Artifact," *Impressions* 30 (2009): 123.

24. Coates, "The Shape-Shifting Diva," 23–38. See also Sharalyn Orbaugh, *Japanese Fiction of the Allied Occupation: Vision, Embodiment, Identity* (Leiden, Netherlands: Brill, 2007), 389–416; Yoshikuni Igarashi, *Bodies of Memory: Narratives of War in Postwar Japanese Culture, 1945–1970* (Princeton, N.J.: Princeton University Press, 2000), 35–38.

25. Postwar Japan's collective memories of its wartime deeds are more complicated than what I can describe here. For more detailed analyses, see Franziska Seraphim, *War Memory and Social Politics in Japan, 1945–2005* (Cambridge, Mass.: Harvard University Asia Center, 2006); Mariko Asano Tamanoi, *Memory Maps: The State and Manchuria in Postwar Japan* (Honolulu: University of Hawai'i Press, 2009).

26. Stephenson, "A Star by Any Other Name," 10.

27. See Hirano, *Mr. Smith Goes to Tokyo;* Hiroshi Kitamura, *Screening Enlightenment: Hollywood and the Cultural Reconstruction of Defeated Japan* (Ithaca, N.Y.: Cornell University Press, 2010). For documentary films, see Yuka Tsuchiya, "Imagined America in Occupied Japan: (Re-)Educational Films Shown by the U.S. Occupational Forces to the Japanese, 1948–1952," *Japanese Journal of American Studies* 13 (2002): 193–213.

28. Zeiger, *Entangling Alliances,* 1–9.

29. Zeiger, *Entangling Alliances,* 131–133, 179–182; Peggy Pascoe, *What Comes Naturally: Miscegenation Law and the Making of Race in America* (New York: Oxford University Press, 2009), 199–201.

30. Madeleine Y. Hsu, *The Good Immigrants: How the Yellow Peril Became the Model Minority* (Princeton, N.J.: Princeton University Press, 2015); Michael G. Davis, "Impetus for Immigration Reform: Asian Refugees and the Cold War," *Journal of American–East Asian Relations* 7, nos. 3–4 (Fall–Winter 1998): 127–156.

31. Mae M. Ngai, *Impossible Subjects: Illegal Aliens and the Making of Modern America* (Princeton, N.J.: Princeton University Press, 2004): 234–248; Caroline Chung Simpson, *An Absent Presence: Japanese Americans in Postwar American Culture, 1945–1960* (Durham, N.C.: Duke University Press, 2001), 149–185.

32. Larry Tajiri, "The Vanishing Opposition," *Pacific Citizen,* April 7, 1951, 4; "Fear Walter Omnibus Bill May Become Fuel for Red Propaganda," *Rafu Shimpo,* March 11, 1952, 1; Richard Akagi, "An Open Letter," *Chicago Shimpo,* October 11, 1952, 1; S. I. Hayakawa, "Letters to the Editor, Part 2," *Chicago Shimpo,* November 22, 1952, 1; "Naturalized Issei Given Tribute for Hard Work in Attaining US Status," *Rafu Shimpo,* December 1, 1956, 1.

33. Maureen Honey and Jean Lee Cole, eds., *"Madame Butterfly" by John Luther Long and "A Japanese Nightingale" by Onoto Watanna (Winnifred Eaton): Two Orientalist Texts* (New Brunswick: N.J.: Rutgers University Press, 2002), 25–79. An excellent analysis of Long's *Madame Butterfly* is in Susan Koshy, *Sexual Naturalization: Asian Americans and Miscegenation* (Stanford, Calif.: Stanford University Press, 2004), 29–49.

34. David Brody, *Visualizing American Empire: Orientalism and Imperialism in the Philippines* (Chicago: University of Chicago Press, 2010); David Weir, *American Orient: Imagining the East from the Colonial Era through the Twentieth Century* (Amherst: University of Massachusetts Press, 2011).

35. See Matthew Frye Jacobson, *Barbarian Virtues: The United States Encounters Foreign Populations at Home and Abroad, 1876–1917* (New York: Hill and Wang, 2001); John Kuo

Wei Tchen, *New York before Chinatown: Orientalism and the Shaping of American Culture, 1776–1882* (Baltimore: Johns Hopkins University Press, 1999); Kristin L. Hoganson, *Consumers' Imperium: The Global Production of American Domesticity, 1865–1920* (Chapel Hill: University of North Carolina Press, 2007); Mari Yoshihara, *Embracing the East: White Women and American Orientalism* (New York: Oxford University Press, 2003).

36. Honey and Cole, "Introduction," in *"Madame Butterfly" and "A Japanese Nightingale,"* 1–5.

37. Koshy, *Sexual Naturalization,* 32–35.

38. Shibusawa, *America's Geisha Ally,* 1–12; Yamamoto, *Masking Selves, Making Subjects,* 9–61; Gina Marchetti, *Romance and the "Yellow Peril": Race, Sex, and Discursive Strategies in Hollywood Fiction* (Berkeley: University of California Press, 1993), 158–201; John W. Dower, *War without Mercy: Race and Power in the Pacific War* (New York: Pantheon, 1986), 301–317.

39. Zeiger, *Entangling Alliances,* 183–187.

40. "Who's Losing Japan?" *Washington Post,* May 24, 1950, 10; "Second Chance in Asia," *Commonweal,* June 29, 1951, 277; "Reluctant Ally," *Nation,* September 10, 1955, 215.

41. Hugh H. and Mabel M. Smythe, "Race, Culture, and Politics in Japan," *Phylon* 13 (3rd Quarter 1952), 192; "Reluctant Ally," 214; "Japan: The Cost of Arming," *Newsweek,* April 18, 1955, 46.

42. "Another Ally Grows Restive," *U.S. News and World Report,* December 17, 1954, 42; "Japan Eyes America for Signs of Wobbling," *Saturday Evening Post,* June 11, 1955, 10; Eric Johnston, "Japan: Partner or Problem?," *Look,* April 5, 1955, 104; Cameron Hawley, "Are We Driving Japan Into Red China's Arms?" *Saturday Evening Post,* August 10, 1957, 18–19+; "Editorials: U.S.-Japanese Relations," *Pacific Citizen,* April 15, 1955, 8.

43. "Invitation to Dance," *Newsweek,* February 14, 1955, 36; N[orman] C[ousins], "They Love Us for the Wrong Reasons," *Saturday Review of Literature* 35 (January 1952): 20–21.

44. Simpson, *An Absent Presence,* 164–171; Shibusawa, *America's Geisha Ally,* 47–50; Pascoe, *What Comes Naturally,* 233–234.

45. Janet Wentworth Smith and William L. Worden, "They're Bringing Home Japanese Wives," *Saturday Evening Post,* January 19, 1952, 26–27+; Peter Kalischer, "Madame Butterfly's Children," *Collier's,* September 20, 1952, 15–18; William L. Worden, "Where are Those Japanese War Brides?" *Saturday Evening Post,* November 20, 1954, 38–39+; James A. Michener, "Pursuit of Happiness by a GI and a Japanese," *Life,* February 21, 1955, 124–126+; Chester Morrison, "East Meets West," *Look,* October 29, 1957, 73–77.

46. Zeiger, *Entangling Alliances,* 140–150. See also Elaine Tyler May, *Homeward Bound: American Families in the Cold War Era,* rev. and updated 20th anniv. ed. (New York: Basic Books, 2008).

47. Igarashi, *Bodies of Memory,* 13.

48. Zeiger, *Entangling Alliances,* 148–149, 187–189; Shukert and Scibetta, *War Brides of World War II,* 186–189.

49. See Susan L. Carruthers, *Cold War Captives: Imprisonment, Escape, and Brainwashing* (Berkeley: University of California Press, 2009).

50. "GI Tells Japanese Bride He Won't Give Up Reds," *Los Angeles Times,* December 20, 1953, 18.

51. J. P. McEvoy, "America through the Eyes of a Japanese War-Bride," *Reader's Digest* 66 (April 1955): 95–99.

52. Hirano, *Mr. Smith Goes to Tokyo,* 160–162.

53. "Story of a 'Japanese War Bride,'" *New York Times,* January 30, 1952, 22; "War Bride's Story Unique," *Los Angeles Times,* February 5, 1952, C6.

54. Harry Brand, "Biography of Shirley Yamaguchi," 1, Core Biographical Clippings, *House of Bamboo,* n.d., Margaret Herrick Library, Beverly Hills, Calif.

55. What has been written about *Japanese War Bride* focuses mainly on issues of gender dynamics occurring in the United States. See Marchetti, *Romance and the "Yellow Peril,"* 158–175. For a different take on the film's spatial politics, see David Palumbo-Liu, *Asian/American: Historical Crossings of a Racial Frontier* (Stanford, Calif.: Stanford University Press, 1999), 225–232. For a transnational perspective from a historian of modern Japan that examines the film's marketing, see Brandt, "'There Was No East or West When Their Lips Met.'"

56. Simpson, *An Absent Presence,* 149–185.

57. Shibusawa, *America's Geisha Ally,* 255–287; Yamamoto, *Masking Selves, Making Subjects,* 9–61.

58. Larry Tajiri, "And the Twain Shall Meet," *Pacific Citizen,* September 1, 1951, 4; Tajiri, "Love Story via Hollywood," *Pacific Citizen,* July 14, 1951, 4; Tajiri, "'Japanese War Bride,'" *Pacific Citizen,* December 1, 1951, 4.

59. "The Treaty Conference: Formal Peace with Japan Brings Obligation to Nisei," *Pacific Citizen,* September 1, 1951, 4, 7; Al Miyadi, "Oriental Orchid," *Scene,* August 1950, 16.

60. Yamaguchi Yoshiko, quoted in "Book and Humanities Day Lecture Trace History of Japan's Postwar Period through Popular Music," *UChicagoNews,* https://news.uchicago.edu/article/2012/10/17/book-and-humanities-day-lecture-trace-history-japan-s-postwar-period-through-popu (accessed January 7, 2017). See also Brownie Furutani, "Japanese Actress Will Sing before Mainland Audiences," *Pacific Citizen,* June 3, 1950, 2; Michael K. Bourdaghs, *Sayonara Amerika, Sayonara Nippon: A Geopolitical Prehistory of J-Pop* (New York: Columbia University Press, 2012), 58–60, 75–77.

61. "Shirley 'Rikoran' Yamaguchi Slated to Sign Contract for Hollywood Film Role," *Nichi Bei Times,* August 18, 1950, 1; Tajiri, "Love Story via Hollywood," 4. See also Furutani, "Japanese Actress Will Sing before Mainland Audiences," 2; "Rikoran's American Film on Screen Soon," *Chicago Shimpo,* January 12, 1952, 1; "Yamaguchi Film Here," *Chicago Shimpo,* March 8, 1952, 1; "Rikoran Studies Scripts in Hollywood, Receives Publicity in Many Columns," *Nichi Bei Times,* July 26, 1950, 1.

62. After 1952, some popular periodicals still remained wary of Japanese intentions. See for instance, Johnston, "Japan: Partner or Problem?," 104; "Another Ally Grows Restive," *U.S. News and World Report,* December 17, 1954, 45; Peter Kallischer, "Japan," *Collier's,* March 2, 1956, 58.

63. Larry Tajiri, "Notes from Hollywood," *Pacific Citizen,* July 8, 1950, 4; "Japanese War Bride," *Time,* February 4, 1952, 74; Koshiro, *Trans-Pacific Racisms,* 84.

64. "Story of a 'Japanese War Bride,'" *New York Times,* January 30, 1952, 22. See also "Japanese War Bride," *Time,* February 4, 1952, 74; Rod Nordell, "Don Taylor in Problem Film with Shirley Yamaguchi," *Christian Science Monitor,* February 8, 1952, 5; Ray Falk, "Japanese Screen Scene: East Meets West with Varying Reactions as American Producers Invade Nippon," *New York Times,* February 3, 1952, X5.

65. Koshiro, *Trans-Pacific Racisms,* 84; Masayo Duus, *The Life of Isamu Noguchi: Journey without Borders,* translated by Peter Duus (Princeton, N.J.: Princeton University Press, 2004), 231.

66. Wang, "Affective Politics and the Legend of Yamaguchi Yoshiko/Li Xianglan," 153, 160.

67. Isamu Noguchi, *A Sculptor's World* (New York: Harper and Row, 1968), 19–24; Hayden Herrera, *Listening to Stone: The Art and Life of Isamu Noguchi* (New York: Farrar, Straus and Giroux, 2015), 205–214; Duus, *The Life of Isamu Noguchi,* 11–136.

68. Duus, *The Life of Isamu Noguchi,* 224–226.

69. Robert J. Maeda, "Isamu Noguchi: 5–7-A, Poston, Arizona," *Amerasia Journal* 20, no. 2 (1994): 61–76.

70. Duus, *The Life of Isamu Noguchi,* 221–222, 224–225; Herrera, *Listening to Stone,* 279–280.

71. Duus, *The Life of Isamu Noguchi,* 235–237.

72. Noguchi, *A Sculptor's World,* 32.

73. Noguchi, quoted in Herrera, *Listening to Stone,* 285; Noguchi, *A Sculptor's World,* 163.

74. Noguchi, *A Sculptor's World,* 32.

75. See Daisuke Miyao, *Sessue Hayakawa: Silent Cinema and Transnational Stardom* (Durham, N.C.: Duke University Press, 2007).

76. Samuel Fuller, with Christa Lang Fuller and Jerome Henry Rudes, *A Third Face: My Tale of Writing, Fighting, and Filmmaking* (New York: Knopf, 2002), 323.

77. "House of Bamboo," *Time,* August 1, 1955, 61; "Under the Color," *Newsweek,* July 18, 1955, 83; Bosley Crowther, "Term Examination," *New York Times,* July 3, 1955, X1; Ray Falk, "Americans in the Nipponese Cinema Scope," *New York Times,* July 3, 1955, X5; Hollis Alpert, "The House of Bamboo," *Saturday Review,* July 23, 1955, 23; Moira Walsh, "Films: House of Bamboo," *America,* July 23, 1955, 419.

78. On "the imperial gaze," see E. Ann Kaplan, *Looking for the Other: Feminism, Film, and the Imperial Gaze* (New York: Routledge, 1997). See also Mary Louise Pratt, *Imperial Eyes: Travel Writing and Transculturation, Second Edition* (New York: Routledge, 2007); Ella Shohat and Robert Stam, *Unthinking Eurocentrism: Multiculturalism and the Media* (New York: Routledge, 1994), 100–136.

79. Lucy Herndon Crockett, "GI Holidays in Japan," *Travel* 89 (August 1947): 32.

80. Miriam Troop, "I've Got a Yen for Japan," *American Magazine* 159 (June 1955): 100.

81. Fuller, *A Third Face,* 323.

82. Alpert, "The House of Bamboo," 23.

83. "House of Bamboo," *Time,* August 1, 1955, 61; "Under the Color," *Newsweek,* July 18, 1955, 83.

84. Harry Brand, "Vital Statistics on 'House of Bamboo,'" 1, Core Production Clippings, n.d.; Fuller, quoted in "Orient Beckons CinemaScope," 2, *Exhibitor's Campaign Book, House of Bamboo,* n.d., Margaret Herrick Library, Beverly Hills, Calif.

85. Fuller, *A Third Face,* 315–316.

86. Bosley Crowther, "Screen: Starring Tokyo," *New York Times,* July 2, 1955, 13.

87. "Japanese Attack Hollywood Policy in Film Selection," *Christian Science Monitor,* September 8, 1955, 4. See also "Threat to Ban All U.S. Movies Made by Japanese Theater-Owner," *Pacific Citizen,* September 16, 1955, 2.

88. Larry Tajiri, "New Cycle of Orient-Caucasian Romances," *Pacific Citizen,* April 15, 1955, 1; Tajiri, "East Meets West on Screen," *Pacific Citizen,* July 22, 1955, 8.

89. Tamotsu Murayama, "'Blackboard Jungle' Cheapens U.S. in Eyes of Japanese as Controversial Movie Arouses Press, Parents and Educators," *Pacific Citizen,* September 16, 1955, 2; "Threat to Ban All U.S. Movies Made by Japanese Theater-Owner," 2.

90. Shinichi Hasagawa, "Shirley Starts Anew—As Diplomat's Wife," *Japan Times,* March 8, 1958, 7.

91. *Exhibitor's Campaign Book, House of Bamboo,* 1.

92. Quoted in Bert Winther, "The Rejection of Isamu Noguchi's Hiroshima Cenotaph: A Japanese American Artist in Occupied Japan," *Art Journal* 53, no. 4 (Winter 1994): 26.

93. Winther, "The Rejection of Isamu Noguchi's Hiroshima Cenotaph," 26. See also

Bert Winther-Tamaki, *Art in the Encounter of Nations: Japanese and American Artists in the Early Postwar Years* (Honolulu: University of Hawai'i Press, 2001).

94. Duus, *The Life of Isamu Noguchi,* 252–258; Herrera, *Listening to Stone,* 308–309.

95. Noguchi, quoted in Winther, "The Rejection of Isamu Noguchi's Hiroshima Cenotaph," 26.

96. Winther, "The Rejection of Isamu Noguchi's Hiroshima Cenotaph," 26–27.

97. Duus, *The Life of Isamu Noguchi,* 260–266.

98. Ibid., 269–271; Herrera, *Listening to Stone,* 314–315.

99. John L. Scott, "Fortune Bolt Puts Miiko in Top Film Spot," *Los Angeles Times,* May 5, 1957, E3.

100. Wang, "Affective Politics and the Legend of Yamaguchi Yoshiko/Li Xianglan," 161–162, Wang, "Between the National and the Transnational," 7.

CHAPTER 3

1. Henry Sugimoto, Typed statement of testimony before the Commission on Wartime Relocation and Internment of Civilians (CWRIC), circa 1981, 1, in Henry Sugimoto, "Interviews," Department of Special Collections, Stanford University Libraries, SC 929, Box 15, Folder 2 (hereafter cited as Sugimoto, "Interviews," Stanford University Libraries); Kristine Kim, *Henry Sugimoto: Painting an American Experience* (Berkeley, Calif.: Heyday, 2000), 105–106; Alice Yang Murray, *Historical Memories of the Japanese American Internment and the Struggle for Redress* (Stanford, Calif.: Stanford University Press, 2008), 185–381.

2. Henry Sugimoto, "From Paris to Mexico in 1963," in "Life Story," translated and prepared by Emily Anderson (unpublished manuscript, 2000), 1; Kim, *Henry Sugimoto,* 11–31, 104.

3. Murray, *Historical Memories of the Japanese American Internment,* 185–381.

4. Gordon H. Chang, Mark Dean Johnson, Paul J. Karlstrom, and Sharon Spain, eds., *Asian American Art: A History, 1850–1970* (Stanford, Calif.: Stanford University Press, 2008), 126.

5. Debates about what various ideas define "cosmopolitanism" can be found in Pheng Cheah and Bruce Robbins, eds., *Cosmopolitics: Thinking and Feeling beyond the Nation* (Minneapolis: University of Minnesota Press, 1998); Bruce Robbins and Paulo Lemos Horta, eds., *Cosmopolitanisms* (New York: New York University Press, 2017).

6. My definition of "racialized cosmopolitanism" overlaps with, but also differs from, Susan Koshy's phrase, "minority cosmopolitanism" (as discussed in Chapter 1). Similar to Koshy, I link the idea of cosmopolitanism to ethnic studies, with a focus that shifts away from European-centered subjects. However, I am also framing a more evident tension between a state's power to define and incarcerate a racialized population and Sugimoto's response, from a cosmopolitan worldview, to transcend, but also to protest, that specific historical moment of confinement. See Koshy, "Minority Cosmopolitanism" *PMLA* 126 (May 2011): 592–609.

7. Lawrence M. Small, "Foreword," and Karen Higa, "Introduction," in Kim, *Henry Sugimoto,* viii, ix.

8. Kim, *Henry Sugimoto,* 103–104.

9. By claiming Sugimoto's fit in a "Japanese/American" configuration, I complicate previous work on him and on other Japanese American artists that also interrogate the transformation of Japanese immigrants into American citizens. See Kim, *Henry Sugimoto;* ShiPu Wang, *Becoming American? The Art and Identity Crisis of Yasuo Kuniyoshi* (Honolulu: University of Hawai'i Press, 2011).

10. Henry Sugimoto, Handwritten notes expressing his views on art, n.d., 3, in Sugimoto, "Interviews," Stanford University Libraries.

11. Ibid.

12. Greg Robinson, "Henry Sugimoto," *Densho Encyclopedia,* http://encyclopedia.densho.org/Henry%20Sugimoto/#cite_ref-ftnt_ref3_3-0 (accessed July 22, 2017); Kubo Sadajiro, "History of the Sufferings of the Japanese Citizens," in Henry Sugimoto, *North American Japanese People in Relocation Camps* (Self-Publication, 1983), 11.

13. Boris Musich, "Interview with Henry Sugimoto," December 1986 (unpublished manuscript), 6, in Sugimoto, "Interviews," Stanford University Libraries.

14. Kim, *Henry Sugimoto,* 3–6, 11–13; Typed transcript of unindentified interview with Henry Sugimoto, circa 1982, 1–2, in Sugimoto, "Interviews," Stanford University Libraries.

15. Michael D. Brown, *Views from Asian California, 1920–1965* (San Francisco: Michael Brown, 1992), 6–7.

16. Sugimoto, "Because I Wanted to See Paintings by Old and New Masters," in "Life Story," 1; Kim, *Henry Sugimoto,* 12–13.

17. Kim, *Henry Sugimoto,* 12–17.

18. Jean Selz, *Vlaminck,* translated from the French by Graham Snell (New York: Crown, 1963). For context on the Postimpressionists, see T. J. Clark, *The Painting of Modern Life: Paris in the Art of Manet and His Followers* (New York: Knopf, 1985); Sue Roe, *In Montmartre: Picasso, Matisse and the Birth of Modernist Art* (New York: Penguin, 2015).

19. These and other works of Sugimoto's can be viewed on the Japanese National American Museum site: http://www.janm.org/collections/henry-sugimoto-collection/.

20. *Exhibition of Paintings by Henry Sugimoto,* quoted in Kim, *Henry Sugimoto,* 34.

21. Kim, *Henry Sugimoto,* 35.

22. "17 Paintings by Nippon Artist[s] in Exhibition," *Kashu Mainichi,* January 27, 1935, n.p.; "Open First Oriental Modern Art Exhibit at Gallery in L.A.," *Kashu Mainichi,* April 27, 1934, 1; "Young Nisei Artists to Exhibit at Wilshire Art Gallery Showing," *Rafu Shimpo,* April 4, 1934, 1, all in Henry Sugimoto, "Press," Department of Special Collections, Stanford University Libraries, SC 929, Box 15, Folder 1 (hereafter cited as Sugimoto, "Press," Stanford University Libraries).

23. Kim, *Henry Sugimoto,* 36–37.

24. Sugimoto, quoted in Ruth Gomes, "Sugimoto Exhibit Coming to Kings Art Center," *Hanford Sentinel,* June 16, 2000, B1, in Sugimoto, "Press," Stanford University Libraries.

25. Sugimoto, "Sketching in Carmel," in "Life Story," 2–3; Sugimoto, "Because I Wanted to See Paintings by Old and New European Masters," in "Life Story," 7.

26. Sugimoto, "Sketching Trip in Mexico," in "Life Story," 1.

27. Ibid., 3–4.

28. James Oles, *South of the Border: Mexico in the American Imagination, 1914–1947* (Washington, D.C.: Smithsonian Institution Press, 1993).

29. Stacy I. Morgan, *Rethinking Social Realism: African American Art and Literature, 1930–1953* (Athens: University of Georgia Press, 2004), 45–48; Rebecca Schreiber, *Cold War Exiles in Mexico: U.S. Dissidents and the Culture of Critical Resistance* (Minneapolis: University of Minnesota Press, 2008), 30–34.

30. Kim, *Henry Sugimoto,* 38–39.

31. Higa, "Introduction," in Kim, *Henry Sugimoto,* xiii.

32. See Jane E. Dusselier, *Artifacts of Loss: Crafting Survival in Japanese American Concentration Camps* (New Brunswick, N.J.: Rutgers University Press, 2008); Delphine Hirasuna, Terry Heffernan, and Kit Hinrichs, *The Art of Gaman: Arts and Crafts from the*

Japanese American Internment Camps, 1942–1946 (Berkeley, Calif.: Ten Speed Press, 2005); Jasmine Alinder, *Moving Images: Photography and the Japanese American Incarceration* (Urbana: University of Illinois Press, 2010); Kristine C. Kuramitsu, "Internment and Identity in Japanese American Art," *American Quarterly* 47, no. 4 (December 1995): 619–658; Karin M. Higa, *The View from Within: Japanese American Art from the Internment Camps, 1942–1945* (Los Angeles: Japanese American National Museum, UCLA Wight Art Gallery, and UCLA Asian American Studies Center, 1992); Deborah Gesensway and Mindy Roseman, *Beyond Words: Images from America's Concentration Camps* (Ithaca, N.Y.: Cornell University Press, 1987), 30–40.

33. Alinder, *Moving Images,* 44–74; Elena Tajima Creef, *Imaging Japanese America: The Visual Construction of Citizenship, Nation, and the Body* (New York: New York University Press, 2004), 18–37; Thy Phu, *Picturing Model Citizens: Civility in Asian American Visual Culture* (Philadelphia: Temple University Press, 2011), 60–67.

34. Linda Gordon and Gary Y. Okihiro, eds., *Impounded: Dorothea Lange and the Censored Images of Japanese American Internment* (New York: Norton, 2006); Alinder, *Moving Images* 23–43; Creef, *Imaging Japanese America,* 37–57.

35. Alinder, *Moving Images,* 3.

36. Ibid., 3–4, 12–18; Creef, *Imaging Japanese America,* 19–22, 41–43, 45–46; Phu, *Picturing Model Citizens,* 54–83. See also Marita Sturken, "Absent Images of Memory: Remembering and Reenacting the Japanese American Internment," *positions* 5, no. 3 (Winter 1997): 687–707. For works on aspects of nineteenth- and early twentieth-century visual culture and Orientalism, refer to Anthony W. Lee, *Picturing Chinatown: Art and Orientalism in San Francisco* (Berkeley: University of California Press, 2001); Robert G. Lee, *Orientals: Asian Americans in Popular Culture* (Philadelphia: Temple University Press, 1999), 15–144; John Kuo Wei Tchen, *New York before Chinatown: Orientalism and the Shaping of American Culture, 1776–1882* (Baltimore: Johns Hopkins University Press, 1999), 131–154; David Brody, *Visualizing American Empire: Orientalism and Imperialism in the Philippines* (Chicago: University of Chicago Press, 2010); Laura Wexler, *Tender Violence: Domestic Visions in an Age of U.S. Imperialism* (Chapel Hill: University of North Carolina Press, 2000).

37. Alinder, *Moving Images,* 75–102; Creef, *Imaging Japanese America,* 57–64. See also Eric L. Muller, *Colors of Confinement: Rare Kodachrome Photographs of Japanese American Incarceration in World War II* (Chapel Hill: University of North Carolina Press, 2012); Lane Ryo Hirabayashi with Kenichiro Shimada, *Japanese American Resettlement through the Lens: Hikaru Carl Iwasaki and the WRA's Photographic Section, 1943–1945* (Boulder: University Press of Colorado, 2009); Kim Kodani Hill, ed., *Topaz Moon: Chiura Obata's Art of the Internment* (Berkeley, Calif.: Heyday, 2000); Hisako Hibi, with Ibuki H. Lee, *Peaceful Painter: Memoirs of an Issei Woman Artist* (Berkeley, Calif.: Heyday, 2004).

38. Sugimoto, Handwritten notes expressing his views on art, 2, in Sugimoto, "Interviews," Stanford University Libraries.

39. Lee, *Orientals,* 145–179.

40. Typed transcript of unindentified interview with Sugimoto, circa 1982, 10–11, in Sugimoto, "Interviews," Stanford University Libraries.

41. See Alejandro Anreus, Robin Adèle Greeley, and Leonard Folgarait, eds., *Mexican Muralism: A Critical History* (Berkeley: University of California Press, 2012); Matthew Affron, Mark A. Castro, Renato González Mello, and Dafne Cruz Porchini, eds., *Paint the Revolution: Mexican Modernism, 1910–1950* (New Haven, Conn.: Yale University Press, 2016).

42. Nancy Sparks, "Tragic Artwork from Rohwer," (newspaper clipping, no publication title, n.d.), 8B, in Sugimoto, "Interviews," Stanford University Libraries; Collette

Chattopadhyay, "Henry Sugimoto at the Japanese American National Museum," *Artweek* 32 (July–August 2001): 22, in Sugimoto, "Press," Stanford University Libraries.

43. Kim, *Henry Sugimoto,* 54–55.

44. Michi Nishiura Weglyn, *Years of Infamy: The Untold Story of America's Concentration Camps,* updated ed. (Seattle: University of Washington Press, 1996), 33–102; Greg Robinson, *A Tragedy of Democracy: Japanese Confinement in North America* (New York: Columbia University Press, 2009), 59–153.

45. Gesensway and Roseman, *Beyond Words,* 34; Typed transcript of unidentified interview with Sugimoto, circa 1982, 22, in Sugimoto, "Interviews," Stanford University Libraries. Most currency converters estimate that ten thousand dollars in 1942 would have been the equivalent to well over one hundred thousand dollars in the 1980s, when Sugimoto made this statement about the worth of his lost art.

46. Typed transcript of statements by Henry Sugimoto and members of the CWRIC, circa 1981, 276, in Sugimoto, "Interviews," Stanford University Libraries.

47. Ibid.; Kim, *Henry Sugimoto,* 66–67.

48. Typed transcript of unidentified interview with Sugimoto, circa 1982, 15, in Sugimoto, "Interviews," Stanford University Libraries.

49. Ibid., 15.

50. Ibid., 9; Musich, "Interview with Henry Sugimoto," 6.

51. Sugimoto, "Continuing My Education on My Own in California," in "Life Story," 2; Typed transcript of unindentified interview with Sugimoto, circa 1982, 19, in Sugimoto, "Interviews," Stanford University Libraries.

52. Wendy Kozol, "Madonnas of the Fields: Photography, Gender, and 1930s Farm Relief," *Genders* 2 (Summer 1988): 1–23. See also James Curtis, *Mind's Eye, Mind's Truth: FSA Photography Reconsidered* (Philadelphia: Temple University Press, 1989), 46–67; William Stott, *Documentary Expression and Thirties America, with a New Afterword* (Chicago: University of Chicago Press, 1986); Carl Fleischhauer and Beverly W. Brannan, eds., *Documenting America, 1935–1943* (Berkeley: University of California Press, 1988), 114–127.

53. Robert Hariman and John Louis Lucaites, *No Caption Needed: Iconic Photographs, Public Culture, and Liberal Democracy* (Chicago: University of Chicago Press, 2007), 56–60.

54. Colleen Lye, *America's Asia: Racial Form and American Literature, 1893–1945* (Princeton, N.J.: Princeton University Press, 2005), 156.

55. Lye, *America's Asia,* 153–173. See also Brian Masaru Hayashi, *Democratizing the Enemy: The Japanese American Internment* (Princeton, N.J.: Princeton University Press, 2004); Phu, *Picturing Model Citizens,* 58–75.

56. The film clips are from the documentary *Harsh Canvas: The Art and Life of Henry Sugimoto,* directed by John Esaki (Los Angeles: Japanese American National Museum Media Arts Center, 2001), 30 min.

57. Typed transcript of unidentified interview with Sugimoto, circa 1982, 17, in Sugimoto, "Interviews," Stanford University Libraries; Kim, *Henry Sugimoto,* 84.

58. In her postwar memoir, *Citizen 13660* (1946), Miné Okubo conveyed in text and in illustrations a similar scene to that rendered by Sugimoto. Her drawing of the mess hall is comparable to his, with eight people sitting four to each side of a table in flattened perspective, as they eat, talk, sneeze, or squirm in their seats. Her text description of the scene verifies the lack of sufficient food. "Before mess tickets were issued," she writes, "most of us were hungry after one meal, so we would dash to another mess hall for a second meal." See Okubo, *Citizen 13660* (Seattle: University of Washington Press, 1983), 89.

59. Sugimoto, Handwritten notes on his wartime removal and confinement, n.d., 5, in Sugimoto, "Interviews," Stanford University Libraries.

60. *Personal Justice Denied: Report of the Commission on Wartime Relocation and Internment of Civilians,* foreword by Tetsuden Kashima (Washington, D.C.: Civil Liberties Public Education Fund; Seattle: University of Washington Press, 1997), 185–212; T. Fujitani, *Race for Empire: Koreans as Japanese and Japanese as Americans during World War II* (Berkeley: University of California Press, 2011), 163–205; Eric L. Muller, *Free to Die for Their Country: The Story of the Japanese-American Draft Resisters in World War II* (Chicago: University of Chicago Press, 2001); Weglyn, *Years of Infamy,* 134–173.

61. Paul Faris, "Special to Art News," n.d., in Sugimoto, "Interviews," Stanford University Libraries. See also John Howard, *Concentration Camps on the Home Front: Japanese Americans in the House of Jim Crow* (Chicago: University of Chicago Press, 2008), 160–161.

62. Robert W. Meriwether, "Hendrix History: The Sugimoto Exhibition, 1944," August 1987, (unpublished manuscript), 2–3, in Sugimoto, "Interviews," Stanford University Libraries.

63. Jason Morgan Ward, "'No Jap Crow': Japanese Americans Encounter the World War II South," *Journal of Southern History* 73 (February 2007): 85–86; Russell Bearden, "Life inside Arkansas's Japanese-American Relocation Centers," *Arkansas Historical Quarterly* 48, no. 2 (Summer 1989): 191. The author thanks Greg Robinson for the information on Sugimoto's trip to New Orleans.

64. Chang et al., *Asian American Art,* 128–129.

65. Grace Elizabeth Hale, *Making Whiteness: The Culture of Segregation in the South, 1890–1940* (New York: Pantheon, 1998), 121–197.

66. Ward, "'No Jap Crow,'" 75–104; Howard, *Concentration Camps on the Home Front,* 95–197; Leslie Bow, *Partly Colored: Asian Americans and Racial Anomaly in the Segregated South* (New York: New York University Press, 2010), 130–131.

67. Typed transcript of unidentified interview with Sugimoto, circa 1982, 19, in Sugimoto, "Interviews," Stanford University Libraries.

68. Ibid., 12; Sugimoto, "New Year's Day Thoughts," in "Life Story," 1–5.

69. Typed transcript of unidentified interview with Sugimoto, circa 1982, 7–8, in Sugimoto, "Interviews," Stanford University Libraries.

70. The historical periodization of these works is imprecise, and I have relied on the Japanese American National Museum's online collection of Sugimoto's paintings that date them as "circa 1965." See http://www.janm.org/collections/henry-sugimoto-collection/.

71. Kim, *Henry Sugimoto,* 103.

72. Typed transcript of unidentified interview with Sugimoto, circa 1982, 17–18, in Sugimoto, "Interviews," Stanford University Libraries; Kim, *Henry Sugimoto,* 104.

73. Jane de Hart Mathews, "Art and Politics in Cold War America," *American Historical Review* 81, no. 4 (October 1976): 762–787; Serge Guilbaut, *How New York Stole the Idea of Modern Art: Abstract Expressionism, Freedom, and the Cold War* (Chicago: University of Chicago Press, 1983).

74. David Craven, *Abstract Expressionism and the Cultural Logic of Romantic Anti-Capitalism: Dissent during the McCarthy Period* (Cambridge: Cambridge University Press, 1999); Greg Barnhisel, *Cold War Modernists: Art, Literature, and American Cultural Diplomacy* (New York: Columbia University Press, 2015); Frances Stonor Saunders, *The Cultural Cold War: The CIA and the World of Arts and Letters* (New York: New Press, 2000); Andrew N. Rubin, *Archives of Authority: Empire, Culture, and the Cold War* (Princeton, N.J.: Princeton University Press, 2012).

75. Musich, "Interview with Henry Sugimoto," 3, in Sugimoto, "Interviews," Stanford University Libraries.

76. Morgan, *Rethinking Social Realism,* 42–105.

77. Amalia K. Amaki and Andrea Barnwell Brownlee, *Hale Woodruff, Nancy Elizabeth Prophet, and the Academy* (Seattle: University of Washington Press, 2007).

78. Morgan, *Rethinking Social Realism,* 43–48; Schreiber, *Cold War Exiles in Mexico,* 27–57.

79. Morgan, *Rethinking Social Realism,* 46–48.

80. Matthew Frye Jacobson, *Whiteness of a Different Color: European Immigrants and the Alchemy of Race* (Cambridge, Mass.: Harvard University Press, 1999); David R. Roediger, *Working toward Whiteness: How America's Immigrants Became White: The Strange Journey from Ellis Island to the Suburbs* (New York: Basic, 2006).

81. Tom Engelhardt, *The End of Victory Culture: Cold War America and the Disillusioning of a Generation,* rev. ed. (Amherst: University of Massachusetts Press, 2007), 3–65.

82. Ibid., 61–65. See also Paul R. Boyer, *By the Bomb's Early Light: American Thought and Culture at the Dawn of the Atomic Age* (Chapel Hill: University of North Carolina Press, 1994).

CHAPTER 4

1. Yoshiko Uchida to Dwight and Iku Uchida, [letter fragment] 1950, Box 61, Folder 3, Yoshiko Uchida Papers, BANC MSS 86/97 c, Bancroft Library, University of California, Berkeley (hereafter cited as Uchida Papers, Bancroft Library).

2. For scholarship on Uchida and the wartime confinement, see Ann Rayson, "Beneath the Mask: Autobiographies of Japanese-American Women," *MELUS* 14 (Spring 1987): 43–57; Masami Usui, "Regaining Lost Privacy: Yoshiko Uchida's Story Telling as a Nisei Woman Writer," *Studies in Culture and the Humanities* [*Ningen bunka kenkyu*] 3 (1994): 1–22; Violet H. Harada, "Caught between Two Worlds: Themes of Family, Community, and Ethnic Identity in Yoshiko Uchida's Works for Children," *Children's Literature in Education* 29 (March 1998): 19–30; Danton McDiffett, "Prejudice and Pride: Japanese Americans in the Young Adult Novels of Yoshiko Uchida," *English Journal* 90 (January 2001): 60–65; Montye P. Fuse, "Under the Burden of Yellow Peril: Race, Class, and Gender in Yoshiko Uchida's *Picture Bride* (1987)," in *Women in Literature: Reading through the Lens of Gender,* ed. Jerilyn Fisher and Ellen S. Silber (Westport, Conn.: Greenwood Press, 2003), 230–233; Rocio G. Davis, "Ethnic Autobiography as Children's Literature: Laurence Yep's *The Lost Garden* and Yoshiko Uchida's *The Invisible Thread,*" *Children's Literature Association Quarterly* 28 (Summer 2003): 90–97; Fu-jen Chen and Su-lin Yu, "Asian North-American Children's Literature About the Internment: Visualizing and Verbalizing the Traumatic *Thing,*" *Children's Literature in Education* 37 (April 2006): 111–124; Matthew Teorey, "Untangled Barbed Wire Attitudes: Internment Literature for Young Adults," *Children's Literature Association Quarterly* 33 (Fall 2008): 227–245.

3. John Okada's novel *No-No Boy* (1957) presents the most recognized example of how a postwar text could be ignored if it went too far against the commemorative grain regarding the "Good War." A few Japanese Americans, however, managed to achieve public recognition for their writings on the removal and incarceration. The artist Miné Okubo's *Citizen 13660* (1946) depicted her hardships through a combination of text and drawings. Monica Sone's memoir *Nisei Daughter* (1953) traced her childhood in Seattle, Washington, during the 1930s and then her adolescence in the camps. Two novels, Shelley Ota's *Upon Their Shoulders* (1951) and Kazuo Miyamoto's *Hawaii: End of the Rainbow* (1964), portray generations of family struggles and triumphs in Hawai'i, with the mainland incarceration playing a part in these narratives. The *Pacific Citizen* and other periodicals throughout

the 1950s printed short stories by Toshio Mori, Hisaye Yamamoto, and others about the aftereffects of the imprisonment on Japanese American communities. Sympathetic white authors also contributed fictional work on this topic, including Karen Kehoe's *City in the Sun* (1946) and James Edmiston's *Home Again* (1955). Florence Crannell Means, a writer of children's books, won a Newbery Honor award in 1946 for *The Moved-Outers* (1945).

4. Catherine E. Studier Chang, "Profile: Yoshiko Uchida," *Language Arts* 61 (February 1984): 192–193; Barbara Bader, "Multiculturalism Takes Root: Yoshiko Uchida," *Horn Book Magazine* 79 (March–April 2003): 143–145; Katharine Capshaw Smith, "Introduction: The Landscape of Ethnic American Children's Literature," *MELUS* 27 (Spring 2002): 3–8.

5. Yoshiko Uchida, *Desert Exile: The Uprooting of a Japanese-American Family* (Seattle: University of Washington Press, 1982), 5–6. Future page citations appear parenthetically in the chapter.

6. Dwight Uchida, letters to family (December 1941 to April 1942), Online Archives of California, http://www.oac.cdlib.org/ark:/13030/tf367n99st/?brand=oac4 (accessed June 20, 2015).

7. Yoshiko Uchida, diary entry, September 27, 1942, Box 63, Folder 13, Uchida Papers, Bancroft Library.

8. See also Sandra C. Taylor, *Jewel of the Desert: Japanese American Internment at Topaz* (Berkeley: University of California Press, 1993).

9. Uchida, diary entry, September 27, 1942.

10. Ibid.

11. Ibid.

12. Christina Klein, *Cold War Orientalism: Asia in the Middlebrow Imagination, 1945–1961* (Berkeley: University of California Press, 2003). See also Naoko Shibusawa, *America's Geisha Ally: Reimagining the Japanese Enemy* (Cambridge, Mass.: Harvard University Press, 2006).

13. Jack Zipes, *Fairy Tale as Myth, Myth as Fairy Tale* (Lexington: University of Kentucky Press, 1994), 19.

14. Yoshiko Uchida, *The Dancing Kettle and Other Japanese Folk Tales* (New York: Harcourt, Brace, 1949), vii.

15. *Saturday Review of Literature,* May 21, 1949, 38, Box 16, Folder 5, Uchida Papers, Bancroft Library.

16. Review of *The Dancing Kettle, New York Herald Tribune,* May 8, 1949, 13, Box 16, Folder 5, Uchida Papers, Bancroft Library.

17. F.S.C. Northrop, *The Meeting of East and West: An Inquiry Concerning World Understanding* (New York: Macmillan, 1946), 4.

18. Review of *The Magic Listening Cap, San Francisco Chronicle,* May 22, 1955, 22, Box 16, Folder 6, Uchida Papers, Bancroft Library.

19. For biographical information on Taro Yashima, refer to Naoko Shibusawa, "'The Artist Belongs to the People': The Odyssey of Taro Yashima," *Journal of Asian American Studies* 8 (October 2005): 257–275.

20. Taro Yashima, *The Village Tree* (New York: Viking, 1953), 4.

21. Pat Clark, "Japanese Boyhood: The Village Tree," *New York Times,* November 15, 1953, BRA43.

22. Maxine LaBounty, "First Climb of Matterhorn Made Memorable in Fiction," *Washington Post,* December 5, 1954, B6.

23. Nancy Barr Mavity, "Oakland Girl Writes Tales of Old Japan," *Oakland Tribune,* March 6, 1955, 2-C, Box 28, Folder 6, Uchida Papers, Bancroft Library.

24. *Virginia Kirkus Bookshop Service Bulletin,* March 15, 1949, 148, Series I, Box 1, Folder 7, Yoshiko Uchida Papers, Ax 549, Special Collections and University Archives, University of Oregon Libraries, Eugene, Oregon (hereafter cited as Uchida Papers, University of Oregon Libraries).

25. Uchida, *Dancing Kettle,* 9; Uchida, *The Magic Listening Cap: More Folk Tales from Japan* (New York: Harcourt, Brace, 1955), 3.

26. Larry Reed [Wichita, Kansas] to Yoshiko Uchida, December 4, 1959, Box 13, Folder 14, Uchida Papers, Bancroft Library.

27. Mary O. Pottenger [General Supervisor of Elementary Education, Public Schools of Springfield, Massachusetts] to Yoshiko Uchida, July 19, 1949, Box 16, Folder 8, Uchida Papers, Bancroft Library.

28. Yoshiko Uchida to Mrs. Eula Ruth [Springdale, Arkansas], February 26, 1952, Series I, Box 1, Folder 6, Uchida Papers, University of Oregon Libraries.

29. *Nichi Bei Times,* March 15, 1949 (clipping, n.p.), Box 16, Folder 5, Uchida Papers, Bancroft Library; "Book Reviews: Dancing Kettle/Nisei Writer Retells Famous Old Folk Tales of Japan," *Pacific Citizen,* March 26, 1949 (clipping, n.p.), Series I, Box 1, Folder 7, Uchida Papers, University of Oregon Libraries.

30. Yoshiko Uchida to Margaret McElderry, January 19, 1949. See also Uchida to McElderry, February 16, 1953, Series I, Box 1, Folder 2, Uchida Papers, University of Oregon Libraries.

31. Yuri Iwabuchi [Tokyo, Japan] to Yoshiko Uchida, July 26, 1949, Box 16, Folder 8, Uchida Papers, Bancroft Library.

32. Sanshiro Ikeda [Nagano, Japan] to Yoshiko Uchida, March 9, 1955, Box 4, Folder 14, Uchida Papers, Bancroft Library.

33. Yoshiko Uchida, *The Invisible Thread* (New York: Julian Messner, 1991), 14. Hereafter, page citations appear parenthetically in the text.

34. Rayson, "Beneath the Mask," 53–55; Harada, "Caught between Two Worlds," 22–29; Davis, "Ethnic Autobiography as Children's Literature," 94–97. See also Traise Yamamoto, *Masking Selves, Making Subjects: Japanese American Women, Identity, and the Body* (Berkeley: University of California Press, 1999), 102–140.

35. Yoshiko Uchida (Tokyo) to parents (Oakland, CA), October 20, 1952; Uchida (Tokyo) to parents (Oakland, CA), October 22, 1952, Box 61, Folder 3, Uchida Papers, Bancroft Library.

36. Yoshiko Uchida (Tokyo) to parents (Oakland, CA), November 5, 1952, Box 61, Folder 3, Uchida Papers, Bancroft Library.

37. Yoshiko Uchida, "We Want You to Be Happy: A Nisei in Japan," 3–4 (unpublished manuscript, March 1953), Box 46, Folder 17, Uchida Papers, Bancroft Library.

38. Yoshiko Uchida (Kyoto) to parents (Oakland, CA), January 16, 1953, Box 61, Folder 4, Uchida Papers, Bancroft Library.

39. Frances Wrenn Moto-o, "All Children Live in One World; 'International Education' Stressed (Miss Uchida in Kyoto on Ford Foundation Fellowship)," *Mainichi,* March 23, 1953, Box 61, Folder 4, Uchida Papers, Bancroft Library.

40. "A Portrait of Modern Japan," *Arrietty's Notes,* no. 12, February 1958, 2, Series V, Box 1, Folder 36, Uchida Papers, University of Oregon Libraries.

41. Nicole Sackley, "Cosmopolitanism and the Uses of Tradition: Robert Redfield and Alternative Visions of Modernization during the Cold War," *Modern Intellectual History* 9, no. 3 (November 2012): 566, 569–570.

42. It is unknown whether or not Uchida was aware of the more complex history of

mingei and its ambiguous relationship to the Japanese state and imperialism, to industrial development, and to the changes within middle-class consumerism. See Kim Brandt, *Kingdom of Beauty: Mingei and the Politics of Folk Art in Imperial Japan* (Durham, N.C.: Duke University Press, 2007).

43. Yoshiko Uchida, "Folk Art of Japan," *Craft Horizons,* September–October 1955, 22, Box 45, Folder 7, Uchida Papers, Bancroft Library.

44. Ibid., 25.

45. Yoshiko Uchida, *Takao and Grandfather's Sword* (New York: Harcourt, Brace, 1958), 19.

46. Yoshiko Uchida, *The Full Circle* (New York: Friendship Press, 1957), vii. Hereafter, page citations appear parenthetically in the text.

47. Louise DeForest to Uchida, March 30 [no year], Box 3, Folder 9, Uchida Papers, Bancroft Library.

48. Yoshiko Uchida, *Journey Home* (New York: Aladdin, 1992), 104.

49. Yoshiko Uchida, *New Friends for Susan* (New York: Charles Scribner's Sons, 1951), 184.

50. Form letter from Alice Dalgliesh, Editor, Books for Younger Readers, Charles Scribner's Sons, re: *New Friends for Susan,* December 7, 1952, Box 2, Folder 10, Uchida Papers, Bancroft Library; Dust jacket, *New Friends for Susan,* Box 28, Folder 18, Uchida Papers, Bancroft Library.

51. Gladys Grofoot Castor, clipping from *New York Times Book Review,* November 4, 1951, Box 28, Folder 19, Uchida Papers, Bancroft Library.

52. "Scribner's Publishes Another Book by Yoshiko Uchida," clipping from *Rafu Shimpo,* n.d., n.p.; "Former Berkeley Nisei Pens Second Children's Book," clipping from *Nichi Bei Times,* November 16, 1951, n.p.; "'New Friends for Susan,' But No Tears for Tolerance in Kids' Book by Nisei," clipping from *Hokubei Shimpo,* November 1951, n.p., all in Box 28, Folder 19, Uchida Papers, Bancroft Library.

53. Yoshiko Uchida, "An Autobiography," 8–9, (unpublished manuscript, 1952), Box 50, Folder 5, Uchida Papers, Bancroft Library.

54. Charles Scribner's Sons, 1951 *Books for Younger Readers* catalogue, n.p., Box 28, Folder 19, Uchida Papers, Bancroft Library.

55. Clipping from *Nichi Bei Times,* December 25, 1951, n.p., Box 28, Folder 19, Uchida Papers, Bancroft Library.

56. "Annual Report of Stateside Activities Supporting the Reorientation Program in Japan and the Ryukyu Islands," Washington, D.C.: Reorientation Branch, Office for Occupied Areas, Office of the Secretary of the Army, October 1950, 1. For more information on the role of literature in the reorientation program, see Hiromi Ochi, "Democratic Bookshelf: American Libraries in Occupied Japan," in *Pressing the Fight: Print, Propaganda, and the Cold War,* ed. Greg Barnhisel and Catherine Turner (Amherst: University of Massachusetts Press, 2010), 89–111; Marlene J. Mayo, "Literary Reorientation in Occupied Japan: Incidents of Civil Censorship," in *Legacies and Ambiguities: Postwar Fiction and Culture in West Germany and Japan,* ed. Ernestine Schlant and J. Thomas Riner (Washington, D.C.: Woodrow Wilson Center Press; Baltimore: Johns Hopkins University Press, 1991), 135–161; Yuka Moriguchi Tsuchiya, "Military Occupation as Pedagogy: The U.S. Re-education and Reorientation Policy for Occupied Japan, 1945–1952" (Ph.D. diss., University of Minnesota, December 2004).

57. John I. Pray, Lt. Colonel GSC Chief, NY field office, to Miss Joanna Foster, Assistant Editor, Books for Younger Readers, Charles Scribner's Sons, October 31, 1951, Box 2, Folder 10, Uchida Papers, Bancroft Library.

58. Nancy Larrick, "The All-White World of Children's Books," *Saturday Review of Literature,* September 11, 1965, 63.

59. Yoshiko Uchida, *The Promised Year* (New York: Harcourt, Brace, 1959), 14. Hereafter, page citations appear parenthetically in the text.

60. Charlotte Jackson, "California Authors—New Work by Familiar Personalities," *San Francisco Sunday Chronicle,* November 13, 1960, 4, Box 28, Folder 11, Uchida Papers, Bancroft Library.

61. Olga Hoyt, "New Books for the Young Readers' Library," *New York Times Book Review,* January 22, 1961 (newspaper clipping, n.p.), Box 28, Folder 11, Uchida Papers, Bancroft Library.

62. Ellen D. Wu, *The Color of Success: Asian Americans and the Origins of the Model Minority* (Princeton, N.J.: Princeton University Press, 2014). See also Cindy I-Fen Cheng, *Citizens of Asian America: Democracy and Race during the Cold War* (New York: New York University Press, 2013); Madeline Y. Hsu, *The Good Immigrants: How the Yellow Peril Became the Model Minority* (Princeton, N.J.: Princeton University Press, 2015).

63. Yoshiko Uchida to Margaret McElderry, November 27, 1959, Series VII, Box 2, Folder 12, Uchida Papers, University of Oregon Libraries.

64. Margaret McElderry to Yoshiko Uchida, January 6, 1960, Series VII, Box 2, Folder 14, Uchida Papers, University of Oregon Libraries.

65. Uchida, *The Invisible Thread,* 125–129; Uchida, "An Autobiography," 10.

66. Uchida, "An Autobiography," 10.

67. Yoshiko Uchida, "Courage of the Issei," 5, April 1949, Box 46, Folder 14, Uchida Papers, Bancroft Library.

68. A fellow teacher with Uchida at the Frankford Friends School in Philadelphia wrote to the author about this published work: "It almost broke my heart when I realized once again what had been done to the Japanese-Americans." Reba S. Lammey to Uchida, October 28, 1952, Box 5, Folder 1, Uchida Papers, Bancroft Library.

69. The story has no specific date on it, but its likely composition was around 1952, like Uchida's other adult short fiction about the wartime confinement. "Crepe Paper Flowers," Box 39, Folder 7, Uchida Papers, Bancroft Library.

70. Taylor, *Jewel of the Desert,* 136–146.

71. Yoshiko Uchida, diary entry, April 12, 1943, Box 63, Folder 14, Uchida Papers, Bancroft Library.

72. Miné Okubo, *Citizen 13660* (Seattle: University of Washington Press, 1983), 180–181. See also Heather Fryer, "Miné Okubo's War: *Citizen 13660*'s Attack on Government Propaganda," in *Miné Okubo: Following Her Own Road,* ed. Greg Robinson and Elena Tajima Creef (Seattle: University of Washington Press, 2008), 89, 95.

73. Yoshiko Uchida, "The Crepe Paper Flowers," 1, Box 39, Folder 7, Uchida Papers, Bancroft Library.

74. Harriet Wolf to Yoshiko Uchida, August 26, 1952, Box 7, Folder 12, Uchida Papers, Bancroft Library.

75. Lee [no surname] to Harriet Wolf, November 18, 1952, Box 7, Folder 12, Uchida Papers, Bancroft Library.

76. Michi Nishiura Weglyn, *Years of Infamy: The Untold Story of America's Concentration Camps,* updated ed. (Seattle: University of Washington Press, 1996), 156–173; Greg Robinson, *A Tragedy of Democracy: Japanese Confinement in North America* (New York: Columbia University Press, 2009), 162–167.

77. Yoshiko Uchida, *Journey to Topaz* (Berkeley, Calif.: Heyday, 2009), 121.

78. Yoshiko Uchida, *Picture Bride* (New York: Fireside, 1987), 216.

CONCLUSION

1. Janet Hoskins and Viet Thanh Nguyen, eds., *Transpacific Studies: Framing an Emerging Field* (Honolulu: University of Hawai'i Press, 2014), 3.

2. Ibid., 8.

3. The philosopher Anthony Kwame Appiah argues for a "rooted cosmopolitanism," which contrasts against comprehending worldliness as transcending, or being detached from, specific localities. In his framing, persons are "attached to a home of his or her own, with its own cultural particularities, but taking pleasure from the presence of other, different, places that are home to other, different people." See Appiah, "Cosmopolitan Patriots," in *Cosmopolitics: Thinking and Feeling beyond the Nation,* ed. Pheng Cheah and Bruce Robbins (Minneapolis: University of Minnesota Press, 1999), 91.

4. Lisa Lowe, *The Intimacies of Four Continents* (Durham, N.C.: Duke University Press, 2015); Anthony Pagden, "Stoicism, Cosmopolitanism, and the Legacy of European Imperialism," *Constellations* 7, no. 1 (2000): 3–22. See also Eduardo Mendieta, "From Imperial to Dialogical Cosmopolitanism," *Ethics and Global Politics* 2, no. 3 (2009): 241–258. A recent collection of essays assessing the merits, limits, and changing nature of cosmopolitanism as a Western and a global alternative construct is Bruce Robbins and Paulo Lemos Horta, eds., *Cosmopolitanisms* (New York: New York University Press, 2017).

5. Silviano Santiago, "The Cosmopolitanism of the Poor," translated by Magdalena Edwards and Paulo Lemos Horta, in Robbins and Horta, *Cosmopolitanisms*; Sheldon Pollock, Homi K. Bhabha, Carol A. Breckenridge, and Dipesh Chakrabarty, "Cosmopolitanisms," *Public Culture* 12, no. 3 (2000): 577–589; James Clifford, "Traveling Cultures," in *Cultural Studies,* ed. Lawrence Grossberg, Cary Nelson, and Paula A. Treichler (New York: Routledge, 1992), 96–116.

6. Ed Pilkington, "Japanese American Internment Survivor Hears Troubling Echoes in Trump Rhetoric," *Guardian,* May 28, 2016, https://www.theguardian.com/us-news/2016/may/28/japanese-american-internment-survivor-donald-trump-rhetoric (accessed February 15, 2018).

7. For cultural perspectives on this matter, see Melani McAlister, *Epic Encounters: Culture, Media, and U.S. Interests in the Middle East since 1945,* updated ed., with a post-9/11 chapter (Berkeley: University of California Press, 2005), 266–307; Tom Engelhardt, *The End of Victory Culture: Cold War America and the Disillusioning of a Generation,* rev. ed. (Amherst: University of Massachusetts Press, 2007), 305–333.

8. Jodi Kim, *Ends of Empire: Asian American Critique and the Cold War* (Minneapolis: University of Minnesota Press, 2010); Josephine Nock-Hee Park, *Cold War Friendships: Korea, Vietnam, and Asian American Literature* (New York: Oxford University Press, 2016); Cathy J. Schlund-Vials, *War, Genocide, and Justice: Cambodian American Memory Work* (Minneapolis: University of Minnesota Press, 2012); Lisa Yoneyama, *Cold War Ruins: Transpacific Critique of American Justice and Japanese War Crimes* (Durham, N.C.: Duke University Press, 2016).

9. For Henry Sugimoto, see Kristine Kim, *Henry Sugimoto: Painting an American Experience* (Berkeley, Calif.: Heyday, 2000). For examples that mention Yoshiko Uchida on the wartime confinement, see David K. Yoo, *Growing Up Nisei: Race, Generation, and Culture among Japanese Americans, 1924–49* (Urbana: University of Illinois Press, 2000), 92–93, 124; Traise Yamamoto, *Masking Selves, Making Subjects: Japanese American Women, Identity, and the Body* (Berkeley: University of California Press, 1999), 102–140. Scholarship on Japan that references Hanama Tasaki includes John J. Stephan, *Hawai'i under the Rising Sun: Japan's Plans for Conquest after Pearl Harbor* (Honolulu: University of Hawai'i

Press, 1984), 35–36; Alvin D. Coox, "Evidences of Antimilitarism in Prewar and Wartime Japan," *Pacific Affairs* 46, no. 4 (Winter 1973–1974): 502–514. For Yamaguchi Yoshiko, see Jennifer Coates, "The Shape-Shifting Diva: Yamaguchi Yoshiko and the National Body," *Journal of Japanese and Korean Cinema* 6, no. 1 (2014): 23–38. Yamaguchi, however, is the only figure among the four who is still the subject of transnational-based scholarship (regarding her relationships with China and Japan).

Selected Bibliography

This bibliography underscores selected endnote citations, highlighting works (books, journal articles, films) that have been important to the specific focus of my analysis and that may appear more than once in the endnotes.

BOOKS AND JOURNALS

Alinder, Jasmine. *Moving Images: Photography and the Japanese American Incarceration.* Urbana: University of Illinois Press, 2010.

Azuma, Eiichiro. *Between Two Empires: Race, History, and Transnationalism in Japanese America.* New York: Oxford University Press, 2005.

Baskett, Michael. *The Attractive Empire: Transnational Film Culture in Imperial Japan.* Honolulu: University of Hawai'i Press, 2008.

Bow, Leslie. *Partly Colored: Asian Americans and Racial Anomaly in the Segregated South.* New York: New York University Press, 2010.

Brandt, Kim. "'There Was No East or West When Their Lips Met': A Movie Poster for Japanese War Bride as Transnational Artifact." *Impressions* 30 (2009): 119–127.

Brown, Michael D. *Views from Asian California, 1920–1965.* San Francisco: Michael Brown, 1992.

Chang, Gordon H., Mark Dean Johnson, Paul J. Karlstrom, and Sharon Spain, eds. *Asian American Art: A History, 1850–1970.* Stanford, Calif.: Stanford University Press, 2008.

Cheah, Pheng, and Bruce Robbins, eds. *Cosmopolitics: Thinking and Feeling beyond the Nation.* Minneapolis: University of Minnesota Press, 1999.

Cheng, Cindy I-Fen. *Citizens of Asian America: Democracy and Race during the Cold War.* New York: New York University Press, 2013.

Coates, Jennifer. "The Shape-Shifting Diva: Yamaguchi Yoshiko and the National Body." *Journal of Japanese and Korean Cinema* 6, no. 1 (2014): 23–38.

Creef, Elena Tajima. *Imaging Japanese America: The Visual Construction of Citizenship, Nation, and the Body.* New York: New York University Press, 2004.

Davis, Rocio G. "Ethnic Autobiography as Children's Literature: Laurence Yep's *The Lost Garden* and Yoshiko Uchida's *The Invisible Thread.*" *Children's Literature Association Quarterly* 28 (Summer 2003): 90–97.

Dower, John W. *Embracing Defeat: Japan in the Wake of World War II.* New York: Norton, 1999.

———. *War without Mercy: Race and Power in the Pacific War.* New York: Pantheon, 1986.

———. *Ways of Forgetting, Ways of Remembering: Japan in the Modern World.* New York: New Press, 2012.

Dudziak, Mary L. *Cold War Civil Rights: Race and the Image of American Democracy.* Princeton, N.J.: Princeton University Press, 2000.

Duus, Masayo. *The Life of Isamu Noguchi: Journey without Borders.* Translated by Peter Duus. Princeton, N.J.: Princeton University Press, 2004.

Engelhardt, Tom. *The End of Victory Culture: Cold War America and the Disillusioning of a Generation.* Rev. ed. Amherst: University of Massachusetts Press, 2007.

Fujitani, T. *Race for Empire: Koreans as Japanese and Japanese as Americans during World War II.* Berkeley: University of California Press, 2011.

Fuller, Samuel, with Christa Lang Fuller and Jerome Henry Rudes. *A Third Face: My Tale of Writing, Fighting, and Filmmaking.* New York: Knopf, 2002.

Gallicchio, Marc, ed. *The Unpredictability of the Past: Memories of the Asia-Pacific War in U.S.–East Asian Relations.* Durham, N.C.: Duke University Press, 2007.

Gesensway, Deborah, and Mindy Roseman. *Beyond Words: Images from America's Concentration Camps.* Ithaca, N.Y.: Cornell University Press, 1987.

Harada, Violet H. "Caught between Two Worlds: Themes of Family, Community, and Ethnic Identity in Yoshiko Uchida's Works for Children." *Children's Literature in Education* 29 (March 1998): 19–30.

Hariman, Robert, and John Louis Lucaites. *No Caption Needed: Iconic Photographs, Public Culture, and Liberal Democracy.* Chicago: University of Chicago Press, 2007.

Hein, Laura. "Revisiting America's Occupation of Japan." *Cold War History* 11, no. 4 (November 2011): 579–599.

Herrera, Hayden. *Listening to Stone: The Art and Life of Isamu Noguchi.* New York: Farrar, Straus and Giroux, 2015.

Higa, Karin M. *The View from Within: Japanese American Art from the Internment Camps, 1942–1945.* Los Angeles: Japanese American National Museum, UCLA Wight Art Gallery, and UCLA Asian American Studies Center, 1992.

Honey, Maureen, and Jean Lee Cole, eds. *"Madame Butterfly" by John Luther Long and "A Japanese Nightingale" by Onoto Watanna (Winnifred Eaton): Two Orientalist Texts.* New Brunswick, N.J.: Rutgers University Press, 2002.

Hoskins, Janet, and Viet Thanh Nguyen, eds. *Transpacific Studies: Framing an Emerging Field.* Honolulu: University of Hawai'i Press, 2014.

Howard, John. *Concentration Camps on the Home Front: Japanese Americans in the House of Jim Crow.* Chicago: University of Chicago Press, 2008.

Hsu, Madeleine Y. *The Good Immigrants: How the Yellow Peril Became the Model Minority.* Princeton, N.J.: Princeton University Press, 2015.

Igarashi, Yoshikuni. *Bodies of Memory: Narratives of War in Postwar Japanese Culture, 1945–1970.* Princeton, N.J.: Princeton University Press, 2000.

Kim, Jodi. *Ends of Empire: Asian American Critique and the Cold War.* Minneapolis: University of Minnesota Press, 2010.

Kim, Kristine. *Henry Sugimoto: Painting an American Experience.* Berkeley, Calif.: Heyday, 2000.

King, Richard, Cody Poulton, and Katsuhiko Endo, eds. *Sino-Japanese Transculturation: From the Late Nineteenth Century to the End of the Pacific War*. Lanham, Md.: Lexington Books, 2012.

Klein, Christina. *Cold War Orientalism: Asia in the Middlebrow Imagination, 1945–1961*. Berkeley: University of California Press, 2003.

Koshiro, Yukiko. *Trans-Pacific Racisms and the U.S. Occupation of Japan*. New York: Columbia University Press, 1999.

Koshy, Susan. "Minority Cosmopolitanism." *PMLA* 126 (May 2011): 592–609.

———. *Sexual Naturalization: Asian Americans and Miscegenation*. Stanford, Calif.: Stanford University Press, 2004.

Kozol, Wendy. "Madonnas of the Fields: Photography, Gender, and 1930s Farm Relief." *Genders* 2 (Summer 1988): 1–23.

Kramer, Paul A. "Power and Connection: Imperial Histories of the United States in the World." *American Historical Review* 116 (December 2011): 1348–1391.

Kuramitsu, Kristine C. "Internment and Identity in Japanese American Art." *American Quarterly* 47, no. 4 (December 1995): 619–658.

Lowe, Lisa. *The Intimacies of Four Continents*. Durham, N.C.: Duke University Press, 2015.

Lye, Colleen. *America's Asia: Racial Form and American Literature, 1893–1945*. Princeton, N.J.: Princeton University Press, 2005.

Marchetti, Gina. *Romance and the "Yellow Peril": Race, Sex, and Discursive Strategies in Hollywood Fiction*. Berkeley: University of California Press, 1993.

Michener, James A. *The Voice of Asia*. New York: Random House, 1951.

Miyamoto, Kazuo. *Hawaii: End of the Rainbow*. Rutland, Vt.: Charles E. Tuttle, 1964.

Morgan, Stacy I. *Rethinking Social Realism: African American Art and Literature, 1930–1953*. Athens: University of Georgia Press, 2004.

Murray, Alice Yang. *Historical Memories of the Japanese American Internment and the Struggle for Redress*. Stanford, Calif.: Stanford University Press, 2008.

Nadel, Alan. *Containment Culture: American Narratives, Postmodernism, and the Atomic Age*. Durham, N.C.: Duke University Press, 1995.

Ngai, Mae M. *Impossible Subjects: Illegal Aliens and the Making of Modern America*. Princeton, N.J.: Princeton University Press, 2005.

Nguyen, Viet Thanh. *Race and Resistance: Literature and Politics in Asian America*. New York: Oxford University Press, 2002.

Noguchi, Isamu. *A Sculptor's World*. New York: Harper and Row, 1968.

Northrop, F.S.C. *The Meeting of East and West: An Inquiry Concerning World Understanding*. New York: Macmillan, 1946.

Okubo, Miné. *Citizen 13660*. Seattle: University of Washington Press, 1983.

Oles, James. *South of the Border: Mexico in the American Imagination, 1914–1947*. Washington, D.C.: Smithsonian Institution Press, 1993.

Orbaugh, Sharalyn. *Japanese Fiction of the Allied Occupation: Vision, Embodiment, Identity*. Leiden, Netherlands: Brill, 2007.

Ota, Shelley Ayame Nishimura. *Upon Their Shoulders*. New York: Exposition Press, 1951.

Pagden, Anthony. "Stoicism, Cosmopolitanism, and the Legacy of European Imperialism." *Constellations* 7, no. 1 (2000): 3–22.

Palumbo-Liu, David. *Asian/American: Historical Crossings of a Racial Frontier*. Stanford, Calif.: Stanford University Press, 1999.

Park, Josephine Nock-Hee. *Cold War Friendships: Korea, Vietnam, and Asian American Literature*. New York: Oxford University Press, 2016.

Personal Justice Denied: Report of the Commission on Wartime Relocation and Internment of

Civilians. Foreword by Tetsuden Kashima. Washington, D.C.: Civil Liberties Public Education Fund; Seattle: University of Washington Press, 1997.

Phu, Thy. *Picturing Model Citizens: Civility in Asian American Visual Culture*. Philadelphia: Temple University Press, 2011.

Pollock, Sheldon, Homi K. Bhabha, Carol A. Breckenridge, and Dipesh Chakrabarty. "Cosmopolitanisms." *Public Culture* 12, no. 3 (2000): 577–589.

Rademaker, John A. *These Are Americans: The Japanese Americans in Hawaii in World War II*. Palo Alto, Calif.: Pacific Books, 1951.

Rayson, Ann. "Beneath the Mask: Autobiographies of Japanese-American Women." *MELUS* 14 (Spring 1987): 43–57.

Robbins, Bruce, and Paulo Lemos Horta, eds. *Cosmopolitanisms*. New York: New York University Press, 2017.

Robinson, Greg. *After Camp: Portraits in Midcentury Japanese American Life and Politics*. Berkeley: University of California Press, 2012.

———. *A Tragedy of Democracy: Japanese Confinement in North America*. New York: Columbia University Press, 2009.

Sackley, Nicole. "Cosmopolitanism and the Uses of Tradition: Robert Redfield and Alternative Visions of Modernization during the Cold War." *Modern Intellectual History* 9, no. 3 (November 2012): 565–595.

Schreiber, Rebecca. *Cold War Exiles in Mexico: U.S. Dissidents and the Culture of Critical Resistance*. Minneapolis: University of Minnesota Press, 2008.

Sherry, Michael S. *In the Shadow of War: The United States since the 1930s*. New Haven, Conn.: Yale University Press, 1995.

Shibusawa, Naoko. *America's Geisha Ally: Reimagining the Japanese Enemy*. Cambridge, Mass.: Harvard University Press, 2006.

———. "'The Artist Belongs to the People': The Odyssey of Taro Yashima." *Journal of Asian American Studies* 8 (October 2005): 257–275.

Shukert, Elfrieda Berthiaume, and Barbara Smith Scibetta. *War Brides of World War II*. Novato, Calif.: Presidio Press, 1988.

Simpson, Caroline Chung. *An Absent Presence: Japanese Americans in Postwar American Culture, 1945–1960*. Durham, N.C.: Duke University Press, 2001.

Slaymaker, Douglas N. *The Body in Postwar Japanese Fiction*. New York: Routledge Curzon, 2004.

Sone, Monica. *Nisei Daughter*. Seattle: University of Washington Press, 1979.

Stahl, David C. *The Burdens of Survival: Ooka Shohei's Writings on the Pacific War*. Honolulu: University of Hawai'i Press, 2003.

Stephan, John J. *Hawaii under the Rising Sun: Japan's Plans for Conquest after Pearl Harbor*. Honolulu: University of Hawai'i Press, 1984.

Stephenson, Shelley. "A Star by Any Other Name: The (After) Lives of Li Xianglan." *Quarterly Review of Film and Video* 19 (2002): 1–13.

Stoler, Ann Laura, ed. *Haunted by Empire: Geographies of Intimacy in North American History*. Durham, N.C.: Duke University Press, 2006.

Sturken, Marita. "Absent Images of Memory: Remembering and Reenacting the Japanese American Internment." *positions* 5, no. 3 (Winter 1997): 687–707.

Sugimoto, Henry. "Life Story." Translated and prepared by Emily Anderson. Unpublished manuscript, 2000.

———. *North American Japanese People in Relocation Camps*. Self-Publication, 1983.

Tang, Edward. "Reorienting Empires: Hanama Tasaki's Long the Imperial Way and Postwar American Culture." *Journal of Asian American Studies* 17, no. 1 (February 2014): 31–59.

Tasaki, Hanama. *Long the Imperial Way*. Boston: Houghton Mifflin, 1950.

———. *The Mountains Remain*. Boston: Houghton Mifflin, 1952.

Taylor, Sandra C. *Jewel of the Desert: Japanese American Internment at Topaz*. Berkeley: University of California Press, 1993.

Uchida, Yoshiko. *The Dancing Kettle and Other Japanese Folk Tales*. New York: Harcourt, Brace, 1949.

———. *Desert Exile: The Uprooting of a Japanese-American Family*. Seattle: University of Washington Press, 1982.

———. *The Full Circle*. New York: Friendship Press, 1957.

———. *The Invisible Thread*. New York: Julian Messner, 1991.

———. *Journey Home*. New York: Aladdin, 1992.

———. *Journey to Topaz*. Berkeley, Calif.: Heyday, 2009.

———. *The Magic Listening Cap: More Folk Tales from Japan*. New York: Harcourt, Brace, 1955.

———. *New Friends for Susan*. New York: Charles Scribner's Sons, 1951.

———. *The Promised Year*. New York: Harcourt, Brace, 1959.

———. *Takao and Grandfather's Sword*. New York: Harcourt, Brace, 1958.

Wang, Yiman. "Between the National and the Transnational: Li Xianglan/Yamaguchi Yoshiko and Pan-Asianism." *IIAS Newsletter* 38 (September 2005): 7.

Ward, Jason Morgan. "'No Jap Crow': Japanese Americans Encounter the World War II South." *Journal of Southern History* 73 (February 2007): 75–104.

Watt, Lori. *When Empire Comes Home: Repatriation and Reintegration in Postwar Japan*. Cambridge, Mass.: Harvard University Asia Center, 2009.

Weglyn, Michi Nishiura. *Years of Infamy: The Untold Story of America's Concentration Camps*. Updated ed. Seattle: University of Washington Press, 1996.

Winther, Bert. "The Rejection of Isamu Noguchi's Hiroshima Cenotaph: A Japanese American Artist in Occupied Japan." *Art Journal* 53, no. 4 (Winter 1994): 23–27.

Wu, Ellen D. *The Color of Success: Asian Americans and the Origins of the Model Minority*. Princeton, N.J.: Princeton University Press, 2014.

Yamaguchi, Yoshiko, and Fujiwara Sakuya. *Fragrant Orchid: The Story of My Early Life*. Translated and with an introduction by Chia-ning Chang. Honolulu: University of Hawai'i Press, 2015.

Yamamoto, Traise. *Masking Selves, Making Subjects: Japanese American Women, Identity, and the Body*. Berkeley: University of California Press, 1999.

Yashima, Taro. *The Village Tree*. New York: Viking, 1953.

Young, Louise. *Japan's Total Empire: Manchuria and the Culture of Wartime Imperialism*. Berkeley: University of California Press, 1998.

Zeiger, Susan. *Entangling Alliances: Foreign War Brides and American Soldiers in the Twentieth Century*. New York: New York University Press, 2010.

Zhang, Yingjin, ed. *Cinema and Urban Culture in Shanghai, 1922–1943*. Stanford, Calif.: Stanford University Press, 1999.

Zipes, Jack. *Fairy Tale as Myth, Myth as Fairy Tale*. Lexington: University of Kentucky Press, 1994.

FILMOGRAPHY

Fuller, Samuel, dir. *House of Bamboo*. Los Angeles: Twentieth Century–Fox, 1955.

Vidor, King, dir. *Japanese War Bride*. Los Angeles: Twentieth Century–Fox, 1952.

Index

Edward Tang is an Associate Professor of American Studies at the University of Alabama.

Also in the series *Asian American History and Culture:*

Kathleen S. Yep, *Outside the Paint: When Basketball Ruled at the Chinese Playground*

Benito M. Vergara Jr., *Pinoy Capital: The Filipino Nation in Daly City*

Jonathan Y. Okamura, *Ethnicity and Inequality in Hawai'i*

Sucheng Chan and Madeline Y. Hsu, eds., *Chinese Americans and the Politics of Race and Culture*

K. Scott Wong, *Americans First: Chinese Americans and the Second World War*

Lisa Yun, *The Coolie Speaks: Chinese Indentured Laborers and African Slaves in Cuba*

Estella Habal, *San Francisco's International Hotel: Mobilizing the Filipino American Community in the Anti-eviction Movement*

Thomas P. Kim, *The Racial Logic of Politics: Asian Americans and Party Competition*

Sucheng Chan, ed., *The Vietnamese American 1.5 Generation: Stories of War, Revolution, Flight, and New Beginnings*

Antonio T. Tiongson Jr., Edgardo V. Gutierrez, and Ricardo V. Gutierrez, eds., *Positively No Filipinos Allowed: Building Communities and Discourse*

Sucheng Chan, ed., *Chinese American Transnationalism: The Flow of People, Resources, and Ideas between China and America during the Exclusion Era*

Rajini Srikanth, *The World Next Door: South Asian American Literature and the Idea of America*

Keith Lawrence and Floyd Cheung, eds., *Recovered Legacies: Authority and Identity in Early Asian American Literature*

Linda Trinh Võ, *Mobilizing an Asian American Community*

Franklin S. Odo, *No Sword to Bury: Japanese Americans in Hawai'i during World War II*

Josephine Lee, Imogene L. Lim, and Yuko Matsukawa, eds., *Re/collecting Early Asian America: Essays in Cultural History*

Linda Trinh Võ and Rick Bonus, eds., *Contemporary Asian American Communities: Intersections and Divergences*

Sunaina Marr Maira, *Desis in the House: Indian American Youth Culture in New York City*

Teresa Williams-León and Cynthia Nakashima, eds., *The Sum of Our Parts: Mixed-Heritage Asian Americans*

Tung Pok Chin with Winifred C. Chin, *Paper Son: One Man's Story*

Amy Ling, ed., *Yellow Light: The Flowering of Asian American Arts*

Rick Bonus, *Locating Filipino Americans: Ethnicity and the Cultural Politics of Space*

Darrell Y. Hamamoto and Sandra Liu, eds., *Countervisions: Asian American Film Criticism*

Martin F. Manalansan IV, ed., *Cultural Compass: Ethnographic Explorations of Asian America*

Ko-lin Chin, *Smuggled Chinese: Clandestine Immigration to the United States*

Evelyn Hu-DeHart, ed., *Across the Pacific: Asian Americans and Globalization*

Soo-Young Chin, *Doing What Had to Be Done: The Life Narrative of Dora Yum Kim*

Robert G. Lee, *Orientals: Asian Americans in Popular Culture*

David L. Eng and Alice Y. Hom, eds., *Q & A: Queer in Asian America*

K. Scott Wong and Sucheng Chan, eds., *Claiming America: Constructing Chinese American Identities during the Exclusion Era*

Lavina Dhingra Shankar and Rajini Srikanth, eds., *A Part, Yet Apart: South Asians in Asian America*

Jere Takahashi, *Nisei/Sansei: Shifting Japanese American Identities and Politics*

Velina Hasu Houston, ed., *But Still, Like Air, I'll Rise: New Asian American Plays*

Josephine Lee, *Performing Asian America: Race and Ethnicity on the Contemporary Stage*

Deepika Bahri and Mary Vasudeva, eds., *Between the Lines: South Asians and Postcoloniality*

E. San Juan Jr., *The Philippine Temptation: Dialectics of Philippines–U.S. Literary Relations*

Carlos Bulosan and E. San Juan Jr., eds., *The Cry and the Dedication*

Carlos Bulosan and E. San Juan Jr., eds., *On Becoming Filipino: Selected Writings of Carlos Bulosan*

Vicente L. Rafael, ed., *Discrepant Histories: Translocal Essays on Filipino Cultures*

Yen Le Espiritu, *Filipino American Lives*

Paul Ong, Edna Bonacich, and Lucie Cheng, eds., *The New Asian Immigration in Los Angeles and Global Restructuring*

Chris Friday, *Organizing Asian American Labor: The Pacific Coast Canned-Salmon Industry, 1870–1942*

Sucheng Chan, ed., *Hmong Means Free: Life in Laos and America*

Timothy P. Fong, *The First Suburban Chinatown: The Remaking of Monterey Park, California*

William Wei, *The Asian American Movement*

Yen Le Espiritu, *Asian American Panethnicity*

Velina Hasu Houston, ed., *The Politics of Life*

Renqiu Yu, *To Save China, To Save Ourselves: The Chinese Hand Laundry Alliance of New York*

Shirley Geok-lin Lim and Amy Ling, eds., *Reading the Literatures of Asian America*

Karen Isaksen Leonard, *Making Ethnic Choices: California's Punjabi Mexican Americans*

Gary Y. Okihiro, *Cane Fires: The Anti-Japanese Movement in Hawaii, 1865–1945*

Sucheng Chan, *Entry Denied: Exclusion and the Chinese Community in America, 1882–1943*